MANUFACTURING PROCESSES

AUTHOR

Dr. Dheerendra Kumar Dwivedi
Professor
Department of Mechanical and Industrial Engineering
Indian Institute of Technology Roorkee

REVIEWER

Dr. Ajay Muljibhai Sidpara
Associate Professor
Indian Institute of Technology, Kharagpur

KHANNA BOOK PUBLISHING CO. (P) Ltd.
4C/4344, Ansari Road, Darya Ganj,
New Delhi, India

All India Council for Technical Education
Nelson Mandela Marg, Vasant Kunj,
New Delhi, India

Dear Readers,

To prevent the piracy, this book is secured with HIGH SECURITY HOLOGRAM on the front title cover. In case you don't find the hologram on the front cover title, please write us to at contact@khannabooks.com or whatsapp us at +91-99109 09320 and avail special gift voucher for yourself.

Specimen of Hologram on front Cover title:

Moreover, there is a SPECIAL DISCOUNT COUPON for you with EVERY HOLOGRAM.

How to avail this SPECIAL DISCOUNT:

Step 1: Scratch the hologram

Step 2: Under the scratch area, your "coupon code" is available

Step 3: Logon to www.khannabooks.com

Step 4: Use your "coupon code" in the shopping cart and get your copy at a special discount

Step 5: Enjoy your reading!

ISBN: 978-93-5538-723-3

Book Code: UG484EN

Manufacturing Processes

by Dr. Dheerendra Kumar Dwivedi

First Edition: 2026

Originally Published by:
All India Council for Technical Education, Ministry of Education, GOI

Exclusively Published & Distributed by:
Khanna Book Publishing Co. (P) Ltd.
4C/4344, Ansari Road, Daryaganj,
New Delhi (INDIA)

Visit us at: **www.khannabooks.com**
Write us at: **contact@khannabooks.com**

To view complete list of books, Please scan the QR Code:

KPH

Printed in Bharat.

प्रो. टी. जी. सीताराम
अध्यक्ष
Prof. T. G. Sitharam
Chairman

सत्यमेव जयते

आज़ादी का अमृत महोत्सव

अखिल भारतीय तकनीकी शिक्षा परिषद्
(भारत सरकार का एक सांविधिक निकाय)
(शिक्षा मंत्रालय, भारत सरकार)
नेल्सन मंडेला मार्ग, वसंत कुंज, नई दिल्ली–110070
दूरभाष : 011–26131498
ई–मेल : chairman@aicte-india.org

ALL INDIA COUNCIL FOR TECHNICAL EDUCATION
(A STATUTORY BODY OF THE GOVT. OF INDIA)
(Ministry of Education, Govt. of India)
Nelson Mandela Marg, Vasant Kunj, New Delhi-110070
Phone : 011-26131498
E-mail : chairman@aicte-india.org

FOREWORD

Engineers are the backbone of any modern society. They are the ones responsible for the marvels as well as the improved quality of life across the world. Engineers have driven humanity towards greater heights in a more evolved and unprecedented manner.

The All India Council for Technical Education (AICTE), have spared no efforts towards the strengthening of the technical education in the country. AICTE is always committed towards promoting quality Technical Education to make India a modern developed nation emphasizing on the overall welfare of mankind.

An array of initiatives has been taken by AICTE in last decade which have been accelerated now by the National Education Policy (NEP) 2020. The implementation of NEP under the visionary leadership of Hon'ble Prime Minister of India envisages the provision for education in regional languages to all, thereby ensuring that every graduate becomes competent enough and is in a position to contribute towards the national growth and development through innovation & entrepreneurship.

One of the spheres where AICTE had been relentlessly working since past couple of years is providing high quality original technical contents at Under Graduate & Diploma level prepared and translated by eminent educators in various Indian languages to its aspirants. For students pursuing 2nd year of their Engineering education, AICTE has identified 87 books, which shall be translated into 12 Indian languages - Hindi, Tamil, Gujarati, Odia, Bengali, Kannada, Urdu, Punjabi, Telugu, Marathi, Assamese & Malayalam. In addition to the English medium, books in different Indian Languages are going to support the students to understand the concepts in their respective mother tongue.

On behalf of AICTE, I express sincere gratitude to all distinguished authors, reviewers and translators from the renowned institutions of high repute for their admirable contribution in a record span of time.

AICTE is confident that these outcomes based original contents shall help aspirants to master the subject with comprehension and greater ease.

T. G. Sitharam

(Prof. T. G. Sitharam)

ACKNOWLEDGEMENT

The authors are grateful to the authorities of AICTE, particularly Prof. T. G. Sitharam, Chairman; Dr. Abhay Jere, Vice-Chairman; Prof. Rajiv Kumar, Member-Secretary, Dr. Sunil Luthra, Director, and Reena Sharma, Hindi Officer Training and Learning or their planning to publish the books on ***Manufacturing Processes***.

I sincerely acknowledge the valuable contributions of the reviewer of the book Prof. Ajay M. Sidpara, Assoc. Professor, IIT Kharagpur. Author wishes to acknowledge the assistance of Mr. Niwas Kumar Roy, Mr. Rajat Malik, Mr. Ritesh Rai, Mr. Shashank Gupta, Mr. Saurabh Kumar Nishad and Mr. G. Govinda in compiling technical content and figures of Unit 7. I am also thankful to my wife Nirupma, my daughters Shalini and Shagun, as without their support, this work would not have realised.

I would also like to acknowledge the reference books that have been instrumental in the preparation of this book:, "Manufacturing Engineering and Technology" by S Kalpakjian, S R Schmid, "Fundamentals of Modern Manufacturing" by M P Groover, "Manufacturing science" by A Ghosh, A K Malik, "Fundamentals of Metal Joining", by D K Dwivedi "Dissimilar Metal Joining" by D K Dwivedi, "Materials Engineering" by D K Dwivedi, NPTEL Course / MOOCS on "Fundamentals of Manufacturing Processes" by D K Dwivedi.

Additionally, I extend my gratitude to my research scholars and M. Tech. students, over the years, who have made significant contributions that have enriched my experience and expertise in this subject. I am immensely grateful for their valuable input for making this book students' friendly and giving a better shape in an artistic manner.

This book is an outcome of various suggestions of AICTE members, experts and authors who shared their opinion and thought to further develop the engineering education in our country. Acknowledgements are due to the contributors and different workers in this field whose published books, review articles, papers, photographs, footnotes, references and other valuable information enriched us at the time of writing the book.

Dheerendra Kumar Dwivedi

PREFACE

The book titled "Manufacturing Processes" is an outcome of the teaching and R & D experience in field of materials and manufacturing. The main reason behind writing this book is to provide fundamental understanding on approaches, processes and methods related to manufacturing of wide range of materials including metal, plastics, ceramics, in the forms of powder, sheet and bulk materials. Keeping in mind the purpose of wide coverage as well as providing essential supplementary information, topics recommended by AICTE have been presented in a very systematic and orderly manner throughout the book. Efforts have been made to explain the fundamental concepts of the subject using suitable schematic diagrams as far as possible.

The content of the manuscript has been prepared considering international standard textbooks, handbooks and research and development experience of the author. Additionally, each unit is supported with few sections like questions for self-assessment, unsolved subjective and numerical questions and activities for further information, references for further reading etc. Apart from illustrations and examples as required, the unit 7 on mathematical modelling of manufacturing processes has been enriched with numerous solved and unsolved problems for proper understanding of the related topics.

The book entitled "Manufacturing Processes" is largely based on model curriculum of AICTE for third year under-graduate students. This should be equally suitable for under-graduate programs on mechanical, production, manufacturing engineering of other University and Institutions for subject related to Manufacturing Processes. The book comprises seven units in following sequence introduction of manufacturing processes, material shaping processes, materials removal processes, unconventional manufacturing processes, additive manufacturing, welding and joining, mathematical modelling of manufacturing processes.

The book "Manufacturing Processes" is meant to provide a thorough understanding on presented topics related to manufacturing processes which will enable future graduate engineers in comprehending and interpreting the factors to be kept in mind for manufacturing quality products considering the material, geometry and application. The subject matters are presented in a constructive manner so that graduate engineers are better prepared to work in real world at the very forefront of technology.

I sincerely hope that the book will inspire the students to learn and discuss the ideas behind basic principles of manufacturing processes and will surely contribute to the development of a solid foundation of the subject. I would be thankful to all beneficial comments and suggestions which will contribute to the improvement of the future editions of the book. It gives us immense pleasure to place this book in the hands of the teachers, researchers and students. It was indeed a big pleasure to work on different aspects covered in the book. I sincerely hope that this book will be a valuable resource in your journey of learning and discovery. I invite you to immerse yourself in the world of manufacturing technologies and embark on an adventure that will empower you to shape the future.

Happy reading! Happy Learning!

Dheerendra Kumar Dwivedi

OUTCOME BASED EDUCATION

For the implementation of an outcome based education the first requirement is to develop an outcome based curriculum and incorporate an outcome based assessment in the education system. By going through outcome based assessments evaluators will be able to evaluate whether the students have achieved the outlined standard, specific and measurable outcomes. With the proper incorporation of outcome based education there will be a definite commitment to achieve a minimum standard for all learners without giving up at any level. At the end of the program running with the aid of outcome-based education, a student will be able to arrive at the following outcomes:

PO1. Engineering knowledge: Apply the knowledge of mathematics, science, engineering fundamentals, and an engineering specialization to the solution of complex engineering problems.

PO2. Problem analysis: Identify, formulate, review research literature, and analyze complex engineering problems reaching substantiated conclusions using first principles of mathematics, natural sciences, and engineering sciences.

PO3. Design / development of solutions: Design solutions for complex engineering problems and design system components or processes that meet the specified needs with appropriate consideration for the public health and safety, and the cultural, societal, and environmental considerations.

PO4. Conduct investigations of complex problems: Use research-based knowledge and research methods including design of experiments, analysis and interpretation of data, and synthesis of the information to provide valid conclusions.

PO5. Modern tool usage: Create, select, and apply appropriate techniques, resources, and modern engineering and IT tools including prediction and modeling to complex engineering activities with an understanding of the limitations.

PO6. The engineer and society: Apply reasoning informed by the contextual knowledge to assess societal, health, safety, legal and cultural issues and the consequent responsibilities relevant to the professional engineering practice.

PO7. Environment and sustainability: Understand the impact of the professional engineering solutions in societal and environmental contexts, and demonstrate the knowledge of, and need for sustainable development.

PO8. Ethics: Apply ethical principles and commit to professional ethics and responsibilities and norms of the engineering practice.

PO9. Individual and team work: Function effectively as an individual, and as a member or leader in diverse teams, and in multidisciplinary settings.

PO10. Communication: Communicate effectively on complex engineering activities with the engineering community and with society at large, such as, being able to comprehend and write effective reports and design documentation, make effective presentations, and give and receive clear instructions.

PO11. Project management and finance: Demonstrate knowledge and understanding of the engineering and management principles and apply these to one's own work, as a member and leader in a team, to manage projects and in multidisciplinary environments.

PO12. Life-long learning: Recognize the need for, and have the preparation and ability to engage in independent and life-long learning in the broadest context of technological change.

COURSE OUTCOMES

After completion of the course the students will be able to:

1. Understand the different conventional and unconventional manufacturing methods employed for making different products.
2. To motivate and challenge the students to understand and develop an appreciation of the processes in terms of material properties, size and shape of the components.
3. To apply mathematical models related to manufacturing processes to understand related physics and mechanisms.
4. To introduce newer approaches of manufacturing process like additive manufacturing for metal and polymer, laser assisted material processing.
5. To learn about methods suitable for manufacturing components made of polymers, glass, metal and composite materials.

Course Outcomes	Expected Mapping with Programme Outcomes *(1- Weak Correlation; 2- Medium correlation; 3- Strong Correlation)*											
	PO-1	PO-2	PO-3	PO-4	PO-5	PO-6	PO-7	PO-8	PO-9	PO-10	PO-11	PO-12
CO-1	3	3	2	2	2	1	2	-	-	1	1	2
CO-2	3	3	3	2	2	1	2	-	-	1	2	2
CO-3	3	3	2	3	3	2	1	-	-	-	2	2
CO-4	3	2	3	2	3	-	2	-	-	-	-	2
CO-5	3	2	2	3	1	-	-	-	-	-	-	2
CO-6	-	-	-	-	-	-	-	-	-	-	-	-

ABBREVIATIONS AND SYMBOLS

List of Abbreviations

General Terms			
Abbreviations	**Full form**	**Abbreviations**	**Full form**
HAZ	Heat affected zone	TMAZ	Thermo-mechanically affected zone
NDT	Non-destructive test		
PDCA	Plan-DO-Check-Act	TIG	Tungsten inert gas
DOC	Depth of cut	MPa	Mega-Pascal
PCBN	Polycrystalline boron	MRR	Material removal rate
TiB	Titanium boride	Ra	Surface roughness
LCS	Low carbon steel	HSS	High speed steel
HCS	High carbon steel	TiN	Titanium nitride
UMP	Unconventional manufacturing processes	BUE	Built up edge
		SOD	Stand-off distance
HRC	Rockwell hardness C scale	HF	High frequency
AJM	Abrasive jet machining	ECM	Electrochemical machining
EDM	Electric discharge machining	USM	Ultrasonic machining
		W-EDM	Wire-electric discharge machining
PAM	Plasma arc machining		
KE	Kinetic energy	CNC	Computerized numerical control
LBM	Laser beam machining	EBM	Electron beam machining
R & D	Research and development	3D	Three dimensional
STL	Stereolithographic	2D	Two dimensional
WAAM	Wire-arc additive manufacturing	AM	Additive manufacturing
		SLS	Selective laser sintering
UV	Ultraviolet light	SLM	Selective laser melting
MAM	Metal additive manufacturing	DMLS	Direct metal laser sintering
		H_{net}	Net heat input
SMAW	Shielded metal arc welding	GMAW	Gas metal arc welding
GTAW	Gas tungsten arc welding	PAW	Plasma arc welding
DC	Direct current	AC	Alternating current
DCSP	Direct current straight polarity	DCRP	Direct current reverse polarity
		DCEN	Direct current electrode negative
DCEP	Direct current electrode positive		
		IMC	Intermetallic compound
NZ	Nugget zone	FSW	Friction stir welding
SAW	Submerged arc welding	BM	Base metal
		MIG	Metal inert gas

List of Symbols

Symbols	Description	Symbols	Description
Na	Sodium		
K	Potassium/Kelvin	*Pb*	Lead
Mg	Magnesium	Sn	Tin
Cr	Chromium	*FeS*	Iron sulfide
Ni	Nickel	*Tm*	Melting temperature
J	+Joule	*mm*	Millimetre
k	Thermal conductivity	*D*	Diameter
Cu	Copper	*N*	Rotational speed
Mn	Manganese	*RPM*	Rotation per minute
μm	Micrometer	*Co*	Cobalt
α	Thermal expansion coefficient	WC	Tungsten carbine
CO_2	Carbon dioxide	HRA	Rockwell hardness A scale
Ar	Argon	W	Tungsten
He	Helium	V	Vanadium / Voltage
^oC	Degree centigrade	C	Carbon
Zn	Zinc	g	Gram
s	Second	min	Minute
m	Meter	A	Ampere
Cl	Chloride	kg	Kilogram
ρ	Density	NH_3	Ammonia
kW	Kilowatt	S	Welding speed
η	Efficiency	H_2	Hydrogen

LIST OF FIGURES

Unit 5: Additive Manufacturing Processes

Unit 6: Joining and Fastening Processes

Unit 7: Mathematical Models for Manufacturing Processes

GUIDELINES FOR TEACHERS

To implement Outcome Based Education (OBE) knowledge level and skill set of the students should be enhanced. Teachers should take a major responsibility for the proper implementation of OBE. Some of the responsibilities (not limited to) for the teachers in OBE system may be as follows:

- Within reasonable constraint, they should manoeuvre time to the best advantage of all students.
- They should assess the students only upon certain defined criterion without considering any other potential ineligibility to discriminate them.
- They should try to grow the learning abilities of the students to a certain level before they leave the institute.
- They should try to ensure that all the students are equipped with the quality knowledge as well as competence after they finish their education.
- They should always encourage the students to develop their ultimate performance capabilities.
- They should facilitate and encourage group work and team work to consolidate newer approach.
- They should follow Blooms taxonomy in every part of the assessment.

Bloom's Taxonomy

Level	Teacher should Check	Student should be able to	Possible Mode of Assessment
Create	Students ability to create	Design or Create	Mini project
Evaluate	Students ability to justify	Argue or Defend	Assignment
Analyse	Students ability to distinguish	Differentiate or Distinguish	Project/Lab Methodology
Apply	Students ability to use information	Operate or Demonstrate	Technical Presentation/ Demonstration
Understand	Students ability to explain the ideas	Explain or Classify	Presentation/Seminar
Remember	Students ability to recall (or remember)	Define or Recall	Quiz

GUIDELINES FOR STUDENTS

Students should take equal responsibility for implementing the OBE. Some of the responsibilities (not limited to) for the students in OBE system are as follows:

- Students should be well aware of each UO before the start of a unit in each and every course.
- Students should be well aware of each CO before the start of the course.
- Students should be well aware of each PO before the start of the programme.
- Students should think critically and reasonably with proper reflection and action.
- Learning of the students should be connected and integrated with practical and real life consequences.
- Students should be well aware of their competency at every level of OBE.

TABLE OF CONTENTS

1 Manufacturing Processes and Classification

Unit Specific / Learning Objective

Objectives of this unit is to talk about following aspects

- To learn about needs and evolution of manufacturing processes
- To introduce broad approaches of manufacturing to obtain desired products
- To understand the relation between product geometry and choice of a manufacturing process
- To develop understanding on influence of manufacturing process on material characteristics
- To understand various costs related issues of manufacturing processes
- To introduce principles related to design of product for ease of manufacturing
- To learn about approaches on the selection of a manufacturing process

Additionally, a few fundamental questions for self-assessment included in this chapter in form of application, comprehension, analysis and synthesis. Further. some reading references have been included for deep learners and readers assistance.

Rationale

Design and development of a new product made of novel material is a continuous process. Therefore, it needs continuous innovations for developing efficient, economical, eco-friendly, productive and sustainable manufacturing technologies. Manufacturing products in high volume at low cost (using a high productivity manufacturing process) ensures easy availability to society for consumption which in turn improves the livelihood. This chapter introduces common approaches of manufacturing products made of metals, polymers and glasses. Learning about these would help in choosing suitable one or combination of manufacturing process (es) to make products of desired geometry, dimensional accuracy, surface finish and mechanical properties. Additionally, learning fundamentals related to specific manufacturing processes and design considering manufacturing aspects will help in producing sound good/product at low cost and in a short time while reducing wastage, and defective products.

Pre-Requisites

Physics: (Class XII)

Learning outcomes

U1-O1: Ability to differentiate between conventional and unconventional manufacturing processes

U1-O2: Ability to choose and apply suitable manufacturing process considering the product characteristics

U1-O3: Ability to estimate the way material characteristics are affected by manufacturing process

U1-O4: Ability to design a product for ease of manufacturing

U1-O5: Ability to take suitable decision (based on costing) to reduce failure and improve the quality of product

Unit-1 Outcomes	EXPECTED MAPPING WITH COURSE OUTCOMES (1- Weak Correlation; 2- Medium correlation; 3- Strong Correlation)					
	CO-1	**CO-2**	**CO-3**	**CO-4**	**CO-5**	**CO-6**
U1-O1	3	1	-	-	-	-
U1-O2	1	3	-	-	-	-
U1-O3	1	3	-	-	-	-
U1-O4	1	3	-	-	-	-
U1-O5	1	2	-	-	-	-

CO

1. Understand the different conventional and unconventional manufacturing methods employed for making different products.
2. To motivate and challenge the students to understand and develop an appreciation of the processes in terms of material properties, size and shape of the components.

1.1 Introduction

Society needs a variety of products for consumption. Methods of manufacturing these products have been evolving continuously due to varying requirements in form of material, design, quality requirements and volume of products. Further, volume of production and variety of design of product dictated the approach of manufacturing. In the beginning, things were manufactured locally by craftsmen in the form of unit production followed by batch production, mass production, continuous production and smart manufacturing (Fig. 1.1). Recently, increased variety, fast change of technologies, resulted in relatively reduced volume of production led to again change in approach for efficient, economic and productive manufacturing.

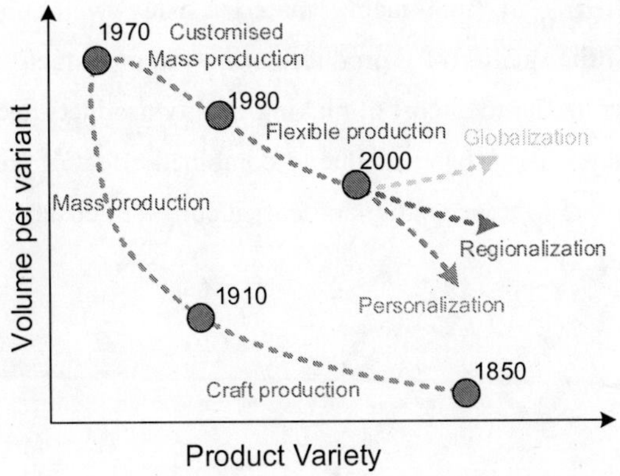

a)

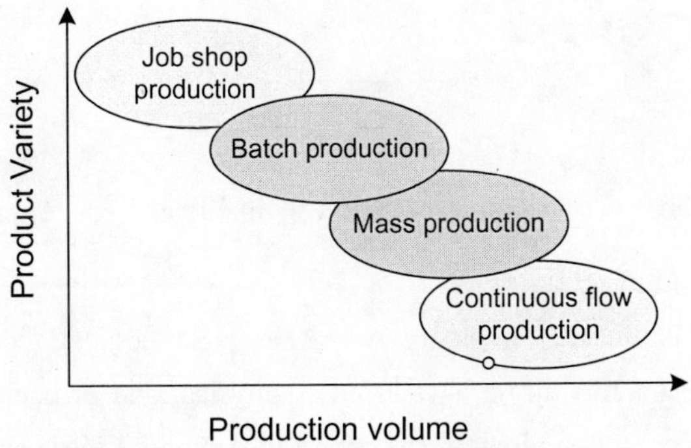

b)

Fig. 1.1 Schematic diagram of manufacturing strategies a) evolution of production strategies and b) effect of product variety and volume on production strategy

The manufacturing involves making products of desired size, shape and characteristics using suitable raw materials. The requirement of size, shape and desired characteristics depends on the application and end use of the products. The raw materials can be plastic, metal, wood, etc. in the form of solid bars, powder, plates, thin sheets, and films to make a wide variety of products for the consumption by the public or industry. How closely size, shape and properties are controlled during the manufacturing of a product affects their quality. The quality of product in turn depends on the approach of manufacturing. Criticality of the application and desired performance during use / service determine the quality requirements for proper functioning and reliability. Quality becomes more critical in the case of systems/products (like nuclear reactors, aircrafts, spacecrafts, pressure vessels) whose performance is extremely important for continuity of operation, mass production, economic performance and safety of human being / users. The quality of the product, however, significantly affects the cost. In general, efforts (in terms of high-quality material using well-controlled manufacturing processes) to increase the quality of a product during the manufacturing increases the cost. However, in the long run, the total cost of making quality products decreases with increasing levels of quality. This primarily happens due to combined effect of cost of the failures (both internal and external) due to poor quality and cost incurred to ensure manufacturing of good quality products (Fig. 1.2).

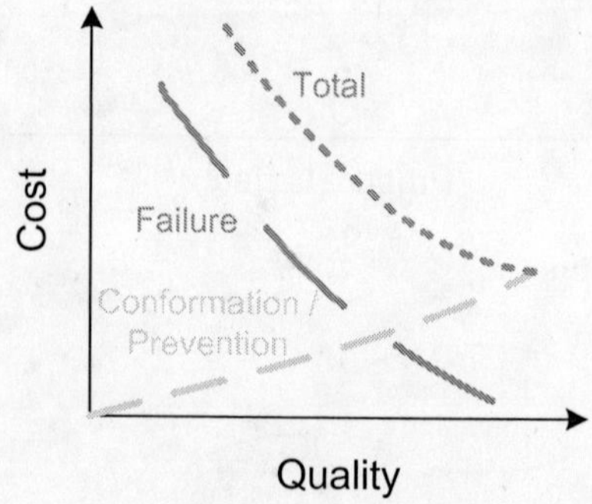

Fig. 1.2 Schematic diagram of relationship between quality and cost of product manufacturing

1.2 Perspective of manufacturing

The manufacturing is defined in many ways i.e. technological, economical (Fig. 1.3). Technologically, the manufacturing is referred as physical and or chemical processes using heat, pressure singly or in combination to convert raw material into useful products while in terms of economics, the manufacturing is a value addition process wherein low value raw material transformed into high value usable goods.

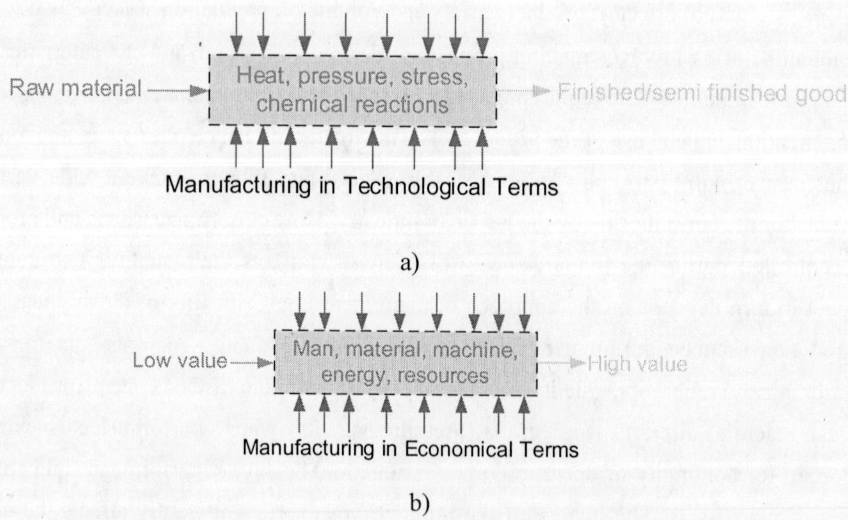

Fig. 1.3 Manufacturing in a) technological and b) economical terms.

The components and parts can be grouped as soft / hard products as per volume and approach of production. Soft products (like plates, nuts and bolts, etc.) are similar in terms of design, material and characteristics and are manufactured in very large volumes by mass production. The design flexibility and frequency of change in design are very limited in case of soft products. Hard products on the other hand are customised ones in terms of design, material, and characteristics and are manufactured in a variety of designs but in very limited volume involving job shop production.

Products (manufactured in industries) based on their end use can be termed as consumer good and capital good. Consumer goods like car, fridge, pen, bicycle, mobile phone, bread, etc. are used by society as per end use while capital goods like rolling and forging machines, lathes, welding machines, etc. are further used to manufacture other products.

Products used by us in our daily life are made of a variety of sizes, materials, and designs for various applications to satisfy a wide range of requirements including ease of use, performance, maintenance, reliability, and cost. As per application, each product requires different material (metal, wood, plastic, etc.), size (few mm to m or mg to tonnes), design (simple shapes like bars to very complex geometries engine block), and characteristics (surface finish, tolerance, mechanical and physical properties). Therefore, it is not feasible or even possible to manufacture all types of products using a single manufacturing process.

1.3 Conventional and Non-conventional Manufacturing Processes

Manufacturing processes just for the ease of understanding are grouped in two broad categories namely conventional manufacturing processes and non-conventional / newer manufacturing processes. The conventional manufacturing processes namely casting, forming, welding and machining are relatively old, developed long time ago. These are very commonly used in industries. The conventional manufacturing processes are quite efficient and effective for manufacturing products of relatively less challenging geometries and materials like cast iron, steel, aluminium, copper, magnesium, plastics, etc.

The non-conventional manufacturing processes (ultrasonic machining, electric discharge machining, electro chemical machining, laser machining, diffusion bonding, friction stir welding, incremental forming, thixoforming, etc.) are preferred when conventional manufacturing processes are unable to produce the parts with the desired

- Size
- Aspect ratio
- Shape
- Dimensional accuracy
- Tolerance

- Surface roughness
- Production rate
- Low-level of waste generation
- Productivity
- Low environmental issues
- Disposal of wastages
- Mechanical, metallurgical, corrosion characteristics

It is always preferred to realize the desired size, shape and characteristics in the manufactured products using minimum time, cost, power, wastage, material, environmental damage and any other resource(s) used for manufacturing. These factors in turn determine the economics of manufacturing and cost at which products are produced for the end usage. High productivity means less material, power, labour, time, wastage, etc., which indirectly results in low cost of product (Fig. 1.4).

Since the approach of each of the conventional manufacturing processes (like casting, welding, forming, and machining) is different, therefore each one offers unique performance in respect of effectiveness, efficiency, eco-friendly, productivity, economics, technological capability and production capacity.

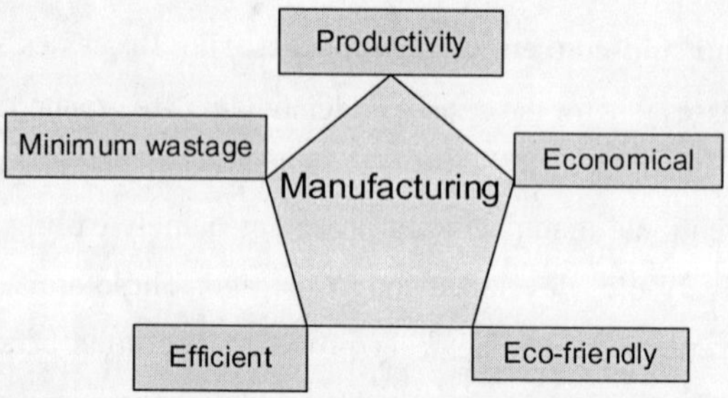

Fig. 1.4 Desired features of a manufacturing process

1.4 Classification of Manufacturing Processes

There are six broad categories of manufacturing processes used for obtaining the desired size, shape, surface finish, dimensional accuracy and tolerance, surface and bulk material properties (Fig. 1.5). The first four groups of processes (primary shaping, joining, machining and additive manufacturing) are used to obtain the desired size, shape and geometry while the last two (surface engineering and heat treatment) are used for improving the surface and bulk material characteristics of the products.

Casting involves melting of metal followed by pouring the same (after melt treatment, if any) into mould cavity, which subsequently on solidification produces the product / casting of desired size and shape. Forming primarily uses shifting of metal from one region to another through the controlled plastic deformation of bulk metal/sheet metal using suitable systems like press and die to realize the desired product. Theoretically, both casting and forming processes are zero waste processes as these are largely based on constancy of volume through shifting of metal / material from one zone to another to realize the desired size and shape. However, approaches in these two manufacturing processes are different i.e. casting involves melting followed by solidification in mould cavity while forming is based on plastic deformation using a combination of stresses like compressive, tensile, shear, bending, etc. These processes are classified as primary shaping processes or zero processes (without any addition/removal of metal). Powder metallurgy uses raw material in the form of powders, which are compacted, sintered and then subjected to secondary treatment like finishing (if required) to get the desired product. Therefore, powder metallurgy is also considered as a primary shaping process.

Welding is a joining process based on partial / localised melting and solidification of molten weld metal to fabricate products of desired size and shape. Components of relatively simple shape and smaller size are joined together to produce large and complex shape products. Brazing, soldering, adhesive joining and solid-state joining processes like forge welding, friction welding, friction stir welding, and diffusion bonding are other common joining processes. Additive manufacturing processes are also based on the approach of combining layers together to get a product of the desired size and shape. Therefore, all these are classified as additive processes. Additive manufacturing is a relatively new approach of manufacturing products using layer-by-layer deposition. A lot of work is being undertaken currently to develop these processes for metallic material, while additive manufacturing technologies are well established for manufacturing products of low melting point materials like polymers and plastics.

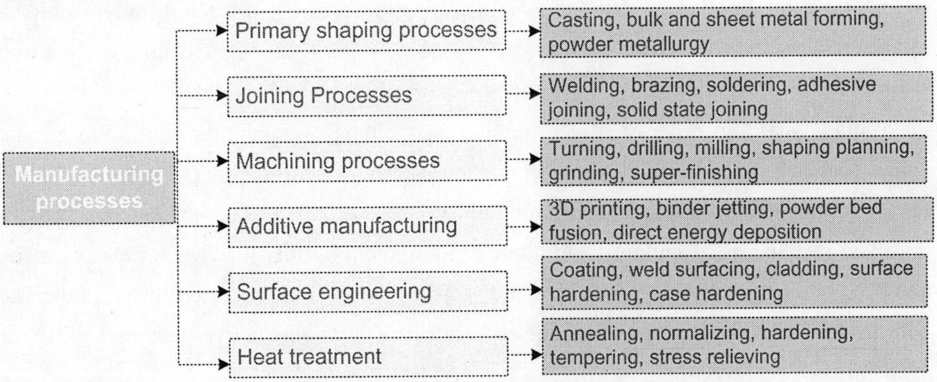

Fig. 1.5 Classification of manufacturing processes

The machining is another important conventional manufacturing process. The machining involves removal of unwanted and extra material from the stock or unfinished component, generally obtained after casting, welding, forming, powder metallurgy or any other manufacturing process. The machining mainly helps to realize the final size, dimension accuracy, tolerance, surface finish and other required dimensional characteristics like straightness, flatness as per application requirement. The material is removed using a hard and sharp wedge shape tool through the controlled relative motion between tool and workpiece to achieve the desired size and shape of the components. Since the approach of machining is based on removal of unwanted extra material from the raw materials / stock to get the final product, therefore, it is called a subtractive process. Additionally, the material is removed in the form of chips (pieces) during the machining to produce a component. These chips are simply loss of metal worth, as these cannot be used for any other purpose except recycling by re-melting.

1.5 Capabilities of Manufacturing Process

The capability of a manufacturing process can be examined in terms of technological capability, ability to handle size, weight of components and production rate (Fig. 1.6). The scope of technological capability of a manufacturing process includes control over dimensions of product (accuracy, tolerance), surface finish, defect-formation tendency, residual stress, thermo-mechanical and metallurgical damage of the material affecting the reliability and performance of the product during service.

The size of the products can vary from a few microns/millimetres to few hundred meters and weight from a few mg to tonnes. Small to medium size /weight components can be produced using casting, forming, machining but very large size components like ship, spacecraft, aircraft, etc. certainly need welding / joining based processes to realize the desired size and shape. Relatively simple shape components of moderate size are generally produced by casting and forming. Thereafter, machining is done for realizing the final dimensional control (tolerance) and surface finish. Further, very large size/complex shape components obtained using welding/joining. Production rate of manufacturing process indicates how many units are produced in unit time (per hour, per day, per week, etc.). Welding and machining are relatively slower than forming and casting. Forming processes offer the highest possible production rate. Each manufacturing process offers unique technological capability, ability to produce component of a size / size range and production capacity due to the unique approach of each family of manufacturing processes as mentioned earlier. Choice of a manufacturing process, however, dictated by economics, and quality requirement besides many other factors such as ability to process a given material, size and shape of component, surface finishing, tolerance, defect-tolerance, production rate required, need of non-destructive testing (NDT) and availability of resources.

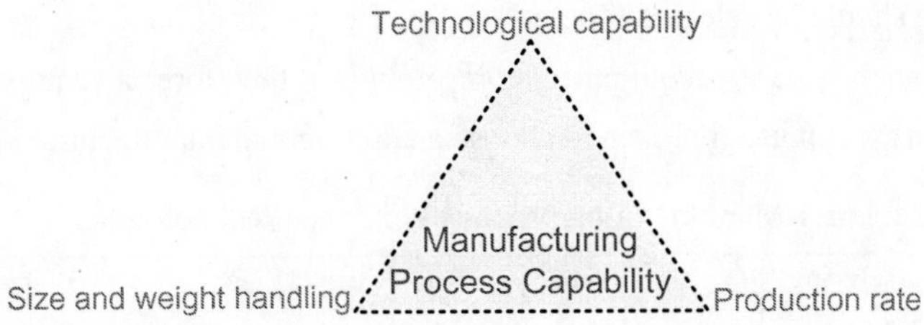

Fig. 1.6 Factor indicating capability of manufacturing process

1.6 Interdependence of Geometry, Material and Manufacturing Process

Manufacturing of a metallic product to obtain the desired size, shape and characteristics generally (but not necessarily) follow three stages:

- Primary shaping: In the initial stage, the primary size and shape (which is close to the desired one) is achieved. Therefore, this stage may be called as primarily processing/shaping. Three conventional manufacturing processes (casting, welding, forming, and powder metallurgy) are generally used to complete this stage. However, non-conventional manufacturing processes can also be used to process exotic materials (having very high hardness, melting point, work hardening behaviour) apart from realizing complex shapes which are not otherwise easily achievable by conventional manufacturing processes.
- Secondary processing: In this stage, the desired dimensional accuracy, tolerance, surface finishing and other required dimensional properties (straightness, roughness, flatness, concentricity, etc.) are obtained as per requirement of application. Secondary processing includes processes like machining, grinding, superfinishing, polishing, etc.
- Property enhancement: In this stage desired surface and bulk material properties (mechanical, tribological, metallurgical, corrosion, etc.) are realised through surface engineering, case hardening and heat treatment to develop product with desired performance for longer life and great reliability.

The performance of a product in a given application is significantly governed by geometry, material properties and quality of the components realized after manufacturing. The geometry of a product affects the choice of a suitable manufacturing process for productive, efficient, economic, effective, eco-friendly production with minimum possible resources as not every manufacturing process can satisfy these requirements of production. Somehow, efforts can be made to manufacture a product using any available process but certainly it will not be a productive, efficient, economic, effective, and eco-friendly. Unsuitable manufacturing process imposes many challenges in realising the desired size, shape and characteristics. Therefore, considering geometry, size and other material requirements of the product, an appropriate manufacturing should be selected (Table 1.1). Since products of hundreds of designs (size and shape) with various quality requirements are produced, therefore, it requires a great deal of experience and systematic approach to choose an appropriate manufacturing process.

Table 1.1 Manufacturing processes and their technological features

S. No.	Manufacturing process	Geometry	Size	Tolerance	Roughness
1	Casting	Simple to complex shapes	Small to large	Moderate	High
2	Welding	Relatively simple shapes	Small to very large	High	High
3	Forming	Relatively simple shapes	Small to medium	Moderate	High
4	Machining	Simple to complex shapes	Small to medium	Low	Low

Material and manufacturing processes both affect the achievable part geometry (simple / complex). Inter-relation between three aspects is schematically shown in Fig. 1.7. Mechanical properties such as yield strength, ductility, thermal softening and work hardening affect the section thickness and complexity of geometry that can be realized through deformation-based processes like forming, forging, and rolling. Similarly, physical properties namely coefficient of thermal expansion, and thermal conductivity of metal affect the tolerance and dimensional accuracy of a component having varied geometrical features. The components fabricated by hot forming, casting, and welding are also subjected to differential thermal expansion and contraction at different locations owing to variation in thermal cycle imposed during manufacturing. Further, it is almost impossible to realize all types of geometrical features (including size and shapes) in a product made of any material by any available manufacturing process due to their limited technological capabilities.

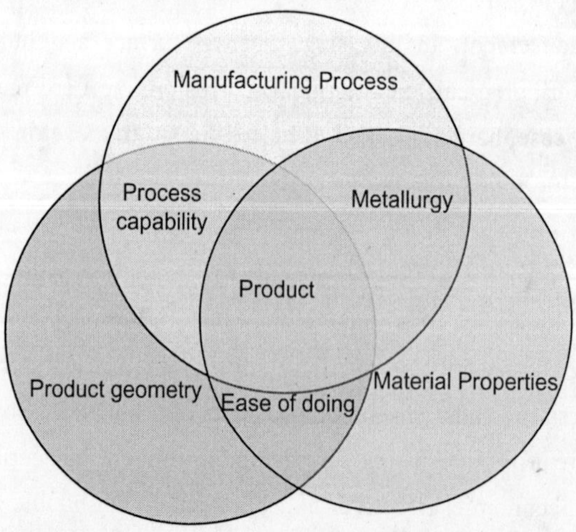

Fig. 1.7 Inter-relationship amongst material, geometry and manufacturing process

1.6.1 Materials and Manufacturing Processes

Material and manufacturing processes are closely related and exhibit significant inter-dependency on two aspects a) ease of manufacturing of a material determines the choice of a suitable manufacturing and b) influence of manufacturing process on microstructure and mechanical, tribological properties of material affects the functionality and performance of the product/component during the service.

Effect of material on manufacturing

The following properties of material need to be considered in manufacturing and performance of the component.

- Physical properties: thermal conductivity, coefficient of thermal expansion, melting point, solidification temperature range, etc.
- Chemical properties: chemical affinity, corrosion, oxidation, etc.
- Mechanical properties: hardness, strength, ductility, toughness, creep, fatigue, fracture toughness, strain hardening, etc.
- Dimensional characteristics: straightness, flatness, roundness, surface roughness, length, etc.

The desired properties in metals vary significantly considering ease of manufacturing process as evident from Table 1.2. Low melting point temperature, narrow solidification temperature and low thermal expansion coefficient metals are preferred for casting and welding processes (involving melting and solidification) for ease of melting; reduce defect formation tendency like hot tears, solidification cracking; and residual stress and distortion tendency (Fig.1.8). Similarly, low affinity of metal to atmospheric gases like oxygen and nitrogen at high temperature and that in the molten condition reduces the defects like inclusions during welding and casting.

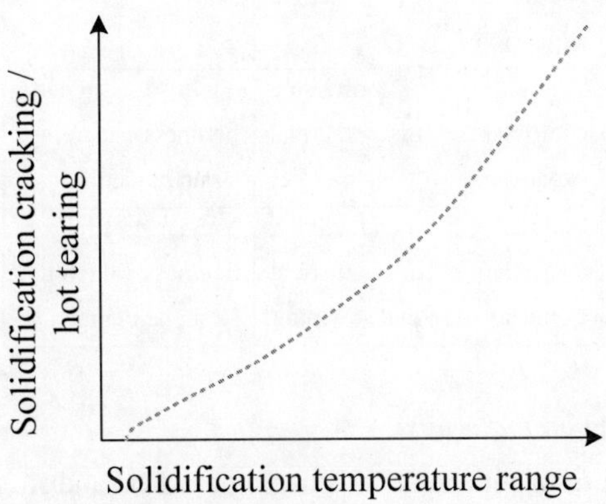

Fig. 1.8 Schematic diagram shows effect of solidification temperature range on hot tearing / solidification cracking

Mechanical properties of metals like hardness, yield strength, ductility, strain hardening, and thermal softening tendency affect the ease of manufacturing by machining, forming and solid state joining. A metal of low yield strength and high ductility facilitates easy plastic deformation during forming and shaping of the metals. Heating of hard, brittle and high strength metals above their recrystallization temperature / critical temperature also facilitates forming (hot rolling, hot forging, etc.) by increasing ductility and lowering yield strength.

Removal of material during machining needs penetration of the cutting edge of the tool into the workpiece followed by relative motion between the tool and workpiece. In addition to hardness, strain-hardening tendency and ductility are other two important mechanical properties affecting ease of machining. Low strain hardening metals offer higher machinability while an optimum ductility is important for good machinability. Low chemical affinity of metal with atmospheric gases, low coefficient of thermal expansion and high thermal conductivity generally improve machinability due to a) low chemical reaction at the surface, b) better dimensional control and c) longer tool life.

Table 1.2. Properties of metals important for various manufacturing processes

S. No.	Manufacturing process	Physical properties	Mechanical properties	Chemical properties
1	Casting	Melting point, solidification temperature range, coefficient of thermal expansion	Yield strength and ductility	Affinity of gases, solid and liquid state solubility
2	Welding	Melting point, solidification temperature range, coefficient of thermal expansion	Yield strength, hardness, ductility	Affinity of gases, solid and liquid state solubility
3	Forming	Thermal softening, coefficient of thermal expansion	Yield strength, hardness, ductility, strain hardening	Oxidation tendency
4	Machining	Thermal conductivity, coefficient of thermal expansion, thermal softening	Yield strength, hardness, ductility, strain hardening	Affinity with coolant, water, oil

Effect of manufacturing on materials

The manufacturing processes for sizing and shaping use heat and stress either separately or in combination. Heating / Temperature rise during manufacturing processes like casting, welding, machining and forming alters the microstructure and mechanical properties of metal, which in turn affect the quality, performance and reliability of manufactured components during the service. Usage of high heat for melting during casting and welding alters the microstructure of metals. Tendency of formation of defects like porosity, inclusion and cracks during these processes is very high due to development of tensile residual stresses and interaction of gases with metal. Forming and machining processes involve use of stress for plastic deformation and shearing of metals, respectively for manufacturing. The plastic deformation at low temperature (cold working) causes work/strain hardening while at high temperature the strain hardening becomes negligible (Fig. 1.9). Strain/work hardening of metal (depending on the strain hardening exponent) increases hardness, and strength due to plastic deformation during forming and machining but at the cost of ductility and toughness.

It is pertinent to mention that inherent heat generation or controlled external heat application during forming and machining above certain critical temperatures changes the microstructure and mechanical properties. However, the extent of these changes depends on strengthening mechanism of material. Conversely, the strengthening mechanism of the metal being processed determines how far plastic deformation and heat affect the microstructure and mechanical properties of material. Metals designed based on strengthening mechanisms (Table 1.3) namely grain refinement, work/strain hardening, transformation and precipitation hardening are very sensitive to thermal cycle (heating, peak temperature, soaking time and cooling). Metals which gain their strength from solid solution strengthening, and dispersion hardening are not much affected by heat and deformation.

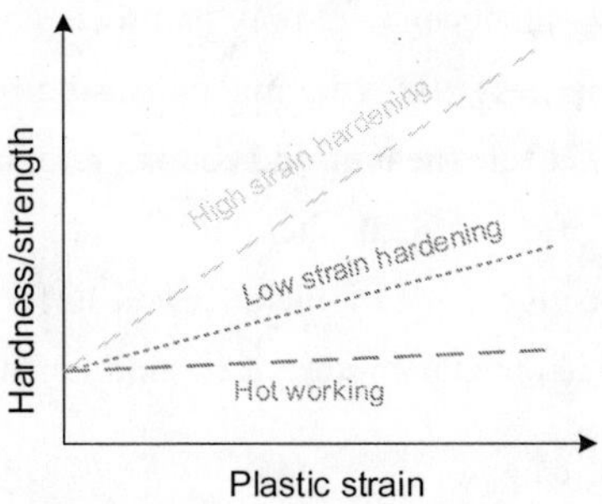

Fig. 1.9 Schematic showing the effect of plastic strain for cold working (different strain hardening materials) and hot working

Further, a metal may gain strength not necessarily from a single metal strengthening mechanism as the mechanisms like grain refinement, and work hardening will always have their contribution in the manufacturing process. Therefore, influence of a manufacturing process on microstructure and mechanical properties must be considered to ensure product functionality and performance during the service. It is therefore inevitable to consider the geometrical and material aspect of a product while considering the impact of manufacturing process on product functionality and performance.

Table 1.3 Relevance of metal strengthening mechanism and manufacturing processes

S. No.	Manufacturing process	Metal Strengthening Mechanism					
		Grain refinement	Strain hardening	Precipitation hardening	Transformation hardening	Solid solution strengthening	Dispersion hardening
1	Casting	As per cooling rate and refiners	No strain hardening left	No	Possibility of elimination of transformation hardening effect as per cooling rate	Not much affected	Not much affected except segregation
2	Welding	As per heat input/cooling rate and refiners	No strain hardening left	No	Increases transformation hardening tendency	Not much affected	Not much affected except segregation
3	Forming	Refinement and elongation of grain	Strain hardening in cold condition only	Not much affected except in hot forming	Possibility of deformation assisted transformation hardening	Not much affected	Not much affected
4	Machining	Not much affected	Strain hardening of surface layers	Not much affected	Possibility of transformation hardening	Not much affected	Not much affected

Similarly, the desired dimensional properties like roundness, flatness, circularity, concentricity, tolerance, surface roughness, etc. depend not only on process but also on the relevant process parameters and material properties such as thermal expansion / contraction behaviour, thermal conductivity affecting thermal cycle (heating and cooling rate) imposed during manufacturing. Each manufacturing process offers a unique thermal cycle due to varying heat input (Fig. 1.10) Common processes and respective range of tolerance and surface roughness are given in Table for reference to have an idea about capabilities of common manufacturing processes.

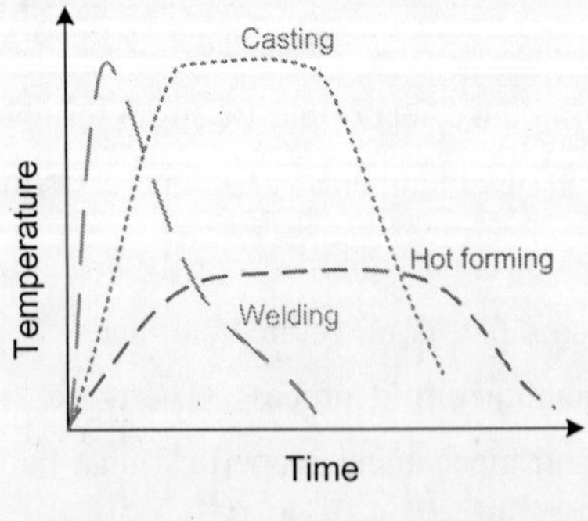

Fig. 1.10 Schematic of indicative thermal cycles of casting, welding and forming process

1.7 Product quality and cost

The quality has been defined in many ways like conformance to the specification or meeting the customers' expectations. There are nine dimensions related to the product/service used to examine the quality namely performance, features, conformance, reliability, durability, service, aesthetics, response of the firm to customer, and reputation of the firm (Fig. 1.11). These factors can be grouped under three headings namely performance, service, and features. All factors used to define quality of a product in fact depend on materials, and manufacturing before making it available to the customer. If a product fails to meet one or more of the above parameters, then it is categorised as a defective product. Cost of product comprises two types of costs: a) cost incurred to achieve the desired product quality and b) costs associated with failure of product either during manufacturing at the factory or during service. Former cost is also known as good quality product cost and latter is termed as failure cost (Fig. 1.12).

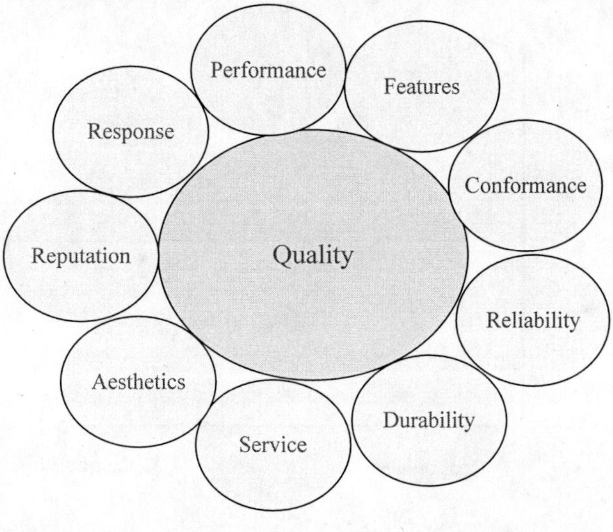

Fig. 1.11 Nine dimensions of a product defining quality

1.7.1 Cost of good quality

To ensure the manufacturing of a quality product a system is developed through a) use of the most appropriate manufacturing process, tools, process parameters, etc., b) identification of defective products at early stages by appropriate quality control, c) taking corrective measures like repair/discard, and making appropriate changes in manufacturing procedure, etc., and d) proper training to manpower, etc. The expenditure in taking care of above activities is termed as good quality cost. Conversely, cost incurred in developing such a system for reducing defects during manufacturing and increasing quality is called prevention and appraisal cost (Fig. 1.12).

Efforts are required to produce a quality product through prevention of causes, detection of defects by increasing investment in the machinery, manufacturing processes, labour training and sensitization, inspection and testing, quality control. Costs associated with these actions are called cost of good quality. Increasing cost of quality reduces the costs due to poor quality and failures.

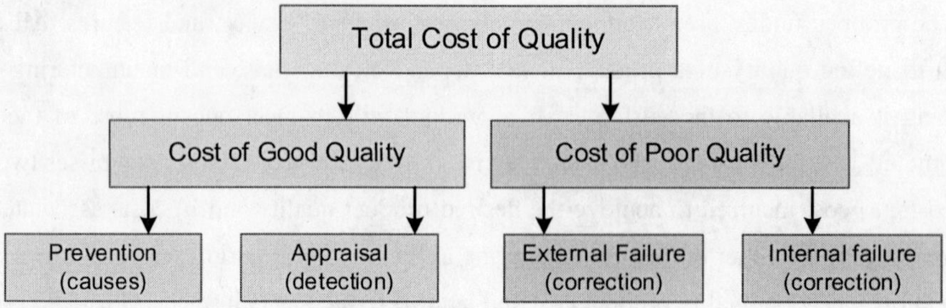

a)

b)

Fig. 1.12 Relationship between cost and quality of product a) block diagram and b) schematic diagram

1.7.2 Cost of poor quality

Lack of proper implementation of the plan, procedure and precaution during manufacturing results in failure to produce the desired quality. Such costs are called internal failure costs. Once the ownership of the product is transferred to the customer and then failure of the product causes losses in terms reputation, potential customers, litigations, calling product back from market apart from costs associated with maintenance and repair. Losses to the firm because of these failures of the product are called external failure cost due to poor quality

1.8 Design for manufacturability

The part design for manufacturing primarily involves designing a product for ease of manufacturing at low cost without compromise on the quality, reliability and performance. The product design affects material, manufacturing processes, labour cost, production time, quality, time to launch a new product to market, etc. Therefore, designing a product considering the manufacturing, quality requirement and performance at the product development stage itself significantly reduces per unit cost of product. As per estimates, the contribution of product design can be much higher (up to 70% of the total cost) than other important factors like manufacturing process, labour, quality control, materials, etc. (accounts for remaining 30% of the product cost).

The design for manufacturability is a general and fundamental approach to design the product in the development stage itself based on inputs from the relevant internal stakeholders (within organization) like people from engineering, marketing (inputs for market needs), design, material, manufacturing, assembly, quality, packaging, etc. A product developed based on comprehensive inputs of all the stakeholders for efficient manufacturing and launch of the product in general offers multiple advantages: a) effective material selection, b) reduced manufacturing time, c) reduced defects, d) reduced time to launch a product in market, e) reduced per unit cost, and f) improved quality. These factors realised through "design for manufacturability" which in turn improves the competitiveness of the product in market and its penetration. In general, the following key aspects are kept in mind for designing a product for manufacturability (Fig.1.13).

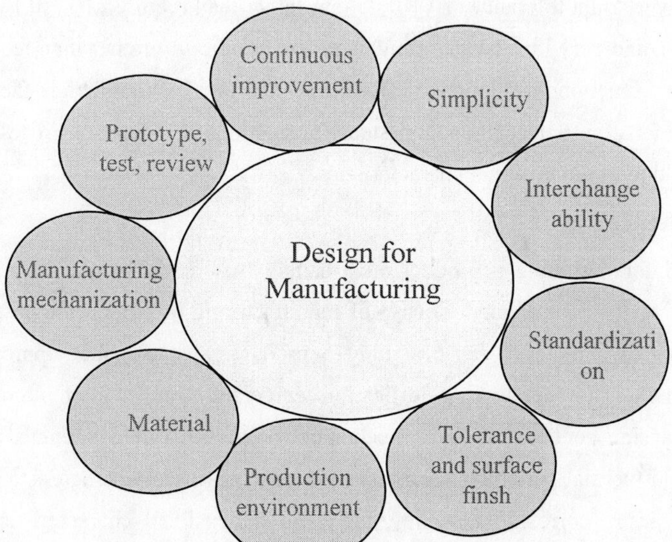

Fig. 1.13 Important aspects for consideration in design for manufacturing

Simple design

The design of a product being developed must be simple with a few parts/components without compromising the functionality and performance. A simple product design facilitates easy and effective manufacturing; reduces error, increases quality, reliability, and reduces manufacturing cost.

Standardization

Develop the product design considering standard size-raw material, manufacturing process, inspection and test methods for which systems and expertise are easily available. Standardization therefore reduces production cost and time to manufacture and launch a product to the market.

Interchangeability and modularity

The product designed for manufacturability must be modular allowing interchangeability to facilitate ease of assembly, replacement during manufacturing and subsequent repairs and manufacturing using standard size nuts/bolts, pipes, wrenches, etc. A modular product design therefore reduces manufacturing cost, improves ease of repair/ maintenance.

Dimensional characteristics (tolerance and surface quality)

Design engineers must establish optimal dimensional characteristics (neither too tight nor loose) such as tolerance, surface roughness, flatness, circularity, concentricity, etc. for different parts of a product. Setting of skewed (too high or low either way) tolerance and surface characteristics adversely affects the ease of manufacturing, cost and performance. For example, unnecessary very tight tolerance (10 ± 0.05 mm rather than required 10 ± 0.1 mm for given a functionality), and very low surface roughness (0.2 ± 0.02 μm rather than required 1.2 ± 0.2 μm for given a functionality) increase effort, time, and cost to manufacture the product due to need of additional systems, procedural steps, precautions, and special processes required to realize such kind of dimensional characteristics.

Material selection

The material for designing a product must satisfy two requirements: a) performance and functionality of the product and b) ease of manufacturing to reduce the cost. Accordingly, characteristics of a material for designing a product must consider appropriate physical properties (melting temperature, solidification temperature range, thermal conductivity, and thermal expansion coefficient, etc.), mechanical properties (yield strength, ductility, work hardening and thermal softening behaviour, etc.) and chemical characteristics (affinity with atmospheric gases, corrosion tendency, etc.) and dimensional characteristics (size, shape, roughness, etc.).

Mechanization

Mechanization of manufacturing, inspection, materials handling, packaging, etc. reduces human / manual intervention. The design of the product therefore must support the mechanization at the different stages of material flow during manufacturing as applicable from raw material to finished product and finally packaging. Mechanisation lowers the chances of defects, improves the quality, reduces the production time and labour cost, reduces requirement of inspection and testing, and improves the consistency in quality.

Manufacturing Process

The product design must consider the available cost-effective manufacturing processes and required technical expertise. Attempts are made to design product such that it allows use of a cost effective and efficient manufacturing process considering the quality requirement, material of the product and the desired production rate.

Production Environment

It is also important to keep the environment (temperature, ambient, inert / vacuum / controlled environment) within the specified range for fabrication of a component using different the manufacturing processes. Lack of consideration of the production environment at the product design stage will increase defect tendency, production time, cost of manufacturing, and reduce productivity.

Feasibility of prototype

The prototype of a designed product is developed (using all relevant aspects of product design like material, tolerance, manufacturing, inspection and testing, packaging) for examination of quality, functionality, and performance. In case of any deviation of quality, functionality and performance of the prototype, design of the product must be reviewed, and appropriate changes are made for improvement accordingly.

Review and continuous improvement

Today's world is very dynamic in terms of rate of change in technological development related to material, manufacturing, inspection and testing, packaging, requirement of customer, and market competition. Timely change in the design stage of the product saves a lot of time, cost and resources (Fig. 1.14). Therefore, it is always good to review product design, performance, aesthetics, and cost of the product to make suitable changes in design for improvement, remain competitive, and retain customers. Continuous improvement can be realised through suitable techniques, like PDCA (plan-do-check-act), FMEA (failure-mode-effect-analysis), and process capability improvement.

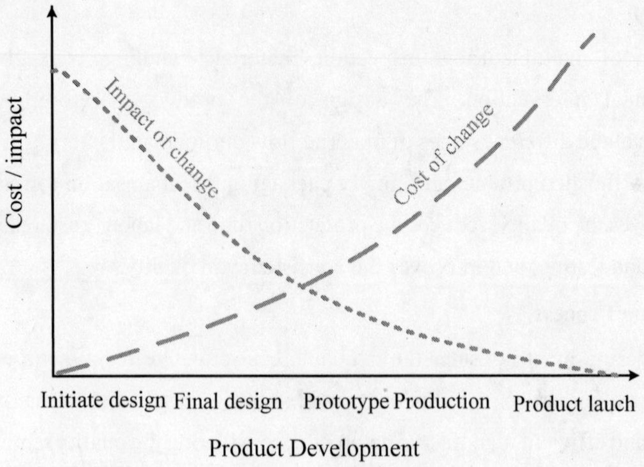

Fig. 1.14 Stages in product design and their influence on cost and impact

Selection of manufacturing process

Selection of a manufacturing process to produce components eventually governed by economics and quality of the product. It is very important to manufacture the desired quality products at minimum possible cost to remain competitive and relevant in the market for customer retention and growth of business. The selection of the manufacturing process depends on multiple factors.

- Size
- Shape
- Material
- Weight
- Properties required
- Post processing requirement
- Production rate
- Batch size
- Volume of production
- Tolerance
- Quality desired
- Surface roughness
- Allowable defect
- Availability of machinery and expertise
- Waste disposal and related regulation
- Cost (energy, environment, labour, materials and other consumables)

The list of factors is suggestive only and can vary with material, product, quantity, and quality requirement (Fig. 1.15). Once the primary shape of the product is achieved then final size, tolerance, surface-finish, mechanical and metallurgical properties and other desired characteristics are obtained through secondary processing / post processing like cleaning, impregnation, machining, finishing, coating, case hardening, heat treatment, painting, stress relieving, etc.

The selection of a single process or combination of a few manufacturing processes to produce a product can be done using various approaches depending on the type of product (custom/standard), availability of resources, volume of production, type of production (batch / mass). Generally, the selection of the manufacturing process is qualitative in nature and is usually based on the collective inputs of all the relevant experienced stakeholders (design, engineering, material, manufacturing, quality control, packaging, etc.).

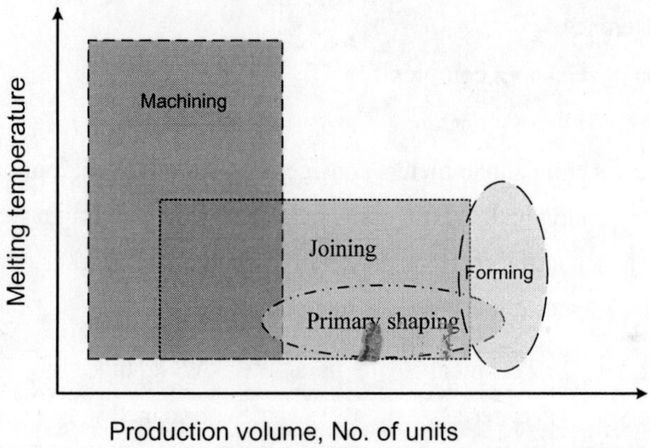

Fig. 1.15 Schematic showing preferred manufacturing processes considering melting temperature of material and volume of production

A team of experts/stakeholders based on the material of the product to be manufactured, shortlists of a few suitable manufacturing processes. Then further narrowing down of the shortlisted processes is done to achieve the desired tolerance, surface finish and production rate. Additionally, other factors like economics, availability of expertise, waste disposal, applicable rules and regulations may significantly affect the choice. This approach is relatively simple and effective for less complicated cases where not much is at stake due to low volume, high product variety, limited capabilities and availability of resources.

The matrix approach is more comprehensive and systematic to arrive at the most appropriate manufacturing process for producing a component. The following steps are used in the decision matrix approach for the selection of a manufacturing process considering all the relevant factors and available manufacturing processes.

1. Prepare a list of all the relevant technical parameters (criteria) for manufacturing a product through brainstorming with a team of experts and different stakeholders e.g.
   a. Material
   b. Tolerance
   c. Surface finish
   d. Production rate
   e. Job (size/shape) complexity
   f. Volume of production
   g. Cost of manufacturing
2. Identify a few most important technical parameters which must be considered in final selection of the manufacturing process e.g.
   a. Material
   b. Tolerance
   c. Job (size/shape) complexity
   d. Cost of manufacturing
3. Prioritise the technical parameters considering their relative importance to manufacture the product economically, efficiently and effectively and assign weight factor to each parameter in scale of 1 to 10 as per relative importance. Higher weight is assigned for criteria with greater importance for manufacturing.

S. No.	Technical parameter (criteria)	Weightage assigned
1	Material	9
2	Cost	8
3	Tolerance	7
4	Job complexity	6

4. Prepare a list of potential manufacturing processes available to produce a product
   a. Casting
   b. Machine forging
   c. Shaping (machining)
   d. Additive manufacturing
5. Assign weight factor to each manufacturing process in scale of 1 to 10 as per their capability to satisfy/fulfil each of the criteria. Higher weight is assigned if suitability of a manufacturing process is more for a given criterion.

S. No.	Technical parameter (weight)	Manufacturing processes			
		Casting	Forging	Shaping	Additive manufacturing
1	Material (9)	8	6	9	8
2	Cost (8)	10	5	4	3
3	Tolerance (7)	8	6	9	7
4	Job complexity (6)	9	7	9	7

6. Calculate sum of product of weightage assigned to technical parameter X that of manufacturing process.

S. No.	Technical parameter	Manufacturing processes			
		Casting	Forging	Shaping	Additive manufacturin g
1	Material (9)	8 X 9: 72	6 X 9: 54	9 X 9: 81	8 X 9: 72
2	Cost (8)	10 X 8: 80	5 X 8: 40	4 X 8: 32	3 X 8: 24
3	Tolerance (7)	8 X 7: 56	6 X 7: 42	9 X 7: 63	7 X 7: 49
4	Job complexity (6)	9 X 6: 54	7 X 6: 42	9 X 6: 54	7 X 6: 42
Sum of combined weights		262	211	230	187

7. A manufacturing process with maximum sum of combined weights suggests the most appropriate manufacturing process for the selected technical parameters. Table above shows that the casting is the most suitable manufacturing process considering material, cost, tolerance and job complexity criteria.

UNIT SUMMARY

This chapter gives an overview of conventional and unconventional manufacturing processes, and their needs. Additionally, relationships between material, product geometry and manufacturing processes have been elaborated. A systematic approach of selection of manufacturing processes has also been described with suitable examples.

EXERCISE

Questions for self-assessment

1. In technological terms, the manufacturing is related to
   a. Trading
   b. Marketing
   c. Producing goods using suitable physical/chemical processes
   d. Earning profit
2. Manufacturing of a drilling machine is an example of
   a. Unique good
   b. Consumer good
   c. Capital good
   d. None of these
3. A single manufacturing process doesn't fit for economical and efficient manufacturing of all type of products due to variation in
   a. Geometry
   b. Materials
   c. Quality requirement
   d. All of these
4. An example of unconventional manufacturing process is
   a. Arc welding
   b. Grinding
   c. Laser machining
   d. Hot rolling
5. A type of primary shaping process is
   a. Gas welding
   b. Shaping
   c. Drilling
   d. Powder metallurgy
6. Layer by layer material deposition approach of manufacturing process is
   a. Casting
   b. Welding
   c. Forming
   d. Additive manufacturing
7. Manufacturing approach used for improving surface properties only is
   a. Welding
   b. Rolling
   c. Surface engineering
   d. Heat treatment
8. Heat treatment of bulk metals help in obtaining desired
   a. Geometry
   b. Accuracy
   c. Finish
   d. Mechanical properties
9. Tendency of metal hot tearing of metal during casting depends on
   a. Melting temperature
   b. Solidification temperature range
   c. Oxidation tendency
   d. Density
10. Properties of metallic product obtained after manufacturing are significantly influenced by
    a. Metallurgy
    b. Biology
    c. Physics
    d. All of these

Answers to Multiple-Choice Questions

Key for MCQ: 1 c, 2 c, 3 d, 4 c, 5 d, 6 d, 7 c, 8 d, 9 b, 10 a

Short and Long Answer Type Questions

1. How did the approaches of manufacturing changes historically over a long-time horizon?
2. Enlist the common approaches of manufacturing
3. What is definition of manufacturing in terms of economics?
4. Distinguish the capital and consumer goods.
5. Differentiate conventional and unconventional manufacturing processes based on suitability.
6. How does additive manufacturing differ from welding for making metallic components?
7. How to examine the capability of a manufacturing process?
8. Elaborate the way materials, manufacturing and product geometry are interrelated.
9. Explain the approaches of any four conventional manufacturing processes.
10. How does material properties affect the selection of a manufacturing process for making any product?
11. What is the importance of physical and mechanical properties of metal in casting and welding?
12. What is significance of mechanical properties of metals by machining and forming processes?
13. How does manufacturing affect the properties of metallic materials?
14. Elaborate relation between cost and product quality in manufacturing.
15. Describe various aspects to be considered for designing a product for ease of manufacturing.
16. Explain approach(es) for selection of a manufacturing process.

PRACTICAL

Select a product that you commonly use. Think about a process or a combination of processes which should be used to manufacture the same with desired characteristics and quality.

KNOW MORE

Explore the ancient and historical way of manufacturing goods from ice, stone, bronze and modern age and try to find how they have evolved over a period of time.

Scan me!

SUGGESTED RESOURCES FOR FURTHER READING/LEARNING

1. D K Dwivedi, Fundamentals of Metal Joining, Springer Nature, (2021)
2. S Kalpakjian, S R Schmid, Manufacturing Engineering and Technology, Pearson (2018)
3. M P Groover, Fundamentals of Modern Manufacturing, John Wiley and Sons, (2010)
4. A Ghosh, A K Malik, Manufacturing science, East-West Press (2010)
5. D K Dwivedi, Surface engineering, Springer Nature (2018)
6. D K Dwivedi, Materials Engineering, AICTE, (2023)
7. D K Dwivedi, NPTEL Course "Joining Technologies for Metals": https://onlinecourses.nptel.ac.in/noc23_me130/preview
8. D K Dwivedi, NPTEL Course "Fundamentals of Manufacturing Processes" https://archive.nptel.ac.in/courses/112/107/112107219/
9. D. K. Dwivedi, Microstructure and abrasive wear behavior of iron base hardfacing developed by SMA welding, Material Science and Technology, 20, 10, (2004) 1326-1330.
10. D. K. Dwivedi, Ashok Sharma, T V Rajan, Influence of silicon morphology and mechanical properties of piston alloys, Materials and Manufacturing Processes, 20, 5, (2005) 777-791.
11. Keshav Prasad, D K Dwivedi, Microstructure and Tensile properties of submerged arc welded 1.25Cr-0.5Mo steel, International Journal of Materials and Manufacturing Processes, 23, 5 (May 2008) 463-868.
12. D. K. DWIVEDI, Heat treatment of cast Al-Si base alloys for improved mechanical properties, Aluminium India, Vol. 28, No. 4, Oct- Dec 2000, 21-24.
13. C P Paul, B K Gandhi, P Bhargava, D K Dwivedi, L M Kukreja, Cobalt Free Laser Cladding on AISI type 316L Stainless Steel for Improved Cavitation and Slurry Erosion Wear Behavior, Journal of Materials Engineering & Performance, 23, (Sep 2014), 4463-4471

2 Material Shaping Processes

Unit Specific / Learning Objective

The objective of this unit is to talk about the following aspects

- To learn about the scope of primary shaping manufacturing processes.
- To introduce casting, forming, powder metallurgy and plastic component manufacturing processes.
- To learn about the suitability and applications of primary shaping processes.
- To develop understanding on the steps of casting, forming and powder metallurgy processes for manufacturing.
- To learn about standard plastic processing methods.
- To understand common casting and forming defects, their causes and remedies.

Additionally, a few questions for self-assessment based on fundamentals have been included in this chapter. These questions are based on applications, comprehension, analysis and synthesis. Suggested further reading and reference have been included for deep learners and readers.

Rationale

Manufacturing is basically the realisation of a component of the desired size, shape and geometry. The raw material is processed using primary shaping processes to obtain the product of size/shape close to the desired one so that need of secondary processing in the form of machining, grinding and super-finishing is minimised. Secondary processing helps in achieving the desired surface finish and tolerance. The engineering industry nowadays uses components made of a wide range of materials such as metals, polymers, glasses and composite materials. Therefore, it is necessary and pertinent to learn about primary shaping processes like casting, forming for processing of metals; powder metallurgy process for making components made of composite materials; many plastic processing methods such extrusion, injection moulding, blow moulding, rotational moulding; glass fibre reinforced polymer matrix composite processing methods such as hand and spray layup. Awareness of these primary shaping methods allows for effective process planning of manufacturing components considering quality and other application requirements.

Pre-Requisites

Physics: (Class XII)

Learning outcomes

U2-O1: Ability to apply primary shaping manufacturing processes to make products of a very wide range of materials

U2-O2: Ability to select appropriate casting, forming, and powder metallurgy process parameters to produce sound products with desired characteristics

U2-O3: Ability to make products made of not just metals but also polymers, glasses and composite materials

U2-O4: Ability to identify defects in casting, forming and take remedial actions

U2-O5: Ability to control the microstructure of the component made by casting, forming and powder metallurgy to control the mechanical properties as per the requirement of the application

Unit-2 Outcomes	EXPECTED MAPPING WITH COURSE OUTCOMES (1- Weak Correlation; 2- Medium correlation; 3- Strong Correlation)					
	CO-1	CO-2	CO-3	CO-4	CO-5	CO-6
U2-O1	3	1	-	-	-	-
U2-O2	3	3	-	-	-	-
U2-O3	3	2	-	-	-	-
U2-O4	1	3	-	-	-	-
U2-O5	1	3	-	-	-	-

CO

1. Understand the different conventional and unconventional manufacturing methods employed for making different products
2. To motivate and challenge students to understand and develop an appreciation of the processes in correlation with material properties which change the shape, size and form of the raw materials into the desirable product.

2.1 Introduction

The material shaping processes help to produce a shape of the product close to the desired one. Products obtained through material shaping processes, also called primary shaping processes, may further need secondary processing and treatment to realize the desired fine features, size, dimensional accuracy, tolerance, surface finish and mechanical properties as per material and application of the product. Primary shaping processes have been developed for processing both metallic and non-metallic material in various forms, e.g. blanks, plates, sheets, bars and rods, powders and moderately complex shapes. The choice of a suitable manufacturing process depends on the multiple factors (material, size, shape, properties, and production rate desired) as described earlier in the last section of Unit 1. In general, the material undergoes through a few or all stages during the manufacturing as shown in Fig. 2.1. However, sequence and all stages are not necessarily followed as these are primarily determined by the available size and shape of raw material, material conditions (heat treatment, temper), surface finish, tolerance, soundness and mechanical properties desired as per application.

In this chapter, the shaping processes for metals like casting, sheet metal and bulk metal forming, and powder metallurgy, apart from processes used to manufacture products of non-metals like plastics, glasses will also be presented covering fundamentals, approaches, process principles, process capabilities and applications.

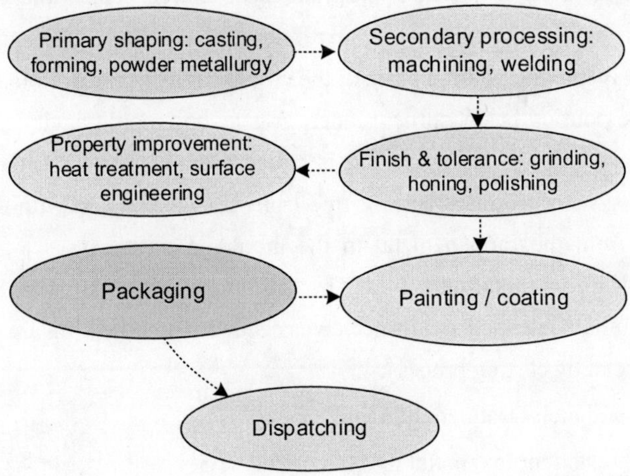

Fig. 2.1 General stages of manufacturing a product

2.2 Metal Shaping Processes

Three material shaping processes commonly used for metals or metals and non-metallic combinations (in the form of composite material) namely casting, forming and powder metallurgy are described in the following section. The approach of each metal shaping process, namely casting, forming and powder metallurgy to realize the desired shape of a product is different and unique. Casting processes (sand mould, die and investment casting) involve the melting of metal followed by solidification of the molten metal in a suitable cavity (called mould). The mould (cavity) is largely close to the shape of the product. Forming processes (depending upon the section thickness of stock material being processed) can be categorised as bulk metal forming (for large section metals) and sheet metal forming (for thin sheets). Bulk metal forming processes (rolling, forging, extrusion) primarily involve controlled plastic deformation (using mainly compressive force) of thick section plates, bars, and rods to achieve the desired shape of the product. Sheet metal forming processes are based on both plastic deformation (bending, compressive, and tensile forces) and shearing (cutting) of thin sheets. Shaping by powder metallurgy uses raw material in the form of powders of metals and constituents of the material of which the product is to be made. In the powder metallurgy process, the powder is compacted/consolidated in a cavity (of the shape corresponding to the desired product) followed by sintering to develop strength, and metallurgical bond. Post-processing of sintered components is carried out as per property requirements. In the following sections, each of these processes have been elaborated.

2.3 Casting

The casting process is based on a simple approach of melting the raw material (including waste material in the form of metallic chips, master alloys, and pure metal as per calculation to realize the desired composition) using an appropriate heat source. The molten metal after melt treatment (degassing, fluxing, alloying, grain refinement, and filtering/cleaning), is then poured in a controlled way into the pouring basin of the mould cavity of the desired shape. A complete channel from the pouring basin, sprue, runner, in-gate, and mould cavity to the riser through which molten metal flows during casting is called a gating system (Fig. 2.2). A properly designed gating system produces casting free from defects coupled with desired production rate. Heat loss from the molten metal to the mould in turn, causes the solidification by transformation of liquid metal into solid. The solid metal in the form of the product is then taken out of the mould, cleaned and inspected as needed. The following are general steps used for shaping of metal by casting process:

- Melting and melt treatment of metal
- Pouring treated molten metal into the mould cavity
- Solidification of molten metal
- Removal of casting from the mould
- Cleaning and inspection of casting

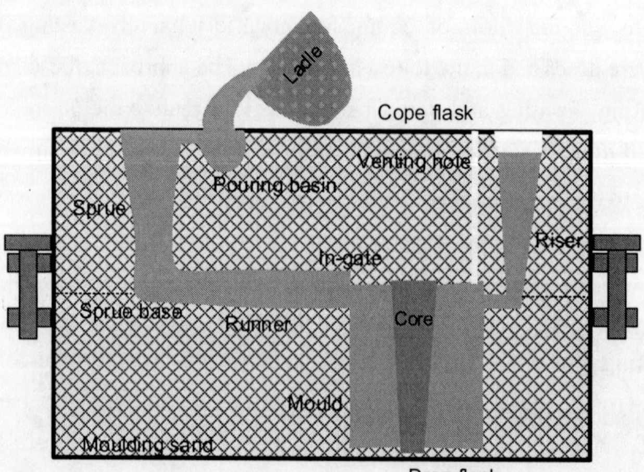

Fig. 2.2 Schematic of gating system used for casting

Gating System

A typical gating system comprises a pouring basin, sprue, runner, in-gate, mould cavity, and riser. The design of the gating system, including the riser has been described in Unit 7. The pouring basin is the first part of a gating system wherein the molten metal is fed from a ladle/furnace. The pouring basin acts as a local reservoir of the molten metal where impurities / solid particles are separated, and then clean molten metal is fed to sprue. Sprue is a vertical channel through which molten metal goes to the runner via sprue base wherein the change in direction and momentum of molten metal takes place. The molten metal then flows to different in-gates through the runner as per casting size and design. The molten metal then enters into the mould cavity through in-gates. The number and location of the runner, and in-gate depend on the size and complexity of mould/casting, the possibility of formation of defects like misrun, cold shut and shrinkage cavity and the need for directional solidification. Molten metal goes to the riser after filling the mould cavity. The riser is a very important part of the gating system, which acts as a temporary reservoir of the molten metal to compensate for shrinkage on account of liquid to solid state transformation. To perform its role effectively, the molten metal in the riser must solidify after completion of solidification in the mould cavity.

Core

A core is an individual element made of core sand and fitted in the mould to realize the special internal geometrical features in casting. A variety of cores are used as per need of part geometry. The core is made of a core sand mixture of greater strength, and refractoriness than the mould.

2.3.1 Melting of metal

The charge having a suitable combination of pure metal, master alloys, and metallic chips is melted using a heat source, which can be a coal/oil/gas fired furnace, arc or induction furnace, depending upon the type of metal, the volume of production, and production rate desired (Fig. 2.3). Coal/oil/gas fired furnaces are used for low melting temperature metals like aluminium, zinc, and lead while arc and induction furnaces are preferred for high-temperature metal like steel, titanium for premium quality castings. The molten metal generally comprises many traces and impurities (in the form of gases, organic compounds, hydrocarbons, and solid particles). Further, metal at high temperature in a molten state tends to interact with atmospheric gases and form their oxides and nitrides. Therefore, the treatment of molten metal is mandatory to take care of these impurities and gases to avoid gaseous defects (porosity, wormholes, blowholes) and oxide/nitride inclusion. The melt treatment involves degassing (to remove gases dissolved in molten metal), fluxing (to remove impurities), and filtering (to remove solid particles). Melting of metal in a protective environment (CO_2 / Argon) and vacuum reduces/avoids the presence of the atmospheric gases from furnace, which in turn reduces the gaseous defects and inclusions occurring due to the reaction between the molten metal, and atmospheric gases. Therefore, a vacuum furnace offers the best quality molten metal and improved quality of casting accordingly. The molten metal of the correct degree of superheat (minimum 50 degree C) after treatment is transferred from the furnace to mould with the help of a suitable ladle. The quality of the molten metal is determined by temperature, absence of gases and impurities, and chemical composition and its homogeneity at the time of pouring.

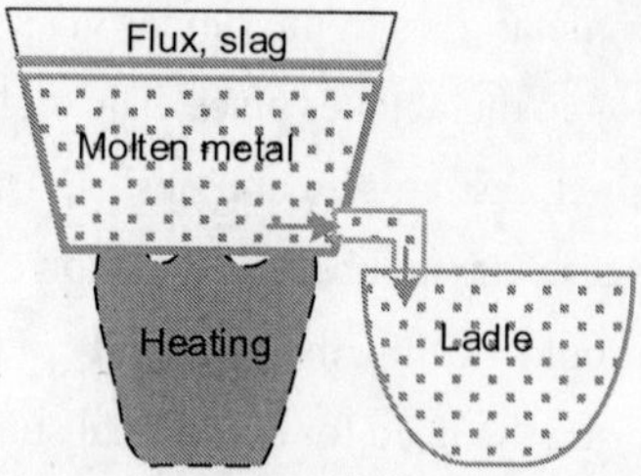

Fig. 2.3 Schematic showing heating to melt the change in crucible and transfer of the molten metal to the ladle

2.3.2 Pouring of molten metal into the mould

The treated molten metal must be poured into the mould in the minimum possible time without causing turbulence in the flow of molten metal in the gating system and the mould (Fig. 2.4). The mould is a cavity of size and shape close to that of casting desired. A slight difference between the two (mould and casting) with respect to size and shape is to accommodate various allowances (like shrinkage allowance, draft allowance, machining allowance, etc.). A turbulent flow of the molten metal in the gating system increases the tendency of a) interaction of molten metal with atmospheric gases leading to their dissolution and chemical reactions like oxidation, b) entrapment of air in the mould causing blow holes and air pocket, and c) damaging the sand mould and gating system leading to change in the shape of mould cavity itself. A well-designed gating system allows smoother and faster filling of molten metal in the mould, which results in a sound and good quality casting with high yield. Further, suitable features like venting holes are made in the mould to facilitate escaping the air from the mould during the filling of the molten metal.

The type of material used for making a mould cavity significantly determines casting characteristics such as surface finish, tolerance, soundness, microstructure and mechanical properties of the product.

Mould materials and its effect

Depending upon the quality requirement, geometrical complexity (size and shape) of the casting and volume of production, the mould can be produced using various materials like sand (sand mould casting), metal (die-casting), and refractory material (investment casting). The mould material affects the cooling rate imposed during solidification of the molten metal. High-conductivity mould materials (like copper, steel, and cast iron) result in a higher cooling rate and so faster solidification of the molten metal than low-conductivity mould materials like sand due to rapid (sensible and latent heat) heat transfer from the hot molten metal to the mould. The high cooling rate imposed by the metallic mould produces fine grain structure, and good mechanical properties, besides good surface finish and dimensional accuracy and high production rate.

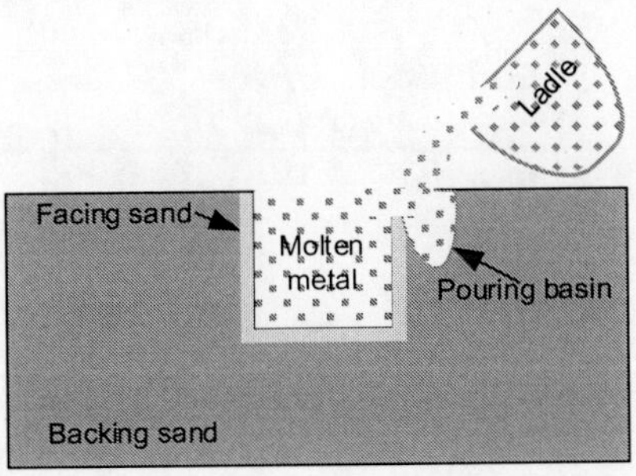

Fig. 2.4 Schematic showing pouring of molten metal into the pouring basin from ladle

2.3.3 Solidification of metals

The solidification of molten metal in the mould primarily involves phase transformation from liquid to solid state due to the loss of sensible and latent heat to the mould wall. The rate of heat transfer to the mould wall determines the cooling rate experienced by the molten metal during the solidification. Depending upon the composition of metal, the solidification can occur either at a constant temperature in the case of pure metal and alloy of eutectic composition or over a range of temperatures in case of alloy of other than eutectic/peritectic composition (Fig. 2.5).

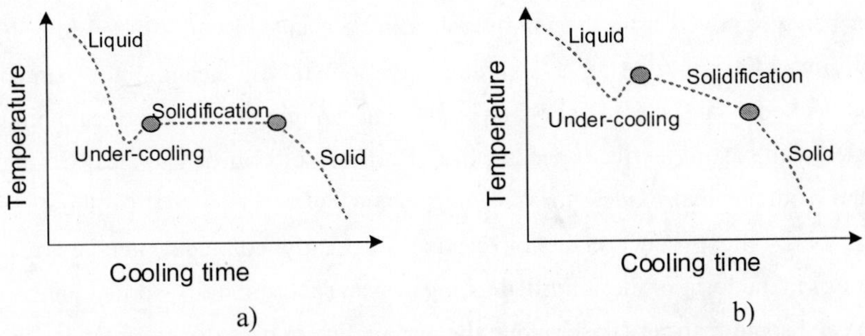

Fig. 2.5 Schematic showing the cooling curve during the solidification of a) pure metal / eutectic alloy solidifying at constant temperature and b) alloys solidifying over a range of temperature

The cooling rate experienced by molten metal during the solidification affects the time available for a) escaping of dissolved gases, inclusions and b) nucleation and growth rate of grains. High cooling rate reduces the time for escaping of gases and inclusions, which promotes porosity and inclusion in casting. Further, high cooling rate increases the nucleation rate and reduces the growth rate, leading to casting with fine grain structure and improved mechanical properties (Fig. 2.6). Additionally, high cooling rate reduces the time available for the growth of grains producing fine grains.

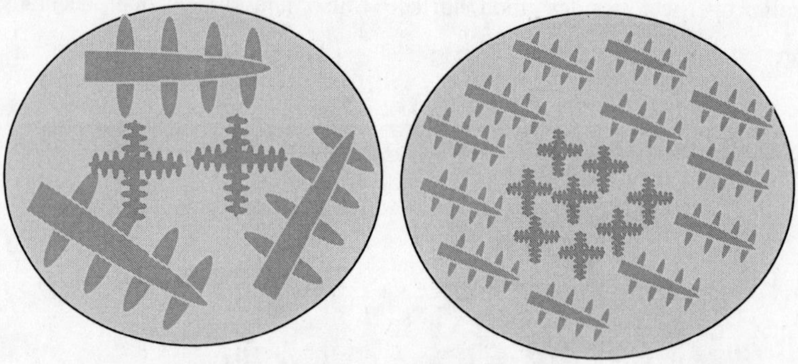

a) b)

Fig. 2.6 Schematic showing the effect of cooling rate during the solidification of molten metal on microstructure a) low cooing rate and b) high cooling rate

2.3.4 Removal of casting from the mould

The removal of casting from the mould at the correct temperature is important to avoid any damage, distortion and fracture of thin section parts. The casting must be allowed to cool down to a low temperature enough before removal from the die or sand mould as casting is weak at high temperature due to strength. The removal of casting can be manual (sand mould casting) or automatic (die casting) depending upon the type of casting process and size of casting

2.3.5 Cleaning of the casting

Castings, after being removed from the sand mould can be cleaned by a) a wire brush, b) a vibratory platform, c) tapping using a hammer, etc. Sometimes, cleaning the hardened moulding sand, and core sand due to excessive binder and ramming (even fusion and mixing of sand particles with casting surface) needs extra effort in the form of chemical treatment (potassium and sodium hydroxide) for cleaning using water/steam jet. to loosen the moulding/core sand. The product made by casting frequently contains many extra and undesired features in the form of the solidified gating system (pouring basis, sprue, runner, in-gate, and riser) and some features (flash) along the parting line in case of split moulds. These are removed using suitable methods like cutting (mechanical / thermal cutting as per section size). Fettling is one the most common words used for cleaning of castings. Fettling primarily involves the removal of rough edges, burrs and fins for achieving good smooth surfaces and edges. Thin, fine fins and protruding materials are removed using shot blasting (directing high-speed steel ball on the surface of casting), air blasting with abrasive and tumbling. For tumbling, (small size) castings to be cleaned are placed in a cylindrical drum/box, then rotation of the box causes continuous rubbing of casting surfaces with each other, which in turn removes fins, burrs, flashes and smoothening of the surfaces of casting.

2.3.6 Inspection

Casting is examined for desired geometrical features, shapes, dimensions, and soundness (presence of defect/discontinuity, if any) using appropriate methods. Visual examination is one of the most common inspection approaches for general observation of the casting condition and quality. However, as per need, casting can be inspected using suitable comparators for dimensional accuracy and tolerance, non-destructive testing (dye penetrant testing, magnetic particle testing, ultrasonic testing, x-ray testing) for evaluating soundness of the casting. Random testing (using acceptance sampling and quality control) for compositional analysis, microstructural consistency and mechanical properties can also be undertaken as per the need and criticality of the casting for the service and requirement of the user.

Dealing with casting defects

Defective casting identified during inspection either reworked or rejected as scrap. For reworking, casting defects are gouged out followed by filling of metal using a suitable low heat input welding process. Additionally, defects located at the surface or in the sub-surface region of casting can be repaired by a) re-melting the surface and near-surface layers using a suitable heat source like TIG & Plasma arc, laser beam and b) controlled surface layer plastic deformation using hammer peening, friction stir process, and contour rolling (Fig 2.7). The control plastic deformation of surface layers breaks and redistributes inclusions and other impurities besides closing gaseous defects like porosity and blowholes.

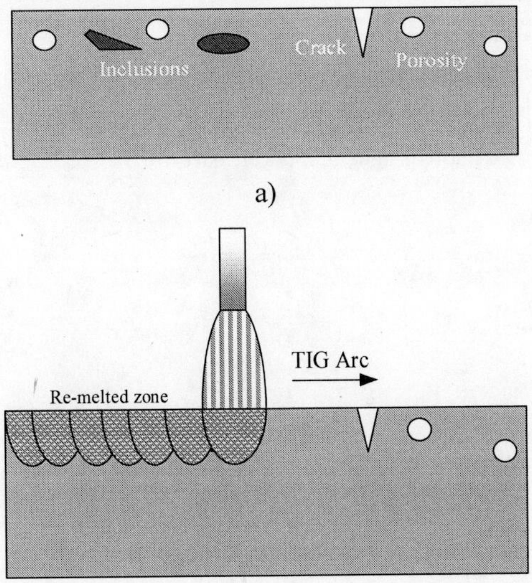

a)

b)

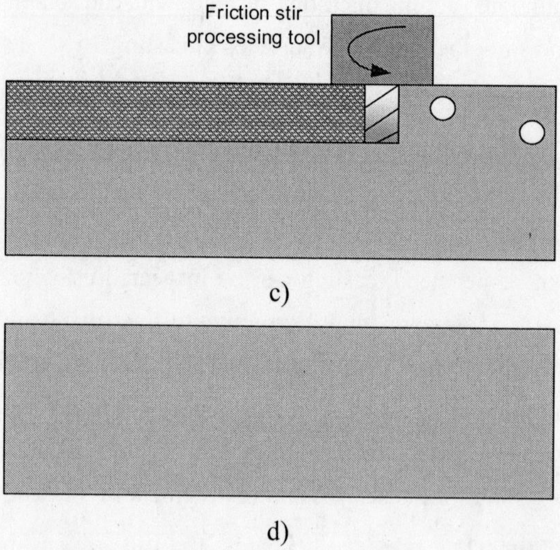

Fig. 2.7 Schematic showing a) casting with variety of defects, b) re-melting by TIG arc approach, c) friction stir processing and d) sound casting after repair

2.4 Fundamentals of casting processes

The molten metal is poured into the mould cavity (prepared using a suitable pattern) under gravity. Due to metallostatic pressure, molten metal fills fine geometrical features/sections of the mould and takes shape accordingly. The heat loss from the molten metal causes the transformation of molten metal to solid casting. The shrinkage in the cooling stage during casting is observed in three stages a) shrinkage of liquid metal due to drop in temperature of the molten metal from superheat temperature to liquidus temperature, b) shrinkage due to liquid to solid state phase transformation during solidification and c) shrinkage due to drop in temperature of solidified casting metal from solidus temperature to room temperature (Fig. 2.8). The first two types of shrinkages are taken care of by feeding extra molten metal to the mould from the riser.

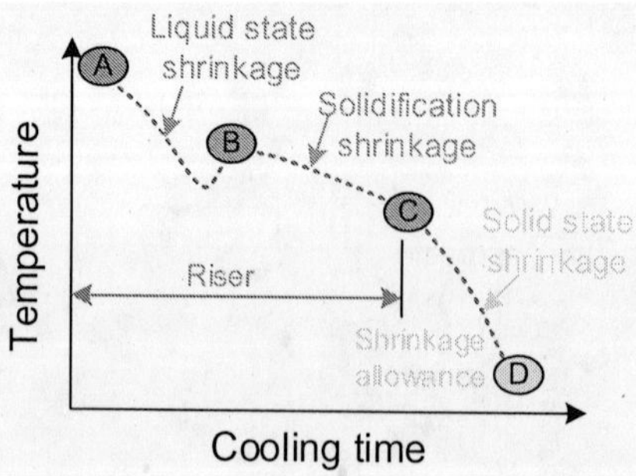

Fig. 2.8 Shrinkages observed during the casting of metal as function of time and role of riser

A riser is an important element, which facilitates the feeding of molten metal to the mould to take care of the molten metal shrinkage. However, the third type of shrinkage occurring in casting in a solid state is taken care of by making a mould (dimensions) a little larger than the required casting size so that after cooling down to the room temperature, a casting of the desired size can be obtained.

Additionally, an extra layer of material is applied on the casting so that after machining, grinding, finishing, the desired surface finish and tolerance can be achieved. Therefore, to accommodate the shrinkage aspect and provide an extra layer of materials for machining and grinding, casting size must be made larger than the final product. To make a casting of size larger than the required size, mould of larger size is made accordingly. To make moulds of larger size, a pattern used for making mould is designed and fabricated accordingly considering shrinkage and machining allowances. Thus, shrinkage and machining allowances are incorporated into the design of the pattern. The shrinkage allowance is added to the external sides while the same is subtracted for internal dimensions when designing a pattern (Fig. 2.9).

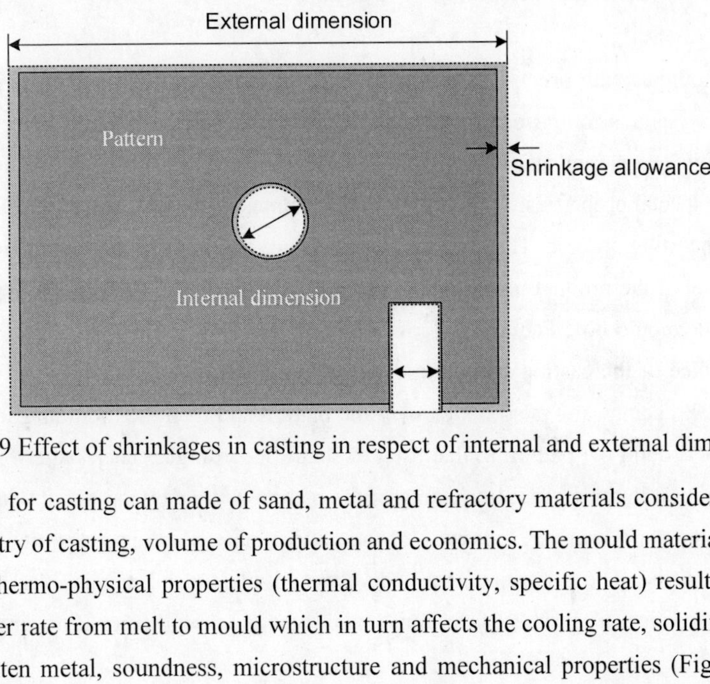

Fig. 2.9 Effect of shrinkages in casting in respect of internal and external dimensions

The mould for casting can made of sand, metal and refractory materials considering the size and geometry of casting, volume of production and economics. The mould material depending upon the thermo-physical properties (thermal conductivity, specific heat) results in varying heat transfer rate from melt to mould which in turn affects the cooling rate, solidification time of the molten metal, soundness, microstructure and mechanical properties (Fig. 2.10). The mould made of sand in case of sand mould casting and refractory material in case of investment casting are broken after each casting cycle. Such types of mould are therefore known as expendable mould and are suitable for low-volume production and a variety of casting designs. Metallic moulds used repeatedly (for producing large volumes of casting) are costlier and therefore justified for high volume and continuous production only.

The mould is made slightly different from the actual product/casting desired. The difference in size and shape of the mould depends on the mould material due to consideration of various allowances. For example, shrinkage, machining, draft and shaking allowance are considered for sand mould, while only the first two types of allowances are used in metallic mould.

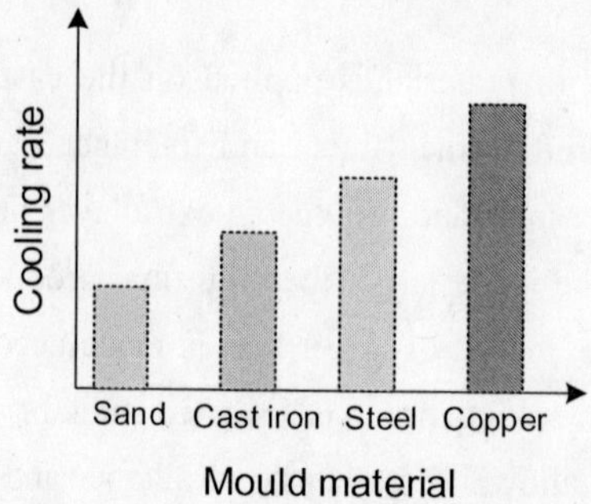

Fig. 2.10 Schematic showing the effect of mould material on cooling rate

2.5 Sand mould casting processes

2.5.1 Fundamental

The sand mould casting process as the name suggests uses a mould made of moulding sand. The moulding sand is composed of green sand, binder, water and additives. Water activates the binder to join green sand particles. Additives like sawdust are added in moulding sand to incorporate special properties. The sand mould is the most important and unique feature of the sand mould casting process. The sand mould is prepared with the help of a pattern, which is a replica/model of the product to be obtained by a casting process. The pattern is placed in the middle of the mould box. Facing sand made of fine particles of high refractoriness ensures a smooth surface of the casting without melting of the mould wall as it is directly exposed to molten metal. Facing sand is sprinkled over the pattern and then the moulding sand is placed and rammed around the pattern to that it takes shape accordingly. Then pattern is withdrawn after loosening it in the mould. Loosening of the pattern is done by tapping it with the help of a wooden hammer. However, loosening of the pattern increases the size of mould and so the size of the casting. The pattern can be made of wood, plastic and metal depending upon the size of the casting, desired surface finish and accuracy, production rate and volume of production.

2.5.2 Pattern allowances

Dimensions of the pattern are slightly different from the actual product to accommodate various allowances such as shrinkage allowance, draft allowance, shaking allowance, machining allowance etc. These allowances are used to finalize the size and shape of pattern, which will accordingly affect the size and shape of the mould.

2.5.2.1 Shrinkage allowance

The shrinkage allowance is provided to the pattern to take care of solid-state shrinkage of the casting after solidification. The allowance provided to a particular dimension of the casting is primarily based on the shrinkage behaviour of casting metal (linear thermal expansion/contraction coefficient Table 2.1) and is expressed as % of a dimension. The consideration of the shrinkage allowance increases the size of the pattern, mould and so casting. Therefore, it is called positive allowance.

Table 2.1 Shrinkage allowance and casting metal

S. No.	Metal	Pattern maker's shrinkage, %
1	Aluminium	1.0 to 1.3
2	Magnesium	1.0 to 1.3
3	Cast iron	0.8 to 1.0
4	Steel	1.5 to 2.0
5	Brass	1.4 to 1.6

2.5.2.2 Draft allowance

Vertical surfaces of the sand mould tend to get damaged during the withdrawal of pattern from the mould. Therefore, to avoid/minimize the damage to the vertical surfaces of the mould, a slight taper (0.5-3°) is given to the respective surfaces of the pattern (Fig. 2.11). This taper-ness provided to vertical surfaces of the pattern is called draft allowance. Internal vertical surfaces need greater draft allowance than external surfaces to facilitate easy withdrawal without damaging the mould surfaces. Material and specific dimension of the pattern also affects the draft allowance e.g., wooden pattern needs a greater draft allowance than plastic and metal. Similarly, increasing the length/height of the pattern needs greater allowance (Table 2.2).

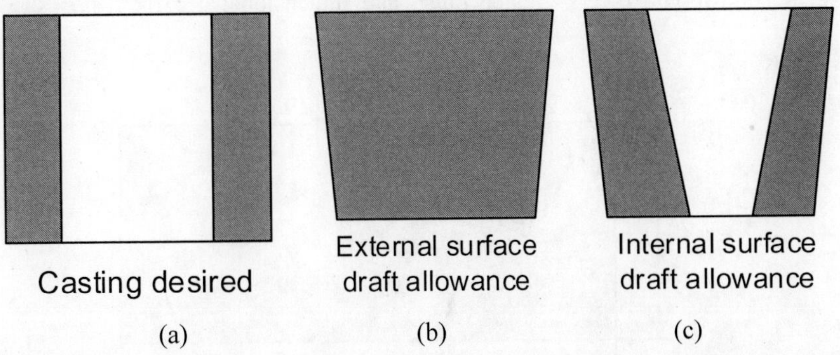

Fig. 2.11 Schematic showing a) casting with vertical internal and external surfaces, b) draft given to the external surface of the pattern and c) draft given to internal surfaces of the pattern.

Table 2.2 Draft (°) recommended as a function of side length, location of surface

S. No.	Pattern material	Side length, mm	Angle: External surface	Angle: Internal surface
1	Wood	< 25	3.0	3.0
2		25 to 50	1.5	2.5
3		50 to 100	1.0	1.5
4		100 to 200	0.75	1.0
5		> 200	0.5	1.0
6	Metal and plastic	< 25	1.5	3.0
7		25 to 50	1.0	2.0
8		50 to 100	0.75	1.0
9		100 to 200	0.5	1.0
10		> 200	0.5	0.75

2.5.2.3 Machining allowance

Actual surface roughness and dimension of components obtained immediately after casting are not found suitable for many applications. Therefore, such rough surfaces are machined to impart the desired surface finish and dimensional accuracy of cast components for satisfying the functional requirements of the castings. The surface to be machined is therefore, made a little larger than the actual product size by providing an extra layer of material which can later be machined out to obtain the desired surface finish and tolerance (Fig. 2.12). An extra layer of material on casting is provided by making a provision of machining allowance to the respective pattern dimensions. The machining allowance given to the pattern depends on the size and metal of casting (Table 2.3). Therefore, the machining allowance is also considered a positive allowance. The machining allowance for die-casting is lower than sand mould casting because metallic mould offers greater finish and dimensional accuracy than sand mould casting.

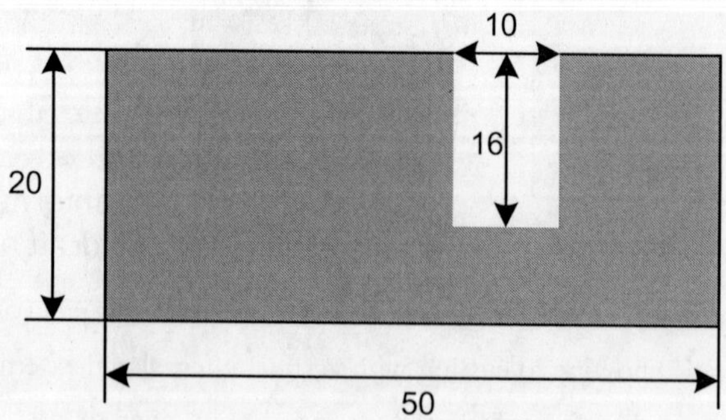

a)

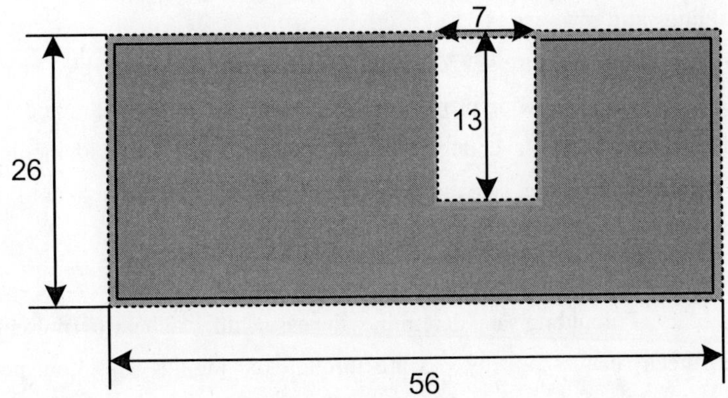

b)

Fig. 2.12 Schematic showing a) final casting with desired dimensions and surface finish, and b) machining allowance given to the pattern.

Table 2.3 Machining allowances (mm) recommended to the pattern as a function of side length, and metal of casting

S. No.	Metal of casting	Side length, mm	Machining allowance, mm
1	Cast steel	< 150	3.0
2		150 to 500	6.25
3		500 to 1000	7.5
4	Cast iron	< 300	3.0
5		300 to 500	5.0
6		500 to 1000	6.25
7	Non-ferrous metal	<200	2.25
8		200-300	3.0
9		300-1000	4.0

2.5.2.4 Wrapping / shaking allowance

Loosening of the pattern for easy withdrawal from the mould during the moulding process increases the size of the mould. This increase in the size of the mould must be kept in mind while designing the pattern by making it slightly smaller than the required size of casting. The reduction in the size of a pattern as compared to the required casting size corresponds to wrapping/shaking allowance. This is a negative allowance as it leads to a smaller pattern size.

2.5.3 Moulding sand properties

The moulding sand is a mixture of green sand, binder, water and additives. The moulding sand is expected to have the following properties to first produce good sand mould and then sound casting. These properties however depend on many factors associated with moulding sand such as type of sand & binder, size, size range and shape of sand particles, extent of ramming done for moulding, etc.

2.5.3.1 Permeability

The permeability of moulding sand determines the ease with which gases (present in the mould and molten metal) can escape by passing through the mould wall. Low permeability of moulding sand increases the tendency of retention and entrapment of gases in the mould cavity during the casting (Fig. 2.13). Low permeability is attributed to fine sand grains, wide size range, excessive moisture, and over-ramming, which in turn restricts the escaping of gases from the mould and therefore promotes gaseous defects like pores, and blow holes.

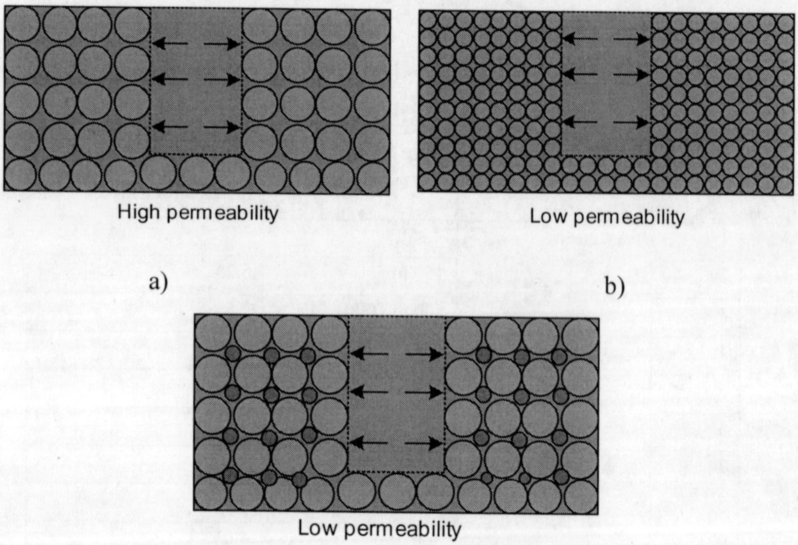

c)

Fig. 2.13 Schematic showing the effect of a) large sand particle size offering greater inter-particle spaces leading to high permeability, b) fine particle size offering less inter-particle spaces leading to low permeability and, and c) a wide size range of mould sand particles reduces inter-particle spaces resulting in low permeability.

2.5.3.2 Mould Strength

The cohesive strength of mould depends on the bonding of sand particles (with each other) due to binder. A binder is a mixture of clay and water. Fine and irregular shape particles allow better bonding due to large bonding surface area and the tendency of more particle interlocking than coarse and spherical shape particles. The strength of green sand mould depends on the type and proportion of clay, size of sand particles and moisture content. In general, the addition of an optimum amount of moisture results in maximum compressive green strength of the mould depending upon the type of clay/binder (bentonite and kaolinite) and size of sand particles (Fig. 2.14 a). The strength of mould (when there is moisture) in unbaked condition is known as green strength. Baking of mould makes it dry by removing the moisture but increases the strength. The strength of the mould in such a baked condition is known as dry strength (Fig. 2.14 b). However, the most important aspect is the ability (strength) of the mould to take the weight of the molten metal (without being damaged) at the high temperature of melt. The strength of the mould at a high temperature (of molten metal) is called hot strength and depends on the type and the size of sand particles and type of binder. The refractoriness of the moulding sand must be high enough to avoid softening/weakening and even melting of the mould surface.

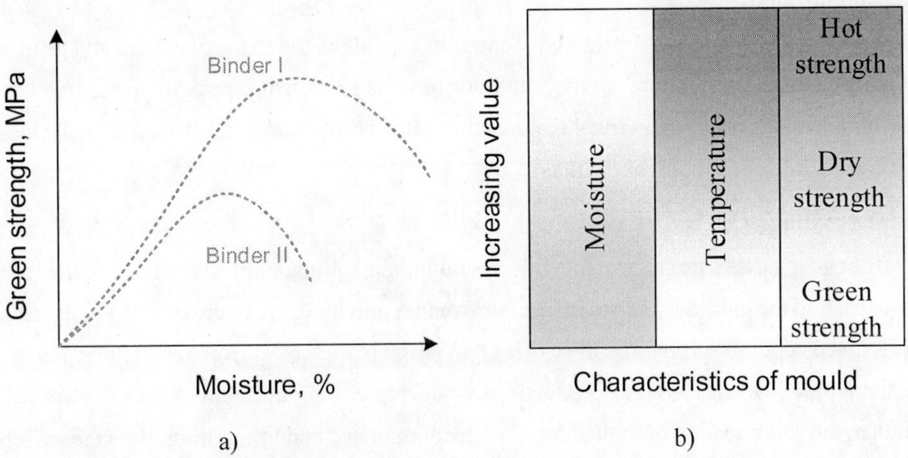

Fig. 2.14 Schematic showing a) effect of moisture (%) in moulding sand on green strength and b) temperature-moisture-mould strength relationship.

2.5.3.3 Adhesive strength

The adhesive strength of the moulding sand shows the bond between the pattern surface and moulding sand/flask so that it can follow and retain the shape accordingly. Poor adhesive strength makes it difficult to realize the mould of the desired shape.

2.5.3.4 Refractoriness

The refractoriness of the moulding sand indicates its ability to withstand high temperature of superheated molten metal without softening and melting. The type of sand and particle size of sand significantly affects refractoriness. Refractoriness of the mould sand is especially important for the casting of high temperature metals like copper and steel. Moulding sand of low refractoriness experiences fusion of the sand particles. Melted sand particles on mixing with molten metal result in hard surfaces of castings, which makes the machining of such surfaces difficult. Further, melting and softening of moulding sand changes the shape of mould leading to modification in casting size and shape.

2.5.3.5 Collapsibility

Collapsibility of mould sand shows the ease of breaking/collapsing mould sand after solidification of the molten metal. High collapsibility allows easy removal of the casting from the mould. Low collapsibility of mould sometimes causes hot tearing/distortion due to contraction of the casting, leading to high residual tensile stress (owing to solid-state shrinkage). Low strength and ductility of metal at high temperature just after solidification of the casting in the presence of tensile residual stresses due to solid-state contraction causes hot cracks/tears.

2.5.3.6 Flowability

Flowability shows how easily moulding sand flows to follow the shape of pattern and geometry to produce the desired mould cavity. The flowability is important especially in casting having fine, thin and complex geometrical features. Low flowability makes it difficult to make mould cavities with fine geometrical features.

2.6 Die casting process

The die casting uses a permanent metallic mould for mass production wherein the molten metal for casting in the mould is fed/solidified either under gravity (gravity die casting) or externally pressurised conditions (pressure die casting). In pressure die-casting, molten metal is fed to the mould rapidly, which increases productivity (reducing casting cycle time) (Fig. 2.15 & 2.16). Further, the solidification of molten metal under pressurised conditions minimizes the tendency of casting defects and increases the soundness of casting. Fast cooling of the molten metal due to rapid heat transfer from the molten metal to metallic mould produces fine grain structure and improved mechanical properties of casting. However, a very high rapid cooling rate may promote the entrapment of dissolved gases due to the limited availability of time for escaping of gases.

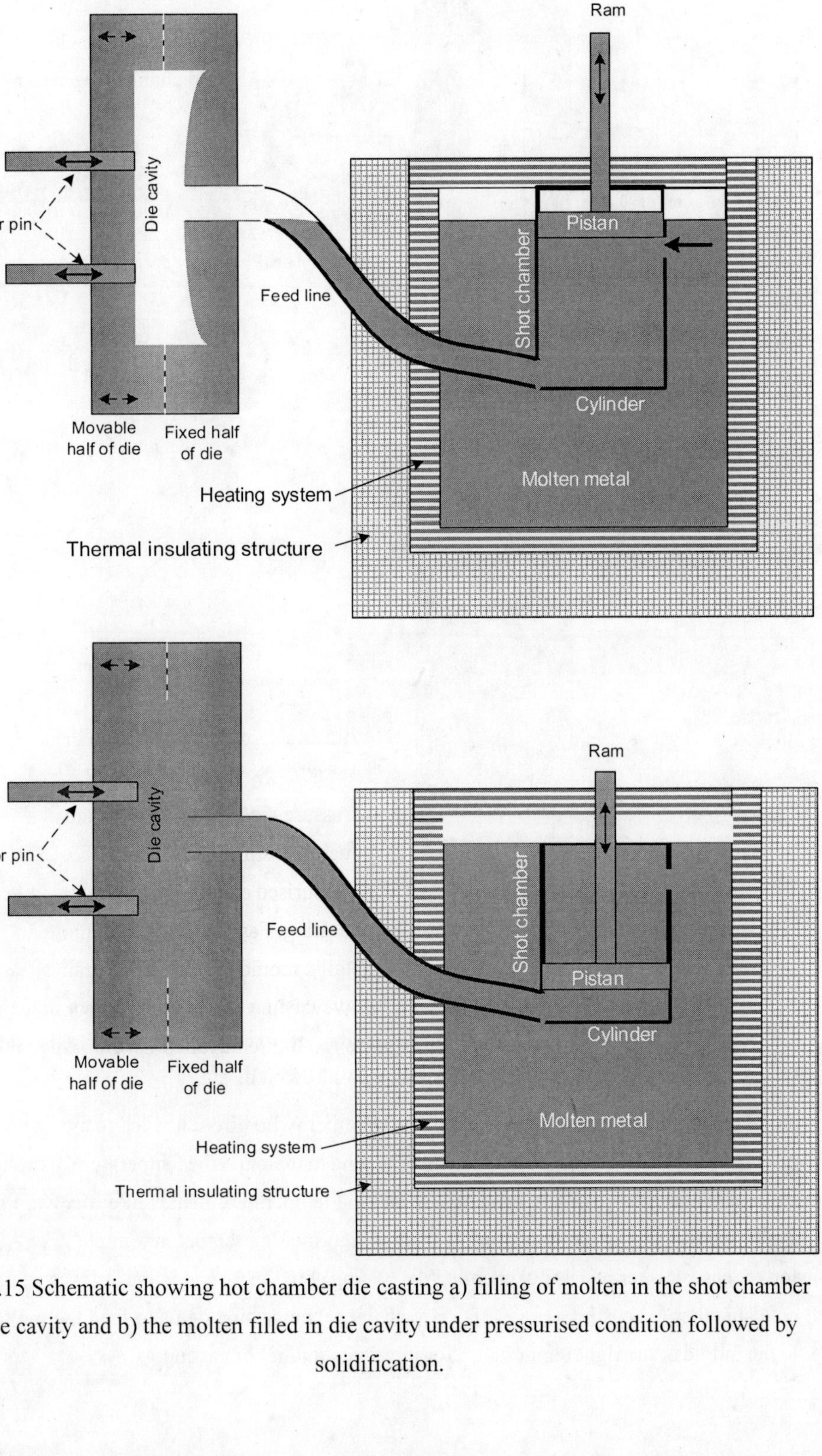

Fig. 2.15 Schematic showing hot chamber die casting a) filling of molten in the shot chamber of die cavity and b) the molten filled in die cavity under pressurised condition followed by solidification.

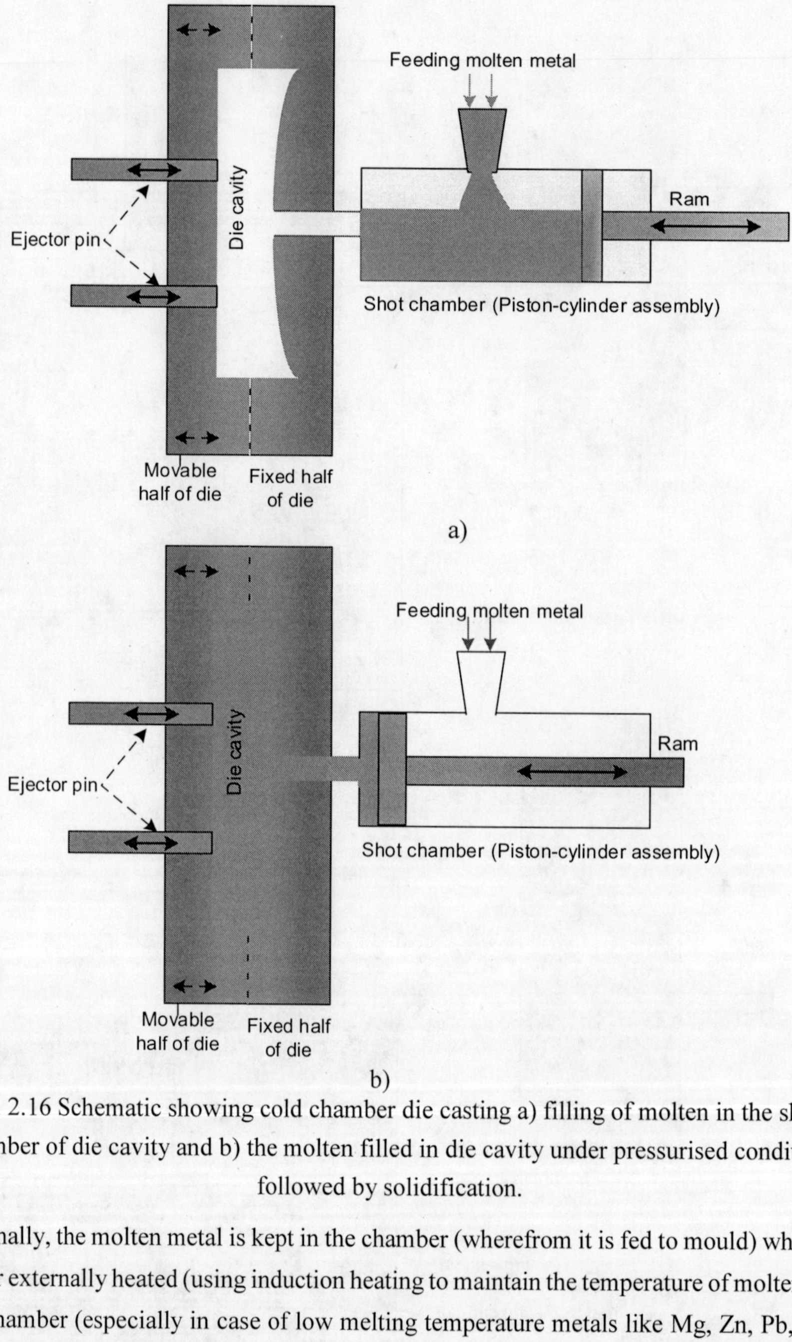

Fig. 2.16 Schematic showing cold chamber die casting a) filling of molten in the shot chamber of die cavity and b) the molten filled in die cavity under pressurised condition followed by solidification.

Additionally, the molten metal is kept in the chamber (wherefrom it is fed to mould) which can be either externally heated (using induction heating to maintain the temperature of molten metal in the chamber (especially in case of low melting temperature metals like Mg, Zn, Pb, Sn) or stored without any external heating (for little high melting temperature metal like Al). In the former case, it is termed as hot chamber die casting (Fig. 2.15), and in the latter case, it is called cold chamber die casting (Fig. 2.16). Hot chamber die-casting helps to feed the molten metal to the mould at the right temperature for improved quality of casting.

2.7 Investment casting

The investment casting process is preferred for making a complex shape with relatively good surface finish like statues, models, and many engineering components using relatively low melting point metals. The process is done in the following stages (Fig. 2.17):

- Preparing a pattern made of wax (via casting route first) using a metallic mould, pouring molten wax in the mould and the solidification and post processing, e.g. finishing, joining etc.
- Developing a mould using wax pattern: Dipping wax pattern into binder-slurry followed by application of refractory powder particles for bonding to obtain a refractory shell mould which is later baked for hardening of the refractory shell and removal of wax (by melting it)
- Pouring the molten metal into the refractory shell mould followed by solidification of melt to produce casting
- Breaking of refractory shell mould to take out the casting,
- Cleaning and inspection of the casting.

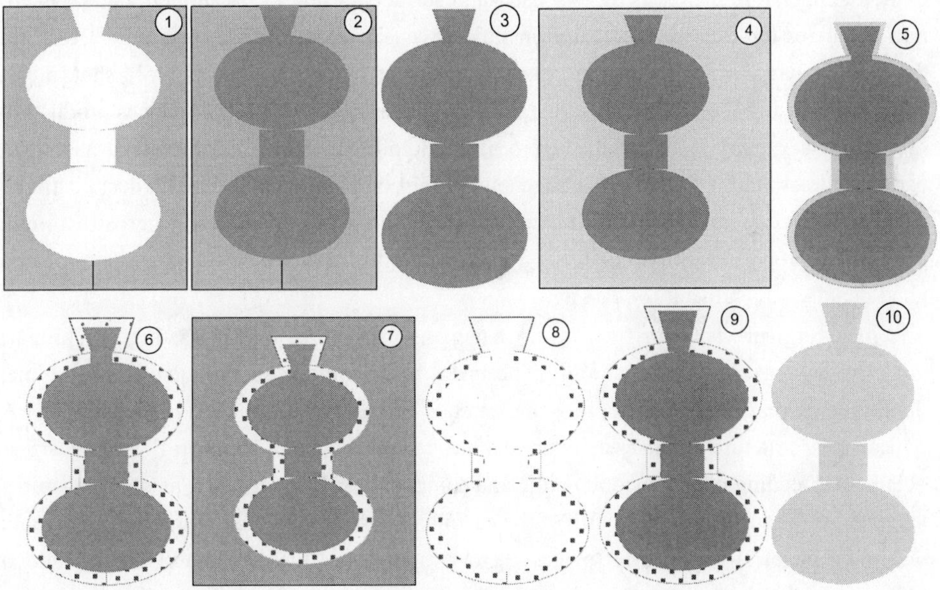

Fig. 2.17 Schematic showing stages of investment casting processes 1) preparation of desired metallic mould, 2) filling the mould with molten wax, 3) taking out the wax pattern, 4) dipping wax pattern in ceramic slurry, 5) wet coating of slurry on the wax pattern, 6) sprinkle and deposit ceramic powder particle over the wet slurry coated wax pattern (steps 4 to 6 may be repeated until ceramic coating of desired thickness obtained), 7) baking of ceramic coated wax pattern, 8) melting, removal of wax leaves behind ceramic shell/mould cavity, 9) pour the molten metal in ceramic shell/mould cavity and 10) break ceramic shell to remove casting after solidification.

Since the mould is made of a very thin wall of refractory/ceramic material, therefore rate of heat transfer from the molten metal to the mould is very low. Low rate of heat transfer causes longer solidification time. Low cooling rate results in coarse grain structure and relatively soft phases. Suitable alloying and grain refinement can be used to refine cast structure and improve the mechanical properties of the investment casting.

2.8 Performance of casting

The performance of the castings primarily depends on two aspects a) soundness of casting and b) metallurgical characteristics. The soundness of a casting indicates how far it is free from defects and discontinuities (inclusion, cracks, porosity). The factors affecting the soundness of casting depend on the quality of the molten metal and those which are specific to a casting process (sand mould in sand mould casting, die/investment casting). Two important aspects related to the quality of molten metal, namely temperature and purity of molten metal affect the tendency of casting defect formation and cracking tendency. The molten must be fed with enough degree of superheat (50-100 °C as per metal) to ensure sufficient fluidity of melt and time to fill the mould cavity before commencement of the solidification. In general, reduction in melt temperature increases the viscosity and surface tension of the molten metal, which in turn decreases the fluidity. Reduction in fluidity causes a longer time requirement for filling the mould cavity, which in turn increases the chances of casting defects (cold shut, misrun) besides increasing the production cycle time. A longer production cycle reduces productivity. Molten metal quality is also judged from a) freedom of the melt from dissolved gases, solid particles, dross, and flux, and b) homogeneity of the composition of melt with desired alloying element for refinement, and modification to develop casting of desired microstructure and mechanical properties. Suitable alloying and filtration of the molten metal is done to supply good quality molten metal for casting.

The metallurgical characteristics (grain and phase structure) of the casting are primarily governed by chemical composition of the metal and cooling rate experienced by the metal during the casting. In the case of most cast metals (except transformation hardening alloys), a typical cast structure (planar, cellular, dendritic and equiaxed grains) of varying sizes is obtained depending upon the cooling rate and composition. The size and type of grain structure varies from the surface to the centre of the casting due to varying cooling rates. Rapid cooling of molten metal at the surface (of casting) by mould wall leads to the extremely fine and equiaxed grain structure resulting in higher hardness than the centre / subsurface region. The rate of cooling experienced by the molten metal in sub-surface regions (on moving from the surface to the centre) will gradually decrease which in turn produces coarser grain sizes and cellular, dendritic grains. Therefore, heterogeneity in the microstructure of cast components results in a significant variation in hardness and other mechanical properties from surface to centre. A very thin layer of a few microns of casting surface experiences a very fine-equiaxed grain structure due to the quenching effect of molten metal with the mould surface. Thereafter, on approaching the centre of the casting, planar, cellular, dendritic and equiaxed grains are observed (Fig. 2.18).

Transformation hardening metals like cast iron and steel undergo solid-state transformation after solidification of the casting. Therefore, a typical cast dendritic structure is usually not observed in casting of such metals. The hard surface layer due to the quenching effect is invariably observed in transformation hardenable ferrous metal casting due to higher tendency of martensitic/bainitic transformation at the surface while centre comprises relatively soft phases like pearlite and ferrite.

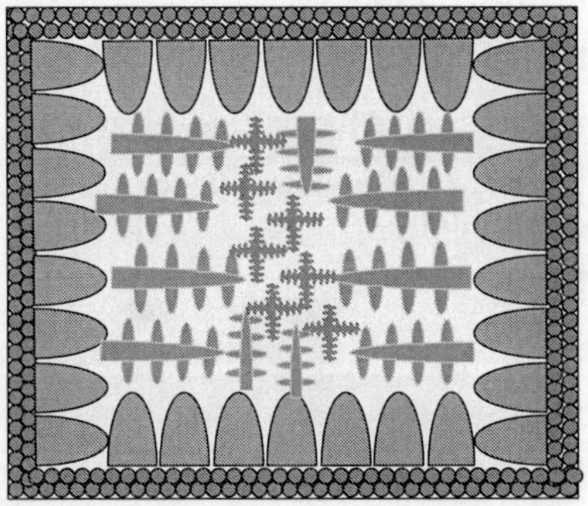

Fig. 2.18 Schematic showing typical microstructural variation in casting from surface to core.

2.9 Casting defect and their remedy

An improper procedure of moulding and casting reflects in the form of casting defects. Casting defects, in general, decrease the mechanical performance of the casting due to a) reduction in net load resisting cross-section and b) stress concentration offered by defect as per size and geometry. The following are broad categories of factors causing defects in casting.

2.9.1 Gases/air

Gaseous casting defects in the form of blow holes, and porosity mainly occur due to the inability of gases to escape from the mould/solidifying molten metal owing to low permeability, poor venting due to faulty grating system design, inefficient degassing, excessive gas generation, too fast cooling (short solidification time) as shown in Fig. 2.19. There are two main sources of gases: a) gases dissolved in the molten metal and b) air present in the mould cavity. Suitable steps are taken after considering the above possibilities (as per the casting process) to reduce gaseous defects.

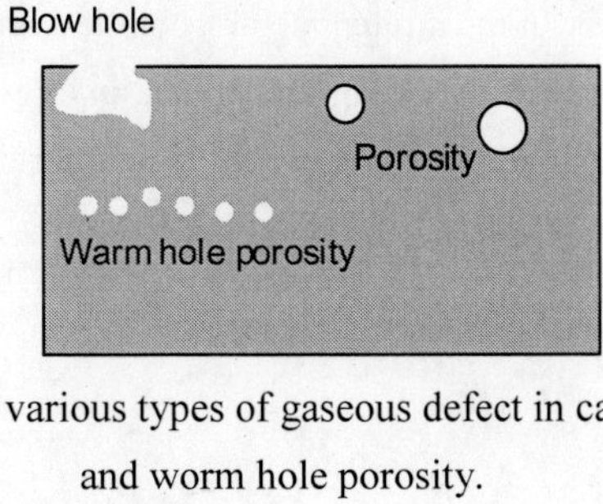

Fig. 2.19 Schematic showing various types of gaseous defect in casting blow holes, porosity, and worm hole porosity.

2.9.2 Improper sand moulding

Casting defects like cuts & washes, rat tails, swell, drop, buckle etc. mainly occur due to the inability of mould sand (owing to low mould strength) to handle the flow of molten metal and its metallostatic load (Fig. 2.20). The turbulent flow of the melt (due to faulty gating system design) and low strength mould surface causes erosion and breaks mould surfaces/features. Similarly, high metallostatic load on low strength mould surface causes expansion/swelling /shifting of the mould wall. Both these factors (erosion and swelling) change the geometry of the mould cavity itself leading to defective casting. Very coarse sand particles cause rough mould surface due to penetration of the molten metal in fine spaces between coarse sand.

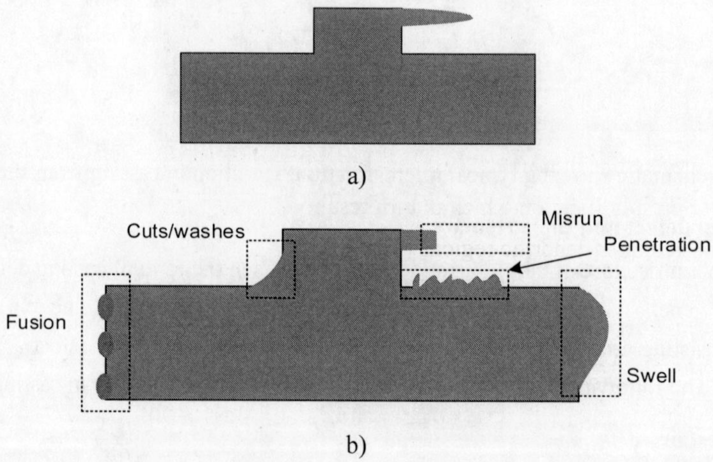

Fig. 2.20 Schematic showing a) desired casting and b) casting with various types of defects (cuts/washes, fusion, misrun, penetration, and swell) due to poor moulding practices.

2.9.3 Poor design of gating system

Casting defects like shrinkage cavity, misrun, and cold shut, cuts & washes, air pockets etc. occur due to faulty gating system design including pouring basin, flow channel and riser leading to lack of directional solidification, turbulent flow, and very long time to fill mould cavity, lack of proper supply of the molten metal from the riser to compensate shrinkage. Cold shut defects occur when streams of molten metal in the mould coming from different gates/directions do not fuse together, leaving behind an interface on solidification (Fig. 2.21).

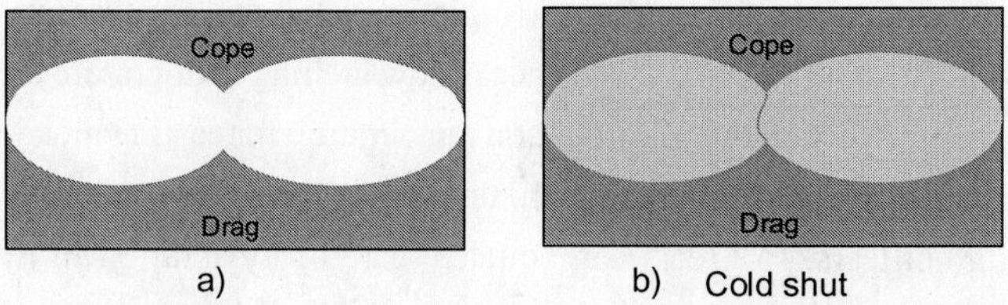

Fig. 2.21 Schematic showing a) desired casting and b) casting with defects like cold shot due to low temperature of the molten metal / faulty gating system design.

2.9.4 Poor quality of molten metal

Casting defects like inclusion, porosity, misrun, and cold shut also occur due to the low quality of molten metal in terms of purity (presence of impurities) and improper pouring temperature into the mould. Improper metal treatment including lack of proper degassing, fluxing, filtration, etc. encourages defects such as inclusion, porosity, and blowholes. Low pouring temperature of the molten metal causes casting defects such as cold shut, misrun, shrinkage cavity etc. The low temperature of molten metal reduces fluidity when it flows through narrow dendritic channels during solidification which in turn results in shrinkage porosity due to the formation of many unfilled inter-dendritic regions (Fig. 2.22)

Fig. 2.22 Schematic showing inter-dendritic shrinkage porosity

2.9.5 Unfavourable metallurgical reactions

Casting defects like hard spots, cold cracks, hot tears are caused by unfavourable metallurgical reactions and transformation hardening during casting (Fig. 2.23). Rapid cooling of hardenable ferrous metals (medium and high carbon steel, alloy steel and cast irons) during casting results in the formation of hard and brittle microstructural constituents like martensite, which promotes hard spots, cold cracking and embrittlement. A combination of dissolved hydrogen, residual tensile stress due to shrinkage and hard & brittle martensite in hardenable ferrous metal castings promotes cold cracking.

Fig. 2.23 Schematic showing localised hard spot formation and hot tears

Hot tearing is also a kind of cracking occurring at elevated temperatures just at the terminal (last) stage of solidification due to the presence of low melting temperature elements like S and Pb. Hot tears occur only when the solidification temperature for casting metal is very large (50° C). Sulphur (frequently added in free machining steel) forms low melting temperature iron sulphide causing hot tears. Hot tears can be taken care of by adding Mn (Mn/S > 7) in low carbon steel. In the presence of Mn, comparatively high melting temperature MnS is formed instead of FeS to avoid hot tearing.

2.10 Bulk Metal Forming

Bulk metal forming is a family of manufacturing processes wherein a large-scale plastic deformation of raw / stock metal (with the help of a suitable load) is used to obtain the desired shape and size. Since the approach of bulk metal forming processes is based on plastic deformation, metal must possess reasonably good ductility and preferably low yield strength and low work hardening tendency at room temperature for easy metal forming. The metals having low ductility and high yield strength can also be subjected to bulk metal forming by heating (using a suitable external heat source like flame, induction, or resistance heating) to a high enough temperature for increasing the ductility and reducing yield strength so that plastic deformation for forming can be achieved easily (Fig. 2.24).

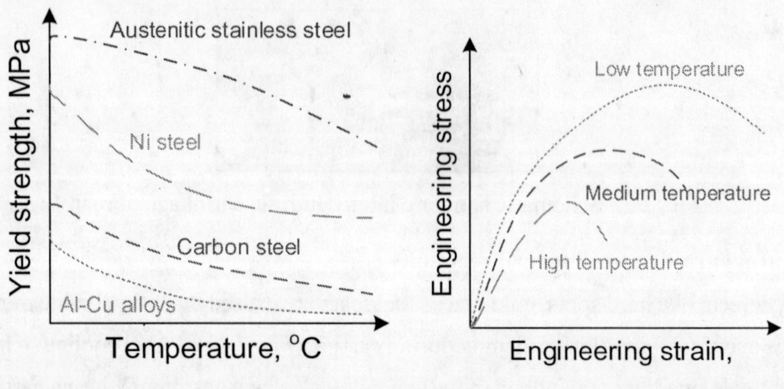

Fig. 2.24 Schematic showing the effect heating temperature on a) yield strength of different metals and b) engineering stress-strain curves for metal like Al, stainless steel

Hot and cold forming

The bulk metal forming processes performed at the room temperature (and below recrystallization temperature) of the metal are called cold forming while those executed above the recrystallization temperature are called hot forming. The forming processes performed between room temperature and recrystallization temperature are called warm forming (Fig. 2.25 a). Since heating of metal above the recrystallization temperature causes recovery, reduces yield strength and work hardening tendency besides increasing the ductility, therefore the force and power consumption for hot forming is found to be much lower than cold forming (Fig.

2.25 b). The absence of work hardening of the metal during hot forming allows continuous and significant plastic deformation without cracking tendency. However, hot forming offers challenges in the form of a) oxidation tendency of metal resulting in relatively high surface roughness, metal loss in the form of oxides and b) thermal expansion/contraction of metal during and after bulk metal hot forming, making it difficult to realize the desired dimensional accuracy and tolerance.

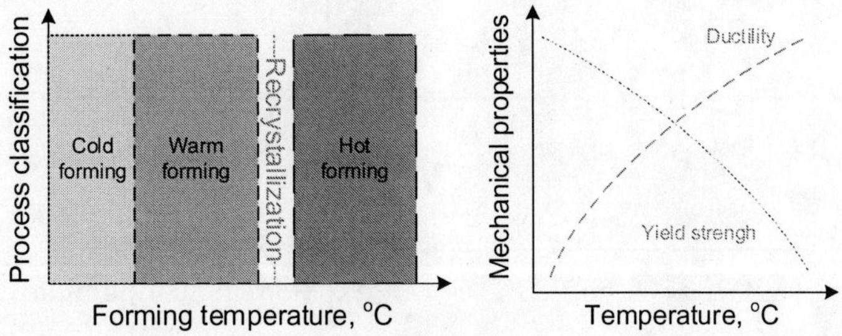

Fig. 2.25 Schematic showing a) forming processes and temperature relationship and b) effect of temperature on yield stress and ductility

On the contrary, the cold forming of metal at room temperature offers greater resistance to plastic deformation (than hot forming) due to high yield strength and low ductility (at room temperature); therefore, cold forming needs a stronger and more robust machine, greater force and power consumption than the hot forming. Further, cold forming offers better surface finish, dimensional accuracy and tolerance due to the absence of both oxidation and thermal expansion/contraction possibilities (Fig. 2.26). However, the extent of deformation, which can be realized during cold forming, is incremental and gradual due to a) work hardening, b) cracking tendency and c) limited system capabilities. Partially deformed metal during cold forming is therefore, subjected to in-process annealing to remove work hardening effect and induce ductility. Process annealing allows further cold forming of metal. Otherwise, tendency of surface cracking of cold-form components increases (Fig.2.27).

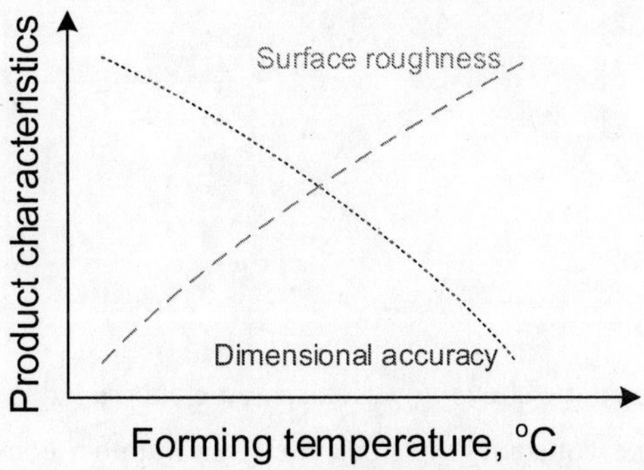

Fig. 2.26 Schematic showing the effect of forming temperature on product characteristics

The soft, ductile, low yield strength and low work hardening tendency metals (Al, Mg, Zn, mild steel) of relatively thin sections can be processed by cold forming involving plastic deformation at room temperature (without any external heating) to realize desired size and shape. While high yield strength, low ductility metals, high work hardening tendency metals (like high strength steel) of heavy section are generally processed by hot forming.

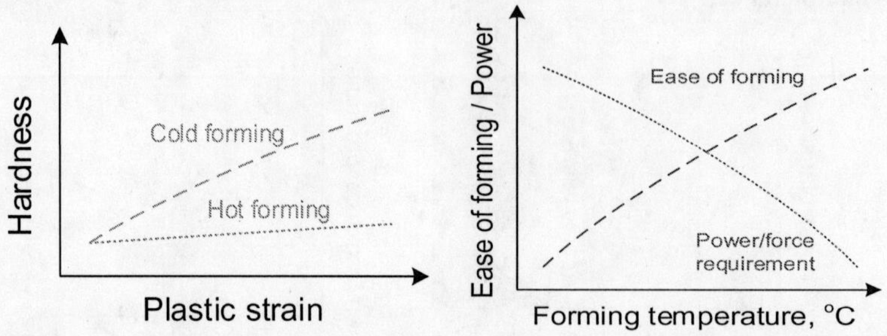

Fig. 2.27 Schematic showing a) effect of plastic strain on hardness under cold/hot forming and b) ease of forming as function forming temperature.

2.10.1 Rolling

The rolling is a bulk metal forming process generally used for making flat plates and sheets of uniform cross-section (of almost uniform thickness and width). The stock material is passed through a controlled gap between two rollers rotating in opposite directions. Inter-roller-stock material friction causes the metal to pass through the rollers. A close gap between rollers (lesser than stock metal thickness) causes plastic deformation of stock metal, leading to a reduction in thickness and increase in length (Fig. 2.28).

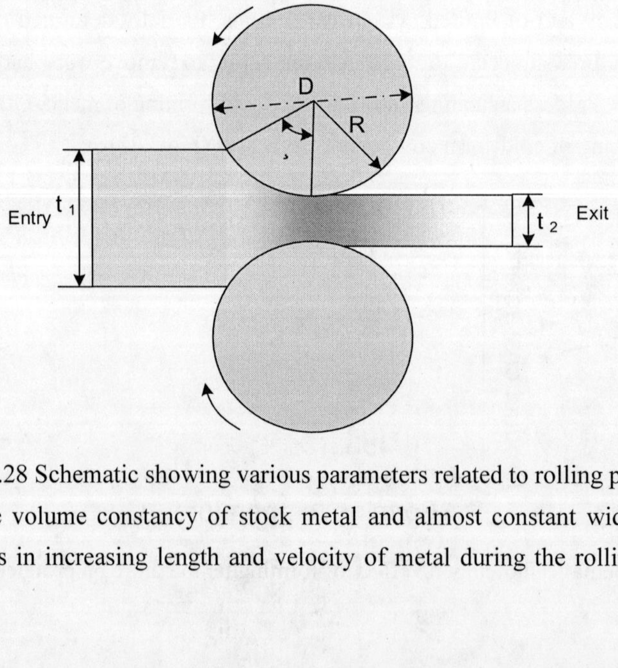

Fig. 2.28 Schematic showing various parameters related to rolling process

Considering the volume constancy of stock metal and almost constant width, reduction in thickness results in increasing length and velocity of metal during the rolling process from entry to exit at a specific rolling stand. The extent of reduction in thickness in a single pass of rolling depends on the radius of roller (R) and inter-roller-stock metal friction (μ).

The ratio of the thickness of plate/sheet after rolling and that of plate/sheet before rolling (t_1/t_2) is called the reduction ratio. Increasing roll diameter and friction coefficient increases reduction ratio for a given stock metal. However, mechanical and metallurgical factors like work hardening, yield strength, ductility, thermal softening and temperature of metal during rolling also affect the maximum achievable reduction ratio. A set of rollers used for rolling is called rolling standing. There are many variants of rolling stands depending on the number of rollers and the direction of movement of material during rolling as presented in Fig. 2.29.

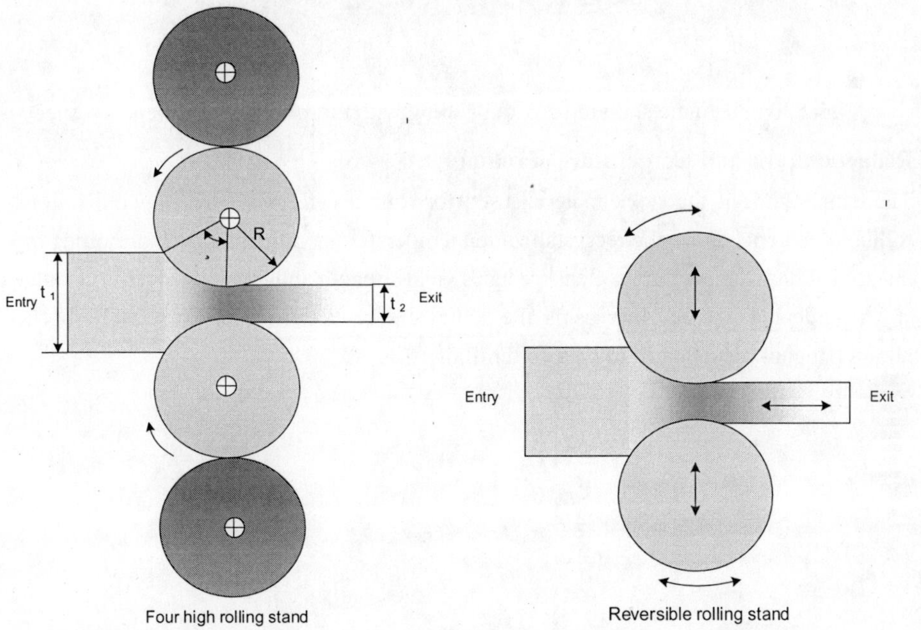

Fig. 2.29 Schematic showing a) four high rolling stand and b) reversible rolling stand

Stages of rolling

The surface features obtained on a rolled plate/sheet depend on the surface topography of the rollers. A smooth and plane surface of the roller produces a flat plate/sheet. As per need, the surface topography of rollers can be made of specific profile like convex, concave etc., to obtain respective mirror surfaces (in the form of gear tooth, threads on cylindrical components and contoured surfaces on plates). Rolling of stock metal to the final product is broadly attained in three stages namely breakdown pass, roughing pass, and final pass. Breakdown pass(es) results in a major reduction in cross-section attained through one / few passes of rolling. Roughing pass(es) helps to attain a shape close to the desired one while finishing pass(es) delivers the final size and shape of the rolled product. Final pass helps to attain desired structure and properties.

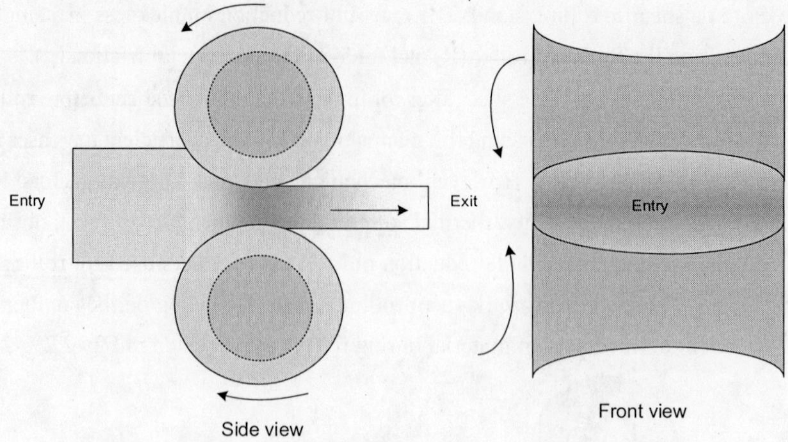

Fig. 2.30 Schematic showing contour rolling with morphology of rollers and sheet.

Reduction ratio and temperature of rolling

The temperature of the stock material used for rolling determines the hot/cold rolling. The rolling of material above the recrystallization temperature is called hot rolling. Rolling of stock material at high temperature softens (reduces yield strength and increases ductility) and avoids strain hardening, thereby increasing the achievable reduction ratio. Conversely, hot rolling allows a higher reduction ratio than cold rolling (Fig. 2.31).

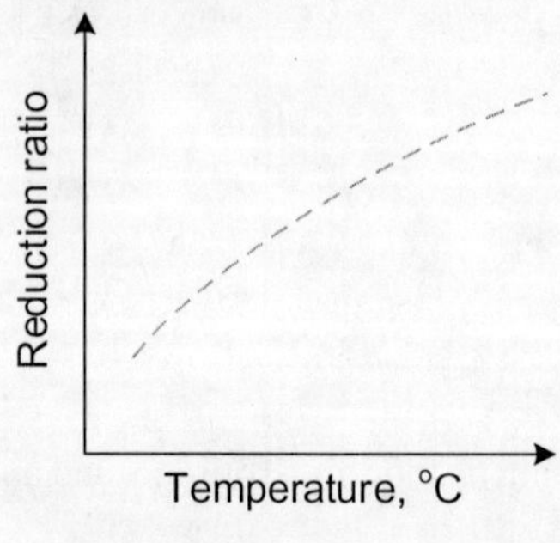

Fig. 2.31 Schematic showing effect rolling temperature on reduction ratio

2.10.2 Plastic Deformation in Forging

The plastic deformation during the forging process broadly occurs in two ways a) upsetting and b) drawing out. The volume of metal largely remains constant except for minor/negligible losses occurring due to oxidation and chipping of metal at the surface. The plastic deformation for forging is realized using compressive force, causing flow in the lateral direction. Plastic deformation by upsetting occurs through the application of compressive force along the axis of material (for bulk metal forging). Upsetting increases the area of cross-section and reduces the height of stock metal. In the case of drawing out, compressive force is applied in the direction perpendicular the axis of metal, which increases the length and reduces the area of cross-section

(Fig. 2.32). Compressive force for upsetting and drawing out actions can be applied either manually or using mechanized hammers/presses. The hammer applies blows in the form of impact load on the metal for drop forging while the press exerts continuously increasing compressive force for machine and press forging. Many bulk metal forming processes like forging, coining and wire drawing manufacturing processes are based on drawing out plastic deformation.

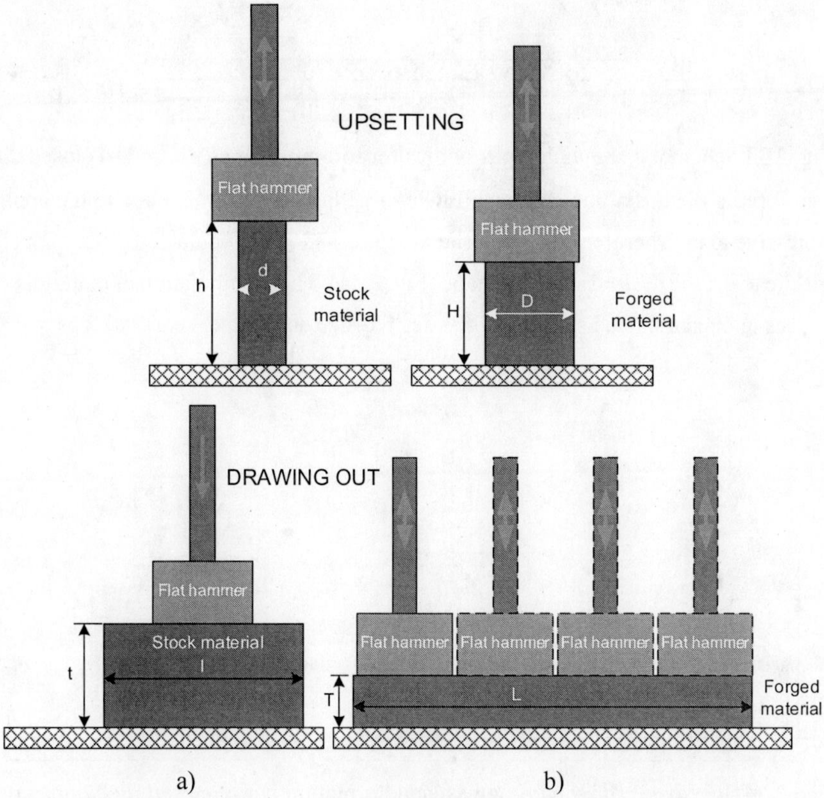

Fig. 2.32 Schematic showing a) upsetting and b) drawing out plastic deformation approaches for forming

Forging Process

The forging process involves controlled plastic deformation/flow of material using compressive load with the help of a suitable open or closed die. The compressive load can be applied in the form a successive impacts/blows using a hammer or gradually increasing pressure using a press to facilitate the flow of metal to take the shape as per the die cavity. The forging die can be opened/closed type and is made of two parts; one half is fixed and mounted on the anvil while another half is attached with a ram of press/hammer to apply a compressive load (Fig. 2.33).

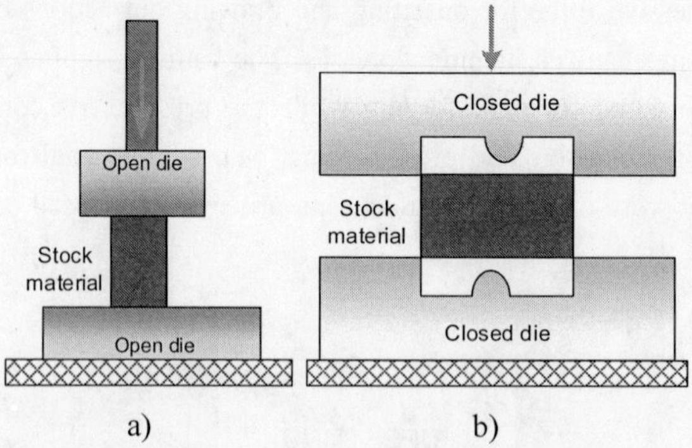

Fig. 2.33 Schematic showing types of dies for forging a) open die and b) closed die

The open forging die has a flat surface, allowing free lateral movement due to the application of compressive load. Therefore, the material being forged is manipulated by the impact of the movable die to get the desired size and shape (Fig. 2.34). The manipulation of material between flat surfaces in open die need skill to get the desired size and shape.

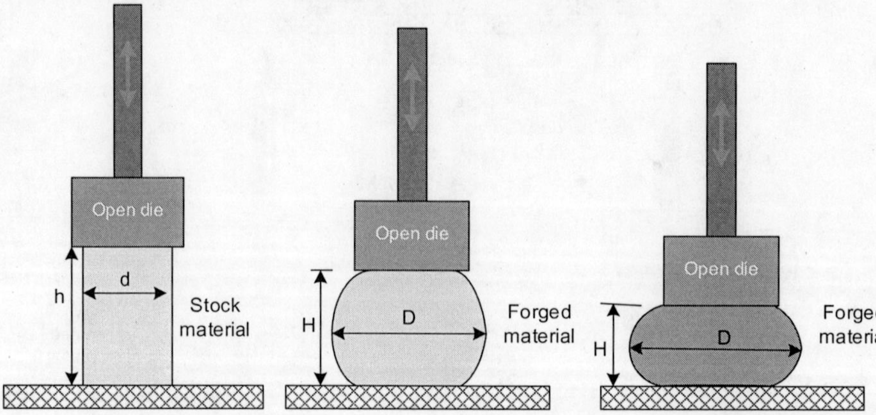

Fig. 2.34 Schematic showing progressive deformation during upsetting by open die

The close (forging) die is just like a mould (in case of casting) forming a cavity corresponding to shape/geometry as per the desired product. The raw material is placed between the upper/lower half of the die and then compressive force is applied to facilitate the flow / plastic deformation of the metal (Fig. 2.33). The compressive load can be applied either in the form of impact/blow in case of drop forging or continuously increasing load in pressure/machine forging.

Compressive load deforms the metal gradually followed by (drawing out approach) lateral flow of the metal to fill the cavity of closed die. Similar to the rolling, the journey of raw material to the final product during forging involves many stages using dies of various designs/geometry, which will gradually converge toward the shape/size of the product (Fig.

2.35). The general steps followed in forging include fullering, edging, bending, blocking, finishing and trimming of flash as the shape of the product.

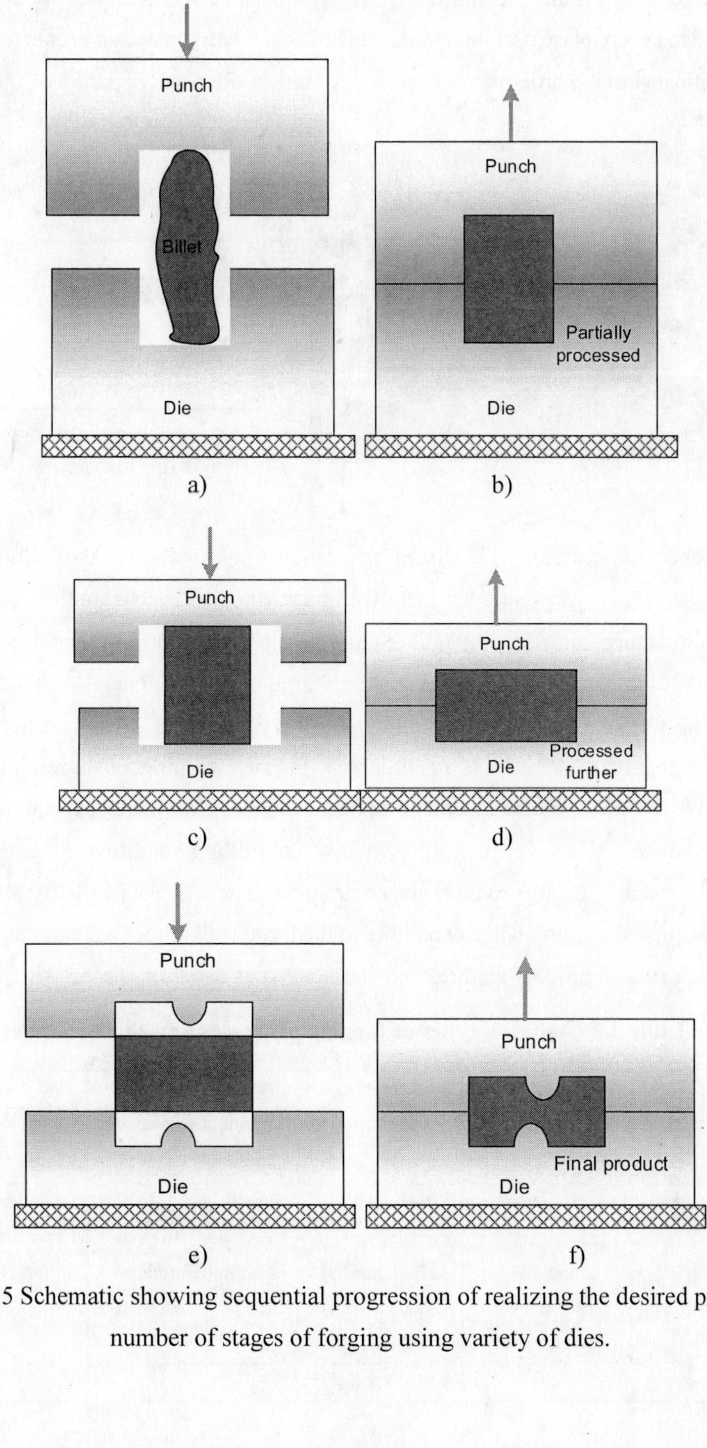

Fig. 2.35 Schematic showing sequential progression of realizing the desired product in number of stages of forging using variety of dies.

Continuous increasing load during press and machine forging causes squeezing action, resulting in a uniform flow of the metal through thickness reducing the severity of anisotropy as compared to drop forging and smith forging. Near surface layers in the case of drop forging are subjected to severe plastic strain, grain refinement and work hardening (cold forging) which causes significant strain hardening of surface layers than the core (Fig. 2.36).

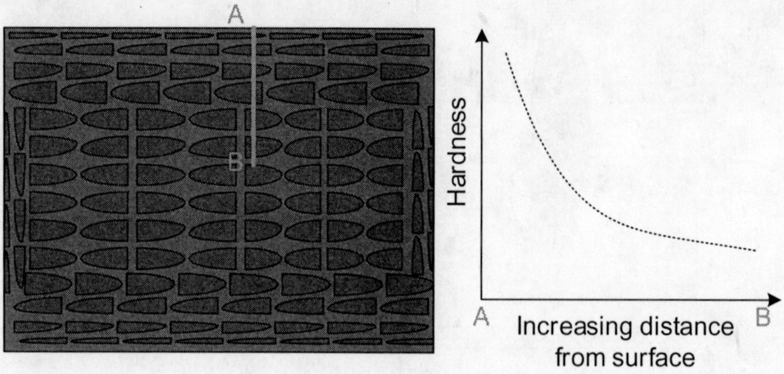

a) b)

Fig. 2.36 Schematic showing a) localized surface layer deformation in the form of elongated grains and b) decreasing hardness with increasing distance from the surface

The continuous squeezing of the metal between the closed dies during press/machine forging needs a very high-capacity press for making large size components. Therefore, size of press/machine forged components is limited by the capacity of press and hence these are preferred for relatively small size components. Further, continuous blows/impacts during drop/smith forging make the surface of component rougher with increased chipping tendency. Additionally, machine and press forging allow controlling the flow of grains and their orientation for manufacturing products and components like gear blanks, shafts, axles, spindles, hooks to maximize the strength and capability of the forged component. A few common forging processes their related process features and characteristics listed in Table 2.4.

Table 2.4 Common types of forging processes and their features

Feature	Smith forging	Drop forging	Pressure forging	Machine forging
Compressive load	Series of impact	Series of impact	Continuous squeezing	Continuous squeezing
Type of die	Open	Closed	Closed	Closed
Surface roughness	Rough / jarred	Rough / jarred	Smoother	Smoother
Anisotropy	Predominant due to localised surface layer deformation	Predominant due to localised surface layer deformation	Less due to more uniform deformation	Less due to more uniform deformation
Flash formation	No	Yes	Yes	Yes

Forging defects

Common issues observed in forged components due to faulty forging procedures include unfilled sections, cold shut, scale/pits, die shift and flakes. Unfilled sections in the forged components occur due to insufficient charge metal in the die cavity and limited flowability of metal during forging. Cold shut is a kind of fine crack observed at the sharp corners of the forged components due to very fine radii of fillet at the corner of the die. Fine radii coupled with limited flowability of metal under forging conditions make it difficult for metal flow and follow the die cavity during the forging. Pits and scale defects occur due to oxidation of surfaces and impurities on the surface under the forging conditions. Die shift is related to the misalignment of the upper and lower parts of a closed die set during forging. Flake are formed due to the continuous impact of upper half of the die on the stock material having limited ductility and flowability. The presence of flakes on the forge component results in a jarred and rough surface.

Cleaning of the stock material, forging at a desired temperature, well-designed forging dies, right volume of stock materials and a robust machine to avoid any possibility of misalignment of dies are a few important parameters which should be optimised and established properly to avoid above forging defects.

2.10.3 Extrusion

Extrusion is a bulk deformation hot working process used to produce long and uniform cross-section (square, circular etc.) bars and rods. The stock material is forced to pass through a nozzle of the die having a shape as per the cross-section of the bar desired (Fig. 2.37). Extrusion facilitates achieving a very large reduction in cross-section in one go. Reduction in cross-sectional area called extrusion ratio can range from 30-50. The extrusion ratio is defined as the ratio of the initial to the final cross-sectional area of stock material after extrusion. The extrusion process can be classified as direct or indirect depending upon the direction of movement of the extruded material with respect to the compressive force applied for extrusion.

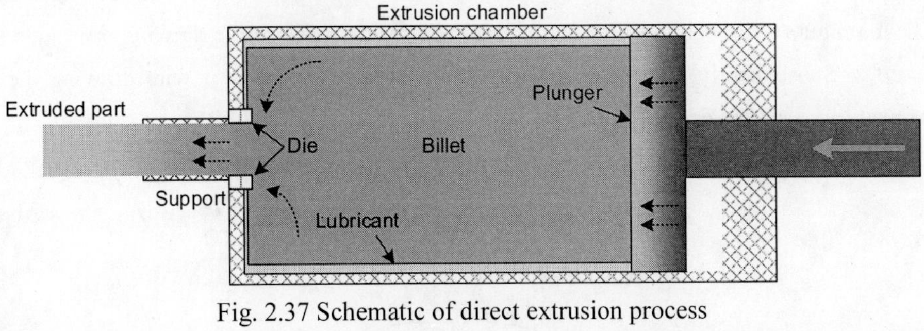

Fig. 2.37 Schematic of direct extrusion process

Direct extrusion involves the movement of material (while coming out of the nozzle) in the direction of applied compressive force, while it is opposite in the case of indirect extrusion (Fig. 2.37 & 2.38). The type of extrusion affects the force required to manufacture products by this process primarily due to the difference in friction encountered between stock material and the wall of extrusion chamber. The direct extrusion experiences high friction force due to relative movement between stock material and the wall of extrusion chamber before taking shape after passing through the nozzle. To reduce the metal stock-wall friction, suitable lubricants (like a combination of molten glass, graphite, grease, and oil) which can withstand elevated extrusion temperature are used. The indirect extrusion avoids the possibility of inter-wall-stock material friction due to the inherent nature of process wherein material flows through a nozzle in a direction opposite to the applied compressive force (Fig.2.28).

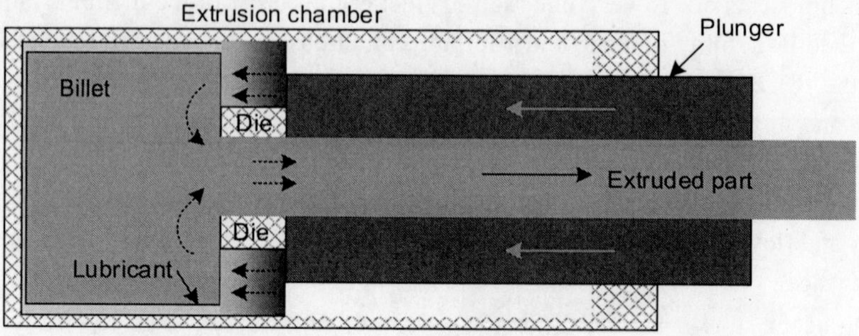

Fig. 2.38 Schematic of indirect extrusion process

Factors affecting the flowability of metal during extrusion are the type of metal (mechanical properties such as yield strength, ductility, thermal softening), temperature, and extrusion speed. All these aspects determine the ease of extrusion, extrusion force, and metallurgical and mechanical properties of extruded components.

2.10.4 Wire Drawing

The wire drawing process is used to produce wires from relatively large diameter cylindrical bars using a suitable wire drawing die (Fig.2.39 a). Initially, the bar is tapered and then passed through the die. The tapered end is pulled by applying tensile force. The design of wire-drawing die is such that the bar being pulled experiences a compressive force, causing yielding / plastic deformation of metal, which in turn results in a reduction in the diameter of bar (Fig. 2.39 b). The maximum reduction in cross-section realized in one pass of wire drawing can range from 40-50%. Subsequently, the bar can be passed through a number of wire drawing die sets sequentially until the desired wire size/diameter is obtained (Fig. 2.39 c).

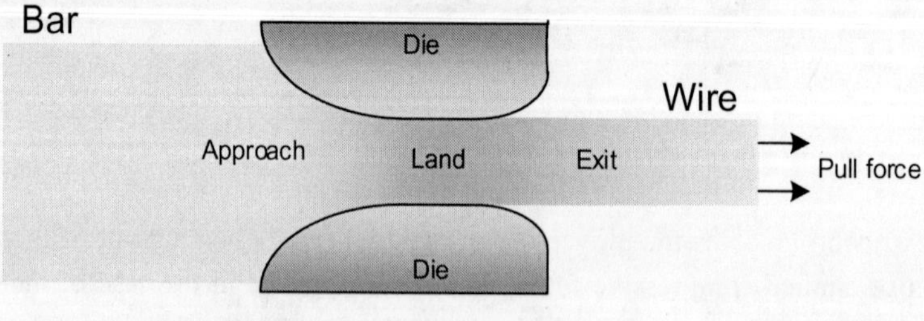

a)

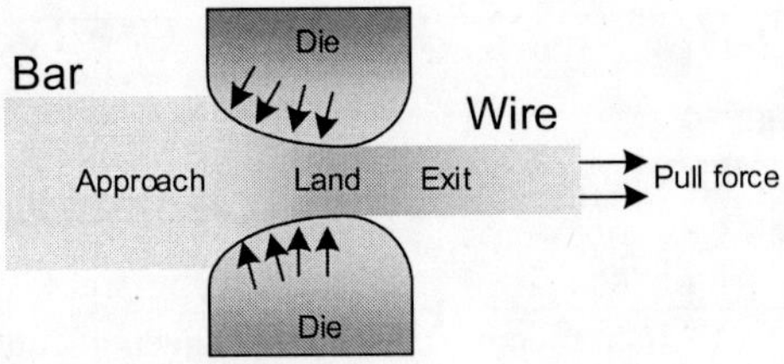

b)

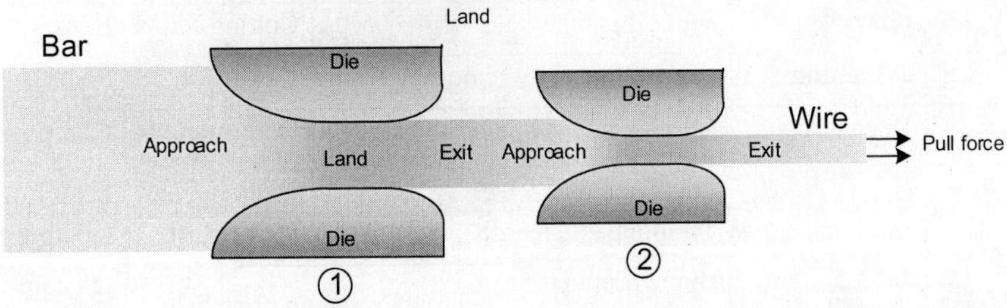

c)

Fig. 2.39 Schematic of wire drawing process (a) and (b) different designs of wire drawing dies with part details and c) wire drawing in multiple stages

The design of die is crucial to avoid breaking material due to the pull force applied during wire drawing. Significant plastic deformation of the metal during wire drawing causes strain hardening. Therefore, in-process annealing is used to restore the ductility and facilitate further wire drawing without cracking. Suitable lubricant is used during wire drawing to reduce wire-die interfacial friction and reduce wear of wire drawing die. Wire drawing die is made of wear resistant material with high thermal stability, like tool steel, tungsten carbide, and diamond. Choice of die material depends on stock metal to be used for wire drawing.

2.11 Sheet metal forming

Thin metallic sheets are extensively used in the form of parts of electronic goods, automotive, tanks and boxes, cutlery utensils, etc. Most of these parts are manufactured by sheet metal forming using sheet metal instead of bulk metal. Sheet metal forming is a family of many forming processes like punching, blanking, bending, drawing and deep drawing, embossing, coining, notching, nibbling, etc. These sheet metal processes involve either cutting by shearing or plastic deformation by bending, compressive, tensile, shear, and bending stress (Table 2.5).

Table 2.5 Common sheet metal forming processes and their features

Sr. No.	Sheet metal forming	Purpose/Application	Approach	Type of stress
1	Punching	Creating hole	Cutting	Shear
2	Blanking	Creating small metal sheets for further processing	Cutting	Shear

Sr. No.	Sheet metal forming	Purpose/Application	Approach	Type of stress
3	Notching	Making special features at the edge	Cutting	Shear
4	Nibbling	Incremental cutting of sheets from the edge following profile	Cutting	Shear
5	Shaving	Smoothening edges	Cutting	Shear
6	Trimming	Sizing blanks by removing flash	Cutting	Shear
7	Deep drawing	Making cup shape products	Deformation	Compression-tension
8	Ironing	Thinning and lengthening of cup shape products	Deformation	Compression-tension
9	Stretch forming	Making axis-symmetric shape products	Deformation	Tension
10	Embossing	Marking, labelling, stiffening of the products	Deformation	Bending, compression
11	Coining	Making coins, souvenir, decorative items	Deformation	Bending, compression

2.11.1 Shearing operation

The sheet metal forming processes like blanking, punching, notching, nibbling, shaving, trimming, etc., use shearing action for cutting metal sheets to get the desired size and shape. A die set is typically used for these operations and comprises two components, namely die and punch or upper/lower blades (Fig. 2.40). A well-controlled clearance is maintained between die and punch for clean and smooth cut edge of sheets. The clearance is a gap between the die and punch (lower/upper blades) and is usually expressed in mm or % of the thickness of sheet metals.

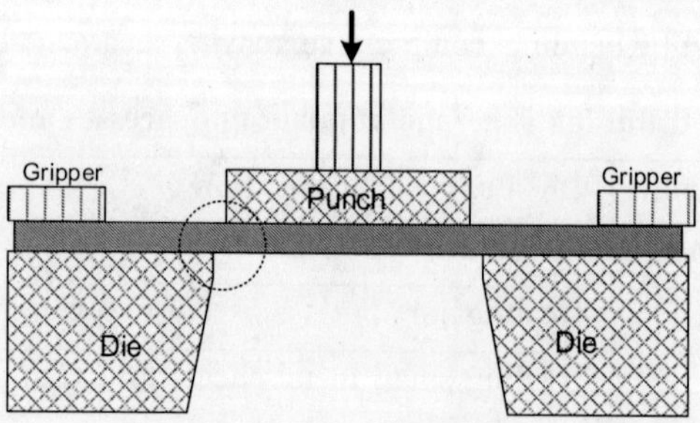

Fig. 2.40 Schematic of die and punch for shearing

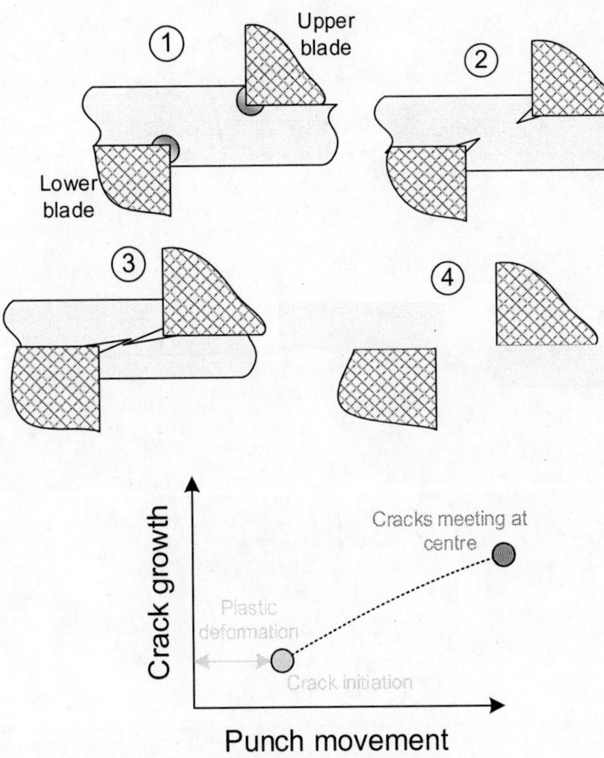

Fig. 2.41 Schematic of sequential progress in shearing action resulting in cutting of sheet metal indirect extrusion process

For shearing action, the movement of the punch in downward direction bends the sheet causing elongation of grains of sheet metal near cutting edges due to localised strain on both die and punch sides. Eventually, fracture of grains is triggered from these locations leading to crack nucleation and propagation. Further, the downward movement of punch causes the propagation of cracks (toward the centre of sheet) from both sides and eventually, coalescence of these cracks occurs at the centre resulting in a clean cut in case of optimum clearance (5-15% of the thickness of sheet metal) as shown in (Fig. 2.41). However, optimum clearance depends on mechanical properties (ductility and hardness) and thickness of sheet metal. High hardness, low ductility and thick sheets need less clearance for clean cutting by shearing (Fig. 2.42 a). A clearance larger than optimum (loose clearance) results in a greater disc shape deformation zone. While less than optimum clearance (tight clearance) produces a rough-cut edge as the cracks propagating from each side do not meet at the centre. An enlarged view of the cut edge of sheet metal is showing deformation, fracture and burr (Fig. 2.42b)

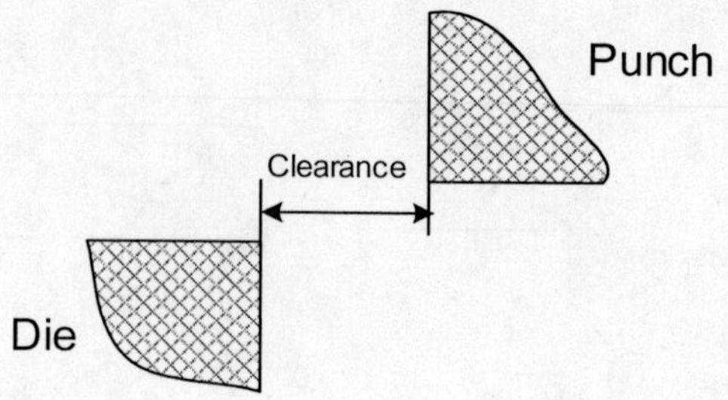

a)

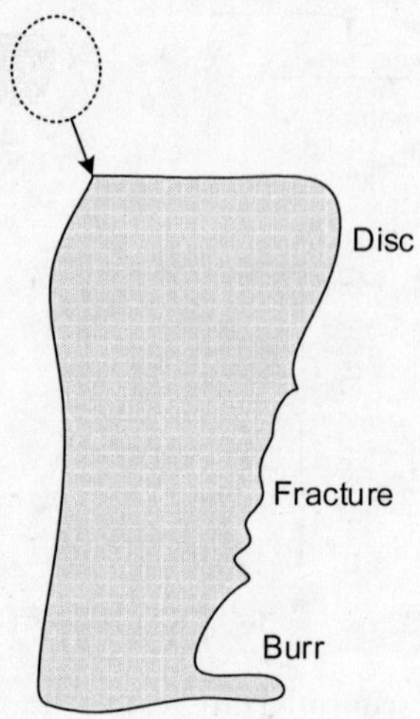

b)

Fig. 2.42 Schematic showing a) clearance between die and punch and b) enlarged view of cut edge by shearing

Punching, blanking, notching, nibbling, trimming and shaving are shearing-based sheet metal operations are shown in Fig.2.43.

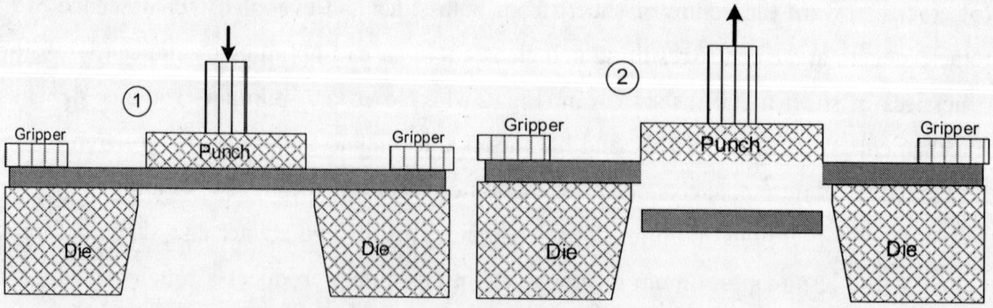

a) b)

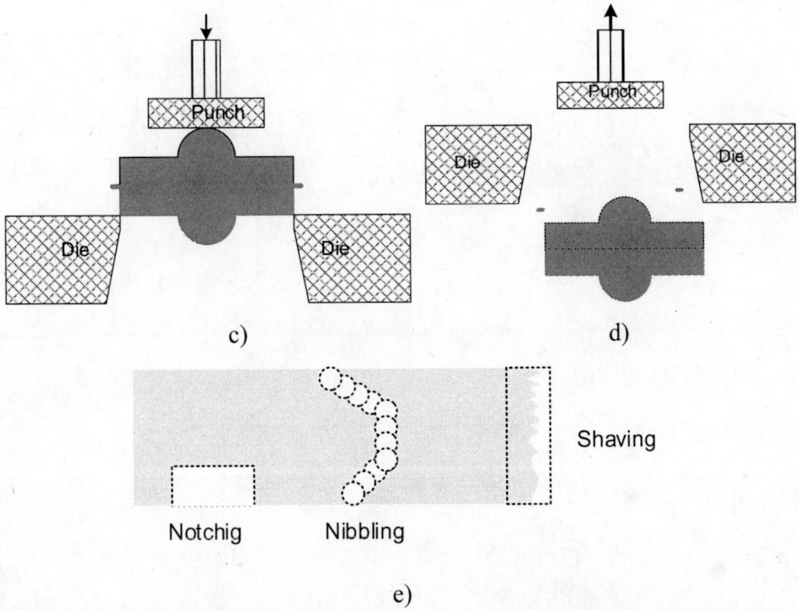

Fig. 2.43 Schematic of shearing-based sheet metal operations a-b) punching / blanking, c-d) trimming, e) notching, nibbling and shaving

2.11.2 Deep Drawing

Drawing operation is based on the plastic deformation of sheet metal to make cup-shaped products with the help of die and punch (with large radii of edges) coupled with large clearance to facilitate controlled deformation while avoiding any shearing action. The drawing operation producing a cup-shape product with a depth greater than its radius is called deep drawing. A blank of the desired size is placed on the die and held loosely (for easy downward movement only without any lateral movement). Sheet metal is then pushed down with the help of punch, leading to radial inward movement. The downward movement of sheet metal between die and punch due to controlled plastic deformation facilitates the production of cup-shaped products (Fig. 2.44). The presence of excess metal during drawing in the latter stages shows the tendency of wrinkle formation. Deep drawing may take repetition of a few steps of drawing to realize the final size and dimension of product. The operation is carried out using the press of suitable capacity and ram speed. This process is extensively used for making sheet metal components in the automotive sector.

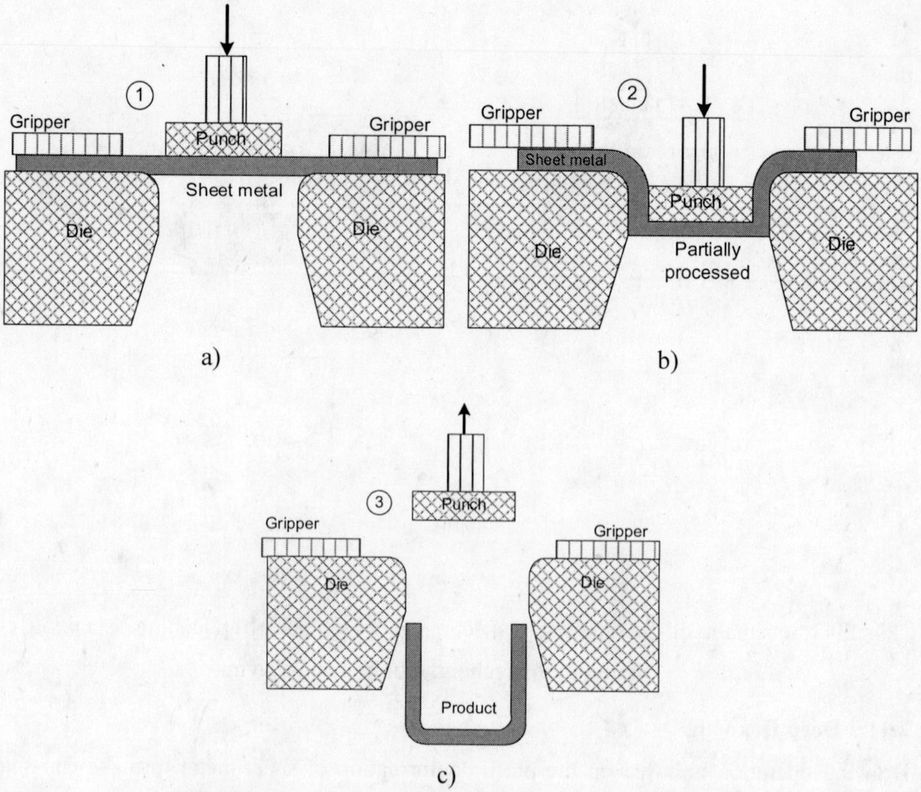

Fig. 2.44 Schematic of the deep drawing process in sequential stages

Ironing (thinning) is a unique variant of drawing where clearance between the die and punch is narrow (but large enough to avoid any shearing action) for controlled plastic deformation involving significant thinning (up to 50% of sheet metal thickness) of wall thickness of cup shape product. The ironing, in fact, increases the length and reduces the diameter of a cup (Fig. 2.45).

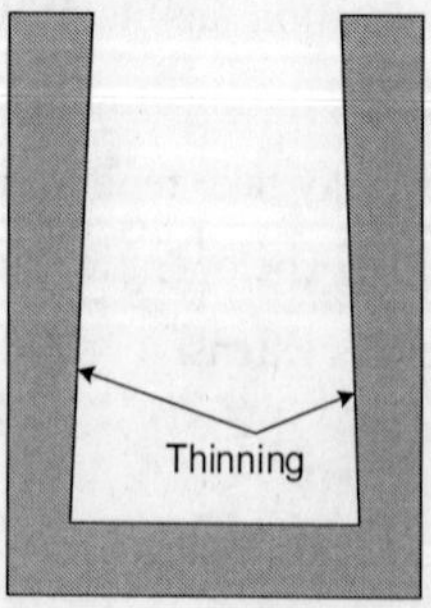

Fig. 2.45 Schematic of deep drawing causing iron of vertical wall of sheet metal cup

2.11.3 Bending

The bending involves the plastic deformation of sheet metal around a straight axis in the neutral plane. The metal on two sides of the neutral plane experiences different stress/ strain (tensile on one side and compressive on the other side). This natural plane lies somewhere between 0.5 to 0.3 times the thickness on the compression side. The sheet metal on the tension side shows a greater tendency to crack and fracture during bending in case of limited ductility and excessive strain hardening. Bending is extensively used in the sheet metal forming industry to make products like cabinets, cases, trunks and boxes. A typical bending sheet metal deformation operation, namely V-shape bending is shown in Fig. 2.46. Other deformation-based sheet metal operations, such as spinning, embossing, and coining, involving plastic deformation are schematically shown in Fig.2.47.

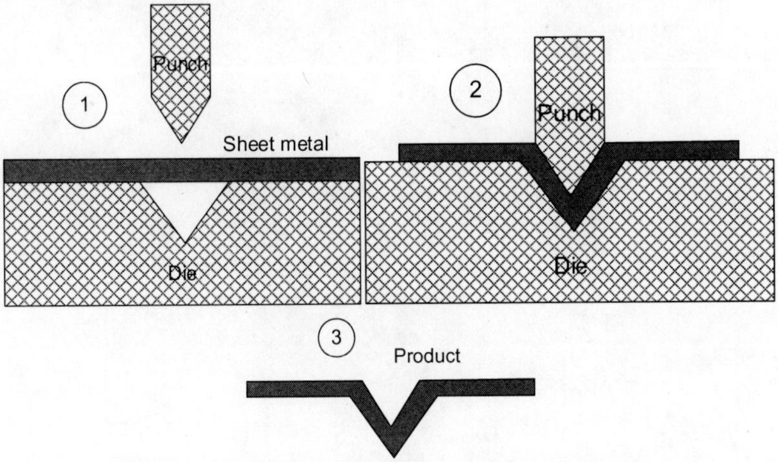

Fig. 2.46 Schematic of V shape being operation

The spinning process is used to make axis-symmetric sheet metal objects by controlled plastic deformation. A round tip tool is pressed against a rotating wooden/metallic mould to cause plastic deformation of the sheet metal to take shape as per mould (Fig. 2.47 a).

Embossing is a process used to a) mark labels in the form of letters, numbers, symbol, etc. and b) localised stiffening/strengthening of sheet metal. This process involves plastic deformation with the help of a die and punch using compressive load. Deformation is such that depression on one side results in corresponding projection on the other side at the same location. Plastic deformation of sheet metal is used to cause work hardening for local strengthening of sheet metal objects (Fig. 2.47 b).

Coining is a process used to make coins, decorative objects, and models using closed die and punch with the help of compressive load. Compressive load in a closed die causes the plastic flow of metal in lateral and multiple directions to fill up the mould/die cavity. The plastic deformation coupled with coining also causes significant work hardening of surface layers (Fig. 2.47 c).

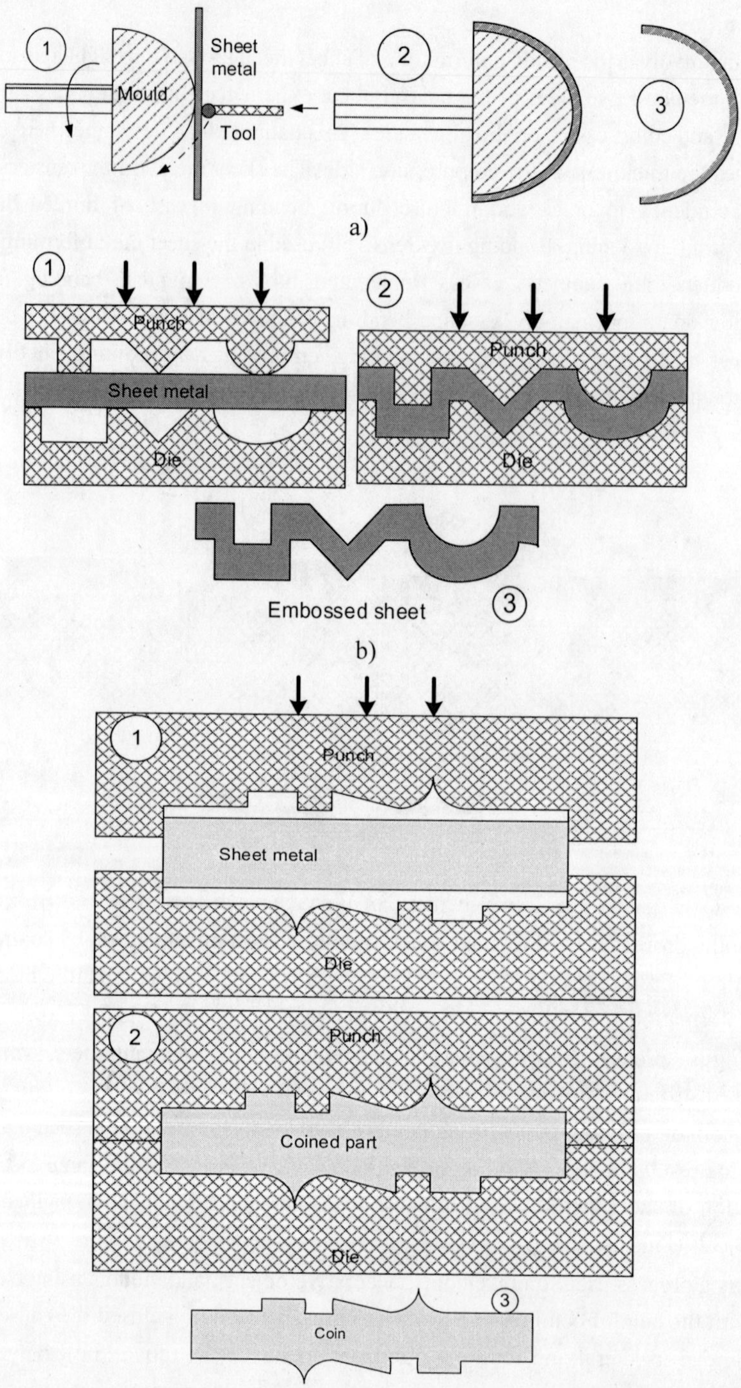

Fig. 2.47 Schematic of deformation-based sheet metal operations a) spinning, b) embossing and c) coining

2.12 Plastic processing

During the last few decades, the application of plastics has increased many folds in various sectors like domestic, automotive, electronics, aerospace, etc. There are two broad categories of plastic in use, namely thermo-setting and thermo-plastic. Thermo-plastics are relatively soft, low strength, high ductility and low melting temperature as compared to thermo-setting plastics. Therefore, thermo-plastic is easier to process than thermo-setting plastics. Thermo-setting plastics allow heating/cooling only once in the course of manufacturing. While thermo-plastics can be heated/cooled multiple times for softening and hardening as per need during manufacturing. Under each category, many types of plastics have also been developed by modification (filler, elastomer, fibres etc.) and reinforcement of external constituents to further enhance mechanical performance and other desired characteristics.

2.12.1 Extrusion

The plastic extrusion in terms of approach is similar to that of the bulk metal forming extrusion process. Still, there are many differences in the form of raw material, temperature and force requirement and condition of the material. Plastic extrusion uses compressive force to push the softened viscous paste-like plastic material through a die having an orifice of the desired shape to manufacture long, slander, and uniform cross-section bars, and rods. A schematic of the plastic extrusion process is shown in Fig. 2.48. This process is used for producing pipes, cables, tubes, and coated electrical wires. These products are generally made of thermo-plastics and rarely of thermosets. Extrusion of plastics involves three steps, namely feeding stock in the form of pellets, followed by heating, and melting/softening in an extrusion barrel/chamber. Then, softened plastic is forced to flow through an orifice in the die. Softening of plastics to facilitate extrusion takes place due to inherent frictional heating (due to rotation of screw plunger) and external heating of the extrusion chamber. Extruded material coming out of the orifice is cooled rapidly using an air/water jet to harden so that any kind of deformation and damage to the extruded component is avoided. Thereafter, the extruded component is cut into suitable lengths, as extrusion is a continuous process.

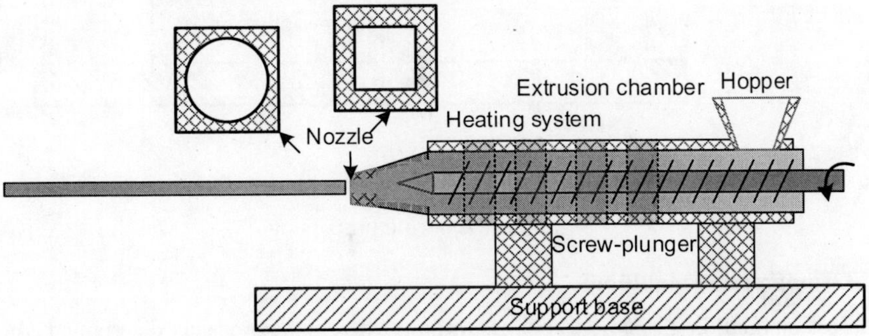

Fig. 2.48 Schematic of plastic extrusion process

2.12.2 Injection moulding

Injection moulding is similar to the die casting process. Injection moulding uses a split die, just like a mould cavity (in die casting), for making products mostly made of thermo-plastics. Plastic granules/fibres fed through a hopper are heated in an injection barrel (using combined external heating and frictional heating by screw-plunger) to a highly plastic state to impart good flowability. The thick, viscous fluid like plastic is then injected into the die (mould cavity) under high pressure (70-200 MPa) as per section thickness and size of the component. The desired injection pressure can be realised either using a hydraulic or screw plunger rotating in the injection barrel. The schematic of injection moulding is shown in Fig. 2.49. The dimensional accuracy and finish of injection mouldings are very good. Therefore, it is useful in manufacturing of near-net shape products. Injection moulding is used to manufacture products like cups, fridge doors, auto bumpers, housing, tool handle, knobs, electrical and communication component, etc.

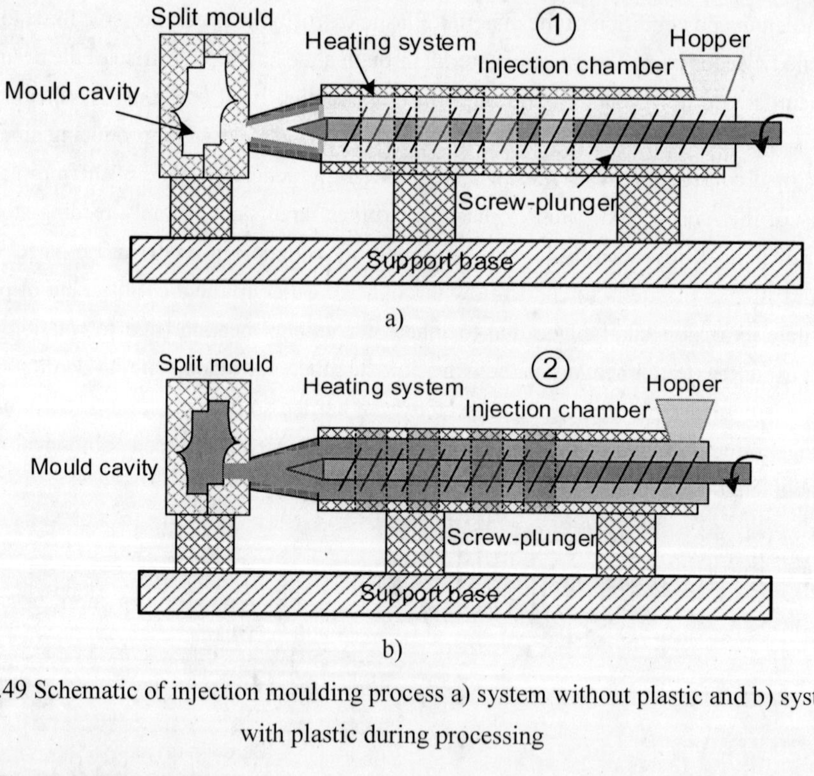

Fig. 2.49 Schematic of injection moulding process a) system without plastic and b) system with plastic during processing

2.12.3 Compression moulding

Compression moulding is similar to press forging wherein the precisely determined amount of plastic (usually thermal setting and elastomer) is placed in the heated lower half of the closed die cavity (in die and punch set). The heating of the plastic imparts the desired flowability. The application of pressure from the punch (upper half of the die set) forces the plastics to flow and fill the cavity to take the shape of the die. Subsequently, on cooling, the plastic product is ejected using a suitable ejection mechanism. A little flash formed at the junction of the dies is trimmed off. Stages of compression moulding are shown in Fig. 2.50. The compression moulding is commonly used for making products like dishes, handles, container caps, fittings, electrical and electronic components, washing machine agitators, and housings.

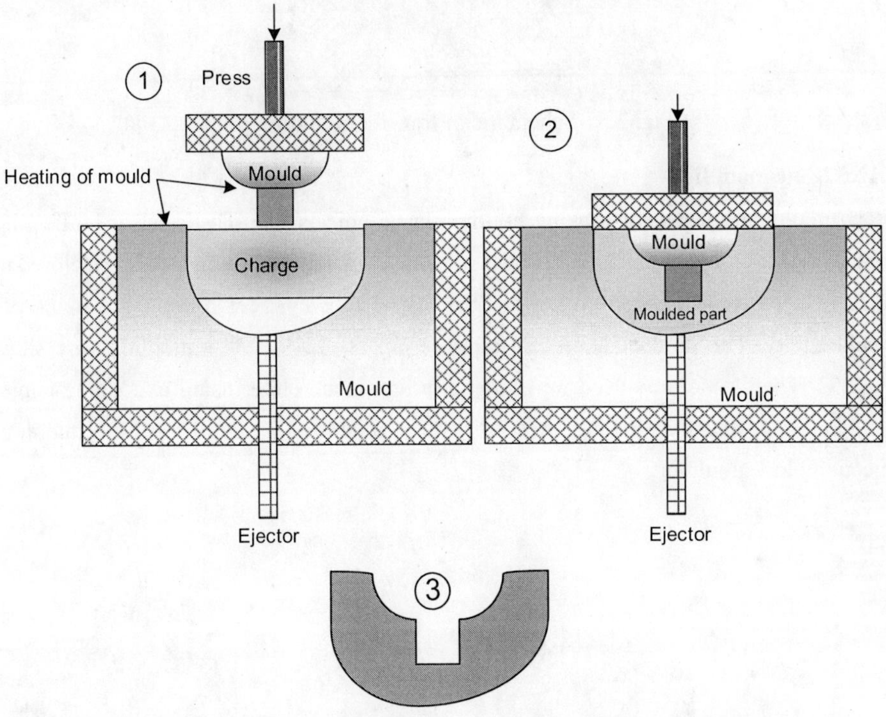

Fig. 2.50 Schematic of sequential steps of compression moulding process

2.12.4 Transfer moulding

This process is a combination of compression and injection moulding. A predetermined quantity of charge (thermosets/elastomers type of plastics) is placed in a chamber (preheated pot). Pressure is applied on the charge with the help of a plunger, which transfers the charge/plastic to a preheated split mould cavity. Pressurised plastic fills entire cavities/features in the mould to make the plastic product. The product is ejected from the mould after curing. The schematic of transfer moulding is shown in Fig. 2.51. The plastic in the preheated pot for transfer moulding can be pressurised using either a hydraulic plunger or an auxiliary ram for pot transfer and plunger transfer moulding, respectively. Extra plastic left in the transfer channel is a waste and should be removed suitably.

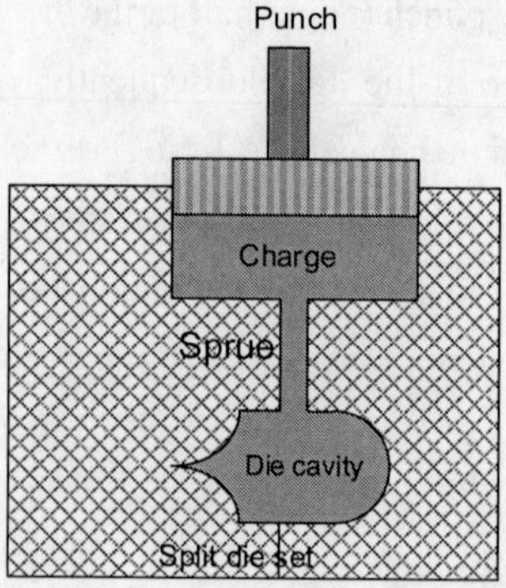

Fig. 2.51 Schematic of transfer moulding process

2.12.5 Blow moulding

Blow moulding is used for making hollow plastic objects like plastic water bottles, hollow containers, etc., by blowing hot air in a plastic tube/cylinder preform placed in the closed mould cavity. On blowing pressurised hot air, the plastic tube/cylinder follows the shape of split mould cavity. The product is ejected after curing. Stages of blow moulding are shown in Fig.2.52. The plastic tube used for blowing is first made either using extrusion or injection moulding followed by blowing. Accordingly, it is termed as extrusion blow moulding or injection blow moulding.

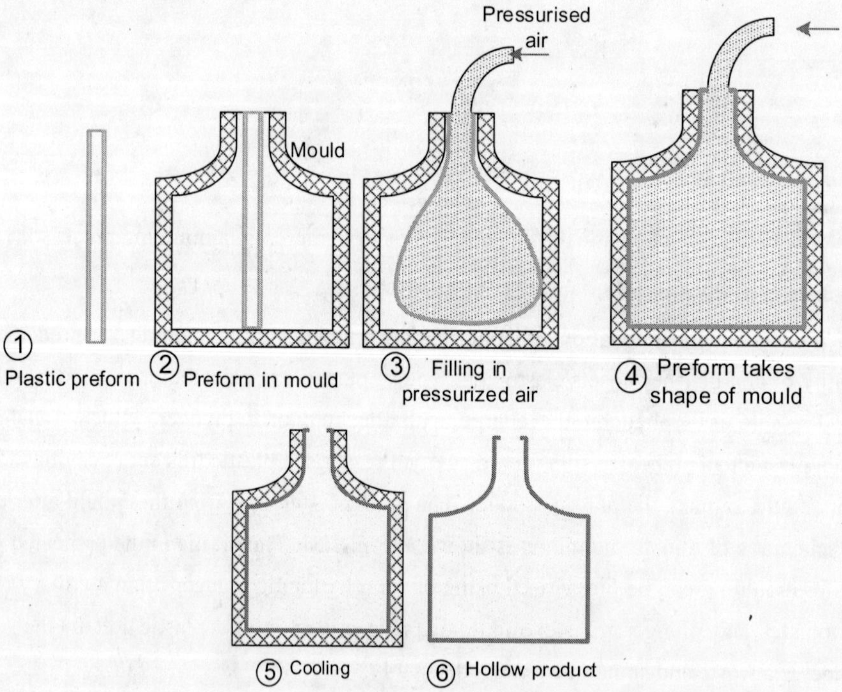

Fig. 2.52 Schematic of sequential steps of blow moulding process

2.12.6 Rotational moulding

The rotational moulding is used for making thin-walled large hollow plastic products like buckets, tanks, trashcans, boat hulls, housings, toys, carry cases, etc. Stages of rotational moulding are shown in Fig.2.53. A predetermined amount of plastic (mostly thermoplastics and a few thermoset plastics) is heated in a thin-walled metallic mould cavity till the molten state. The molten plastic follows the mould cavity surface on rotation in multiple axes. Rotation of the mould cavity about two perpendicular axes help in better distribution of the liquid plastic to make products of uniform wall thickness. Thereafter, cooling of the mould cavity helps to cure the product and then eject it.

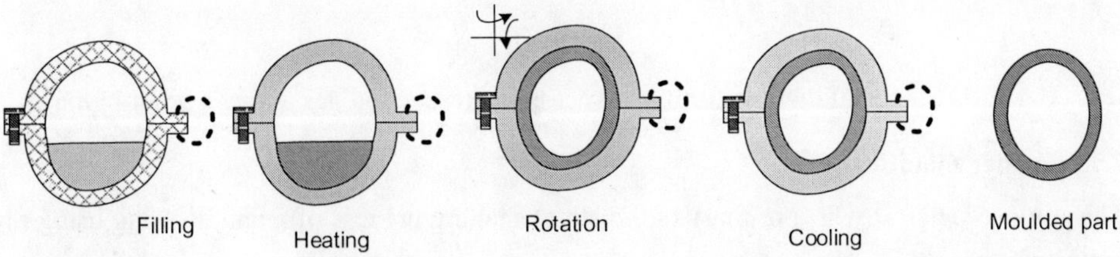

Fig. 2.53 Stages of rotational moulding process

2.12.7 Thermoforming

Thermoforming is performed on a thin thermoplastic sheet/film using a combination of heat for softening of plastic sheet followed by application of (positive/negative) pressure to ensure the shaping of softened sheet as per mould cavity to make products of thermoplastics. The stages of thermo-forming process are shown in Fig. 2.54 (a, b). Heating of plastic sheets can be done using an oven, and radiations followed by application of pressure. Pressure can be applied using compressed air or vacuum. Two plastic sheets can also be formed together to make a multi-colour/material/geometry product.

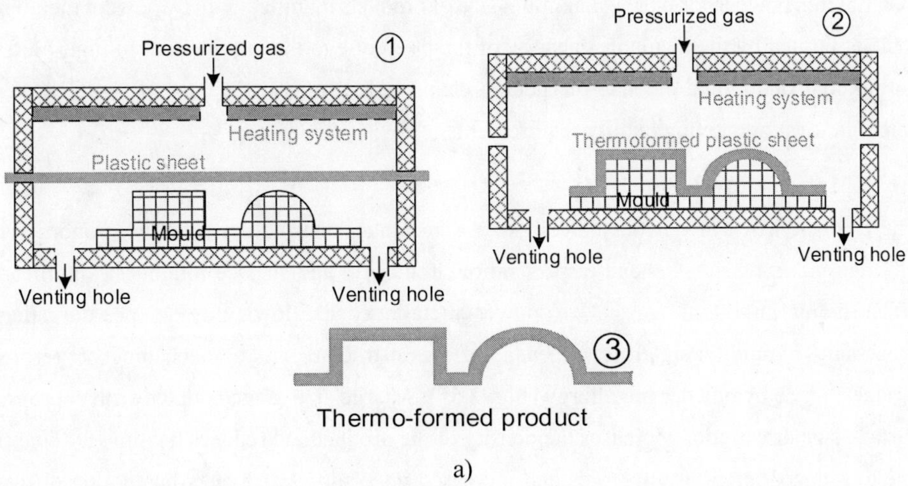

a)

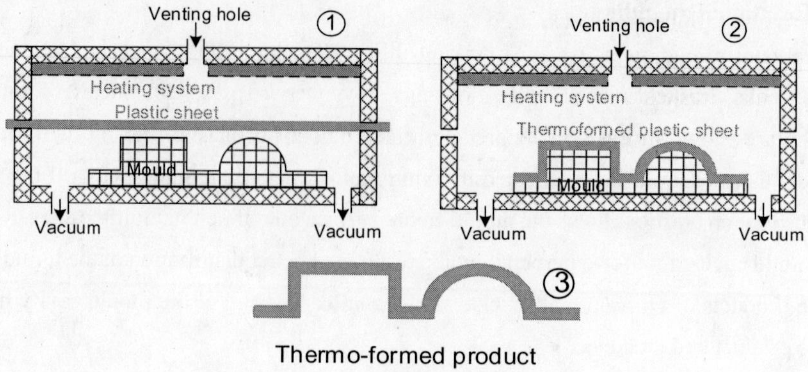

b)

Fig. 2.54 Stages of thermo-forming process a) pressurised gas and b) vacuum type

2.13 Powder metallurgy

The powder metallurgy is a primary (solid state) shaping process of manufacturing using raw material in the form of powders of various constituents as per need. The products made of "metallurgically incompatible material combinations" are generally manufactured by powder metallurgy route using four steps, namely powder blending, compaction, sintering and post processing. Common products like carbide and cermet tools, including those of composite material are made by powder metallurgy. Products made by powder metallurgy route are generally costlier due to the requirement of a) material in powder form, b) special equipment, c) time-consuming process, and is usually limited to small-size products. The powder metallurgy needs equipment like a mixer/blender for uniform mixing of constituent powders, high-capacity press for compaction, and environmentally controlled sintering furnace. Material in powder form is costlier than bulk material as it requires many extra steps to convert bulk material into powder form. The maximum size of products manufactured by powder metallurgy route is limited by the available capacity of the press due to the requirement of high-pressure during compaction and the size of vacuum chamber for sintering in case of certain material combinations for meeting quality requirements.

2.13.1 Material Powders

The characteristics of powder namely size, size range, distribution (relative proportions of different size/ranges %), shape (aspect ratio, circularity) and surface roughness significantly affect many important aspects of power metallurgy a) flowability of powders during processing, b) time for sintering, c) density, d) microstructure, and e) mechanical properties of products made by powder metallurgy (Fig. 2.55). A large size range coupled with appropriate particle size distribution increases the density of the product and reduces the time for sintering due to reduced inter-particle voids and increased inter-particle contacts facilitating diffusion during sintering. Spherical shape particles offer relatively higher flowability, but bonding is limited due to reduced tendency of mechanical interlocking and interfacial contact than irregular shape particles.

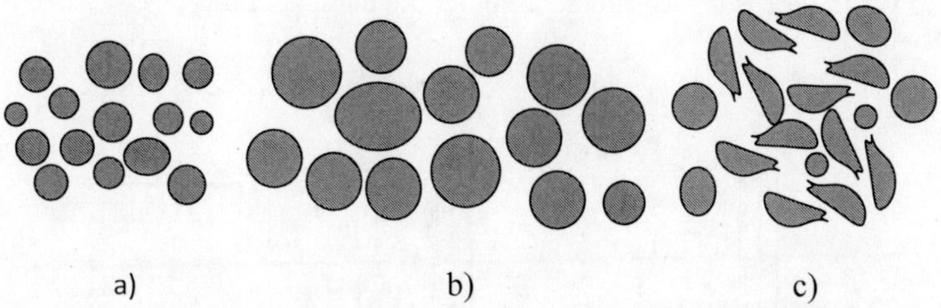

Fig. 2.55 Schematic showing a) fine spherical powder particles, B) large size spherical particles and c) mixed spherical and irregular shaper powder particles

2.13.2 Blending and mixing

The powder metallurgy route of manufacturing is primarily used for manufacturing products made of a combination of metals/materials, which are not (metallurgically) compatible with each other for processing, by casting, forming and welding. Therefore, all constituent materials in powder form must be blended and mixed using suitable mixers and blenders for uniformity of composition, microstructure and mechanical properties (Fig. 2.56).

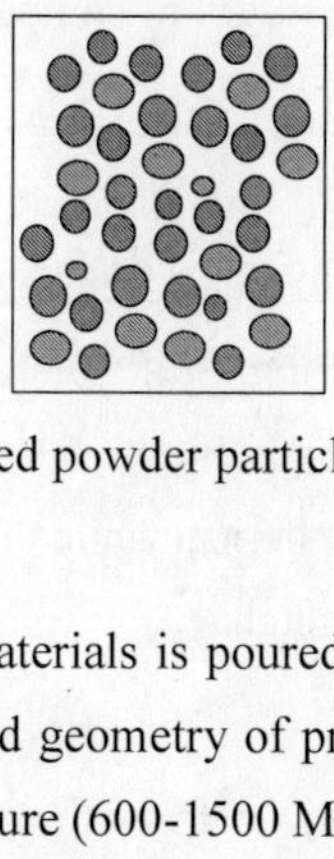

Fig. 2.56 Schematic showing mixed powder particles of different materials and sizes

2.13.3 Compaction

The powder mixture of constituent materials is poured into the die cavity. The die cavity is designed and shaped as per the desired geometry of product. The powder mixture in the die cavity is pressurised to very high pressure (600-1500 MPa) as per material using suitable press to facilitate the inter-powder particle bonding by mechanical interlocking caused by plastic deformation of powders at room temperature. However, the deformation of the fine powder particles needs much-much higher pressure than their yield strength. The pressurization and deformation of powder particles result in mechanical interlocking between them, leading to the development of relatively weak bond between the powder particles (Fig. 2.57). As a result, a low strength product of the desired shape is obtained by this step called ***compaction***. The weak product made after compaction is called a briquette or green compact. To impart the desired mechanical strength to green compact through metallurgical bonding sintering is necessary.

The requirement of very high pressure for compaction, limits the manufacturing of large-size products by powder metallurgy. Ease of compaction is called compactibility. A simple measure of compactibility can be the pressure required to achieve a given level of density in green compact. Lower the pressure requirement higher the compactibility.

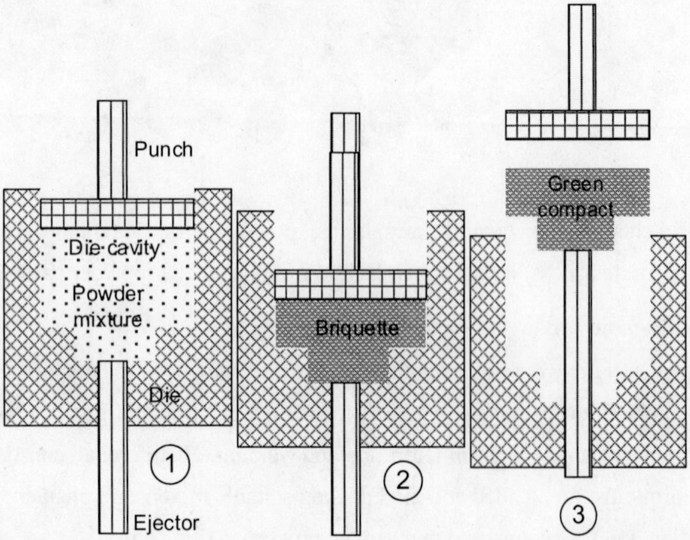

Fig. 2.57 Schematic showing stages of compaction during powder metallurgy

During the compaction, pores and inter-particle gaps are reduced which in turn increases the density of green compact. Compactibility depends on many factors such as hardness of constituent materials, shape, size, size range, surface roughness and intra-particle pores as per methods used for powder manufacturing. Soft, small size, round powder particles of smooth surface with a wide size range in general offer higher compactibility. Powders produced by the atomization method are smooth and spherical while those obtained through reduction of oxides and grinding route are irregular and rough

2.13.4 Sintering

Mechanical interlocking due to plastic deformation of powder particles imparts strength to green compact during compaction but it is not enough for engineering applications. Therefore, the desired strength in the component made through the powder metallurgy route is obtained through metallurgical bonding by sintering. Sintering involves heating of green compact to 0.6 to 0.75 Tm (Tm melting temperature in K) with or without pressure for long enough (time) to facilitate a) inter-particle metallurgical bonding and b) controlled reduction of pores/voids. The atomic diffusion across the powder particle interfaces (having metal-to-metal contact) of green compact at high temperature as function time develops a metallurgical bond without any distinct interfaces (Fig. 2.58). Sintering of components for very long significantly reduces the inert-particle voids (90-95%) through volumetric diffusion. However, it may not be feasible to eliminate all the voids to realise the sound product, as it would be extremely time consuming without much gain in terms of strength.

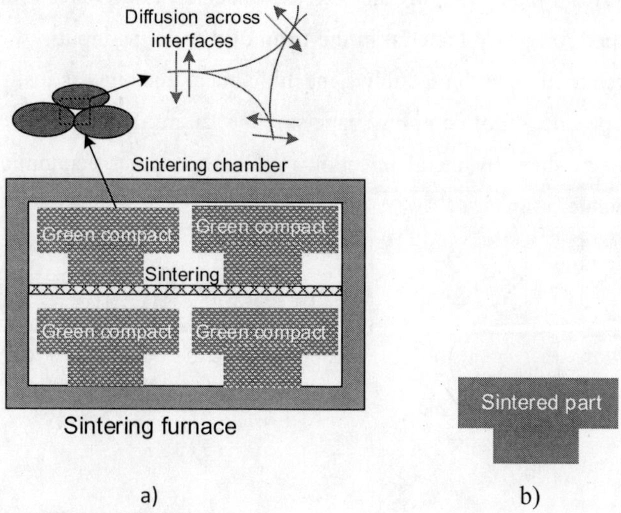

Fig. 2.58 Schematic showing sintering process and mechanism a) system and b) part

2.13.5 Post sintering treatment

The post sintering treatments are applied to obtain the desired surface finish, dimensional accuracy, densification, and sealing of pores, if any, via machining, impregnation and heat treatment as per the functional requirement of the end-product for a given application. These help in improving the performance and characteristics of products made by powder metallurgy route.

2.14 Metal Injection Moulding

The metal injection moulding process combines features of powder metallurgy and plastic injection moulding. This process is primarily used to manufacture very complex parts in very high-volume using powder mixture of constituent materials and thermoplastics (wax and polypropylene). Metal injection moulding involves steps namely blending and mixing of materials in desired proportions, granulation, feed grains/pellets for injection moulding, cleaning of the moulded part, de-binding (removal of thermo-plastic) using chemical and thermal treatment, sintering to develop metallurgical bond and impart desired strength (Fig. 2.59). A mixture comprising thermo-plastic and metal powders in the form of molten and viscous slurry is fed into the mould of a metal injection-moulding machine. On cooling, the product obtained is also called mould. The mould ejected just after metal injection moulding is usually weak and, therefore must be handled carefully to avoid breakage/damage like green compact in powder metallurgy. The thermoplastic binder holding metal/material powder is removed by chemical / thermal treatment. The de-binding step results in many inter-particle pores (30-40%). Sintering of components after de-binding develops metallurgical bonds and reduces porosity, resulting in a significant increase of density (95-99%) and strength of sintered products. The need for costly material in the form of powder as input raw materials coupled with high cost of metal injection moulding machine make this process justifiable only in case of high-volume production of complex shape small (< 20 mm) size jobs. Otherwise, they are uneconomical to produce by metal injection moulding if other economical manufacturing options are available.

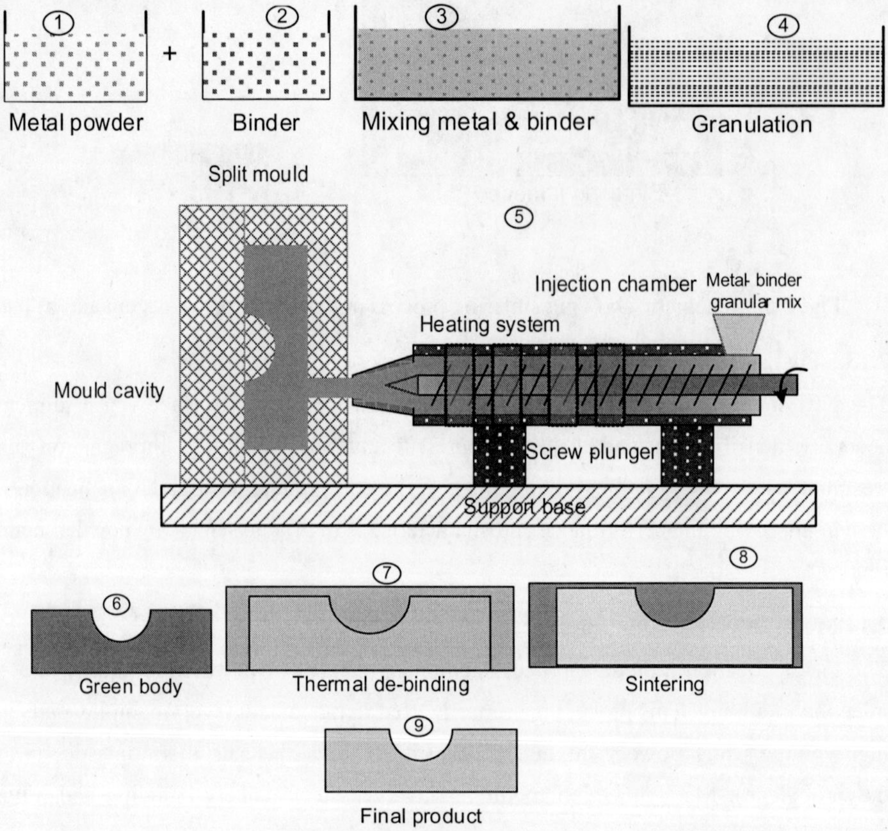

Fig. 2.59 Schematic showing sequential steps of metal injection moulding process

2.15 Lay-up process

This process is mainly used for making fibre reinforced polymer matrix composites offering attractive characteristics like water sealing, chemical and abrasion resistance, and good high strength to weight ratio. First, a gel coating is applied on the surface of mould, followed by application of resin and, a reinforcing agent. Thereafter, alternate layers of resin and reinforcing agent are applied until the desired thickness is obtained. Reinforcing agents (like glass fibre or any other suitable constituent) can applied with appropriate resin/polymer using either hand lay-up or spray lay-up technique on the surface or mould as per the case (Fig. 2.60-2.61). The lay-up process, unlike metal injection moulding, helps to manufacture large-size products of polymer matrix composites (for application in aerospace, automotive, construction and marine industries) at low cost without much investment in machines and tools. The hand lay-up process is a little slower than the spray lay-up process. Other common application of the lay-up process includes sealing of flat roofs, pond bottom surfaces, concrete and timber waterproofing.

In general, the steps of lay-up process include gel/wax coat over the mould surface, application of a layer of glass fibre layer (in the desired orientation) over the gel coat, applying a paste of resin and hardener using a brush. Thereafter, use roller for uniformity of thickness of paste, consolidation and removal of pores, apply another layer of fibre, roller, resin hardener and same process can be repeated maximum (for 3-4 times) to obtain desired thickness of composite mould. Mould is then cured to attain the desired strength.

2.15.1 Hand lay-up

In the hand lay-up process, a layer of fibre and resin/hardener mixture is applied manually on the surface of the mould. The dry reinforcing agent, like glass fibres (in suitable forms like woven, knitted, stitched, or bond fabrics) cut to size and positioned on the mould surface. Polyester resin and hardener paste are then applied using a brush and/or roller to create a fibreglass laminate (Fig. 2.60). A topcoat can be applied for aesthetic and improved protection of laminate.

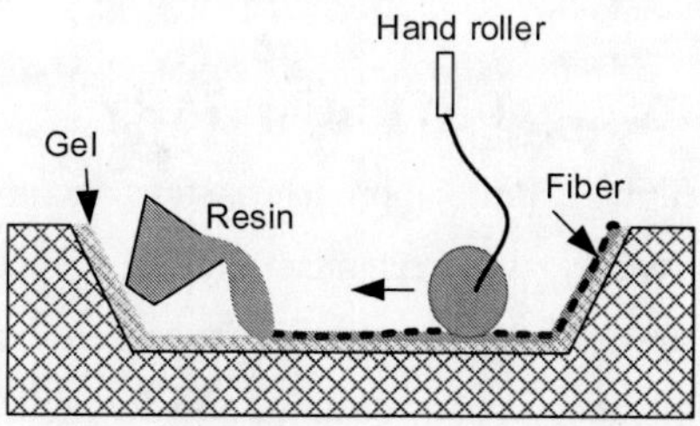

Fig. 2.60 Schematic of hand layup process for making polymer matrix composites

2.15.2 Spray Lay-up

A mixture of glass fibres and resin/hardener in the form of liquid is sprayed over the surface of the mould (Fig. 2.61). Application of controlled pressure and movement of roller over the applied layer of glass fibre and resin/hardener facilitates uniformity of layer thickness and favourable orientation of fibre. This process of spraying and rolling is repeated until the desired thickness of the composite laminates is achieved.

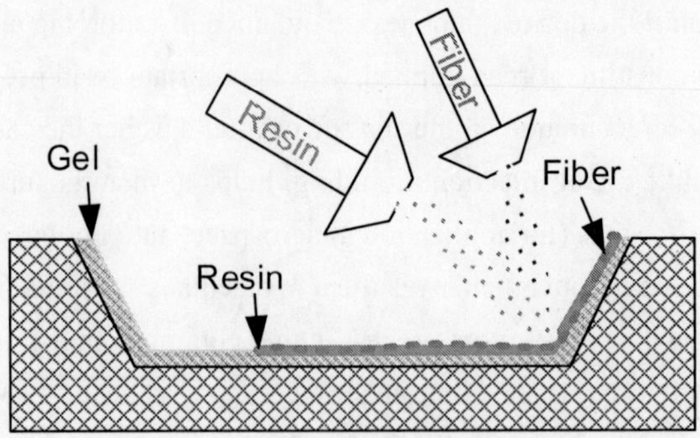

Fig. 2.61 Schematic of spray layup process for making polymer matrix composites

Quality and performance of the product obtained by lay-up process depends on the expertise of the operator besides technical factors like volume fraction, size and orientation of reinforcing agent (glass fibre), porosity as per consolidation of layers and curing of products. Application of pressure using rollers during laying up and use of vacuum helps in consolidation and reducing porosity. Curing is a hardening process involving either simple transformation of liquid resin to solid through evaporation or irreversible chemical reaction for thermo-plastic and thermo-setting resins, respectively, as per the case. Curing depends on both the time and temperature used for hardening purposes. Curing takes a longer time at room temperature to attain peak strength. While, increasing the temperature of curing reduces the time for peak hardening. Under/over exposure of product (in terms of time) for curing at a given temperature is called under/over curing accordingly and both reduce the strength of the composites.

UNIT SUMMARY

This chapter gives detailed insight into approaches, steps and applications of primary material shaping processes. Additionally, the mechanism causes, defect formation, and their remedy during casting, forming and powder metallurgy have been explained. The primary shaping processes like casting, bulk/sheet metal forming, powder metallurgy, plastic processing, and hand/spray layup methods cover the processing of a wide range of materials such as metals, polymers, glasses, and composite materials.

EXERCISE

Questions for self-assessment

1. Blow moulding helps to make
   a. Al castings b. Metallic bars
   c. Plastic bottles d. Composite sheets
2. Blanking operation during sheet metal processing uses
   a. Tensile stress b. Compressive stress
   c. Shear stress d. Bending stress
3. Compaction in powder metallurgy increases
   a. Porosity b. Density
   c. Tolerance d. All of these
4. Casting defect due to the lack of refractoriness of moulding sand is
   a. Porosity
   b. Hot tears
   c. Inter-mixing of molten metal and moulding sand
   d. Swell
5. A type of primary material shaping process is
   a. Welding b. Grinding
   c. Machining d. Rolling
6. A variety of materials in powder form are used for making composite materials products by
   a. Casting b. Forming
   c. Powder metallurgy d. Injection moulding
7. Hot working of metal results in
   a. High power consumption b. High surface finish
   c. High tolerance d. High strain hardening
8. Forming of metal below recrystallization temperature is called
   a. Melt working b. Hot working
   c. Cold working d. Hard working
9. Metal and polymeric binder are used as raw materials in
   a. Extrusion process b. Forging
   c. Blow moulding d. Metal-injection moulding
10. Glass fibre reinforced component material can be processed by
    a. Casting b. Forming
    c. Powder metallurgy d. Hand lay-up

Answers to Multiple Choice Questions

Key for MCQ: 1 c, 2 c, 3 b, 4 c, 5 d, 6 c, 7 c, 8 c, 9 d, 10 d

Short and Long Answer Type Questions

1. What is meaning of primary shaping?
2. What is the importance of pattern in sand mould casting?
3. Explain the permeability of a moulding sand.
4. How does the permeability affect the gaseous defects in casting?
5. What is hot working?
6. What are the properties a material should have for bulk metal forming processes?
7. Compare the cold and hot working processes.
8. What is the importance of strain hardening in metal-forming processes?
9. What are the causes and remedies of hot tearing?
10. What are the typical applications of investment casting?
11. What is the significance of the compaction in powder metallurgy?
12. Why does the sintering help to improve the mechanical properties of components produced by powder metallurgy?
13. Explain the steps used in metal casting.
14. Describe the essential properties a moulding sand should have for producing sound casting.
15. Explain the principle of the investment casting process.
16. How does the casting produced by the sand mould casting process and die Casting process differ in terms of the microstructure and mechanical properties?
17. Why do the forged products show anisotropy?
18. Differentiate open and closed die forging.
19. Explain the principle rolling and extrusion processes.
20. Explain the process used to make hollow plastic products.
21. Describe the spray and hand lay-up processes for making the glass fibre-reinforced polymer composite.
22. Explain the metal injection moulding process and write its applications.
23. What are the common casting defects and their remedies?
24. Write about the forging defects and their remedies.
25. What is the need for secondary processing in powder metallurgy processed components?
26. What is the importance of powder particle characteristics in producing sound products through powder metallurgy route?

KNOW MORE

Explore the how black smiths work to make various good of common use. Try to visit small, medium, large manufacturing units and try to find how real components are manufactured. During industrial training students are expected to expose and learn of real application of technologies. Explore how way of techniques of manufacturing good from bronze to modern age have evolved.

Scan me!

SUGGESTED RESOURCES FOR FURTHER READING/LEARNING

1. D K Dwivedi, Fundamentals of Metal Joining, Springer Nature, (2021)
2. S Kalpakjian, S R Schmid, Manufacturing Engineering and Technology, Pearson (2018)
3. M P Groover, Fundamentals of Modern Manufacturing, John Wiley and Sons, (2010)
4. A Ghosh, A K Malik, Manufacturing science, East-West Press (2010)
5. D K Dwivedi, Materials Engineering, AICTE, (2023).
6. D K Dwivedi, NPTEL Course "Joining Technologies for Metals": https://onlinecourses.nptel.ac.in/noc23_me130/preview
7. D K Dwivedi, NPTEL Course "Fundamentals of Manufacturing Processes" https://archive.nptel.ac.in/courses/112/107/112107219/
8. D K Dwivedi, Production and properties of cast Al-Si alloys, New Age International (2013)
9. https://www.reliance-foundry.com/blog/castings-shakeout
10. D. K. Dwivedi, Ashok Sharma, T V Rajan, molten metal treatment of Al-Si alloys for improved properties, Foundry Journal, Vol. 12, No. 6, Nov-Dec 2000, 9-13.
11. D. K. Dwivedi, Ashok Sharma, T V Rajan, methods to improve the structure and properties of cast Al-Si alloys, Indian Foundry Journal , Vol. 46, No. 12, Dec-2000, 31-39.
12. Prabhkiran kaur, Dheerendra k. Dwivedi, Pushpraj M Pathak, Effects of Electromagnetic stirring and Rare Earth compounds on the Microstructure and Mechanical properties of Hypereutectic Al-Si alloys", International Journal of Advanced Manufacturing Technology , (Dec 2012) 63:415–420

3 Material Removal Processes

Unit Specific / Learning Objective

The objective of this unit is to talk about the following aspects

- To learn about the need and scope of material removal manufacturing processes
- To introduce the concept and approach of removal manufacturing processes to obtain products with the desired finish and tolerance
- To develop an understanding of common material removal processes turning, drilling, milling and grinding for manufacturing
- To learn about common cutting tools and tool materials used in machining
- To familiarise with the concept of quality of machined surface in terms of surface integrity
- To introduce the concept of machinability and various relevant factors

Additionally, a few questions for self-assessment based on fundamentals have been included in this chapter. These questions are based on application, comprehension, analysis and synthesis. Suggested further reading and reference have been included for deep learners and readers.

Rationale

Components and products manufactured by casting, forming and welding routes are generally not good enough for direct applications due to poor surface finish and lack of close control over dimensions. The material removal processes not only allow for achieving the desired size and shape by rough cutting but also help in realising the desired surface finish and close tolerance (using finish cut) needed for many critical applications and proper functioning. Considering the demand to produce high-quality products at low cost, focus is on optimal utilization of the process capabilities of different manufacturing processes involving the use of primary shaping processes followed by secondary processing like machining. Therefore, learning about secondary shaping processes like turning, drilling, milling and grinding are necessary and pertinent. Awareness of these secondary processing methods allows effective process planning of manufacturing components considering surface finish, tolerance and other quality requirements.

Pre-Requisites

Physics: (Class XII)

Learning outcomes

U3-O1: Ability to apply material removal processes to manufacture a product of the desired shape, surface finish and tolerance

U3-O2: Ability to select suitable material removal processes as per design of product, tolerance, and finish requirement

U3-O3: Ability to understand and specify tool geometry using tool signature and select suitable tool materials

U3-O4: Ability to select suitable machining process parameters as per need of productivity and surface quality requirement

U3-O5: Ability to evaluate and interpret machinability of workpiece material

Unit-3 Outcomes	EXPECTED MAPPING WITH COURSE OUTCOMES (1- Weak Correlation; 2- Medium correlation; 3- Strong Correlation)					
	CO-1	CO-2	CO-3	CO-4	CO-5	CO-6
U3-O1	3	2	-	-	-	-
U3-O2	3	3	-	-	-	-
U3-O3	3	2	-	-	-	-
U3-O4	3	3	-	-	-	-
U3-O5	2	3	-	-	-	-

CO

1. Understand the different conventional and unconventional manufacturing methods employed for making different products
2. To motivate and challenge students to understand and develop an appreciation of the processes in correlation with material properties which change the shape, size and form of the raw materials into the desirable product.

3.1 Introduction

The manufacturing by material removal processes is a subtractive approach where unwanted and extra material is removed from the bulk/stock material in the form of fine metallic pieces called chips. The material removal processes are also called machining processes and metal cutting in the case of metallic stock material. The material removed in the form of chips is of no use and just a waste of material worth except recycling. In general, materials by conventional machining processes are removed by shearing action using a suitable cutting tool (Fig. 3.1). A *cutting tool* interacts with the workpiece to remove excess material through direct mechanical contact and applies suitable stresses during conventional machining processes. A m*achine tool* is a complete system including the prime mover and other components such as cutting tool, control devices, etc. to provide necessary relative motion between the workpiece and tool.

The material during machining can be removed by applying mechanical energy, thermal energy and electro/chemical reaction (singly or in combination thereof) to the stock material to obtain the desired shape, dimensional accuracy and tolerance. The scope of this unit includes material removal processes (turning, milling, drilling, grinding) which use mechanical energy for material removal e.g. shearing and abrasion. The material removal by shearing/abrasion mechanism (using mechanical energy) is very gradual, involving material removal in the form of a thin layer-by-layer material removal approach. Therefore, mechanical energy-based material removal processes help in realizing higher dimension accuracy and close control over tolerance and reasonably good surface finish. Hence, machining is one of the most used manufacturing processes in all sectors including aerospace, automotive, pressure vessel, heavy and general engineering applications.

3.2 General approach

The removal of material during machining involves a simple principle wherein a hard, strong and preferably tough cutting tool (with shape-wedge shape cutting edge) penetrates the relatively soft workpiece/stock material followed by controlled relative motion between the two resulting in the removal of material by shearing (Fig. 3.1).

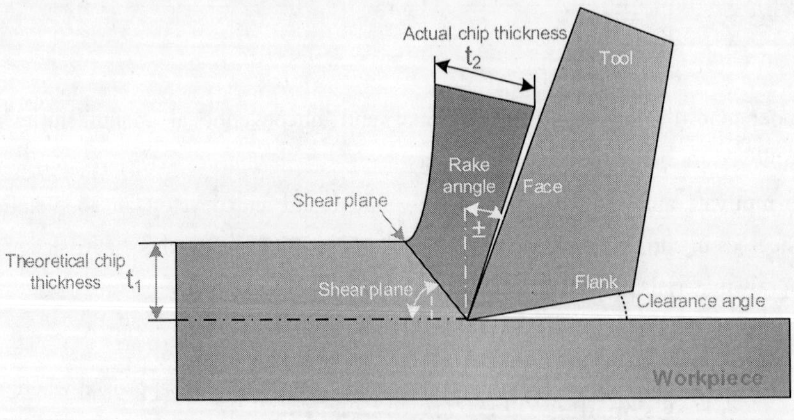

Fig. 3.1 Schematic diagram showing material removal by shearing action

The depth of penetration of the tool into the workpiece is called ***depth of cut*** $(D_1-D_2)/2$), usually expressed in mm. It determines the thickness of the layer removed from the workpiece. Relative velocity between the workpiece and cutting-edge of the tool is called ***cutting speed ($\pi DN/1000$),*** usually expressed in m/min. Cutting speed dictates how fast a material is removed from the workpiece. Additionally, in order to machine the entire length/width of the workpiece to produce the desired shape / size desired, tool/workpiece is given another lateral movement, usually perpendicular to the direction of cutting is called ***feed*** (mm / rev or mm/min) (Fig. 3.2).

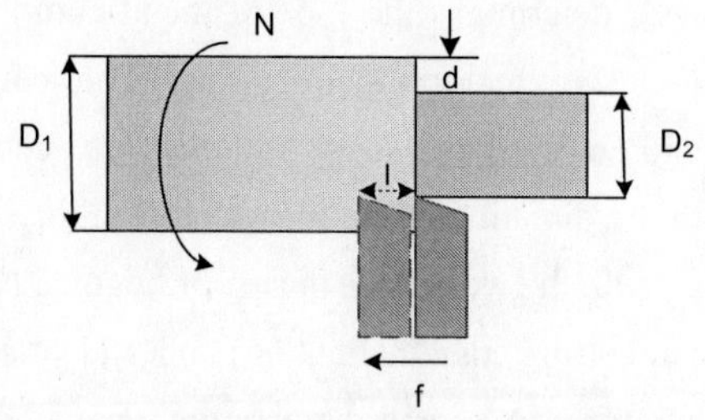

Fig. 3.2 Schematic diagram showing cutting parameters during turning

3.3 Generatrix and Directrix

The shape generated by a tool on the workpiece during the machining depends on two relative movements a) line/path traced by a cutting edge of the tool for metal removal and b) relative lateral movement between tool and workpiece, usually perpendicular to the path traced by cutting edge of the tool (Fig. 3.3). Path traced by cutting edge of the tool in direction of cutting is called generatrix (primary cutting motion as per cutting requirement) and that in direction perpendicular to the cutting is called directrix (secondary cutting motion as per feed requirement). The following table 3.1 shows various combinations of generatrix and directrix used for obtaining various shapes by machining processes.

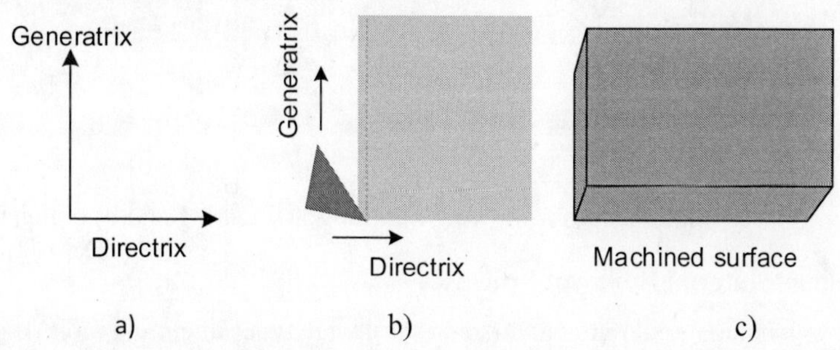

Fig. 3.3 Schematic diagram showing a) a typical generatrix and directrix, b) tool-work relative movement with corresponding generatrix and directrix and c) typical shape produced using said generatrix and directrix

Table 3.1 Generatrix and directrix for common machining processes and shape generated

Sr. No.	Process	Shape	Generatrix	Directrix
1	Turning	Cylindrical / threads	Circular	Linear
2	Drilling	Hole / taps	Circular	Linear
3	Milling	Flat / slots	Linear	Linear
4	Grinding	Flat/cylindrical	Circular/linear	Circular/linear

3.4 Type of metal cutting

The angle of cutting edge of the tool (with respect to direction of cutting) interacting with workpiece during machining determines the type of metal cutting. Metal cutting is broadly classified as orthogonal cutting and oblique cutting. The cutting edge of the tool is perpendicular to the direction of cutting velocity in orthogonal cutting while the cutting edge of the tool is inclined with the direction of cutting velocity (Fig. 3.4). Length/area of cutting-edge contacting/interacting with the workpiece during orthogonal cutting is lesser than oblique cutting (due to difference in cutting edge inclination) under identical cutting conditions of the feed and depth of cut. Therefore, stress and temperature generated during orthogonal cutting are higher than the oblique cutting. Greater area of cutting edge/workpiece interaction/contact area results in a) distribution of cutting force over large area and b) rapid heat transfer to the shank of the cutting tool leading to lower thermal and mechanical stresses. Both these factors, in turn, result in longer cutting tool life during oblique cutting than the orthogonal cutting.

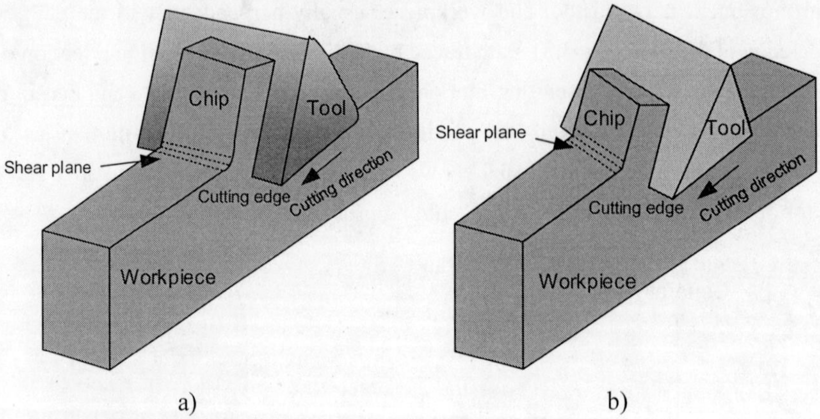

Fig. 3.4 Schematic diagram showing a) orthogonal cutting and b) oblique cutting

3.5 Common Material Removal Processes

The conventional material removal processes use three types of cutting tools (if grouped on the basis size and shape), namely, single-point cutting tool, multiple-point cutting tool and abrasives. Another way to classify tools is tool bit and cutting tool shank type. Then cutting tools are also termed based on the process for which these are used, e.g. turning tool, milling cutter, drill bit, abrasives for grinding, etc. The following section presents the approach, machine tool and common operations related to machining processes such as turning, drilling, milling and grinding.

3.5.1 Turning

The turning is one of the most common machining processes performed on the lathe machine. It produces mostly cylindrical shape products using circular generatrix and linear directrix.

However, the lathe machine can also be used for many other purposes such as creating holes, enlarging holes, making thread, rounded/tapered corners, knurling, parting off, cutting narrow slots, flat and tapered surface, curved surface generation, improving surface finish using operation like taper turning, face turning, shoulder turning, step turning, contour turning, chamfering, grinding, drilling, boring, knurling, threading, reaming, etc. **(Table 3.2)**.

A typical lathe machine has main parts like headstock (electric motor and gear train), tailstock, spindle, carriage, compound rest, tool post, cross-rail, lead screw, feed rod, suitable arrangement of supply of coolant, light and protection from chips (Fig. 3.5).

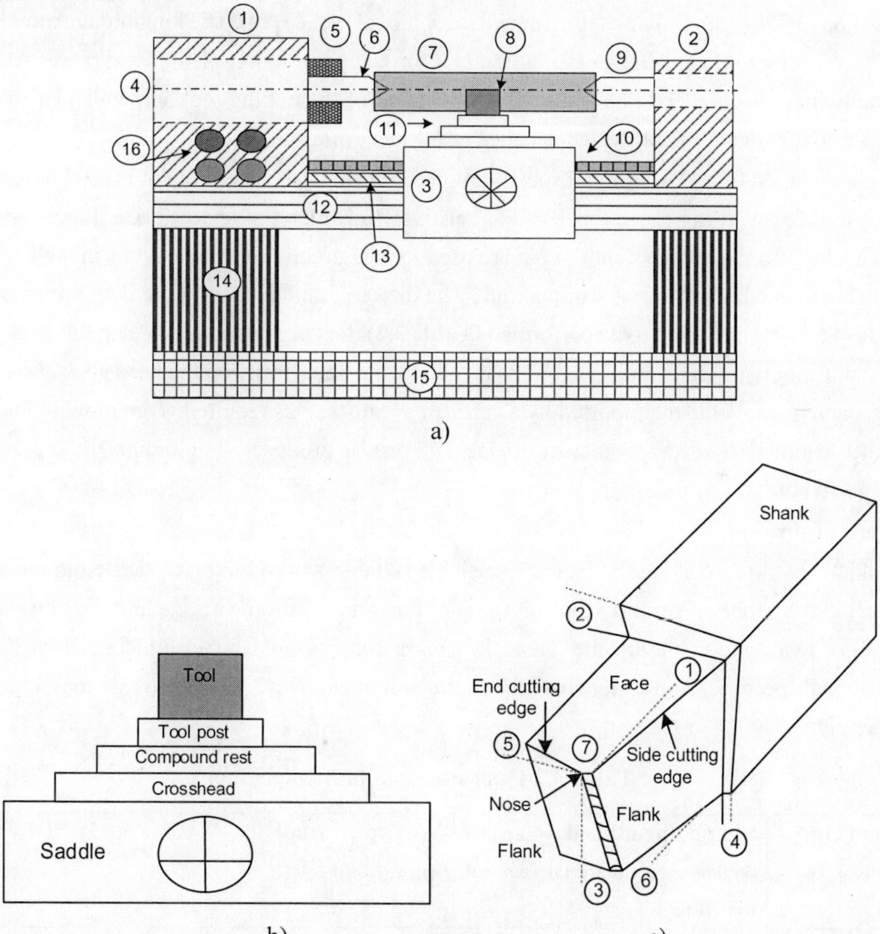

Fig. 3.5 Schematic diagram showing a) lathe machine with major components, b) closure look of carriage with multiple parts and c) single point cutting tool. Parts details are 1, headstock, 2 tail stock, 3 carriage, 4 spindle axis, 5 chuck, 6 live-centre, 7 workpiece, 8 cutting tool, 9 dead centre, 10 leadscrew, 11 compound rest, 12 structural member, 13 feed rod, 14 structural member, 15 base, 16 control panel

Workpiece is mounted on the headstock side of lathe machine using suitable chuck, face plate, live/dead centres. Long workpiece is supported from the tailstock side using a dead centre. The workpiece is power-driven by a spindle on headstock and gives rotational movement for generating circular generatrix. A single point cutting tool is mounted firmly on the tool holder and longitudinal feed to the tool is given by moving the carriage either manually using a hand-wheel or automatically using feed rod.

The required depth of cut (in mm) is given by moving the tool radially inward toward the centre of the workpiece. The diameter (D in mm) and rotational speed (N in rpm) of the workpiece being turned determined the cutting speed (mm/min) with respect to a given cutting tool position (πDN/1000, D diameter in mm, N is rotational speed rpm). The longitudinal movement of the cutting tool (parallel to the lathe axis) for each revolution of the workpiece is called longitudinal feed or feed rate (mm/rev). Movement of the cutting tool perpendicular to lathe axis provides depth of cut, which is called cross-feed (mm).

A combination of high rotational speed, low feed rate and low depth of cut is used for getting low surface roughness (high finish) and a relatively low material removal rate. Low rotational speed, high feed and high depth of cut are used for rough turning which results in high surface roughness and high material removal rate. The directrix and generatrix are determined by the type of turning operation to be performed **(Table 3.2)**. It is important to note that the workpiece in almost all types of turning operations is rotated and held firmly on the headstock and tool is mounted on tool holder supported by a carriage or tailstock as required. Tool moving linearly, either parallel to or perpendicular to the lathe axis, produces longitudinal or cross feed, respectively.

Steps of turning

Hold the workpiece along the lathe axis using a suitable work-holding device. Hold the single point cutting tool or knurling tool on the tool post mounted on carriage and drill bit, boring tool, or reamer mounted on the tailstock using a suitable holder. Set the desired workpiece rotational speed, feed rate, and cross-feed for depth of cut. Now, the stage is set for the turning operation.

Table 3.2 Operations on lathe machine

Turning Process	**Shape produced (hatched section shows material removal needed)**	**Workpiece/tool movement**	**Generatrix**	**Directrix**
Straight turning	Cylinder 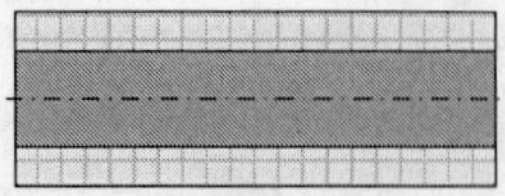	Workpiece: Rotation Tool: longitudinal feed for covering length & cross-feed for depth of cut	Circular	Linear
Taper turning	Taper	Workpiece: Rotation	Circular	Linear

Turning Process	**Shape produced (hatched section shows material removal needed)**	**Workpiece/tool movement**	**Generatrix**	**Directrix**
	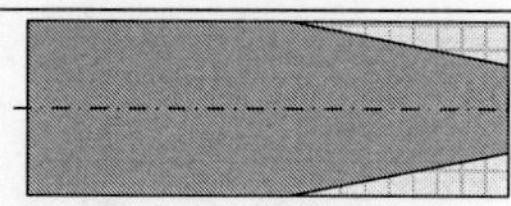	Tool: Lateral feed at an angle & cross-feed for depth of cut		
Face turning (Facing)	Flat surface 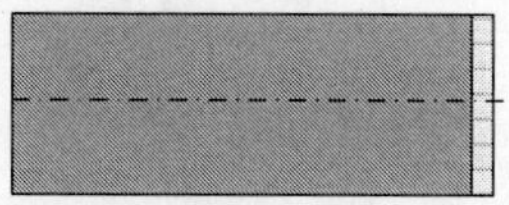	Workpiece: Rotation Tool: Cross feed to cover face Longitudinal feed for depth of cut	Circular	Linear
Shoulder turning	Step cylinder 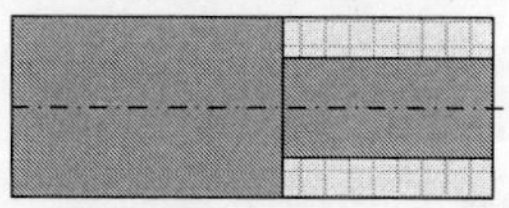	Workpiece: Rotation Tool: longitudinal feed for covering length & cross-feed for depth of cut	Circular	Linear
Contour turning	Curved surface 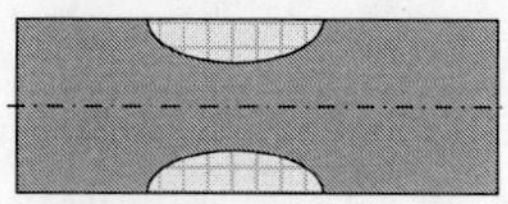	Workpiece: Rotation Tool: longitudinal feed in curve & cross-feed for depth of cut	Circular	Curve
Chamfering	Tapered/round corner 	Workpiece: Rotation Tool: No longitudinal feed and cross-feed for desired dimensions	Circular	Linear
Grinding	Finishing flat/hole 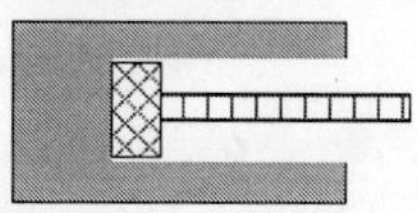	Workpiece: Rotation Tool: Longitudinal feed from tailstock side to cover length and cross-feed for depth of cut	Circular	Linear
Reaming	Finishing hole 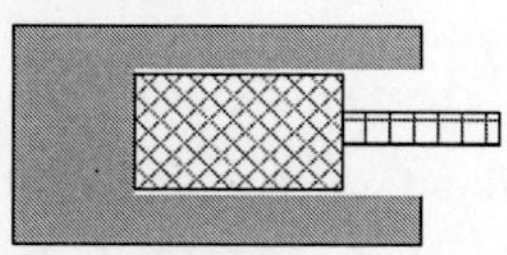	Workpiece: Rotation Tool: Longitudinal feed from tailstock side to cover length and cross-feed for depth of cut	Circular	Linear
Knurling	Roughening cylinder 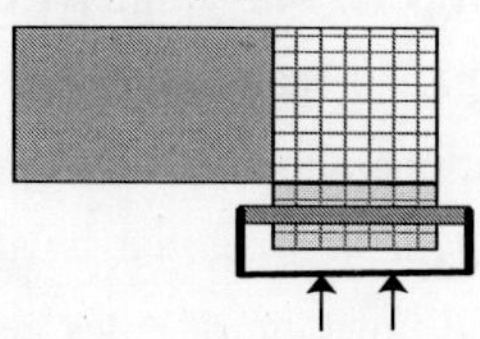	Workpiece: Rotation Tool: rotating to given longitudinal feed to cover length and cross-feed for desired depth of impressions	Circular	Linear
Threading	Thread on cylinder	Workpiece: Rotation Tool: Longitudinal feed to cover length generating	Circular	Linear

Turning Process	Shape produced (hatched section shows material removal needed)	Workpiece/tool movement	Generatrix	Directrix
	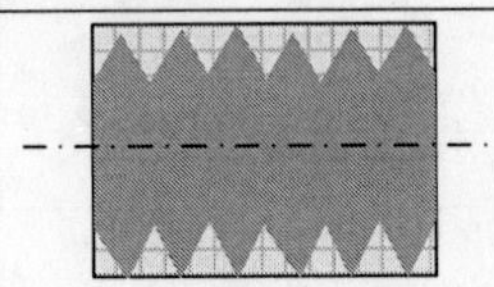	helical pattern and cross-feed for depth of cut		
Drilling	Creating hole 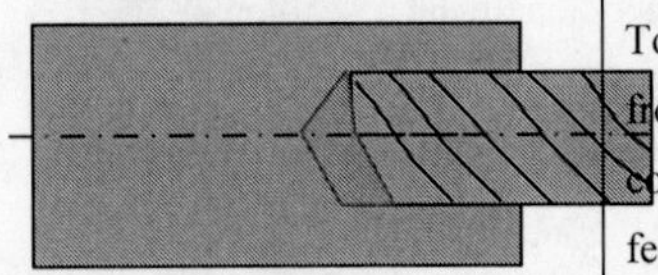	Workpiece: Rotation Tool: Longitudinal feed from tailstock side to cover length and cross-feed for depth of cut	Circular	Linear
Boring	Enlarging hole 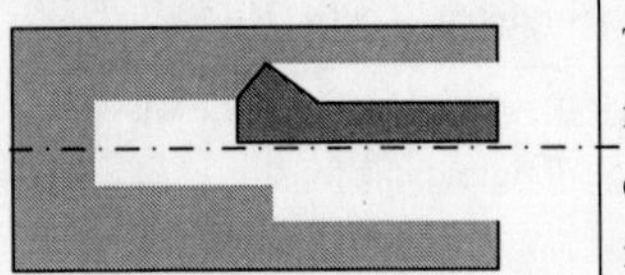	Workpiece: Rotation Tool: Longitudinal feed from tailstock side to cover length and cross-feed for depth of cut	Circular	Linear
Parting off	Cutting and sizing 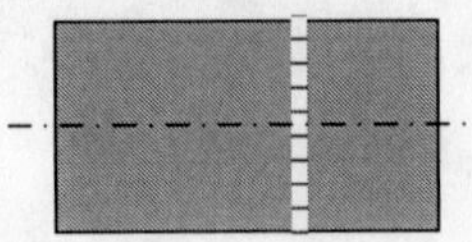	Workpiece: Rotation Tool: No longitudinal feed and only cross-feed for depth of cut	Circular	Linear
Slotting	Slot 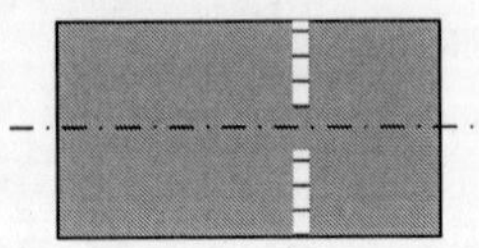	Workpiece: Rotation Tool: Longitudinal feed if required to cover length and cross-feed for depth of cut	Circular	Linear

3.5.2 Drilling

Drilling is an important material removal process and is primarily used for creation of blind or through holes using a rotating cutting tool called a drill bit which interacts with the stationary workpiece mounted firmly on the suitable work holding device (Fig. 3.6). Drilling operation uses circular generatrix and linear directrix to create a hole. Many other secondary drilling operations like counter-boring, countersinking, tapping, and reaming are also performed on drilling machine using twist drill, tap, reamer, etc. as per operation. Drilling operations namely counter-boring, countersinking, tapping, and reaming help in partial enlargement of the cylindrical and conical hole, making internal thread and finishing of holes, respectively. The most common drill tool used on the drilling machine is a twist drill tool having two cutting edges (Fig. 3.7).

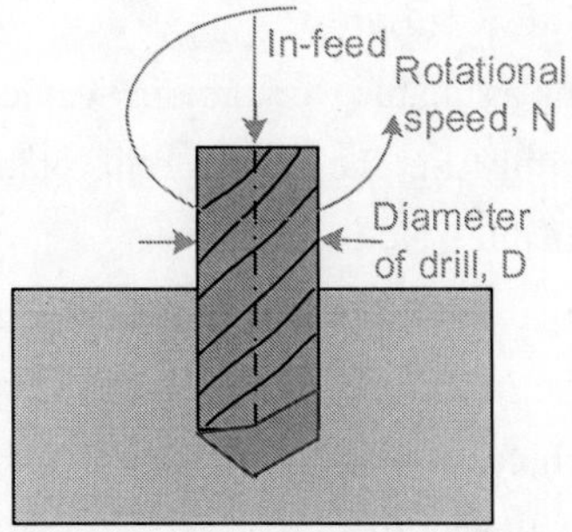

Fig. 3.6 Schematic diagram showing cutting parameters of drilling

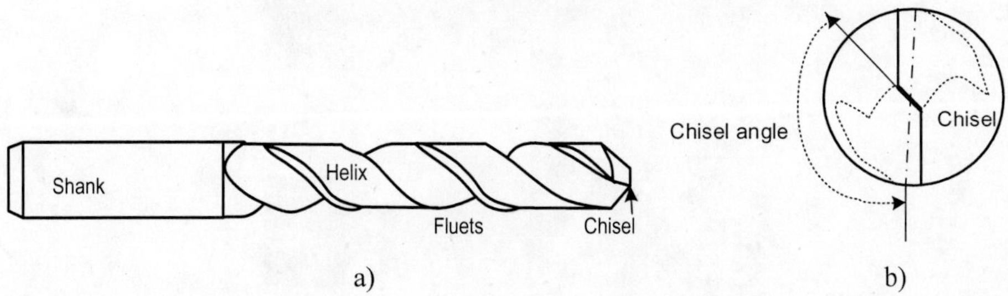

Fig. 3.7 Schematic diagram showing a) front view and b) side view of a twist drill

Drilling operation is performed on a drilling machine having main parts like headstock (electric motor and gear train), drill spindle, column, worktable, work-holding device mounted on the worktable, manual/automatic feed, suitable arrangement of supply of coolant, and light (Fig.3.8).

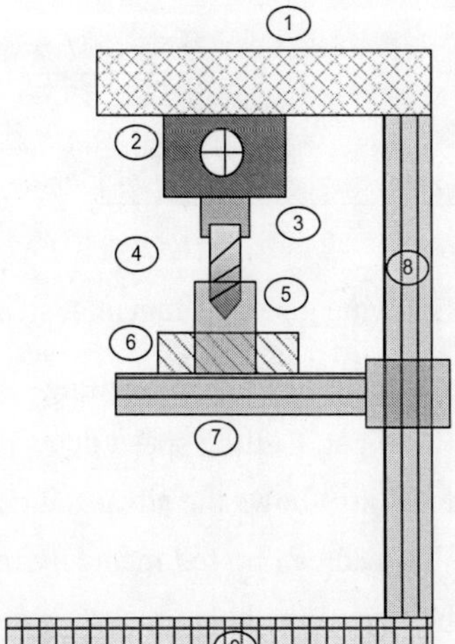

Fig. 3.8 Schematic diagram showing column type drilling machine with different parts 1 overhanging arm, 2 drill head, 3, spindle, 4 twist drill, 5 work-piece, 6 work holding device, 7 work-table, 8 column, 9 base

Steps of drilling

Securely hold the workpiece using a suitable work holding device on worktable. Hold the drill tool bit on the drilling spindle firmly. Set the desired drill rotational speed, and feed rate for depth of cut (for auto-feed if available). Now, the stage is set for the drilling operation.

The following steps are generally followed making a hole as per requirement of desired size, finish and accuracy. First, do the centring at the location where a hole is to be drilled, do countersinking, do drilling of a hole, do boring to create a hole of desired diameter, and do reaming to obtain desired surface finish (Fig. 3.9).

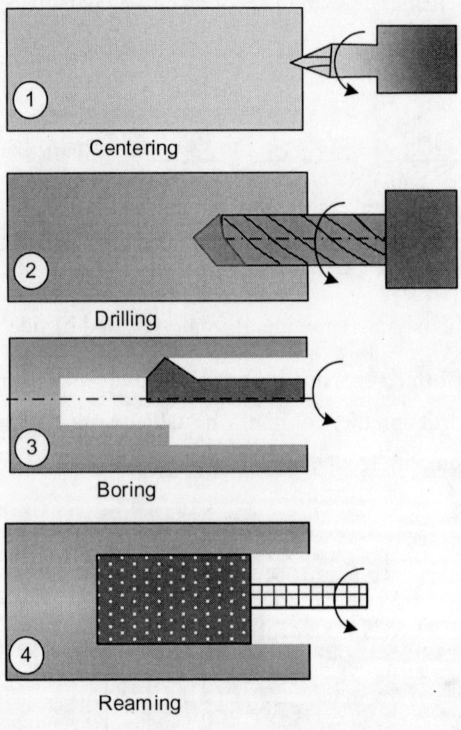

Fig. 3.9 Schematic diagram showing generic sequential steps of making a hole by drilling

Two main cutting parameters used in drilling are cutting speed, and feed rate. There is no drilling parameter namely depth of cut. Cutting speed depends on the diameter and rotational speed of the drill. Feed rate in drilling shows the advancement of drill bit per unit time or per rotation of the drill. The drill bit feed can be fed manually or automatically for drilling. The diameter of drill determines the size of the hole created. If a drill of diameter (D in mm) and rotational speed (N rpm) used to create a hole in a stationary workpiece then the cutting speed (mm/min) is given by $\pi DN/1000$ where D diameter of drill in mm, N is rotational speed rpm. Advancement of drill either per revolution or per unit time is used as in-feed for drilling. Feed determines the rate at which a hole (depth) is created. Increasing the depth of holes reduces accuracy, finish and tolerance of the hole primarily due to reduced stability of drill movement and position of rotation of the drill owing to overhanging / cantilever effect as cutting force during drilling acts at the tip of drill far away from the support to the drill. Various drilling operations and their description is given in Table 3.3.

Table 3.3 Operations on drilling machine

S. No.	**Operation**	**Geometrical feature**	**Process description**
1	Drilling	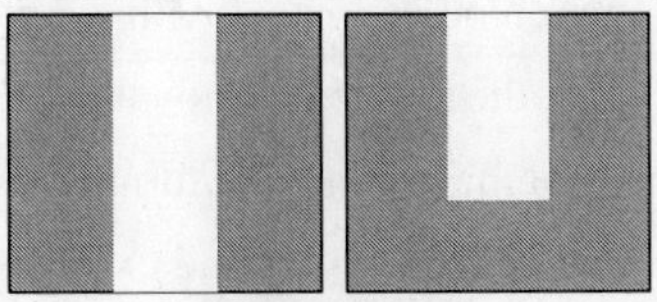	A cylindrical hole of the desired size is created. The hole can be through or partial thickness (blind)
2	Centring		Creation of typical conical/cylindrical geometry for locating position where the hole is to be drilled or providing space for live/dead centre for work holding
3	Counter-boring	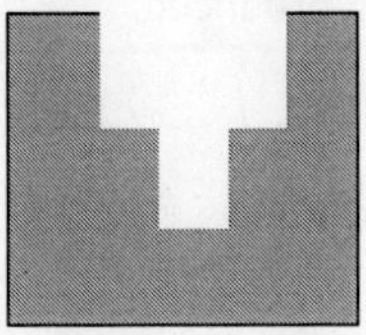	Cylindrical enlargement of the existing hole to some depth to accommodate the head of nut/bolt during assembly
4	Counter-sinking	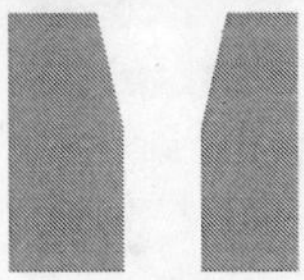	Making a conical hole in existing cylindrical
5	Tapping	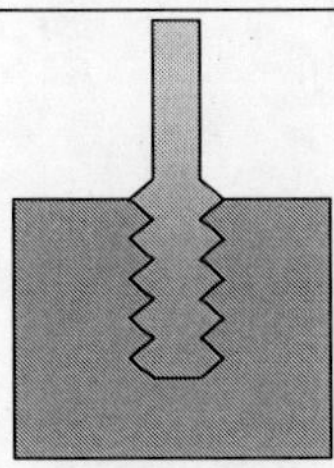	Creating internal threads using tap for assembly using nut/bolt
6	Reaming	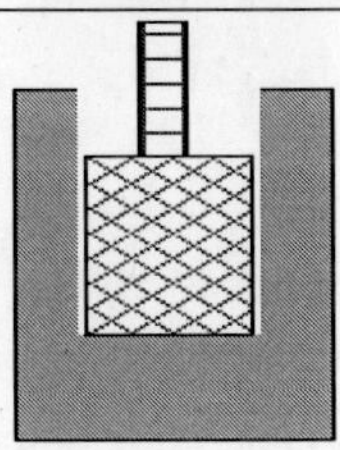	Finishing a hole created by drilling or other processes like casting forming etc. to achieve the desired finish and dimensional accuracy

3.5.3 Milling

Milling is a relatively high material removal rate machining process for producing flat & curved surfaces, keyways, slots, spur and helical gears using a multipoint cutting tool called a milling cutter. A milling cutter rotating at high speed interacts with the workpiece (Fig. 3.10). A milling cutter can be rotated on horizontal or vertical axis and accordingly, a milling machine is categorized as horizontal or vertical milling machine. The workpiece is fed past the rotating cutter. During milling, usually one tooth of the milling cutter removes the material at a time and then all other teeth of the rotating cutter come in contact with the workpiece (in sequence) to remove the material. Therefore, in general, the material removal rate (mm^3/min) obtained by milling is higher than single point cutting tool machining like turning, boring, etc. Conversely, milling involves interrupted cutting coupled with the entry and exit of each tooth one-by-one. Interrupted cutting results in impact loading on the tooth and workpiece. Therefore, milling machine must be robust and milling cutter must be strong and tough (with respect to tool material and tooth geometry). Since generatrix and directrix in milling are linear. Therefore, it produces flat surfaces, keyways and slots. However, computer controlled milling machines allow tool/workpiece movement along a predefined path (straight line / curve line) and accordingly, flat or curved surfaces can also be produced.

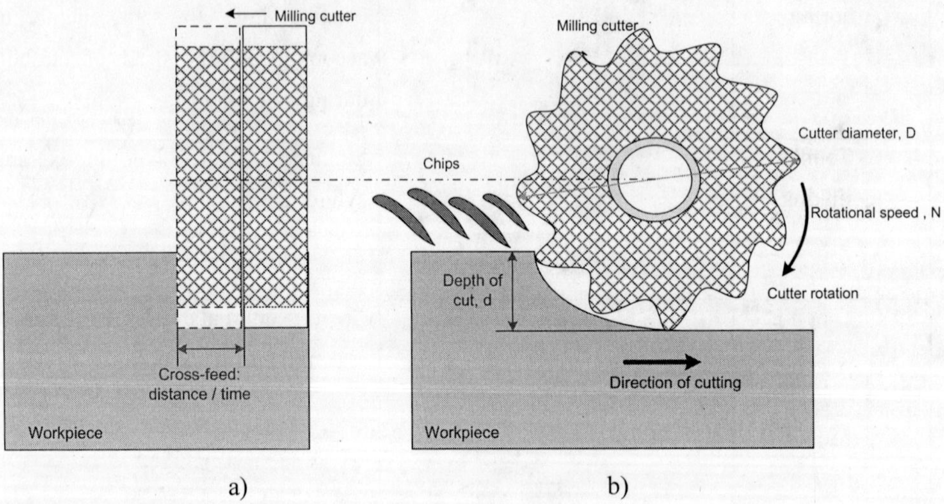

Fig. 3.10 Schematic diagram showing peripheral milling and cutting parameters a) side and b) front view of tool and workpiece interaction.

Milling process parameters

In milling, the workpiece is fed perpendicular to the axis of rotating cutter. While, in drilling, the cutter/drill is fed along the axis of its rotation. Three types of feed movements are given to the workpiece against a rotating milling cutter a) longitudinal feed, b) cross-feed and c) in-feed

(Fig. 3.10-11). Longitudinal feed removes material along the length of workpiece, and it involves moving the workpiece perpendicular to the axis of rotation of the milling cutter. Cross-feed covers the width of workpiece and it involves moving the workpiece perpendicular to the longitudinal feed. In-feed determines the depth of cut and is applied by adjusting the level of workpiece vertically by raising or lowering the worktable by using knee movement. Longitudinal feed is the distance travelled by workpiece per unit time/rotation against the rotating milling cutter and it depends on the mechanical properties of workpiece, section thickness, tool rotational speed and quality requirements (surface roughness and surface integrity) of the machined surfaces. In-feed determines the depth of cut or thickness of the layer of material removed in one pass of the milling cutter. *Cutting speed* in milling operations is determined by the diameter and rotational speed of the milling cutter (Fig. 3.10). Diameter of the milling cutter (D, mm) and rotational speed (rpm) of the cutter determine the cutting speed (mm/min) (πDN/1000, where D is the diameter of milling cutter in mm, N is rotational speed in rpm).

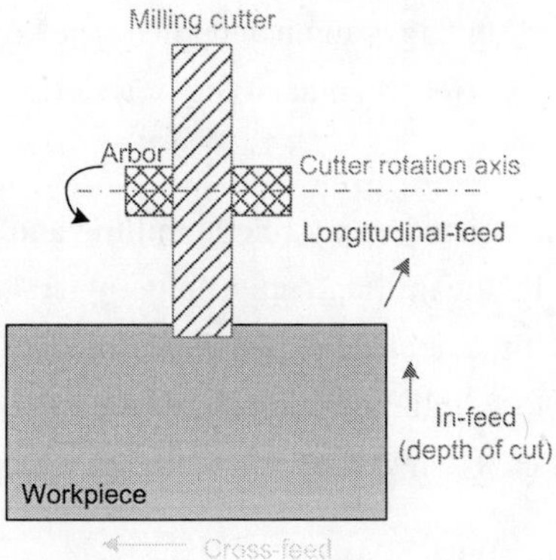

Fig. 3.11 Schematic diagram showing peripheral milling and relevant cutting parameters

Column and knee type milling machine is the most common type of milling machine. Common applications of this machine include slab, side, or straddle milling, face and end milling operations to produce twist drills, milling cutters, helical gear teeth, etc. Bed type milling machine is commonly used for machining heavy workpiece with the help of high material removal rate using heavy cuts and simultaneous milling of two or three surfaces in a single pass. Planar milling machining is preferred for machining a wide variety of surfaces on heavy workpiece in a single setup. Main components of the milling machine are overarm, prime-over (electric motor and gear train), spindle, column, worktable, knee, work-holding device mounted on the work table, manual/automatic feed, suitable arrangement of supply of coolant, and light (Fig.3.12).

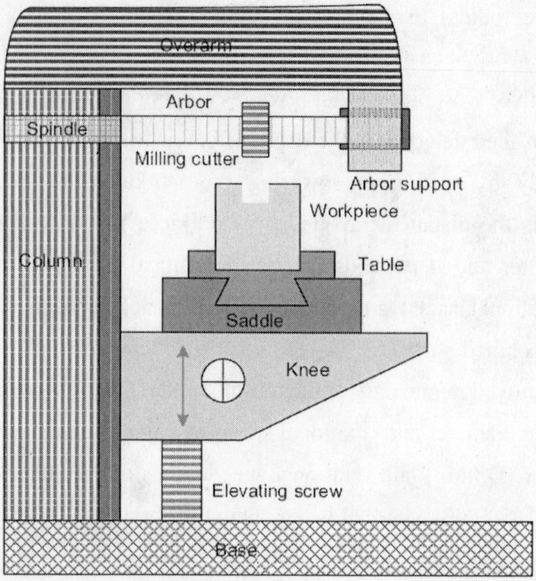

Fig. 3.12 Schematic diagram showing column and knee type horizontal milling machine for peripheral machining of a slot.

Peripheral and face milling

Milling processes are broadly grouped as peripheral milling and face milling depending upon the way cutting is performed by the milling cutter. In peripheral milling, cutting is performed by tooth on the periphery of the cutter having the axis of rotation parallel to the machined surface. While, in the case of face milling, the material is removed by teeth both at the end and periphery of the milling cutter, having the axis of rotation perpendicular to the machined surface (Fig. 3.13).

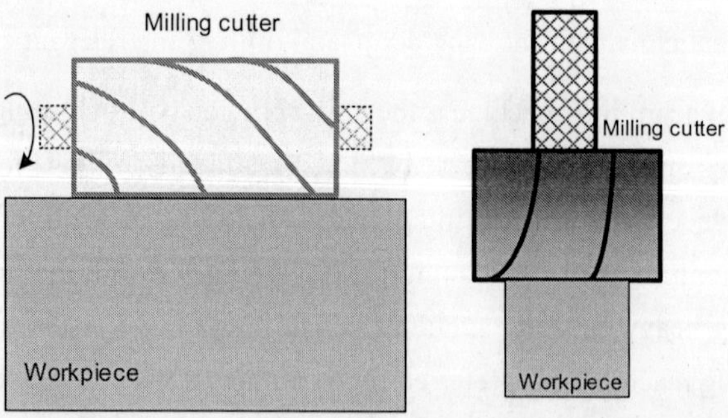

Fig. 3.13 Schematic diagram showing milling cutter and workpiece interaction during a) peripheral milling and b) face milling.

Milling operations like slab milling, slot milling, side milling and straddle milling, fall under peripheral milling. Conventional face milling, profile milling, surface contouring, and pocket milling operations are grouped under face milling. Peripheral milling based on the direction of feed of the workpiece with respect to rotation of the milling cutter, is further categorised as up milling and down milling. Various milling operations based on peripheral and face milling are presented in Fig. 3.14 and Fig. 3.15, respectively. Additionally, a description of these operations is given in Table 3.4.

Table 3.4 Operations on milling machine

S. No.	Milling operation	Description
		Peripheral milling
1	Slab milling	Wider workpiece than cutter for producing a flat surface
2	Slot milling	Making slots, groove and keyways of different shapes
3	Side milling	Machining and finishing of one side vertical surface
4	Straddle milling	Machining and finishing of both sides vertical surface at the same time for enhanced productivity
		Face milling
5	Face milling	For producing flat surfaces
6	Profile milling	For producing specific profiles
7	Surface contouring	For producing curved surfaces
8	Face milling for slots	For cutting slots

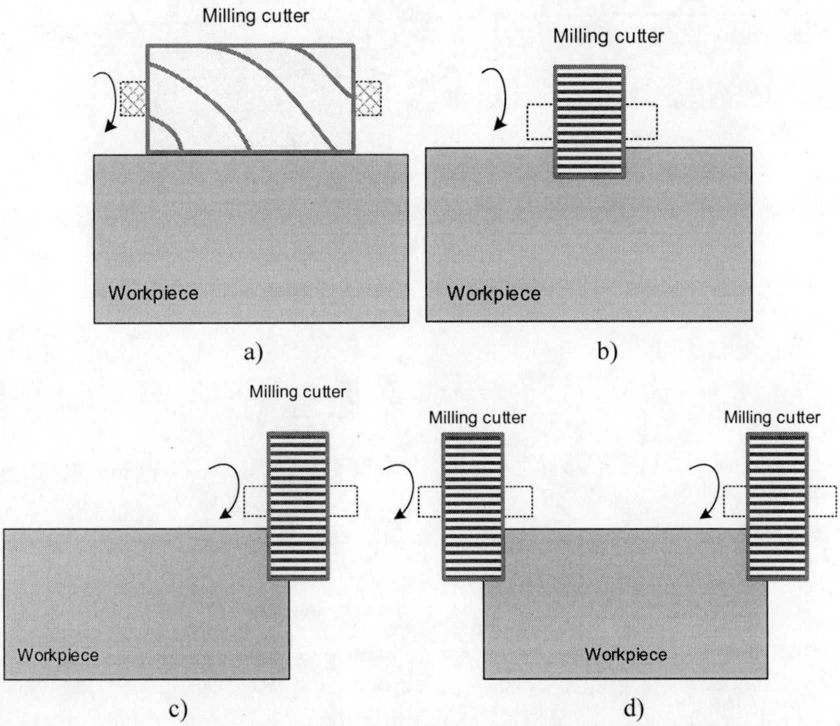

Fig. 3.14 Schematic diagram showing peripheral milling operations a) slab milling, b) slot milling, c) side milling and d) straddle milling.

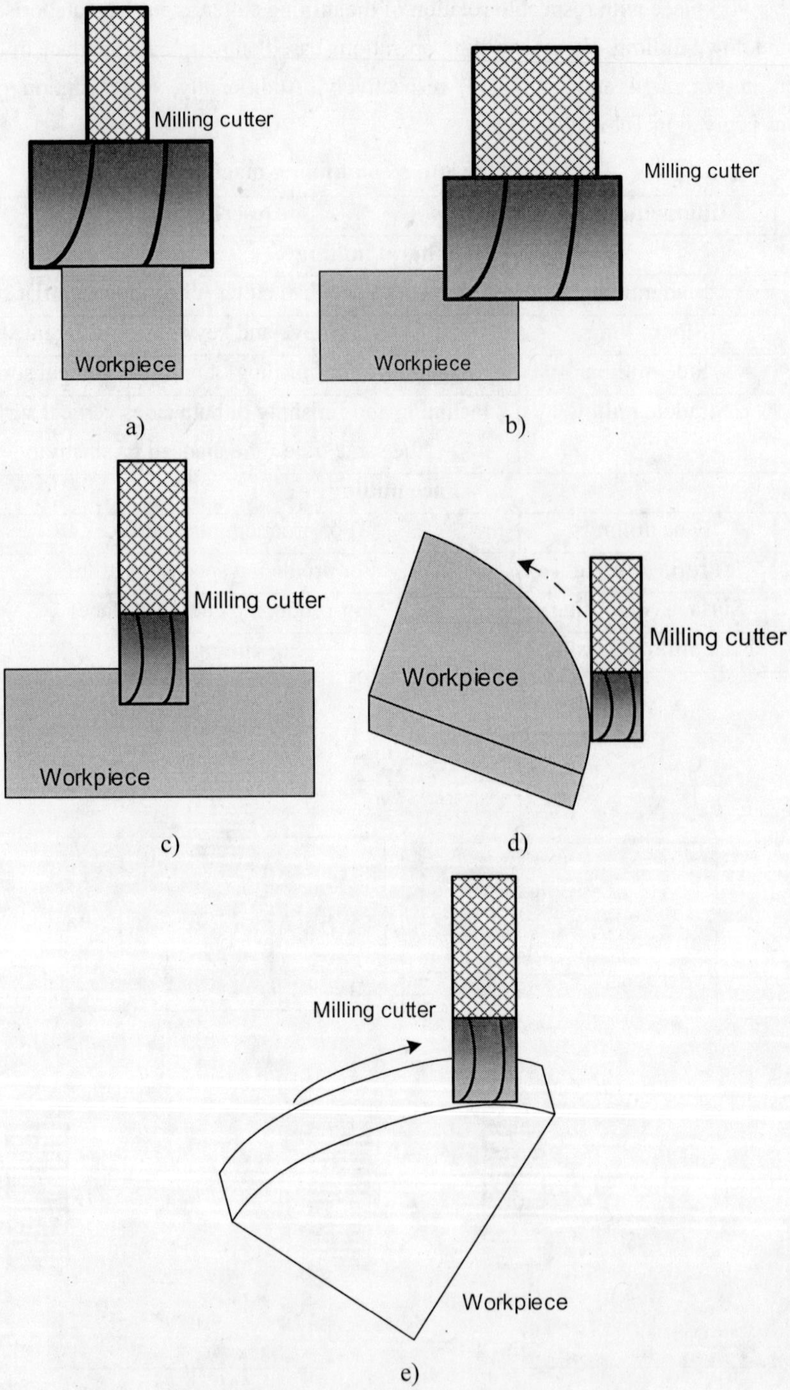

Fig. 3.15 Schematic diagram showing face milling operations a) flat milling, b) side milling, c) slot milling and d, e) surface profiling / contour milling.

Up and down milling

Peripheral milling operations are further classified as up milling and down milling based on relative movement of the workpiece with respect to the rotation direction of milling cutter (Fig. 3.16). Up milling involves workpiece (feed) motion in the direction opposite to that of cutter rotation. The cutting force during up milling tends to lift the workpiece up from the work holding device. In down milling, workpiece (feed) motion is in the same direction as the direction of cutter rotation. Cutting force in down milling tends to force/push the workpiece against the work holding device ensuring its firm seating. Therefore, up milling needs better and more effective workpiece holding than down milling.

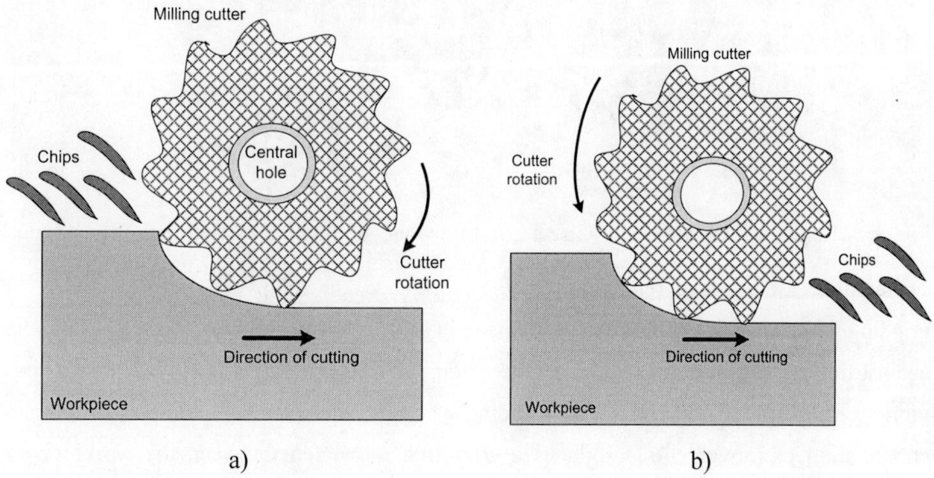

Fig. 3.16 Schematic diagram showing a) up milling and b) down milling.

3.5.4 Grinding

Grinding is an abrasive finishing process wherein a very thin layer of the workpiece material is removed by shearing and abrasive action of fine abrasive particles. These abrasive particles are bonded using a suitable bonding material in the form of a disc shape wheel called grinding wheel. A grinding wheel is composed of abrasives, bonding material and air pockets or porosity (Fig. 3.17). Thousands of abrasive particles of grinding wheel interact with the workpiece and each particle acts as a cutting tool. Therefore, the grinding process can be termed as multi-point cutting type machining process. However, size, shape and orientation vary randomly in a grinding wheel. Therefore, unlike other single and multipoint cutting tools (turning, drilling, milling), cutting tool size in the form of abrasives, and angle of cut (rake/clearance) are found different for each abrasive particle interacting with the workpiece in grinding. The size of abrasives varies from a few tens to hundreds of microns. Therefore, indentation caused by abrasive during grinding for material removal is very shallow. Removal of a thin layer of material in a controlled manner during grinding results in low surface roughness and low material removal rate.

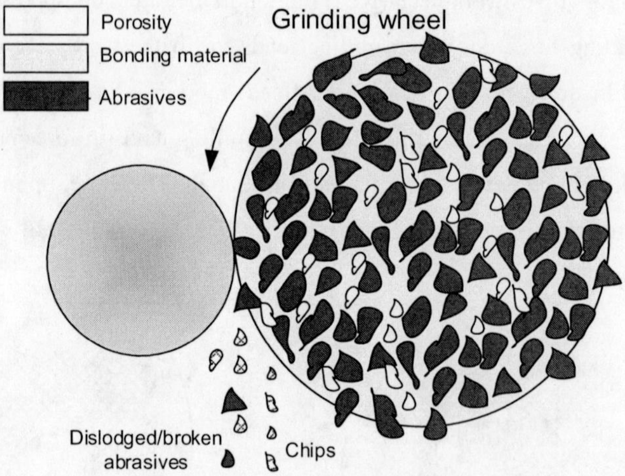

Fig. 3.17 Schematic diagram showing a grinding wheel and its interaction with the workpiece.

To facilitate the material removal from the workpiece, the relative movement between the grinding wheel and workpiece can be realized in different ways: a) workpiece is reciprocated against the rotating grinding wheel, b) the workpiece and grinding wheel both are rotated. A vibratory movement given to either grinding wheel or workpiece (in addition to the above combination of movements) produces a crisscross movement between the workpiece and grinding wheel. The criss-cross movement results in a better surface finish. In general, high relative movement due to high rotational/reciprocating speed (between two) in combination with low feed (transverse / radial in feed) produces a good surface finish. The following are common grinding processes.

Surface grinding

Surface grinding is primarily used for finishing flat surfaces by feeding the workpiece against a rotating grinding wheel. The workpiece can interact with either the face or periphery of the grinding wheel. The workpiece can be given reciprocating or rotary movement (as per size and shape) to ensure surface finishing of the maximum possible length workpiece surface in one setting. In addition to rotary movement, the grinding wheel can be given vibratory motion in a direction perpendicular to the main longitudinal feed. Various type of relative movements given to the grinding wheel, and workpiece for surface grinding is shown schematically in Fig.3.18.

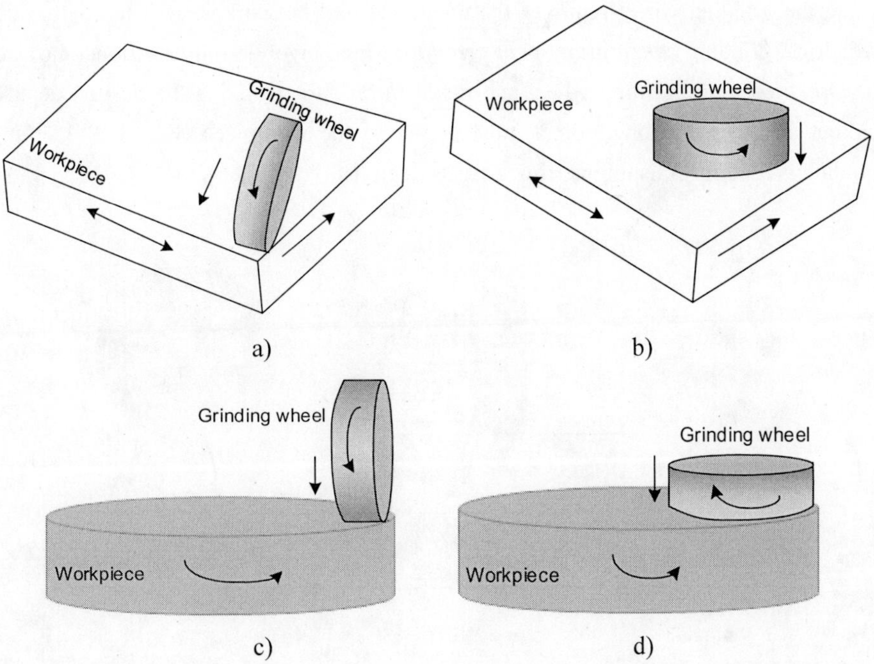

Fig. 3.18 Schematic diagram showing various relative movements given to the grinding wheel and workpiece for surface grinding a) reciprocating movement to the long workpiece for peripheral grinding, b) reciprocating movement to the long workpiece for face grinding, c) rotary movement given for small size workpiece during peripheral grinding and d) rotary movement given for small size workpiece during face grinding.

Cylindrical grinding

Cylindrical grinding can be further classified based on a) the surface processed by grinding as internal and external cylindrical and b) the locating approach i.e. centre type and centreless grinding. Cylindrical grinding is a peripheral grinding process. *The peripheral surface of the grinding wheel* acts on the cylindrical components for abrasive finishing by removing a thin layer of material from the workpiece.

Centre type external & internal cylindrical grinding: The workpiece is held firmly along the centre/axis of grinding machining with the help of a suitable work holding device like chuck at one end. Additional support may be provided at the other end if required in case of long cylindrical jobs to avoid deflection of the workpiece during grinding. The rotating grinding wheel is fed against the rotating workpiece. The workpiece is rotated against the direction of rotation of the grinding wheel. The grinding wheel is fed parallel to the axis of the rotating workpiece to finish the entire length of the workpiece. Rotational and feed movement given to the workpiece and grinding wheel are schematically shown in Fig.3.19 (a). External and internal cylindrical grinding primarily differ with respect to the surface (internal/external) where the grinding wheel removes the material from the workpiece. There is a variant of cylindrical grinding ***called plunge cut grinding*** which involves only rotational movement of the workpiece and grinding wheel and radial in-feed for realizing the desired depth of cut without any lateral / longitudinal movement past the workpiece (Fig. 3.19b). Plunge cut grinding is used for finishing narrow surfaces/regions.

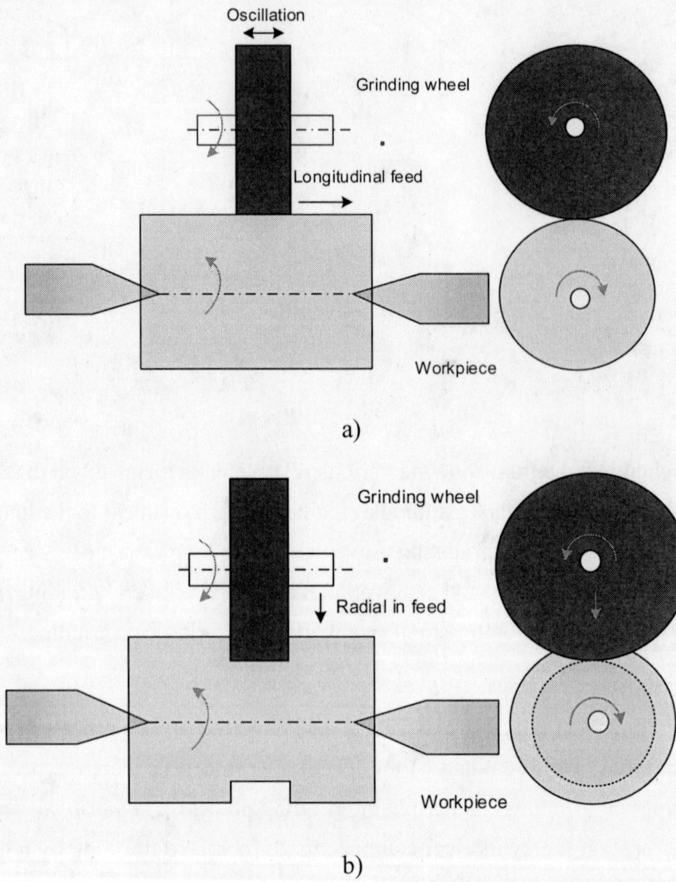

Fig. 3.19 Schematic diagram showing centre type a) external cylindrical grinding and b) plunge-cut external cylindrical grinding.

Centreless type of cylindrical grinding

Centreless grinding does not involve any firm locating & fixing of the workpiece at centre / axis of the grinding wheel. Rather it floats between the grinding wheel, regulating and supporting rolls. This aspect avoids time consuming and tedious task of fixing the workpiece on the centre/axis of the grinding machine, thereby improving the productivity. Additionally, centreless grinding allows the handling of very long cylindrical jobs with the help of suitable support even beyond the length of grinding machines.

External & internal centreless cylindrical grinding

External cylindrical centreless grinding uses a grinding wheel, regulating wheel and support for the workpiece in the middle of the two. Movement given to the grinding wheel, workpiece and regulating wheel for external cylindrical centreless grinding is shown schematically in Fig.3.20. The regulating wheel is kept at a certain angle with respect to the axis of the grinding wheel/workpiece (α, 2-5°) as per feed rate required to move the workpiece past the grinding wheel. Thus, the regulating wheel performs two roles: a) pressurizes the workpiece against the grinding wheel for material removal and b) feeds the workpiece past the grinding wheel. The feed rate depends on the inclination, α (angle of axis of regulating wheel with respect to the axis of the griding wheel/workpiece) diameter, D and rotational speed, N of the regulating wheel. The feed rate past the grinding wheel is expressed by $\pi DN\ \mathrm{Sin}(\alpha)$ (where D diameter of the regulating wheel in mm, N is rotational speed rpm).

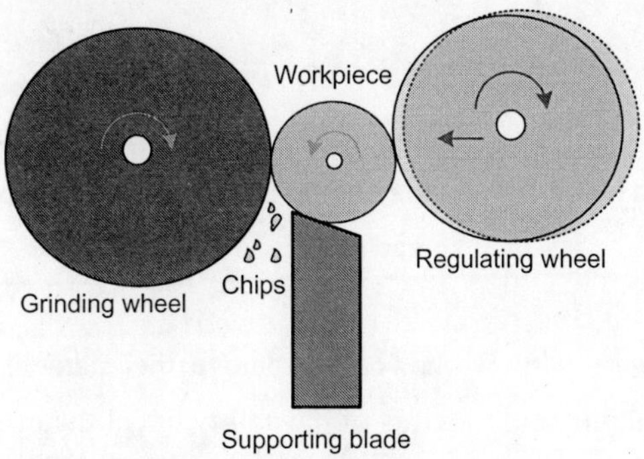

Fig. 3.20 Schematic diagram showing external cylindrical centreless grinding.

Similar to the external cylindrical centreless grinding, the internal centreless cylindrical grinding uses two additional rollers namely pressure and support roller to ensure positioning and grinding. The grinding wheel works on the internal surfaces of the workpiece for finishing. Movement given to the grinding wheel, workpiece and regulating wheel for internal cylindrical centreless grinding is shown schematically in Fig.3.21. Internal cylindrical centreless grinding produces very concentric and uniform wall thickness of hollow cylindrical objects.

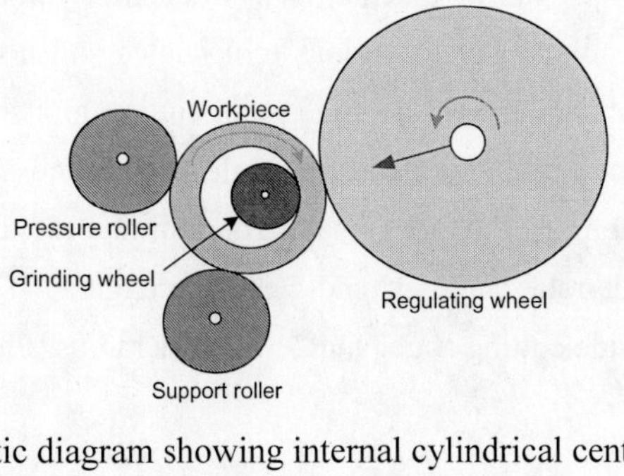

Fig. 3.21 Schematic diagram showing internal cylindrical centreless grinding.

Creep grinding

Creep grinding is a relatively new addition to the grinding processes and is characterised by a very high depth of cut (10-1000 times) and correspondingly a very lower feed rate than conventional grinding. Therefore, creep grinding results in a high material removal rate. The major difference in respect depth of cut given during creep grinding and conventional surface grinding is shown schematically in Fig.3.22

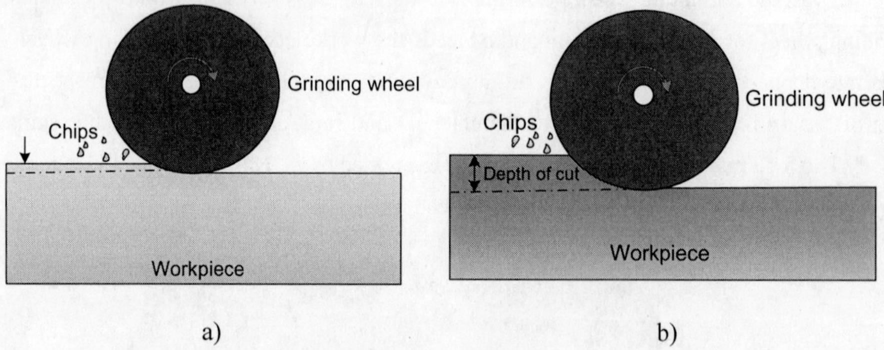

Fig. 3.22 Schematic diagram showing comparison between a) conventional surface and b) creep surface grinding.

3.6 Cutting tool

A cutting tool interacts with workpiece to remove the material for manufacturing. The performance of the cutting tool in terms of the ability to cut the material and life depends on two most important aspects of the tool, namely geometry and b) material of the cutting tool. The following section describes these two aspects in detail.

3.6.1 Single point cutting tool

A single point cutting tool is commonly used for machining by turning, boring, planning, etc. This tool comprises various parts like shank, flank, face, cutting edge, and nose. These parts constitute various tool angles, namely rake, clearance, cutting-edge angle and nose radius (Fig.3.23). These angles and nose radius affects cutting force generated on tool, surface finish, chip formation and tool life during machining. Tool geometry of a single point cutting tool is expressed by tool signature wherein various tool angles and nose radius are mentioned in specific sequence. Tool signature of a single point cutting tool shows: back rake angle, side rake angle, end clearance angle, side clearance angle, end cutting edge angle, side cutting angle and nose radius. For example, the tool signature of a turning tool is 4-6-3-7-4-8-2 indicates 4° back rake angle, 6° side rake angle, 3° end clearance angle, 7° side clearance angle, 4° end cutting edge angle, 8° side cutting angel and 2 mm nose radius (Fig. 3.24).

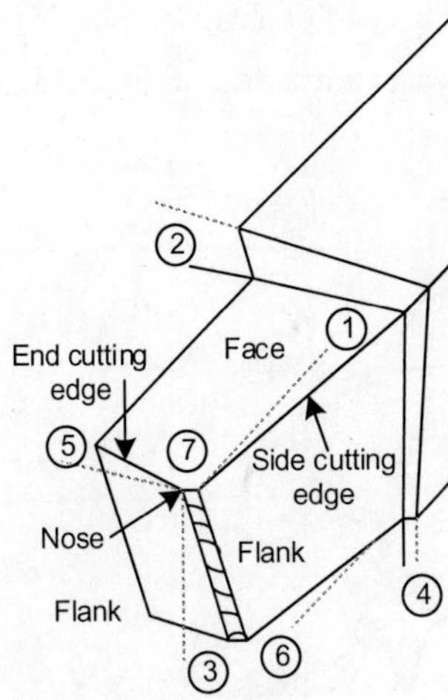

Fig. 3.23 Schematic diagram showing a pictorial view of a single point cutting tool with different parts and angles

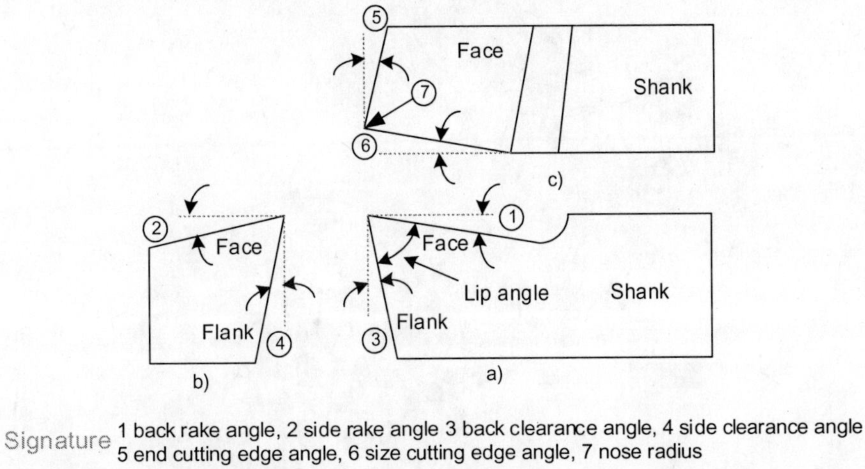

Fig. 3.24 Schematic diagram showing different views of a single point cutting tool with different parts and angles: a) front, b) side and c) top view.

3.6.2 Multi-point cutting tool

Cutting tools like twist drill, milling cutter, and grinding wheel having two or more cutting edges are called multi-point cutting tools. The basic features of each tooth of multi-point cutting tool are similar to those of single point cutting tool except minor differences in size, shape and orientation. Each tooth of multipoint cutting tool has a cutting edge, rake angle, clearance angle, etc. However, in the grinding wheel, the geometry of each tooth (abrasive) in terms of size of cutting edge, rake and clearance angle all vary randomly. Therefore, material in grinding is not just removed by shearing action but also by abrasion, ploughing, cracking, etc. Grinding, in fact, is similar to the two body-abrasion condition. Geometries of two multi-point cutting tools, namely milling cutter and grinding wheel are shown in Fig. 3.25.

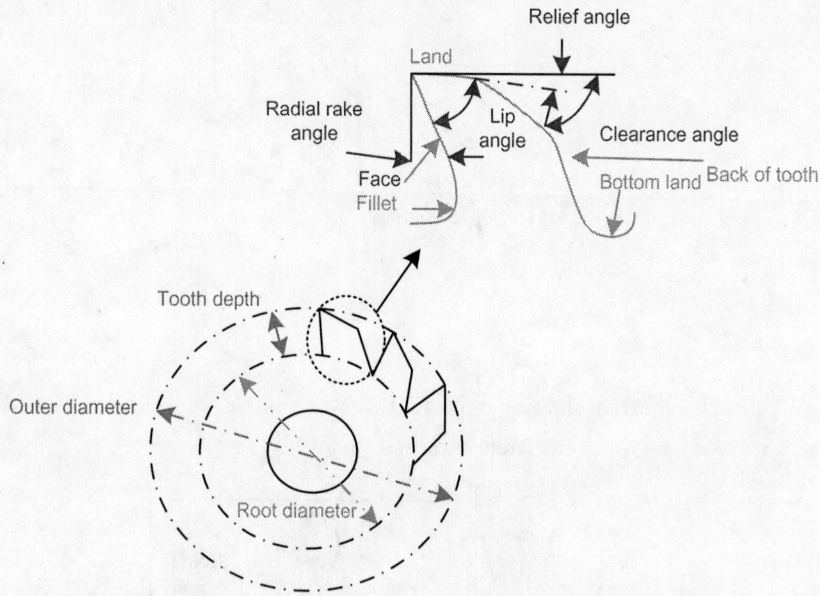

a)

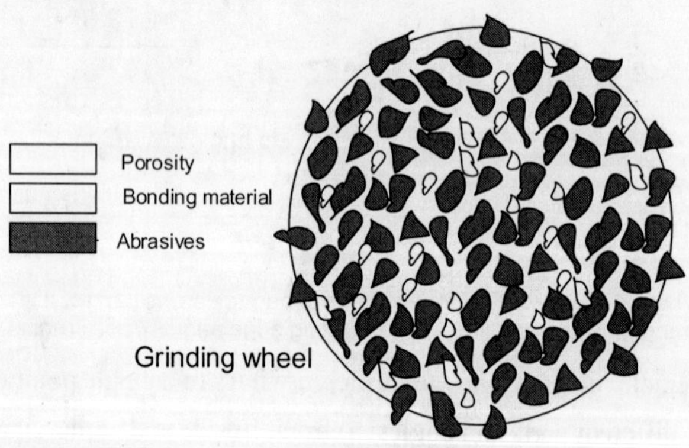

b)

Fig. 3.25 Schematic diagram of multi-point cutting tools a) milling cutter and b) grinding wheel

3.7 Tool material properties

A cutting tool material should be harder than workpiece material to ensure its penetration into the workpiece followed by shearing when the relative motion is applied for material removal. In addition to the harness, tool material must be tough, resistant to wear, heat, and abrasion for longer life to sustain real dynamic cutting conditions. In general, a cutting tool during machining experiences very harsh conditions in the form of thermal softening, impact loading, cyclic heating and cooling, and continuous rubbing of tool with workpiece and chips. Conflicting property requirement of high hardness coupled with good toughness (for efficient, economical and effective cutting) makes selection and development of the cutting tool material difficult and challenging. These difficulties have led to the development of a) composite materials in the form of cermet and b) single / multi-coated tools as these allow benefits of combining properties of high toughness and high hardness both. This is the reason why composite tool material, and coated tools perform better than monolithic tool material for a long tool life. The following properties are desired in cutting tool material for good performance. The most common cutting tool materials include carbon steel, die steel, high speed steel, cast Co alloys, tungsten carbide, ceramic, ceramets, cubic boron nitrides, and diamond. These materials are sequenced in increasing order of hardness and decreasing toughness.

3.7.1 Hot hardness

Machining of hard material generates a lot of heat resulting in significant temperature rise of cutting tool, especially in vicinity of cutting edge. Increase in temperature, in general causes the thermal softening of cutting tool material (Fig. 3.26). That increases the tendency of deterioration of the tool in terms of deformation/bending of cutting edge, blunting of cutting edge, increase in nose radius and reduced cutting ability. Therefore, tool material must exhibit high hardness at elevated temperature (which is expected during machining). The hardness of a material at high temperature is called hot hardness. During the machining, the hardness of the tool at elevated temperature must be greater than the hardness of the workpiece material at room temperature. Increasing the severity of cutting conditions (by increasing cutting speed, feed and depth of cut) increases heat generation and so, the temperature of the cutting tool. Therefore, the use of suitable coolant during machining helps to maintain the temperature (within safe limit) and hardness of the cutting tool.

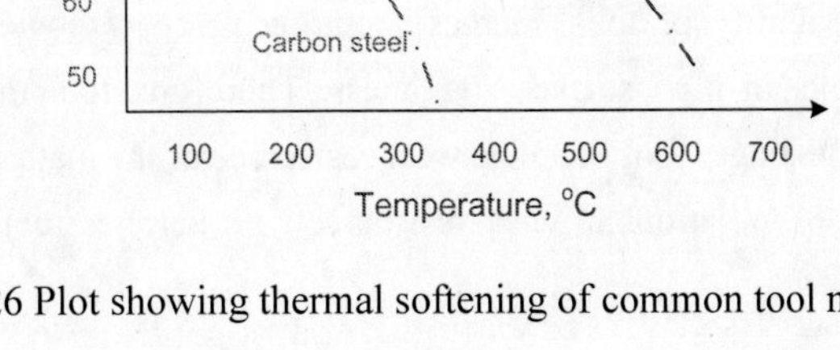

Fig. 3.26 Plot showing thermal softening of common tool material.

3.7.2 Toughness

The cutting tool is subjected to impact loading due to frequent engagement and disengagement with the workpiece during the machining. The impact loading is more severe during interrupted machining processes such as shaping, planning, and milling than the continuous machining processes e.g. turning, boring and drilling. Continuous machining involves continuous machining action of the tool on the workpiece until the entire length of job is machined in one pass. Impact loading of brittle tool materials tends to cause fracture of the cutting edge of the tool. Therefore, tool material must have enough resistance to the impact which is commonly measured in terms of toughness. In general, monolithic materials show increasing toughness at the cost of hardness and vice-versa. The trend of variations in hardness and toughness of common tool materials is shown in Fig. 3.27. Therefore, cutting tools made of composite material (hard particles in the tough matrix), and coated tools offer better machining performance, including longer tool life. Coatings of hard material over the tough substrate / tool material is one of the approaches to realize a combination of both high toughness and high hardness in coated tools. Similar benefits are also realised from composite material like cermet, e.g. composite material of WC / TiC reinforced in Ni / Co matrix (cermet).

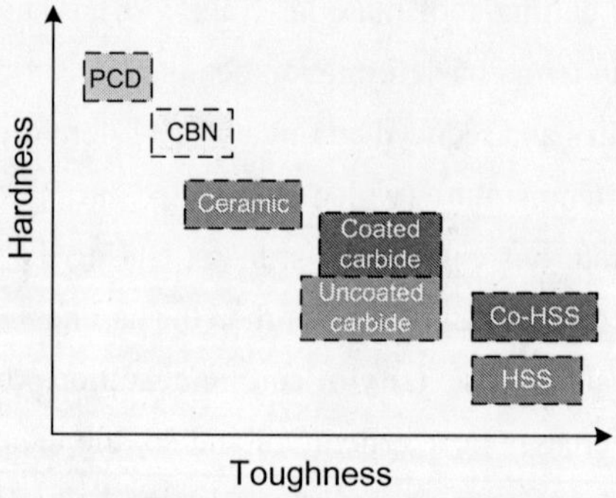

Fig. 3.27 Schematic diagram of hardness vs. toughness relation of common tool materials.

3.7.3 Wear resistance

During machining, material removed from the workpiece in the form of chip, continuously slides over the rake face of cutting tool and the machined surface of the workpiece rubs the flank face of the tool. Continuous rubbing under pressure causes abrasion of the flank, and rake face of the tool and frictional heat generation and tool wear. Continuous wear of cutting tool changes the geometry of cutting tool parts like face, flank, nose and cutting edge. Tool wear reduces the cutting ability of tool, increases cutting forces / power requirement for the machining and results in high surface roughness. Therefore, tool material must be wear-resistant to realize the longer tool life. The wear resistance of the material is directly related to hardness. The trend of variations in wear resistance with hardness common tool materials is shown in Fig. 3.28.

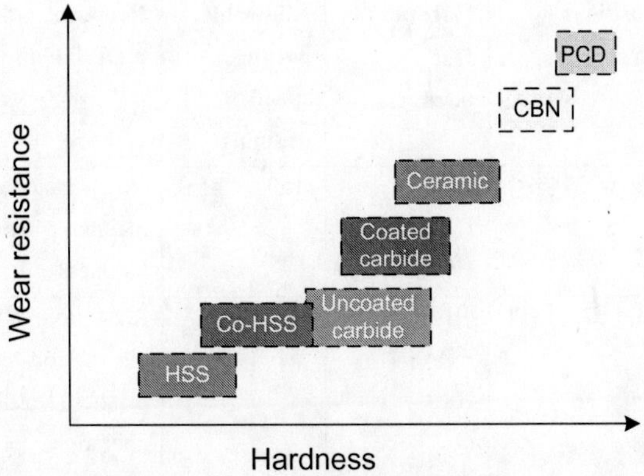

Fig. 3.28 Schematic diagram of showing wear resistance vs. hardness relation of common tool materials.

3.8 Common tool materials

Common tool material includes carbon steel (CS), high speed steel (HSS), cast cobalt alloys, carbide tool (Co-WC, Ni-WC), ceramic (alumina), coated (coating of TiN, TiB, TiC on HSS and cabide tool), cubic boron nitride and polycrystalline diamond. These tool materials are arranged in increasing order of hot hardness and reducing toughness Generic composition, microstructure, hardness, and allowable cutting speed of common tool material are tabulated in below for ease of understanding and comparison (Table 3.5).

Table 3.5 Common tool material and their characteristics

Tool materials	**Compositions (wt.%)**	**Hardness / Hot hardness**	**Allowable cutting speed (m/min)**	**Remarks Workpiece material/ application**	**Impact strength, J**
Carbon steel	C 0.9%, Mn 0.6%, Fe balance	80 HRA	5	Low strength, softer materials, nonferrous alloys, plastics	4-10
High-speed steel	C 0.7-1%, Cr 4%, V 1%, W 2-18%, Mo 0-10%, Co 0-12%, Fe balanced	83-86 HRA/85-87 HRA	90	All materials of low and medium strength and hardness	1.35-8
Cast Co alloy	Cr 30-32%, W 4-17%, Mo 0-1.5%, C 1-2.5%, Mn 1%, Si 1-1.5%, Ni 2.5-3%, Co balanced	82-84 HRA/82-85 HRA	300	-	0.4-1.25

Tool materials	Compositions (wt.%)	Hardness / Hot hardness	Allowable cutting speed (m/min)	Remarks Workpiece material/ application	Impact strength, J
Carbide tool	Co 6%, WC 94%	90-95 HRA/89-94 HRA	150	All materials up to medium strength and hardness	0.34-1.35
Ceramic tool	Al_2O_3, SiC	91-95 HRA/94 HRA	600	Cast iron, Ni-Base super alloys, non-ferrous alloys, plastics (Not for low-speed operations or interrupted cutting. Not for machining Al, Ti alloys)	<0.1
Cermet	WC-Ni, Co-WC				-
Coated tools	TiC, TiC coating on HSS, carbide tool	1900-4000 HV	350	Cast iron, alloy steels, stainless steels, super alloys (Not for titanium alloys)	-
Cubic boron nitrides	CBN	4000 -5000 HK	400	Hardened alloys steels, HSS, Ni – base super alloys, hardened chilled cast iron, commercially pure nickel	<0.5
Diamond (PCD)	C	7000-8000HK	760	Pure copper, pure aluminium, Al-Si alloys, rock, cement, plastics, cemented carbides, nonferrous alloy, hardened high carbon alloy steels (Not for machining low alloy steels, Co, Ni, Zr)	<0.2

3.8.1 Carbon steel

The carbon steel tool is primarily used to manufacture soft workpiece material like wood, polymers, metal, etc. These workpiece materials are machined using milder cutting conditions (low cutting force, low temperature) during machining. Manual cutting tools such as hacksaw, chisel, files, punch and die, etc. are made of carbon steel. Carbon content in carbon steel tools can vary from 0.2 to 1.0% depending upon the combination of toughness and hardness required as per application. Low carbon steel is preferred as a tool material when high toughness and moderately low hardness are acceptable for a given application. While high carbon steel tools are used for conditions requiring high hardness and low toughness.

3.8.2 High speed steel

High speed steel (HSS) is one of the toughest (low hot hardness) and most common tool materials used for turning, drilling, milling, shaping, and planning operations. These are used for machining of low carbon steel, aluminium, copper, magnesium, zinc, etc. High toughness allows the use of high feed and depth of cut but low cutting speed due to relatively low hot hardness (Fig. 3.26, 3.27, 3.28). 18-4-1 is one the most common HSS tool materials, having 18 % W, 4 Cr, 1 V and 0.5% C.

3.8.3 Carbide tool

The carbide tools are basically composite materials with very high fractions of carbide particles like tungsten carbide, and titanium carbide reinforced in tough matrix of cobalt, nickel, etc. These are usually made (by powder metallurgy route) in the form of tool bits, which are mounted (by brazing, screwing) on suitable carbon steel or high-speed steel shank. The tool bit interacts with the workpiece during machining. While, the shank provides suitable support to the tool bit against the cutting forces generated during machining. Carbide tools allow much higher cutting speed than HSS and carbon steel tools due to higher hot hardness (Fig. 3.26).

3.8.4 Ceramics

Ceramic tools are primarily made of alumina and mixture of alumina with other refractory ceramic materials (titanium, magnesium, chromium or zirconium oxides or silicon-carbide, silicon nitrides). Similar to the carbide tools, ceramic materials are also processed by powder metallurgy for making tool bits, which are mounted on tough tool shank. Very high hot hardness of ceramic materials even at elevated temperatures allows higher cutting speed of metals but at very low feed and depth of cut due to poor toughness of ceramic materials (Figs. 3.26, 3.27). Further, low thermal conductivity of ceramics makes them sensitive for thermal shock and cracking due to the development of high temperature gradient. Therefore, ceramics are preferred for continuous cutting and cooling conditions with little or no impact loading operations, such as turning, drilling, boring, etc.

3.8.5 Coated tool

Coated tools are made by developing thin layers (a few microns) of single coating or multiple coatings of hard materials like TiC, TiN, TiB, etc. on tough tool materials (HSS / carbide tool materials). These coatings are developed by chemical and physical vapour deposition techniques. These coatings are primarily developed over the relatively tough tool material like high-speed steel, carbide tool, ceramics, etc. Therefore, coated tools offer a very good combination of high hot hardness of the coating and high toughness of substrate. Sometimes, a thin layer of bond-coat is also developed between the substrate and top coating to increase bond strength between the top coating and substrate through improved physical and metallurgical compatibility (Fig. 3.29). Multi-coated tools offer better performance and longer tool life than single coating tools.

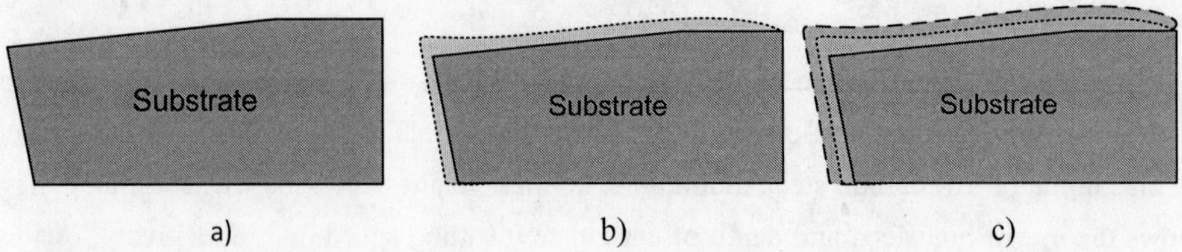

Fig. 3.29 Schematic diagram of cutting tool with negative rake angle a) uncoated substrate, b) single coated tool and c) multi-coated tool

3.8.6 Cubic boron nitride

Polycrystalline boron nitride (PCBN) is the second hardest material after diamond. It offers very high cutting speed during machining of ferrous and non-ferrous metals due to high hot hardness but at low feed and depth of cut (Fig. 3.26, 3.27). In general, the fracture toughness / toughness of tool materials like carbide, ceramic, PCBN and diamond is very low therefore cutting tool / inserts made of these materials are given a negative rake angle to strengthen the cutting edge.

3.8.7 Diamond

Diamond is the hardest known material and a specific carbon variant (cubical hexagonal crystal structure) that offers the maximum hardness. Artificially processed polycrystalline diamonds are commonly used as cutting tools for machining non-ferrous materials, ceramics, glass at very high cutting speed. Diamond cutting tools are not preferred for machining ferrous metals due to high affinity of carbon with iron. Diffusion of carbon atoms at elevated temperature destabilizes the diamond cubical structure which in turn reduces hardness and deteriorates the diamond cutting tool.

3.9 Heat generation during machining

Machining processes consume power for two purposes a) cause shearing to remove materials and b) overcome friction between tool-chip, and tool-workpiece interfaces. Most of the power consumed during the machining is converted into heat. Localised heat generation causes a rapid rise in tool temperature near the cutting edge, rake face and flank (Fig. 3.30). Most of the heat generated during the machining, is carried away by chips. But it still raises the temperature of cutting tool due to the heat dissipating to the tool which results in reduction in tool life. An increase in tool temperature causes the softening of tool materials and promotes various wear mechanisms like adhesion, abrasion and diffusion. Heat generation due to shearing action during machining cannot be reduced to lower the tool temperature but application of cutting fluid reduces friction between tool-workpiece and chip-tool.

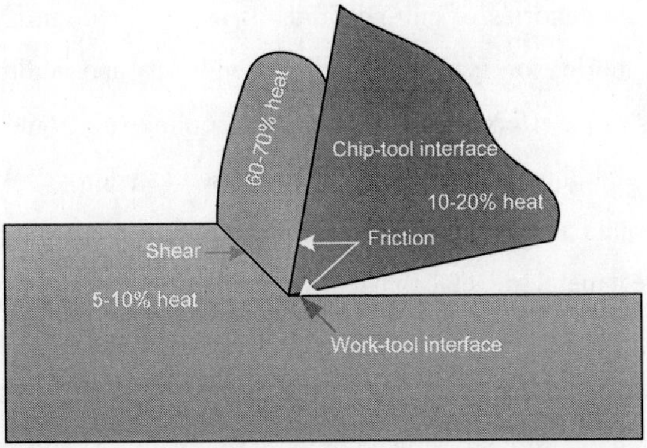

Fig. 3.30 Schematic diagram heat generation and its distribution during machining

3.10 Cutting fluid

Cutting fluid in machining plays mainly two functions; a) lubrication between tool-chip /workpiece interfaces and b) reducing temperature of machining zone and cutting tool. Lubrication reduces the frictional heat generation and temperature of tool and workpiece. Additionally, cutting fluid also acts as a coolant to take away the heat generated during machining. These two functions indirectly offer many advantages like increased tool life, improved surface finish of workpiece, clearing chips from the machining zone and reduced cutting forces and power consumption. The effect of cutting fluid on the temperature profile of machining zone is schematically shown in Fig. 3.31.

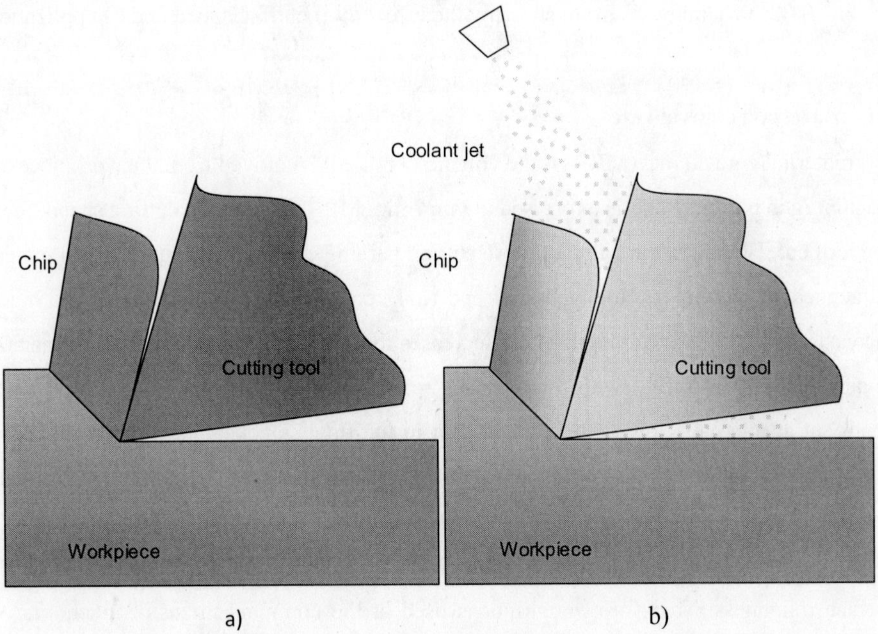

Fig. 3.31 Schematic diagram effect of cutting on thermal profile of machining zone

There are two broad categories of cutting fluids a) water based cutting fluid offering more cooling effect than lubrication (water is modified with oils and additives) and b) oil-based cutting fluid results more effective lubrication than cooling (oil is modified with water and additives). Sulphur and phosphorus compounds are used as additives which react with metal chips to form compound at the chip-tool / workpiece-tool interface. These compounds remain stable and avoid direct metal to metal contact, which in turn provides effective lubrication even under extreme pressure and severe cutting conditions by avoiding direct metal to metal contact between chip and tool interface. The relative efficacy of different types of cutting fluids and their effect on tool temperature are shown in Fig. 3.32.

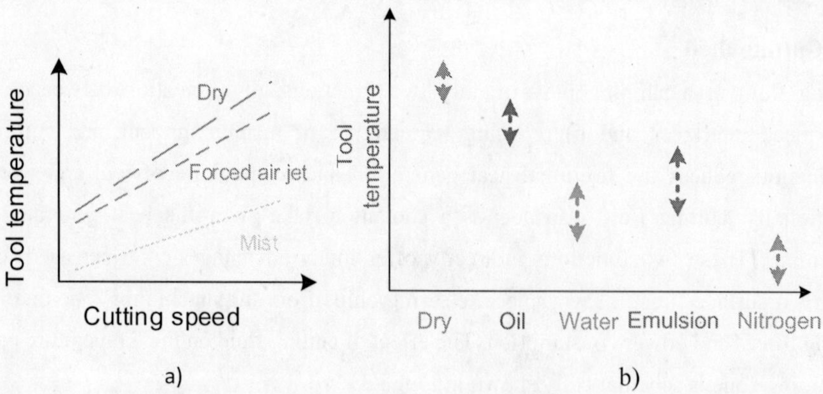

Fig. 3.32: Schematic diagram showing the effect of a) cutting speed and b) application methods on tool temperature.

3.11 Material removal rate

The material removal rate (MRR) is the volume of material removed from the workpiece during machining in unit time and is expressed in mm^3/min. MRR depends on cutting speed, feed and depth of cut. However, the value of these cutting parameters for machining a given material is influenced by the power, tool material and tool geometry, and robustness of the machine. Increasing speed, feed and depth of cut increases the MMR. In the initial stage of machining, usually higher MMR (but with high surface roughness) is obtained by using high feed and depth cut at relatively low cutting speed. But in the final stages of machining, just opposite machining conditions (high cutting speed, coupled with low feed and depth cut) are used to obtain greater dimensional accuracy and low surface roughness. In general, MRR and surface roughness almost move together. High MMR obtained using rough cut is coupled with high surface roughness. Therefore, rough cut is used at the commencement of machining while finish cut is used at the last stage.

3.12 Surface integrity

The surface integrity of a machined surface includes both surface roughness and sub-surface layer characteristics. The surface roughness is a parameter that shows the extent of up/down, undulation, peaks and valleys, and surface irregularities on the surface. The surface roughness based on (area/length) scale is shown in two ways: a) primary surface roughness, also called waviness, measured over a long scale (few tens mm to cm) of ups and downs and b) secondary surface roughness measured on a short scale (few microns to mm) shows the trend of surface asperities (peaks and valleys) as shown in Fig. 3.33

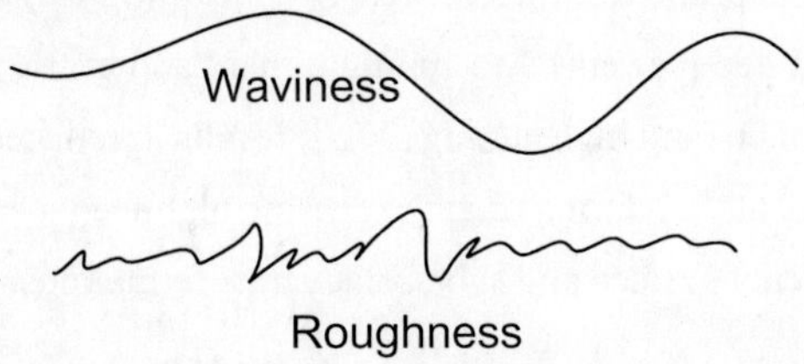

Fig. 3.33 Schematic diagram surface roughness: waviness and secondary roughness

In manufacturing, engineers are primarily concerned with the secondary surface roughness. Therefore, it is the most used roughness parameter and is expressed as R_a. Secondary surface roughness can be measured using various parameters and each shows surface roughness in unique and different ways. The following are the most common secondary surface roughness parameters. One of the ways to represent surface roughness is shown in Fig. 3.34.

R_a: Average roughness

R_z: Average of 5 peaks and 5 valleys (depths) in 5 sampling lengths

R_t: Total height from highest peak to lowest valley in the evaluation length

Representation of surface roughness

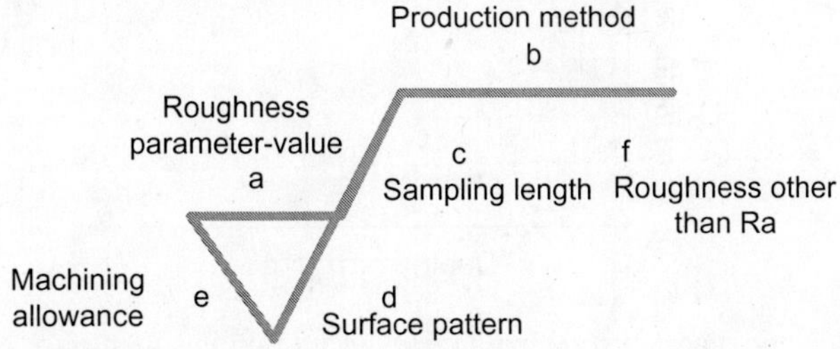

Fig. 3.34 Schematic diagram showing a way of representing surface roughness.

Sub-surface zone

The mechanical, and metallurgical properties of machined components up to a certain depth of surface are affected due to heat generation and plastic deformation experienced by workpiece material during machining. This zone may be termed as machining affected zone (MAZ). A combination of thermo-mechanical stresses imposed during machining changes the microstructure, mechanical properties and residual stress state of material due to temperature rise and surface layer deformation. Just below the machined surface, a very thin plastically/elastically deformed zone is left due to the typical shear mechanism of material removal. The deformed zone in the sub-surface region of a machined component typically comprises three zone: a) highly strained and featureless zone, b) moderately strained zone and c) unaffected zone (Fig. 3.35). The application of cutting fluids reduces the size of these zones due to reduction in temperature and friction. Specific features and size of these zones depend on the workpiece material properties (mechanical and metallurgical) and machining conditions (cutting speed, feed and depth of cut). Machining of hard and brittle materials in finishing cut (using low feed, depth of cut and high cutting speed) results in reduced surface and sub-surface changes. While ductile material during rough cut (using high feed, depth of cut and low cutting speed) results in significant surface and sub-surface transformations.

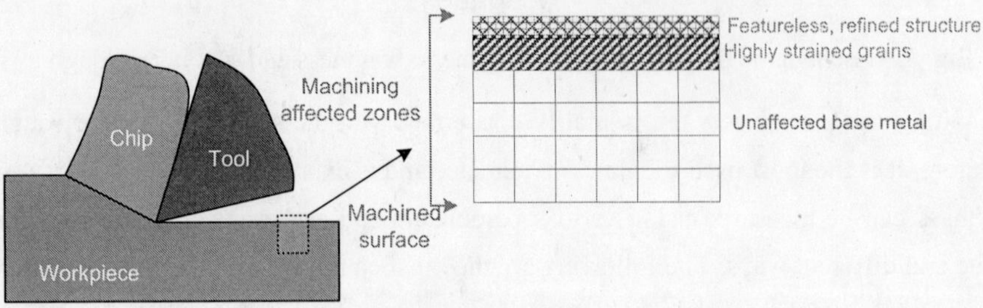

Fig. 3.35 Schematic diagram showing formation of various zones in sub-surface region of machined component.

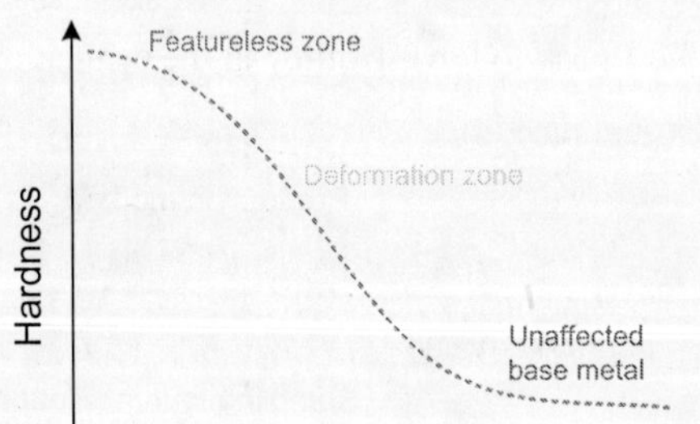

Fig. 3.36 Schematic diagram showing hardness variation in sub-surface region of machined component.

The elastic deformation of a thin layer of material below the plastic deformation zone sets up residual compressive stress on the machined surfaces. While strain hardening (including transformation hardening in the case of hardened metals) results in higher hardness of the top surface than the deep sub-surface region (Fig. 3.36). A combination of high surface hardness and residual compressive stress induced due to machining, in general, increases static and fatigue strength under tensile loading. Hard surfaces take a longer time to nucleate the crack under fatigue conditions. While residual compressive stress (algebraically) negates the effect of fatigue tensile loading responsible for crack nucleation and growth through the crack opening mode of fracture.

3.13 Accuracy and tolerance

The accuracy of a machined component indicates the closeness of dimension with respect to the target/desired dimensions. A high accuracy of the machining process shows the ability to achieve dimensions which are very close to those specified in the design. A smaller difference between the two (achieved and target dimensions) indicates a high accuracy of the machining process and is known as the degree of conformity. Tolerance shows allowable variation in dimensions of a component from the target / design value. Accuracy of machined component shows, how close control over the dimension is possible by a machining process. For example, the machining process can realize tolerance of 10 ± 0.5 or 10 ± 0.02: the later one shows greater accuracy than the former one.

3.14 Machinability

The machinability indicates the ease of machining a material. However, ease of machining is a subjective term depending on a wide range of factors and their relative importance like cost effectiveness, quality of machined surface (accuracy, surface roughness) and surface properties. Therefore, machinability is subjective and relative term and not an absolute thing.

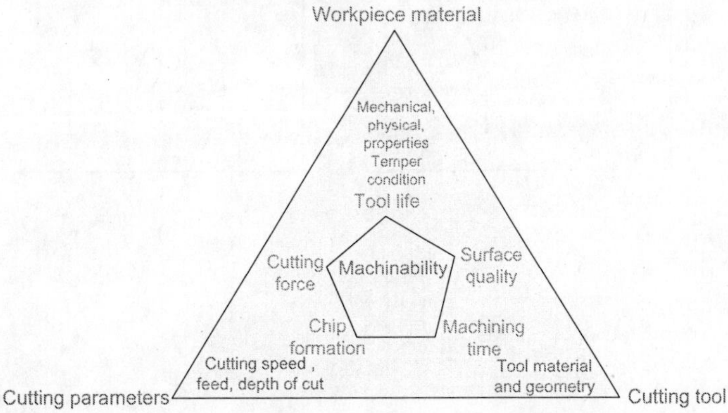

Fig. 3.37 Schematic diagram showing various factors related to the machinability of material.

There are multiple factors affecting machining cost, like machining time (as per maximum permissible cutting condition), tool wear/life, and power consumption. Quality parameters of machined surface include surface integrity including surface roughness, alteration in mechanical and metallurgical characteristics. Traditionally, cutting force/power consumption, machining time, tool wear/life, surface finish, and chip formation/disposal have been used to evaluate the machinability of materials. Therefore, machinability changes with process parameters, type of machining process and operation, the purpose of machining, machine condition (robustness), etc (Fig.3.37). Therefore, machinability (with respect to the above parameters) of a material(s) should be examined under identical conditions of operations, process, process parameter, machine, etc.

For example, it is easier to compare the machinability of varying materials, material conditions, compositions, etc. with respect to one or few aspects such as force/power consumption, machining time, tool wear/life, surface finish, chip formation/disposal and then comment on ease of machining. However, it has been observed that changes in material, condition, composition, etc. may improve machinability in terms of a few aspects (cutting force/power consumption, machining time, tool wear/life, surface finish, chip formation/disposal) while machinability may deteriorate in other aspects. For example, increasing carbon (wt.%) in carbon steel (within limits up to 0.6% C) increases the hardness and reduces ductility which in turn improves the surface finish, and chip removal but decreases the tool wear, cutting force and power consumption (Fig. 3.38).

The machinability of carbon steel is considered 100% and machinability of other materials is expressed with respect to carbon steel. Just for ease of understanding, the machinability of common engineering metals is shown in Fig. 3.39. The machinability of metals has been expressed in range, depending on material conditions, processing methods, and varying alloy composition.

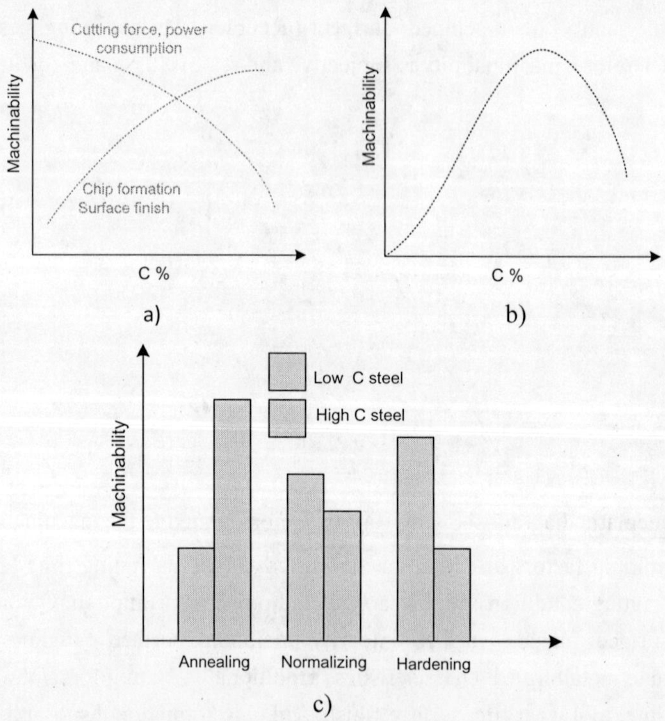

Fig. 3.38 Schematic diagram showing the effect of alloy composition (C %) machinability of common metals.

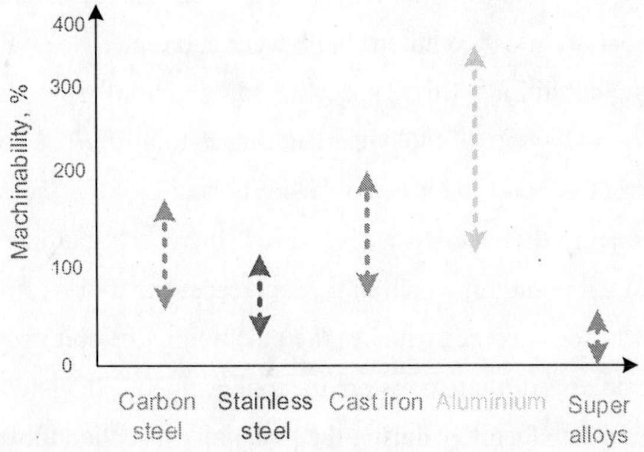

Fig. 3.39 Schematic diagram showing the machinability of common metals.

The following presents the significance of important parameters used to evaluate the machinability

- Cutting force / powder consumption
- Tool life
- Chip formation / disposability
- Surface roughness
- Machining time

3.14.1 Cutting force and power consumption

Depending upon the type of cutting (orthogonal/oblique), the cutting tool experiences three types of cutting forces, namely main cutting force, feed force and thrust force in the case of oblique cutting and the first two types of forces only in the case of orthogonal cutting. The main cutting force predominantly corresponds to the force required for shearing action for material removal and overcoming friction at tool-chip and tool-workpiece interfaces during machining. The main cutting force significantly affects power consumption. Soft and low strength metals, in general, generate lower cutting force than high strength and hard materials. Low shear force and high friction force are observed during machining of soft and low strength materials while reverse happens in case of hard and high strength materials. Low cutting force/power consumption is considered better from the machinability point of view. During the machining of two metals using identical cutting conditions, one which generates lower cutting force is rated high in machinability in terms of cutting force/power consumption.

3.14.2 Tool wear / life

The cutting tool is subjected to high temperature and stress (thermo-mechanical stress) during machining which causes gradual material loss from the face, flank and cutting edge of the tool. The gradual loss of materials from the cutting tool is called tool wear. Wear of cutting tool affects tool geometry (shape and dimensions) due to abrasion, adhesion, and diffusion wear. Two types of tool wear are most common: flank wear and crater wear (Fig.3.40). Abnormal / inappropriate cutting conditions (high speed, feed, depth of cut, long curly chips, dry machining, etc.) increase the rate of tool wear and reduce tool life. The actual machining time, a tool takes to wear out beyond the acceptable limits is one of the measures of the tool life. Tool life is predominantly dictated by cutting speed. Increasing cutting speed increases heat localization, and tool temperature, which in turn increases the tool wear rate and reduces tool life (Fig. 3.40). Loss of tool geometry makes the machining difficult and therefore the cutting tool needs re-sharpening/regrinding to restore the tool geometry. In general, the time for which a cutting tool performs satisfactorily during the machining is called tool life. Tool life can be measured in various ways, such as actual machining time (min), total time (in hours, days, weeks), number of similar units produced, etc. Tool material and cutting conditions in terms of cutting speed and cutting fluid application significantly affect the tool life (Fig. 3.41). The application of cutting fluid during machining increases the tool life due to effective cooling and lubrication. Longer tool life is considered better from the machinability point of view of a workpiece.

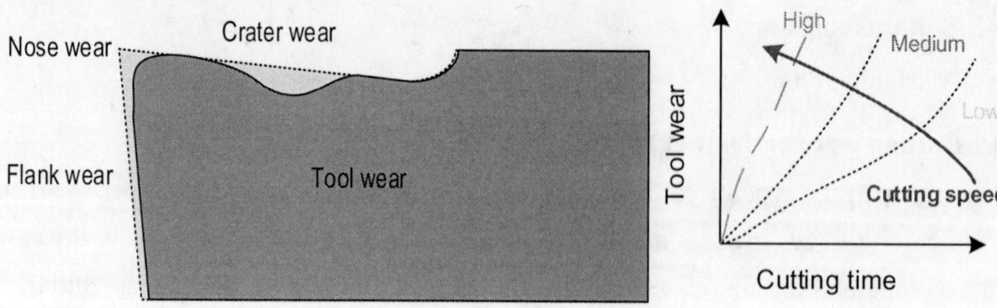

a) b)

Fig. 3.40 Schematic diagram showing a) tool wear and b) tool wear as a function of cutting time and cutting speed.

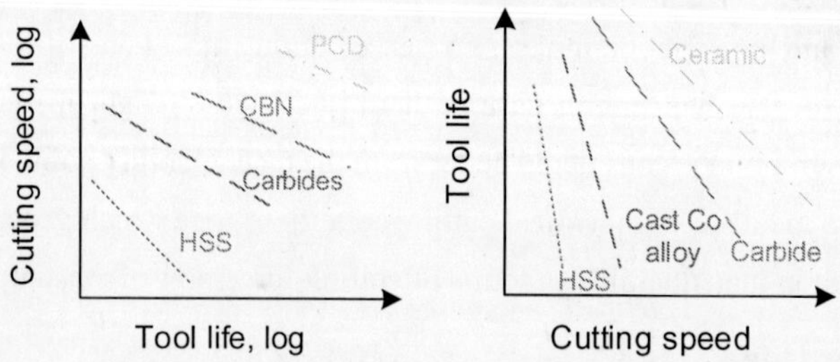

a) b)

Fig. 3.41 Schematic diagram showing effect of tool material and cutting speed on tool life of common tool materials.

3.14.3 Chip formation / disposability

During the machining of workpiece material, a variety of chips are formed by shearing action such as small discontinuous/ fragmented chips, continuous long curly chips, and continuous chips with build-up edge. Small discontinuous chips are formed during the machining of hard and brittle material. These dis-continuous chips easily clear from the machining zone. Apart from the hard workpiece material, other machining conditions like low cutting speed, high feed, depth of cut also results in discontinuous chips. Continuous and long curly chips are formed during the machining of soft and ductile material which tends to wrap around the workpiece in the machining zone. These chips spoil the surface finish and interfere in the cutting process. Machining conditions like high cutting speed, fine feed, and depth of cut promote continuous chips. Continuous chips with built-up edge are formed during the machining of soft and ductile material but inappropriate machining conditions such as low cutting speed, high feed, and depth of cut. Continuous chips with built-up edge (BUE) adversely affects surface finish and reduce tool life. The fragments of BUE metal, after removal, gets deposited on the surface of the workpiece, which adversely affects the surface finish. Short chips easily clear from the machining zone (without affecting machining) are therefore considered better from a machinability point of view.

3.14.4 Surface roughness

The surface roughness indicates the extent of asperities (peaks and valleys) present on the machined surface. The machining process, cutting parameters (cutting speed, feed, depth of cut), robustness and stability of the machine (freedom from vibrations), and mechanical and metallurgical properties of workpiece material affect the surface roughness. For a given set of machining conditions, a workpiece material showing lower surface roughness after machining is considered to have better machinability. A good combination of hardness, ductility, and fine-grained material results in lower surface roughness than material of the same composition but very low hardness, high ductility and coarse grains.

3.14.5 Machining time

The machining time directly affects the productivity i.e. time required to produce a component. High strength, high toughness and work hardened metals (like super alloys, cast iron, stainless steel, etc.) impose many issues in machining such as high tool wear, high heat/temperature generation, and high cutting forces on the tool during the machining. Therefore, these materials are called difficult-to-machine materials, and these take longer time to machine. A workpiece material, which allows the use of high cutting speed, feed and depth of cut generally, takes less time to machine and therefore such materials are considered of higher machinability.

UNIT SUMMARY

This unit gives concepts, and general approaches of making products using material removal processes. Types of metal cutting, generatrix and directrix of common machining processes, common machining processes, namely turning, drilling, milling and grinding are described with the help of schematic diagrams. Further, single and multipoint cutting tools, common tool materials with their capability are presented. The importance of cutting fluid, the concept of tool life and machinability in machining are explained.

EXERCISE

Questions for self-assessment

1. A material removal manufacturing process makes components with

   a. Wide tolerance b. Close tolerance
   c. Very simple shape only d. Less quality control

2. ________ is a material removal manufacturing process.

   a. Die casting b. Extrusion
   c. Drilling d. Soldering

3. Thickness of layer removed in one pass during machining affects.

   a. Production time b. Power consumption
   c. Surface finish d. All of these

4. A machining process which uses a single point cutting tool is

   a. Turning b. Drilling
   c. Milling d. Grinding

5. Abrasives are used as cutting tool in ________ process.

   a. Turning b. Drilling
   c. Milling d. Grinding

6. The tool signature of a single point cutting tool gives information about

   a. Tool material b. Tool geometry
   c. Tool life d. Maximum allowed cutting speed

7. The hardest tool material amongst the following is.

   a. 0. 3% carbon steel tool b. HSS tool
   c. CBN tool d. Carbide tool

8. Maximum allowed cutting speed of tool depends on

   a. Workpiece material b. Hot hardness
   c. Depth of cut and feed d. All of these

9. Grey cast iron during machining produces.
   a. Continuous chips
   b. Continuous chips with BUE
   c. Discontinuous chip
   d. All of these
10. In general, with an increase in cutting speed during machining, tool life
   a. Increases
   b. Decreases
   c. First decreases then increases
   d. Remain unaffected

Answers to Multiple Choice Questions

Key for MCQ: 1 b, 2 c, 3 d, 4 a, 5 d, 6 b, 7 c, 8 d, 9 c, 10 b

Short and Long Answer Type Questions

1. What is the importance of cutting tools in machining?
2. What is the difference between cutting tools and machine tools?
3. Why should the cutting tool material be harder than the workpiece material?
4. What is the general approach to manufacturing by material removal processes?
5. Explain the significance of cutting speed, feed, and depth of cut in machining.
6. What are generatrix and directrix in machining? Write about the generatrix and directrix used for turning and drilling processes.
7. Compare orthogonal and oblique cutting.
8. Why does the oblique cutting offer longer tool life than the orthogonal cutting?
9. What is the turning process? Explain the turning operations using suitable schematics.
10. Explain the methodology used to calculate the cutting speed, feed and depth of cut in the turning process.
11. What are the typical steps used to machine a hole of the desired surface finish and tolerance?
12. What are the cutting parameters used for the drilling process?
13. Using the schematic diagram, explain the purpose of the following operations related to the drilling.
   a. Counter boring
   b. Counter sinking
   c. Reaming
   d. Taping
   e. Centring
14. Compare the milling and turning processes with reference to the approach of material removal.
15. Distinguish peripheral and face milling.
16. Explain the different types of feeds given during the milling process.

17. Using the schematic diagram, explain the purpose of the following operations related to the milling
    a. Slab milling
    b. Slot milling
    c. Side billing
    d. Straddle milling
    e. Face milling
    f. Profile milling
    g. Surface contouring
18. Differentiate up and down milling processes.
19. Compare the milling and grinding processes in terms of material removal.
20. Using a suitable schematic diagram, explain the grinding process.
21. Using schematic diagram, explain the purpose of the following operations related to the grinding.
    a. Surface grinding
    b. Cylindrical grinding
    c. External cylindrical centreless grinding
    d. Internal cylindrical Centreless grinding
    e. Creep grinding
22. Compare the creep and conventional grinding processes
23. Elaborate benefits of centreless grinding processes.
24. Explain the single point cutting tool geometry with the help of a suitable diagram.
25. What is a tool signature and its significance?
26. What important properties should a material have to perform effectively as a cutting tool?
27. How does tool temperature affect the hardness of common tool material?
28. Write about the suitability and applications of common tool materials for different applications.
29. What do you understand regarding heat generation during machining and its effect on tool performance?
30. What are the functions of cutting fluid?
31. How does the application of cutting fluid affect the machining?
32. What is the significance of surface integrity? Explain the surface integrity of the machined surfaces using a suitable diagram.
33. How to represent the surface roughness measurement of a machined surface?
34. Comment on residual stress, microstructure and hardness variation in the sub-surface region of a machine component.
35. What are the common parameters used to evaluate the machinability of a material?

KNOW MORE

Try to visit small, medium, and large manufacturing units and find how real components are machined with the desired tolerance and surface finish. During industrial training, students are expected to learn real applications of machining processes. Explore the evolution of cutting tool material and machining processes.

Scan me!

SUGGESTED RESOURCES FOR FURTHER READING/LEARNING

1. D K Dwivedi, Fundamentals of Metal Joining, Springer Nature, (2021)
2. S Kalpakjian, S R Schmid, Manufacturing Engineering and Technology, Pearson (2018)
3. D K Dwivedi, Surface engineering, Springer Nature (2018)
4. M P Groover, Fundamentals of Modern Manufacturing, John Wiley and Sons, (2010)
5. A Ghosh, A K Malik, Manufacturing science, East-West Press (2010)
6. D K Dwivedi, Materials Engineering, AICTE, (2023)
7. D K Dwivedi, NPTEL Course "Joining Technologies for Metals": https://onlinecourses.nptel.ac.in/noc23_me130/preview
8. D K Dwivedi, NPTEL Course "Fundamentals of Manufacturing Processes" https://archive.nptel.ac.in/courses/112/107/112107219/
9. P S Rao, P K Jain, D K Dwivedi, Electro Chemical Honing (ECH) of External Cylindrical Surfaces of Titanium Alloys, Procedia Engineering 100, 936-945
10. PS Rao, PK Jain, DK Dwivedi Precision Finishing of External Cylindrical Surfaces of EN8 Steel by Electro Chemical Honing (ECH) Process using OFAT Technique, Materials Today: Proceedings 2 (4), 3220-3229
11. D. K. Dwivedi, A. Sharma, T. V. Rajan, Machining of LM 13 and LM 28 Cast Aluminium Alloys: Part I, Journal of Materials Processing Technology, Vol. 196, No.1-3, (2008) pp 197-204.

4 Unconventional Manufacturing Processes

Unit Specific / Learning Objective

The objective of this unit is to develop an understanding of the following aspects

- To learn about the need, scope and suitability of unconventional and micro-manufacturing processes.
- To introduce the concept, and approaches of the micro-manufacturing process.
- To introduce the concept, and approaches of the unconventional and machining processes.
- To develop an understanding of principles and approaches of common unconventional manufacturing processes.
- To learn about the broad classification of newer micro-manufacturing process.

Additionally, a few questions for self-assessment based on fundamentals have been included in this chapter. These questions are based on application, comprehension, analysis and synthesis. Suggested further reading and reference have been included for deep learners and readers.

Rationale

Increasing demand for design, development and manufacturing of components and systems with higher efficiency, capability and reliability has led to the development of many high strength, high melting temperature, heat resistant and hard materials for industrial applications. Manufacturing of such exotic materials by conventional routes using casting, welding, forming and machining becomes challenging, ineffective and inefficient and sometimes even impossible. Further, the requirement of developing features such as high aspect ratio geometrical features in the form of fine holes and slots (which are not achievable using conventional manufacturing processes) has also been a driving force for the development of newer / unconventional manufacturing processes. It is therefore important to learn about these unconventional manufacturing processes to make awareness of various options available for manufacturing such difficult process materials.

Furthermore, manufacturing of small, lightweight and compact components and systems is crucial for aerospace, medical, electronics and computers, automotive and many more devices and systems used by society. Manufacturing miniaturized components using conventional routes becomes very difficult / even impossible because stiffness, and size handling related issues make it difficult to realize the desired quality characteristics (size, shape, tolerance, finish, and properties). Therefore, it is pertinent to learn and study about methods and techniques used for micro-manufacturing.

Learning and awareness about new/unconventional and micro-manufacturing processes will equip mechanical/production/industrial engineers with the latest tools and techniques for efficient and cost-effective manufacturing of products for consumption by society.

Pre-Requisites

Physics: (Class XII)

Learning outcomes

U4-O1: Ability to understand unconventional manufacturing approaches for making components made of difficult to process materials.

U4-O2: Ability to select appropriate unconventional manufacturing process as per the type of material and geometrical features to be realized.

U4-O3: Ability to make products of refractory, hard and brittle materials, and thin section components using unconventional manufacturing processes.

U4-O4: Ability to choose a suitable micro manufacturing approach as per need.

U4-O5: Ability to understand approaches of micro-manufacturing and apply them suitably.

Unit-4 Outcomes	EXPECTED MAPPING WITH COURSE OUTCOMES (1- Weak Correlation; 2- Medium correlation; 3- Strong Correlation)					
	CO-1	**CO-2**	**CO-3**	**CO-4**	**CO-5**	**CO-6**
U4-O1	3	2	-	-	-	-
U4-O2	3	3	-	-	-	-
U4-O3	3	3	-	-	-	-
U4-O4	3	2	-	-	-	-
U4-O5	3	3	-	-	-	-

CO

1. Understand the different conventional and unconventional manufacturing methods employed for making different products
2. To motivate and challenge students to understand and develop an appreciation of the processes in correlation with material properties which change the shape, size and form of the raw materials into the desirable product

4.1 Introduction

The unconventional manufacturing processes (UMPs) are relatively newer machining processes used to produce components a) made of difficult to machine materials (extremely high hardness, very high work hardening characteristics) and b) having unique/ complex geometrical features. These aspects are otherwise difficult to realise effectively, efficiently and economically using conventional methods of manufacturing e.g. casting, welding, machining and forming processes.

Ease of machining by conventional methods depends on hardness, ductility and work hardening characteristics of the material. Requirement of materials with the ability to withstand high stress conditions in hostile operating conditions (temperature, corrosion, erosion, oxidation, etc.) has led to the development of difficult-to-machine materials (composite, titanium alloys, stainless steels, nickel alloys). The conventional machining of these metals offers very low productivity due to short tool life, high surface roughness and low material removal rate (MRR). Similarly, many difficulties are encountered in producing high aspect ratio features like holes, slots, and various fine macro/micro geometrical features.

These new UMPs are based on different mechanisms and approaches such as mechanical (impact, erosion and abrasive) action, chemical reaction (anodic dissolution, corrosion product formation, and passive layer formation), thermal effect (softening, melting, and ablation). Now-a-days, many attempts have been made to combine these approaches to increase the efficiency and effectiveness of UMPs in the form of improved MRR, surface finish, dimensional accuracy and tolerance. This has led to the development of many hybrid unconventional machining processes.

4.2 Classification of UMP on the basis of the approach of material removal

Based on the board mechanism/approach of material removal, the unconventional manufacturing processes can be grouped into the following three categories. Certainly, hybridization of these approaches increases the capability and effectiveness of resulting modified/new (Hybrid) unconventional manufacturing processes.

4.2.1 Mechanical energy

The material removal using mechanical energy-based approach is realized by shearing and cracking as per material characteristics. The mechanical energy is applied on the surface of workpiece in the form of high velocity impact of jet of water, hard abrasive particles carried by compressed water /air/gas jet. The impact of jet and hard particles mainly removes the material from the workpiece by shearing in case of ductile materials and cracking and chipping in the case of brittle materials. Low-angle impact causes abrasive action for removal of relatively soft material, while high-angle impact causes cracking in the case of hard and brittle material. The following unconventional manufacturing processes rely on mechanical energy.

- Water jet machining uses a high-velocity water jet with or without abrasive particles
- Abrasive jet machining uses a high velocity compressed air jet with abrasive particles
- Ultrasonic machining uses the impact of abrasive particles onto the workpiece

4.2.2 Chemical energy

The material removal in chemical energy-based processes can work in multiple ways; a) formation of a relatively soft reaction product after a chemical reaction with workpiece material and followed by removal of reaction product by shearing or abrasive action and b) controlled anodic dissolution of material from the workpiece by electro-chemical reaction. The following unconventional manufacturing processes rely on chemical energy.

- Electro-chemical machining: anodic dissolution of material from the workpiece.
- Electro-chemical grinding: formation of soft chemical reaction product followed by removal by grinding action.
- Chemical machining: selective chemical etching.

4.2.3 Thermal energy

The material removal by thermal energy-based unconventional machining process involves softening, melting, and ablation (evaporation) using a wide range of power densities of various heat sources (flame, plasma, laser and electron beam). All the processes based on the thermal energy-based approach. However, it produces relatively high surface roughness, low dimensional accuracy, high residual stress and even a recast layer with wider heat-affected zone than conventional machining. These issues are primarily due to selective heating causes various thermal cycles experienced by workpiece material during UMPs leading to varying thermal expansion/contraction oxidation, melting and solidification, etc. Additionally, varying thermal cycle exposure affects the mechanical and metallurgical characteristics of machined components.

- Hot machining
- Electric discharge machining
- Plasma arc machining
- Laser beam machining
- Electron beam machining

4.3 Abrasive jet machining

Abrasive jet machining involves the removal of material by directing a jet of high velocity (150-300 m/s) abrasive particles like alumina, and silicon carbide of varying sizes (20-100 μm) with suitable compressed carrier gas (air, carbon dioxide) onto the hard and brittle workpiece material. It uses pressurized air after drying and filtering in which abrasives are mixed in a desired ratio. Then, it impinges on the workpiece surface for machining, as shown in Fig. 4.1.

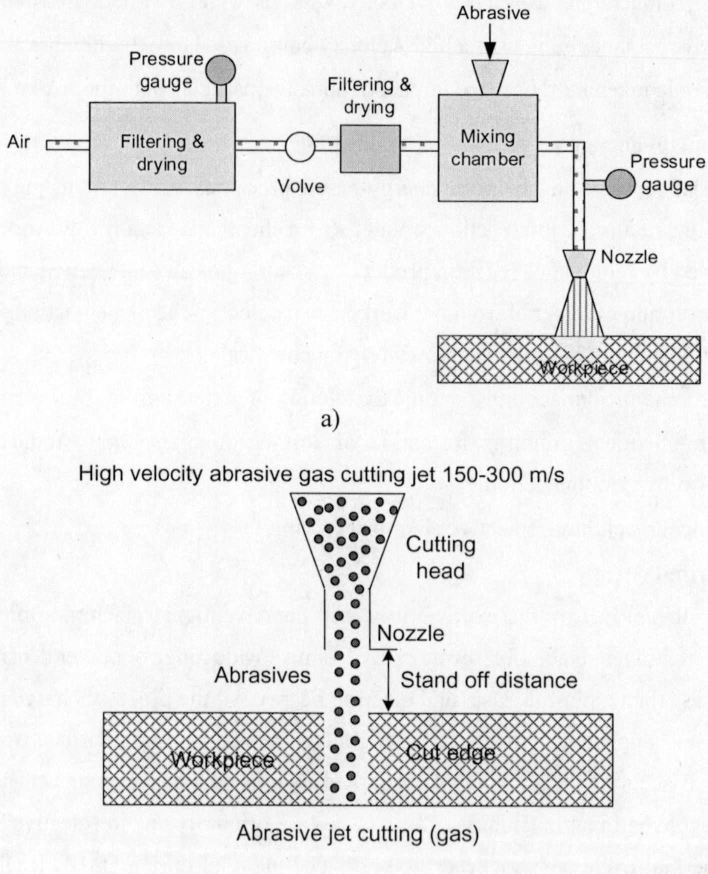

Fig. 4.1 Schematic of abrasive jet machining a) set up and b) closer look of machining zone

The impact of abrasive particles removes the material by cracking and cutting mechanisms. The coalescence of multiple cracks generated due to impact abrasion as hard and brittle surface causes chipping off material in the form of fine chips (Fig. 4.2).

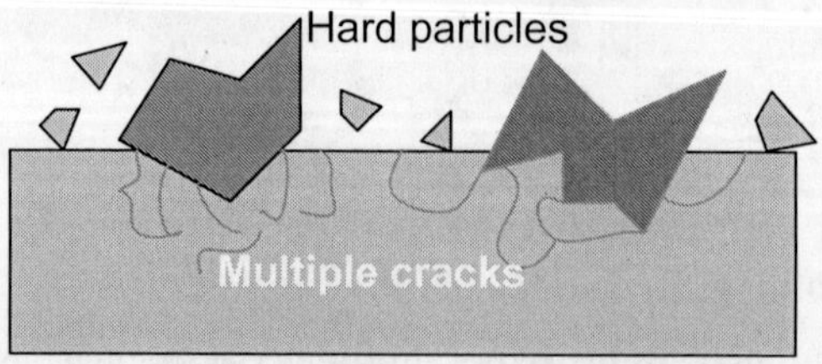

Fig. 4.2 Schematic of material removal mechanism of abrasive jet machining

Machining performance is evaluated in terms of surface roughness, MRR, dimensional accuracy, and nozzle wear rate. Abrasive jet machining process parameters such as size, shape, type, hardness, velocity, flow rate of abrasives, and nozzle to workpiece distance affect the performance of the process. These parameters determine the kinetic energy of the impacting particle, which affect the depth of indentation produced by particles, cracking, and chipping of the workpiece material. The factors related to abrasive jet cutting machine are a) parameters related to abrasives and b) parameters affecting nozzle and carrier gas.

4.3.1 Abrasive Particles

Abrasive particles affect the material removal as per its hardness, size, shape, and kinetic energy of abrasives at the time of impact with the workpiece. All factors affecting the kinetic energy of abrasive particles such as size, density and carrier gas pressure directly/indirectly affect the indentation, cracking, chipping and so MRR. In general, hard abrasives cause higher MRR than the soft ones due to greater indentation/penetration capability under identical conditions.

In general, increasing the size, velocity, hardness, flow rate and sharpness of abrasives initially increases the MRR but up to a certain limit. Increasing the mixing ratio also increases the MRR due to a greater number of abrasives impacting the workpiece surface. However, an excessive number of abrasives in jet starts clogging the nozzle and interfering with particle movement. Similarly, increasing the pressure of carrier gas increases the abrasive particle velocity and kinetic energy which in turn causes a higher MRR. Large size abrasives at a given velocity, produces high kinetic energy (KE) at the time of impact, resulting in deeper and wider craters than fine abrasives. Therefore, increasing particle size up to a certain limit increases materials removal rate and surface roughness. Similarly, increasing particle velocity realized by increasing pressure of carrier gas increases MRR and surface roughness due to higher KE of impacting abrasives (Fig. 4.3).

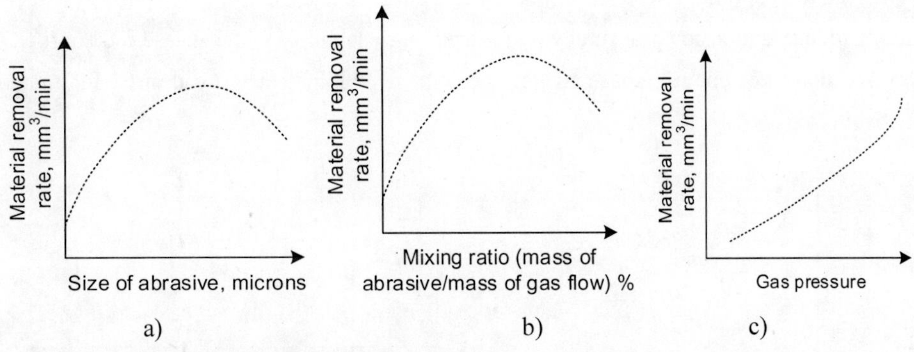

Fig. 4.3 Schematic showing the effect of a) abrasive size, b) mixing ratio, and c) gas pressure on MRR during abrasive jet machining

A combined effect of abrasive flow rate, traverse speed and abrasive particle size on MRR is shown in Fig. 4.4 (a, b). In general, increasing the abrasive flow rate increases the material removal rate. However, there is an optimum value of abrasive flow rate varying abrasive size. Increasing the abrasive flow rate (kg/min) initially increases the metal removal rate (MRR) due to higher number of abrasives impacting the surface to remove the material. Thereafter, further increase of abrasive flow rate either does not affect MRR or it starts decreasing due to higher chance of clogging of nozzle with (large size) abrasives and abrasives impacting one over other. Low traverse speed of jet results in high depth of penetration in single pass because of large number of abrasives impacting for long at a given location to remove the material.

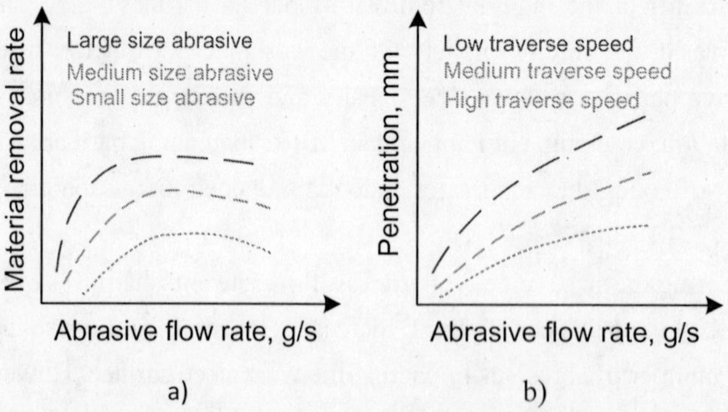

Fig. 4.4 Schematic showing effect of abrasive flow rate a) materials removal rate, b) penetration depth under varying abrasive size and traverse speed during abrasive jet machining

4.3.2 Stand-off distance

It is important to optimize the stand-off distance (gap between nozzle and workpiece) and abrasive flow rate to maximize the MRR and dimensional accuracy (Fig. 4.5). Increasing stand-off distance (SOD) causes divergence of abrasive jet which in turn increases the area over which abrasive impact on the surface of workpiece and reduces velocity of abrasive at the time impact (beyond optimum SOD) resulting in wider cut zone and shallow cut depth. These factors in turn reduce dimensional accuracy and machining capability while incase too short SOD, abresive don't get enough space to get accelerated & kinetic energy desired for material removal.

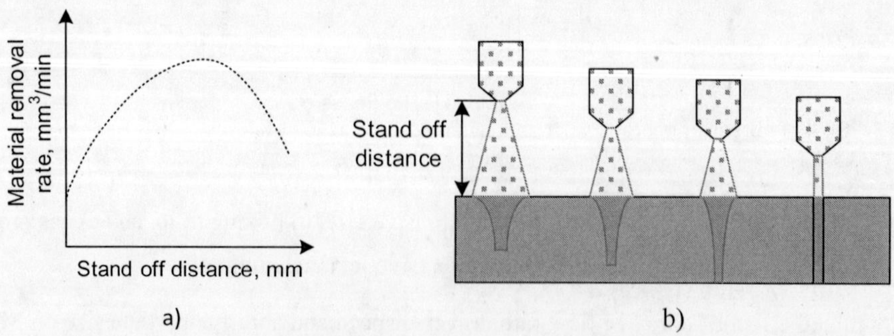

Fig. 4.5 Schematic showing effect of stand-off distance on a) materials removal rate, b) cut morphology during abrasive jet machining.

Typical empirical relations showing effect of process parameters on material removal rate by abrasive jet machining of hard and soft materials is given by the following equations.

Material removal rate (mm^3/min) brittle materials: $1.04 \frac{mv^{\frac{3}{2}}}{\rho^{1/4} H^{3/4}}$

Material removal rate (mm^3/min) ductile materials: $0.5 \frac{mv^2}{H}$

Where v is the velocity of abrasive jet at the time of impact, H is the hardness of the work material, m is mass flow rate of abrasive particles and ρ is density of each abrasive particle.

4.4 Water jet machining

A high velocity (500-2000 m/s) jet of water with / without abrasive (alumina, sand, garnet) is used to cut a wide range of materials such as plastics, wood, rubber, aluminium, composite, steel etc. of relatively thin sections. Material is removed by shear mechanism when pure water jet is used for cutting of soft materials like thin plastic, wood, rubber, and foam. Mixing of abrasives with water in water-jet machining increases cutting ability to process hard materials (like aluminium, copper, steel, composites) due to combined and synergic action of ploughing, abrasion, cracking and shearing in material cutting. It is important to control the path traced by jet using suitable control to cut material and obtain the desired shape. Velocity / pressure distribution across the jet at the time of impact gradually decreases on moving from centre to Surface jet. Depending on the type of material, cutting mechanism varies significantly. In case of ductile and soft metal the materials are predominantly removed by cutting, shearing and ploughing while in case of brittle metal cracking and Chipping remove material (Fig. 4.6(a)). The progress of cut during pure water jet machining of ductile material by ploughing is shown in Fig. 4.6(b).

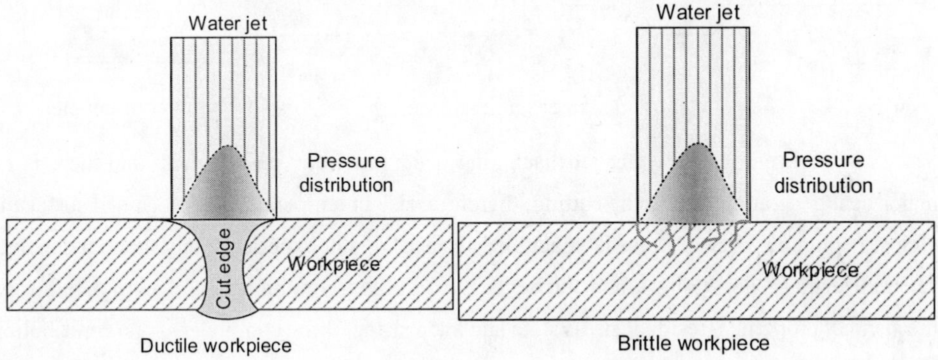

a)

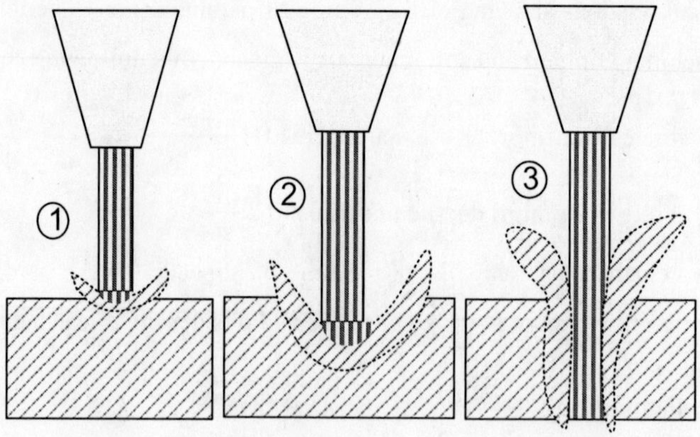

b)

Fig. 4.6 Schematic showing materials removal by water jet machining a) velocity/pressure distribution at the time impact of jet and cutting mechanisms, b) progress of cut in ductile material by ploughing

High velocity jet of water (1000-2000 m/s) is realized by passing pressurised water (2000-6000 bar) through a wear resistant nozzle made of ruby, diamond. Schematic showing a system of water jet machining with different components (water tank, pump, control unit, valve, and nozzle etc.) is shown in Fig. 4.7.

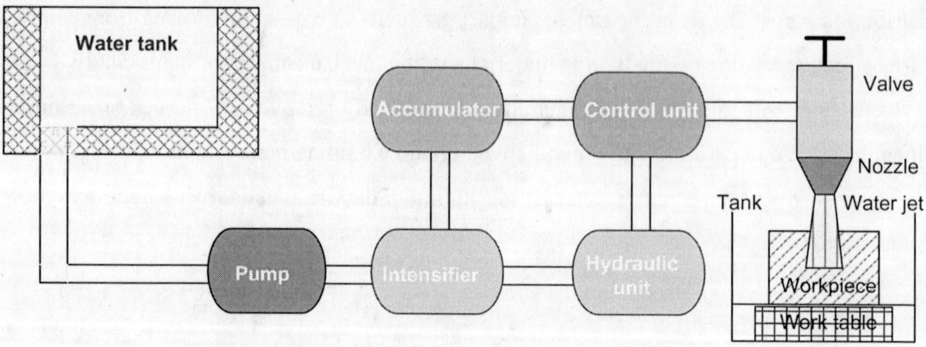

Fig. 4.7 Schematic showing water jet machining system with different components

Since material removal in water jet machining occurs in water environment and there is no major heat generation during the cutting, therefore, rise in temperature of machined surface is almost negligible. Hence, water jet machined surfaces do not experience any thermal damage. Thermal damage depending upon the severity of cutting condition can change metallurgy, mechanical properties, residual stress state and even shape of the component. The contribution of abrasive particles in material removal in water jet machining is similar that described in abrasive jet machining in previous section 4.3. Cutting is water jet machining is further assisted by high velocity water jet through shearing action. Therefore, synergic cutting action of water jet coupled with abrasive increases cuttability, speed of cutting and productivity. Abrasive water jet is more common, effectivity and productive than pure water jet.

The water jet machining performance (in terms of MRR, kerf width, penetration depth, surface roughness, dimensional accuracy and tolerance) affected by process parameters like water jet velocity, feed rate, angle of attack, stand-off distance, jet oscillations, and abrasive particle related parameters (type, size, shape, roughness, flow rate). It is expected that cut edge is smooth and square. Water jet cut edge shows that width of cut is wider at the top surface than lower surface as presented in Fig. 4.8 (a). This is due to reducing cuttability of water jet with increasing penetration depth. Similarly, surface finish along the cut also varies with increasing depth from top surface. Best surface finish is obtained near the top surface of cut edge and worst at the bottom in the form of drag line due to reduced cutting ability of water jet with increasing section depth and reducing jet velocity (Fig. 4.8 a-b).

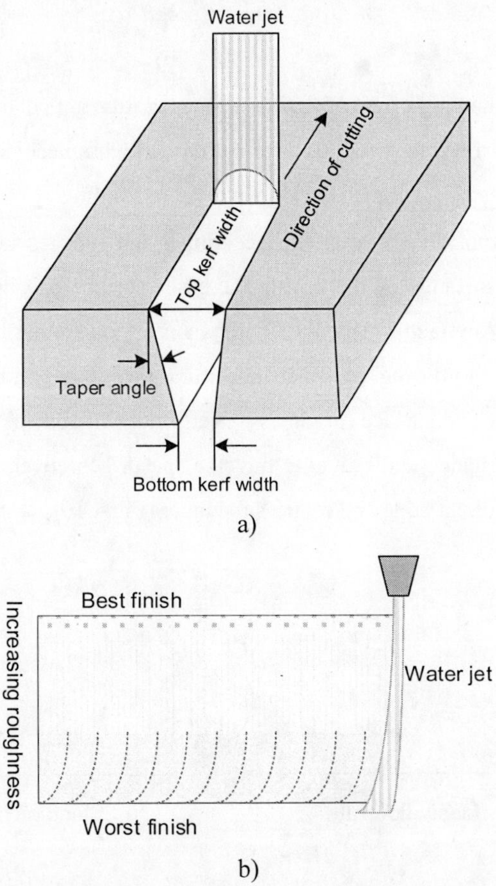

Fig. 4.8 Schematic showing a) morphology of cut edge and b) variation in surface roughness along the depth of cut produced by water jet machining.

Travel speed, oscillation of nozzle and stand-off distance and jet velocity (as per pressure) affect the kerf geometry, surface roughness, depth of penetration significantly. Increasing nozzle travel speed increases surface roughness, kerf formation and reduces penetration depth due to reduced time for removal of material by water jet. In general, increasing angle of impact of water jet increases the cutting ability of water jet and depth of penetration due to increased severity of jet to cut the brittle materials by cracking and chipping (Fig. 4.9).

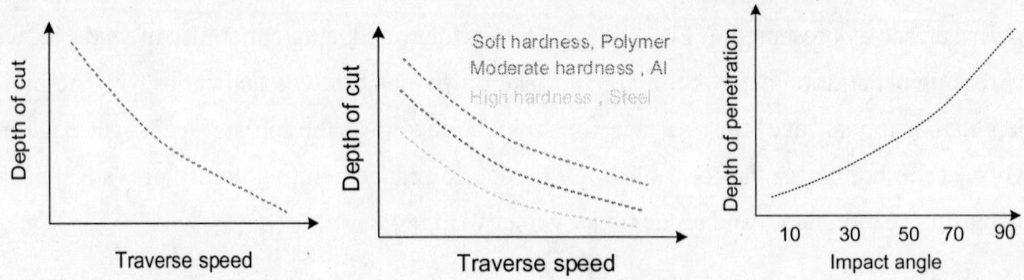

a) b) c)

Fig. 4.9 Schematic showing effect of various process parameters on depth of cut/penetration a) traverse speed, b) traverse speed for different type of workpiece materials and c) angle of impact during water jet machining.

Oscillation given to nozzle improves surface finish and reduces kerf formation tendency. Increasing stand-off distance of the nozzle increases surface roughness due to higher kerf formation tendency. Any factor associated with water jet machining like increase of water jet pressure, mass flow rate during water jet machining increases cutting ability which in turn reduces the kerf taper and surface roughness. Kerf width in general increases with water jet pressure, stand-off distance and reducing traverse speed. Moreover, increase of jet pressure increases squareness of cut edge and reduces the taper (Fig.4.10).

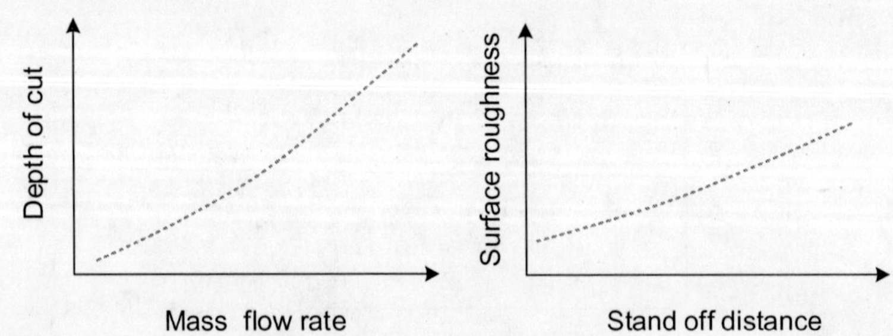

a) b)

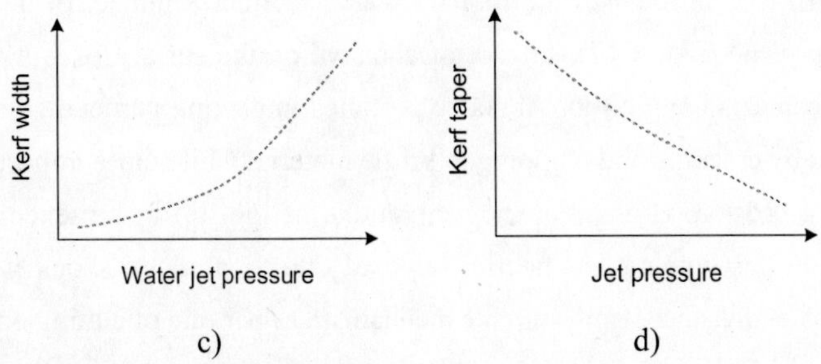

Fig. 4.10 Schematic showing effect of various process parameters a) on depth of cut and mass flow rate relation, b) surface roughness and stand-off distance relation, c) kerf width and water jet pressure relation and d) kerf width and jet pressure relation during water jet machining.

Control over the geometrical features like holes, slot produced by water jet machining is somewhat poor due to converging / diverging nature of water jet after coming out of the nozzle. Generally, rounded upper edges, varying aspect ratio through the thickness are observed on water jet machined components (Fig.4.11). Water jet machining in general offers better surface finish and dimensional accuracy than plasma, laser and electric discharge machining process due to absence of melting and heat.

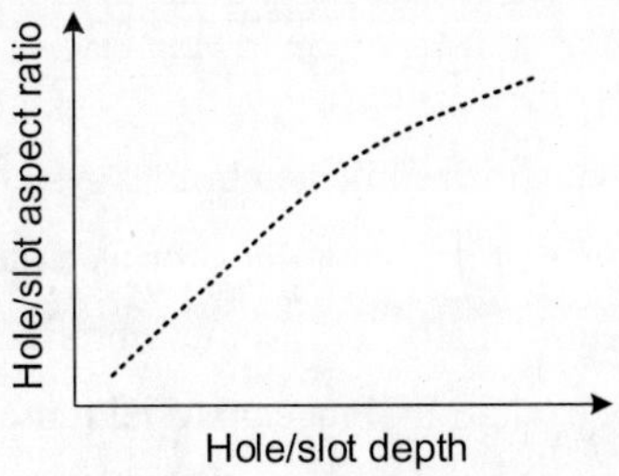

Fig. 4.11 Schematic showing variation hole/slot aspect ratio with hole/slot depth obtained by water jet machining.

4.5 Ultrasonic machining

Ultrasonic machining (USM) is primarily used for manufacturing the components made of very hard and brittle materials (>40 HRC) such as glass, ceramics, cermet, composite materials. The material for shaping by USM is removed by impact of hard and abrasive particles at ultrasonic frequency (20-30 kHz) on to the workpiece through a well-designed tool called sonotrode.

Ultrasonic vibrations are produced using an ultrasonic generator having transducer, amplifier, horn and tool tip. High frequency current supplied to transducer (working on the principle of either piezo-electric or magneto-strictive type) generates high frequency and low amplitude vibrations. Amplifier increases the amplitude of vibrations while a horn concentrates energy of vibrations. Horn is connected to the tool tip which facilitates impact of abrasives onto the surface of workpiece (Fig. 4.12). Impact of abrasive on the surface of workpiece is usually normal but it can at an angle too. Abrasive particles impacting perpendicular to the surface produces crater by cracking and chipping in brittle material while those impacting at low angle causes abrasive erosion. High frequency vibrations of tool tip in presence of slurry create cavitation conditions helping in material removal due to pressure shock wave. As cutting progresses, tool is advanced using suitable mechanism as per rate of cutting obtained to ensure contact feed force during machining.

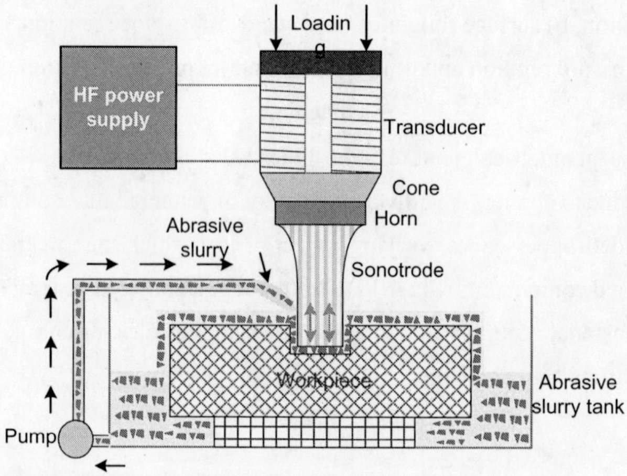

Fig. 4.12 Schematic showing ultrasonic machining system with various components.

Impact of abrasive on the surface of the workpiece forms crater due to shearing and ploughing in case of ductile material. Additionally, ultrasonic vibrations in presence of abrasive slurry causes removal of material by cavitation. Since material removal is primarily due to impact of abrasives caused by vibrating tool tip therefore almost a mirror image of tool tip is produced on the workpiece surface (Fig. 4.13).

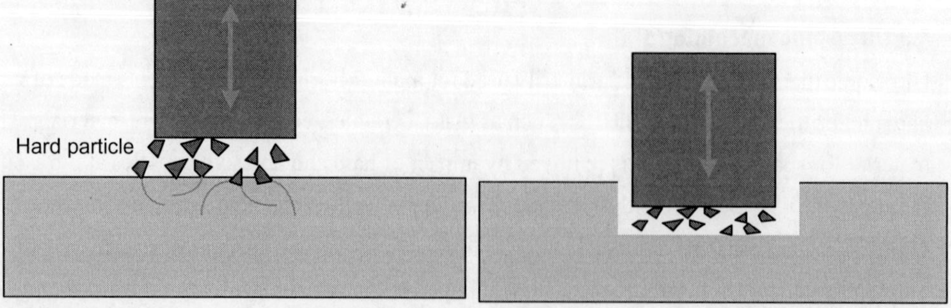

Fig. 4.13 Schematic showing variation hole/slot aspect ratio with hole/slot depth obtained by water jet machining.

These abrasive particles are transferred in machining zone in the form of slurry fed through the gap between sonotrode and workpiece under pressure. Continuous flow of abrasive slurry through the machining zone performs many functions such as providing new/fresh abrasives for machining, flushing out material removed from the workpiece and maintaining the temperature of machining zone.

There are many process parameters related to ultrasonic machining such as vibrations (frequency, amplitude, energy concentration as per design of horn/tool), abrasive slurry (type, hardness, size, shape, concentration of abrasive in slurry, flow rate and tool tip / workpiece gap) and workpiece material properties (hardness) affecting the material removal mechanism, MRR and surface finish. Increasing frequency, amplitude, energy/power, size and hardness of abrasives, concentration of abrasives in slurry, flow rate of slurry increases the MRR (up to a limit) as shown in Fig. 4.14 (a-d). Increasing frequency in general increases the materials removal rate due to more the impacts of abrasives facilitated by vibrating tool tip per unit time leading to higher MRR. Increase of amplitude increases the severity and impact of abrasive in cracking, abrasive erosion and cavitation which in turn results in higher MRR. Increase of normal load increases the depth of penetration obtained through abrasives due to greater impact/load transfer to cause penetration / cracking during ultrasonic machining, which in turn increases MRR and surface roughness. Similarly, increase of abrasive size increases the depth of penetration obtained through abrasives due to greater penetration / cracking during ultrasonic machining. Increase of concentration of abrasive in slurry increases the number of abrasives impacting the surface of workpiece which in turn causes the higher MRR.

However, increase of workpiece to tool hardness ratio decreases materials removal rate because of reduced depth of indentation, penetration and increased chances of blunting of abrasive on impacting with hard workpiece. Similarly, increasing viscosity reduces the material removal rate due to reduce flow of slurry causing slower scavenging, fewer fresh abrasives acting in the machining zone (Fig. 4.15).

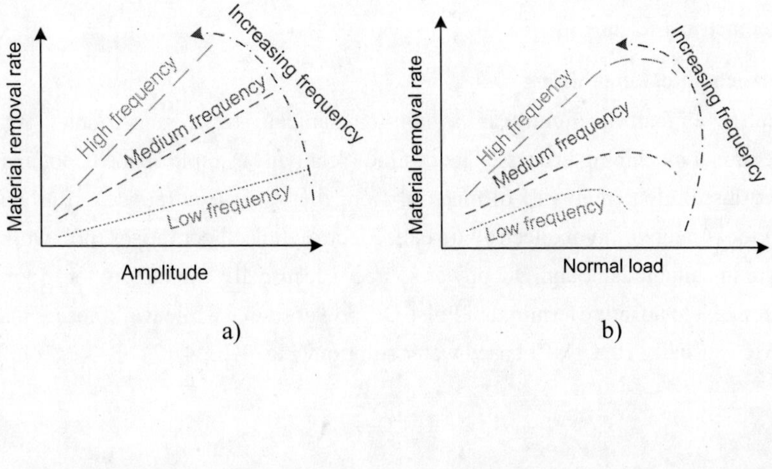

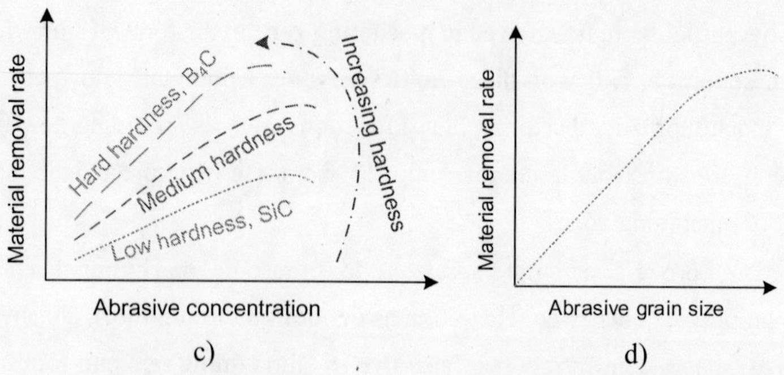

Fig. 4.14 Schematic showing effect of various process parameters on MRR a) amplitude with varying frequency, b) load with varying frequency, c) abrasive slurry concentration with abrasives of different hardnesses and d) abrasive size during ultrasonic machining

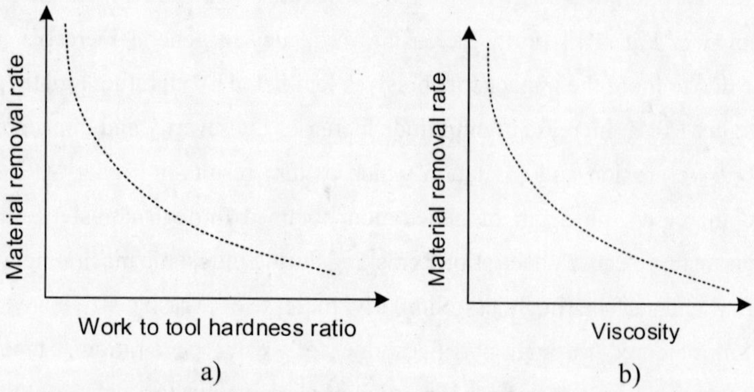

Fig. 4.15 Schematic showing effect of various process parameters on MRR a) work to tool hardness ratio and b) viscosity of slurry during ultrasonic machining.

Gap between the tool tip and workpiece should be optimised as per the need of maximum MRR or geometrical feature requirement. Application of *rotary tool* during ultrasonic machining increases MRR due to improved flushing and cutting by fresh abrasives. This in turn results in a new variant of ultrasonic machining called rotary ultrasonic machining. Taper and overcut are two important measures of dimensional accuracy and ultrasonic process capability. Over cut primarily determined by size of abrasive Overcut indicates difference in size of tool and that of geometrical feature.

4.6 Electrochemical machining

The electrochemical machining is a non-mechanical stress, non-contact type of the Unconventional machining process. The desired (relatively) simple shape is obtained through controlled dissolution (removal) of material from the workpiece (anode) to produce mirror image of tool (cathode) in an electrolytic cell. Electrolytic cell comprises tool, workpiece and electrolyte in suitable tank and DC power source. Electrically conducting tool forms cathode by connecting it to negative terminal of Pulse DC power source while workpiece is made anode. Electrolyte is usually 10% NaCl based water solution (Fig. 4.16, 4.17).

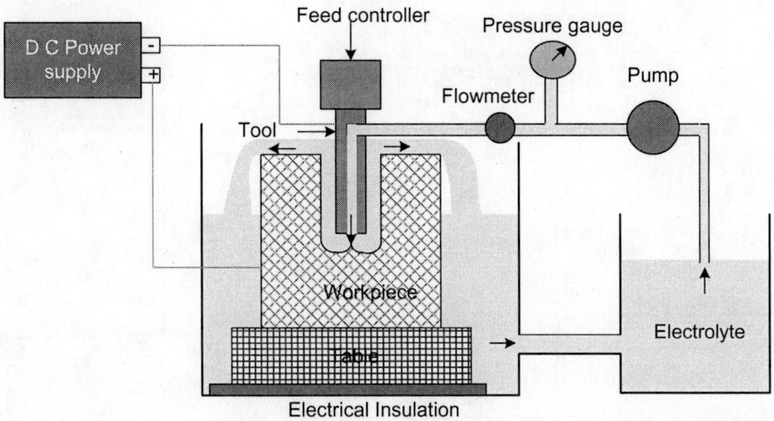

Fig. 4.16 Schematic showing electrochemical machining system with various components.

The current (I), and time (t) for which current flow as per in electrolytic cell determine the material removal from the workpiece of given material (as per electrochemical equivalent, Z: ratio of atomic number and valence). The MRR in electrochemical machining is expressed by the following relation.

MRR (MRR, in g/s)) by ECM: Process efficiency (Current x Electrochemical equivalent)/Faraday's constant: $\eta.I.Z/F \sim \eta.I.(A/v)/F$

Where η is the process efficiency (%), I current (A), Z electrochemical equivalent, A atomic number, v valency, F Faraday's constant (96500), MRR in g/s.

Conversely, material removal rate: $\eta \frac{MI}{\rho FZ}$

M atomic weight (kg/per mole), I current A, F Faradays constant (coulombs), Z valency, η process efficiency, ρ density (kg/m^3) Above equations suggest that

Metal dissolution rate is directly proportional to the current.

MRR can also be expressed using: Tool front area (mm^2) x feed rate (mm/s); ηCI (I current, η efficiency, C specific material removal rate mm^3/s) C is function of material proportion and is expressed as

C: $\frac{M}{\rho FZ}$

Above equation suggests that the current in ECM is dominant parameter in ECM affecting the MRR apart material related parameter (atomic number and valency). ECM is low voltage (10-20 V) and high DC current (2000-10000 A) process. The electrochemical action is adversely affected and MRR is reduced if a passive layer (chemical reaction product) is formed on the workpiece surface due to unfavourable process conditions during machining. Current flow between to cathodic tool and workpiece determines MRR. ECM produces differential MRR in different zone and areas of workpiece surface to obtain the desired shape (Fig. 4.18).

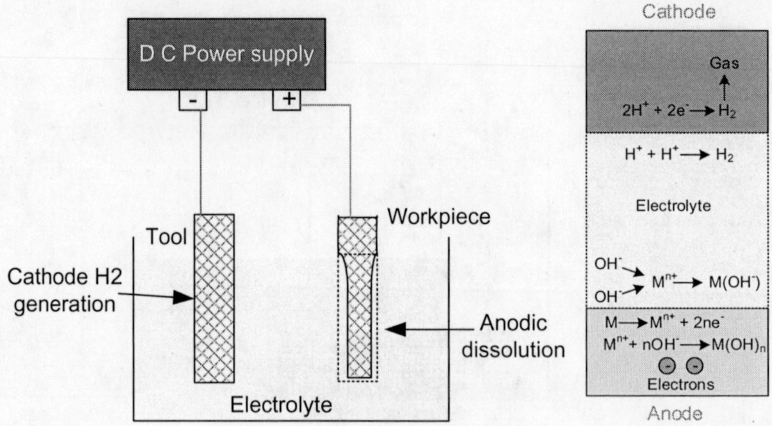

Fig. 4.17 Schematic showing a) anodic dissolution and b) chemical reactions during the electrochemical machining.

A section / region of tool closer workpiece is subjected to higher current flow due to low resistance for the flow of current than the other region. Therefore, a segment having greater distance between tool and workpiece due to higher resistant experiences lower current flow for electrochemical machining hence material is removed at lower rate.

The varying current and so changing material removal as per shape of tool helps to generate the desired shape in the workpiece. As the material is removed, tool is advanced toward the workpiece to maintain the inter-electrode gap (gap between tool and workpiece). A flat face tool generates a flat surface while curved faced tool creates the curved surface accordingly. Application of high current during electrochemical machining generates a lot of heat which raises the temperature of electrolytic cell. Excessive heat generation causes gas generation leading to interference in electrochemical machining, therefore, use of suitable cooling arrangement in ECM is preferred. Except inter-electrode gap, increasing other parameters namely current density, peak current pulse duration, voltage, electrode feed rate and electrolyte concentration increases the MRR and surface roughness due to higher anodic dissolution rate (Fig. 4.18). In fact, MRR and surface finish are inversely related.

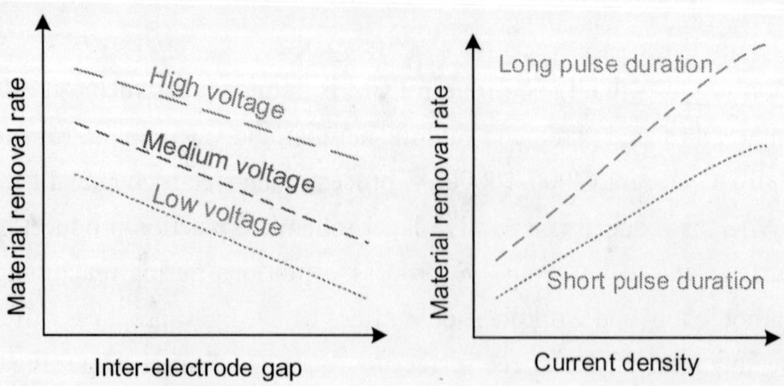

a) b)

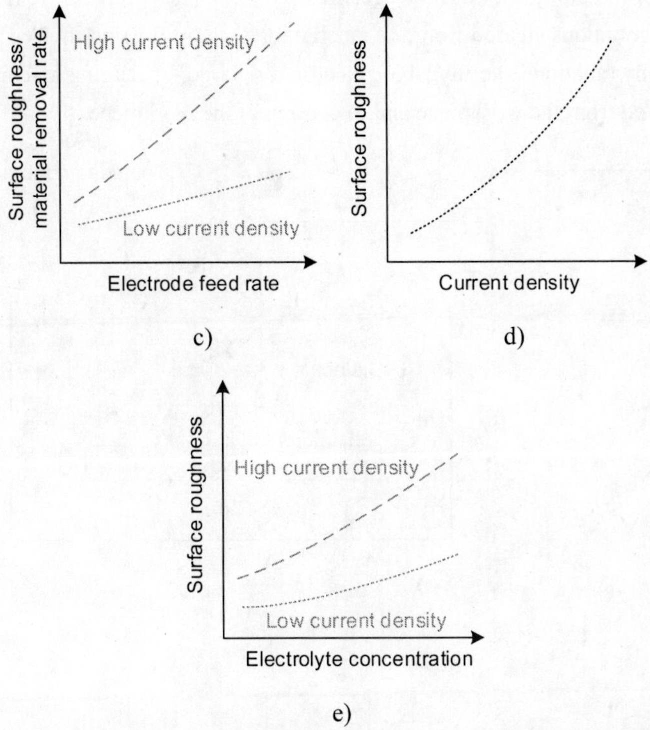

Fig. 4.18 Schematic showing effect of various ECM process parameters on process performance characteristics a) MRR and electrode gap relation with varying voltage, b) MRR and current density relation with varying peak current pulse duration, c) MRR/surface roughness and electrode feed rate relation with varying current density, d) surface roughness and current density relation and, e) surface roughness and electrolyte concentration relation with varying current density.

Absence of any mechanical stress and relatively very low heat generation during ECM eliminates any possibility of thermo-mechanical damage like distortion, heat affected zone, plastic deformation of surface layers. However, presence of deformed-surface layer in conventionally machined components (turned, milled, drilled) causes work-hardening and development residual compressive stresses which in turn increases the tensile load carrying capacity and fatigue resistance under tension. Absence of such a layer in electrochemically machined component surfaces results in relatively lower tensile and fatigue strength than the conventionally machined components.

4.7 Electric Discharge Machining

The electric discharge machining (EDM) is a thermal energy-based process. Controlled electric discharges between (Tungsten usually) tool and electrical conducting workpiece through dielectric generates heat to remove the material from surface of workpiece by melting and evaporation for creating the desired geometrical features. Material removed from the workpiece is continuous cleared from the machining zone by flowing dielectric. Dielectric in EDM plays many functions a) establishing electric discharge, b) clearing machining zone from material removed from the workpiece and c) cooling of the workpiece.

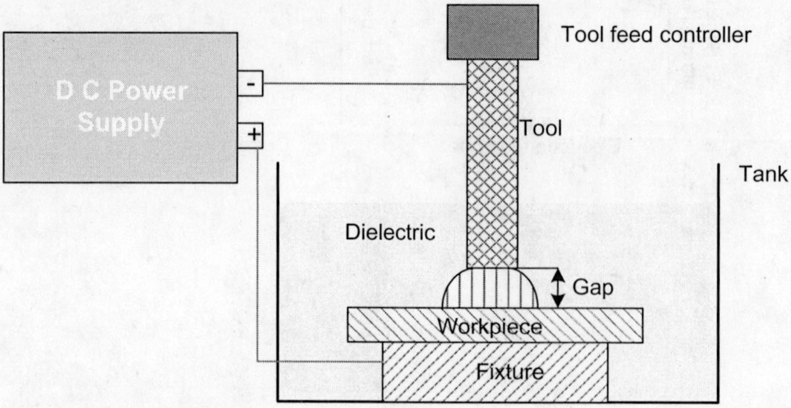

a)

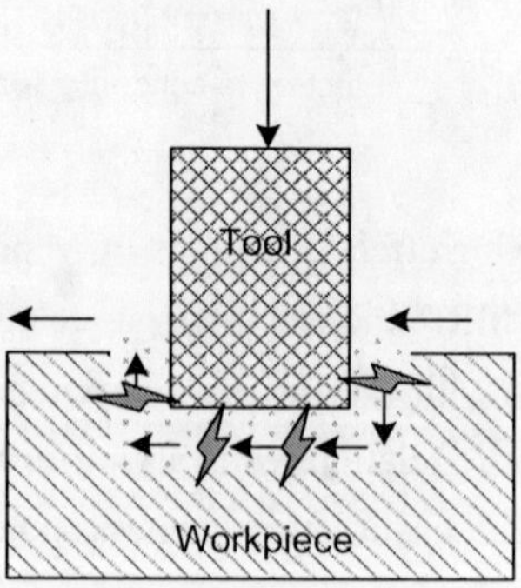

b)

Fig. 4.19 Schematic showing a) electric discharge machining system with main components and b) closer look of machining zone.

The EDM comprises suitable power source, tool (electrode/cathode), dielectric, workpiece (anode) and tank including a platform for holding workpiece. Power source delivers pulses of high voltage current for a short time (between tool and workpiece) which breaks down dielectric and makes it electrical conducting to establish the controlled discharges between tool and workpiece (Fig. 4.19). The discharge produces intense heat and high temperature (10000 to 20000 K).

High temperature and heat generated by controlled discharges melts and evaporates to remove from the surface of workpiece material resulting in crater formation as part of machining process. Various EDM process parameters and their relative importance with respect to MRR and surface roughness of workpiece is shown in Fig. 4.20.

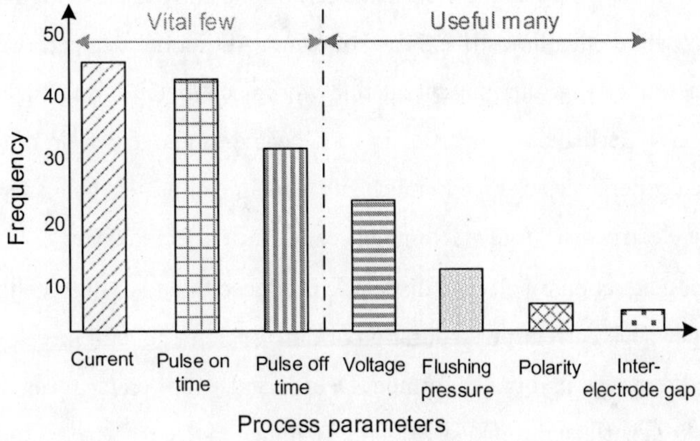

Fig. 4.20 Schematic showing relative importance of various EDM process parameters in the form of pareto diagram

The formation for the deep crater on the surface of workpiece during electric discharge machining in general increases both MRR and surface roughness (Fig. 4.21). EDM generally uses direct current straight polarity (DCEN), therefore more heat is generated by electric discharge on the workpiece side than tool side to facilitate higher MRR. Still high temperature generated by electric discharge causes thermal damage to tool leading to tool wear. Therefore, tool for EDM is made of heat resistant electrical conducting materials and reuires periodic replacement.

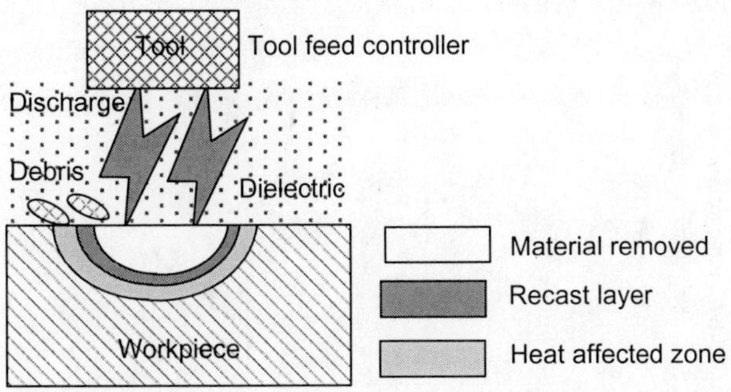

Fig. 4.21 Schematic showing the formation of various zones on the surface produced by EDM

Mechanism of material removal from the workpiece in EDM is by melting evaporation and flushing approach. A thin layer of molten metal which is not completely flushed out from the machining zone results in "recast layer" on solidification having a typical casting structure. Thin recast layer is prone have defect like cracks, pores, inclusion (Fig.4.21). This layer can be hard or soft depending up on the metal strengthening mechanism of workpiece metal subjected to EMD. Transformation hardenable metals like carbon and alloy steels of high carbon equivalent show hardening while others mostly exhibit softening. Additionally, a part of heat generated is dissipated to the underlying thermal conducting workpiece metal during EDM which changes microstructure and mechanical properties in zone heated to above certain critical temperature. This zone which experiences change in mechanical and metallurgical characteristics due to heat supplied during electric discharge machining is called heat affected zone.

Increase of heat generation by electric discharge produced due to a) high voltage, b) high peak current, c) longer peak current pulse duration or duty cycle in general increases the volume of material melted/removed and crater formed. Deeper and wider crater formation increases the MRR but with high surface roughness (Fig. 4.22). In general, surface roughness increases with high heat generation (with high current, voltage, pulse duration) due to deeper crater formation (Fig. 4.23).

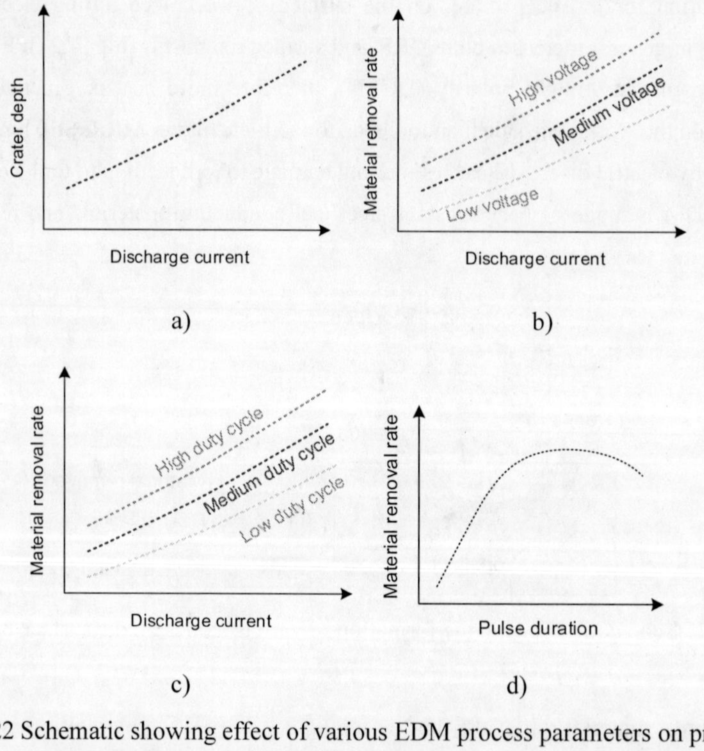

Fig. 4.22 Schematic showing effect of various EDM process parameters on process performance characteristics a) crater depth and discharge current relation, b) MRR and discharge current relation with varying voltage, c) MRR and discharge current relation with varying duty cycle (ratio of pulse current duration to off current duration), and d) MRR and pulse current duration.

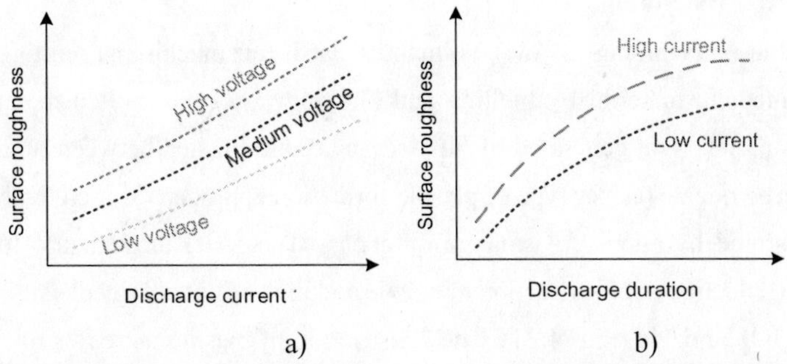

Fig. 4.23 Schematic showing effect of various EDM process parameters on surface roughness variation with a) discharge current with varying voltage relation and b), discharge duration and varying current relation.

Typical empirical relations showing effect of process parameters on material removal rate, surface roughness and tool wear rate of electrode by electric discharge machining are given by the following equations.

Material removal rate (mm^3/min): $(4\ x\ 10^4)iT^{-1.23}$

Surface roughness Ra (µm): $(0.0225)i^{0.29}\ t^{0.38}$

- i = Peak current used for EDM, A
- T = Melting point temperature of the work material °C
- t = Pulse current duration, s

Similarly, erosion (wear) of tool/ electrode during EDM can be expressed using following equation

Tool wear (mm^3/min): $(11\ x\ 10^3)iT_e{}^{-2.38}$

Wear ratio: $2.25\ T_r{}^{-2.3}$

- i = Peak current used for EDM, A
- T_e = Melting point temperature of the electrode material °C
- T_r = Ratio of melting point temperature of the workpiece and electrode material(T/Te)

Wire-EDM

The wire electric discharge machining (W-EDM) is a variant of the electric discharge machining where in electrode is in the form of wire (diameter from 0.05 to 0.25 mm). Electric discharge is established between electrically conducting wire and workpiece to make fine cut, slots, and produce other geometrical features. A controlled relative movement of workpiece (with respect to wire) with help of CNC machine table helps to trace the path (of wire) along which cut is to be made by wire-EDM. Approach wise, W-EDM is like the nibbling process of sheet metal cutting except that material removal in W-EDM based on melting and evaporation while nibbling is based on shearing of material for cutting. Since wire is subjected to thermal damage due to intense heat generated by discharges therefore it frequently breaks during machining which in turn affects the productivity.

4.8 Plasma Arc Machining

The plasma arc machining (PAM) is mainly used for machining/ cutting of electrical conducting metallic material by melting and blowing away the molten metal using a high velocity plasma jet. Heat generated by an electric arc established between tungsten electrode and workpiece / nozzle (as per type of plasma formation approach) is used to produce plasma. Plasma is formed by supply plasma forming gas (CO_2, Air) through arc followed by its constriction (reduction in cross-section of nozzle and increase of energy density) as plasma gas flows through the nozzle (Fig. 4.24). The constriction of plasma increases the power density and accelerates the plasma to high velocity thereby increasing its capability to melt, penetrate and cut the thick plates rapidly. During the plasma cutting an appropriate controlled environment like water, nitrogen, carbon dioxide, argon etc. can be provided to protect hot cut edges of the workpiece from the atmospheric gases to improve the quality of metal cutting. Like EDM, plasma arc machining also uses DCRP polarity to a) increase the heat generation on workpiece side thereby enhancing cutting speed and b) increase tungsten electrode life. Similar to EDM, PAM surface also shows recast layer and heat affected zone. Cut edges show kerfs and drag. Debris/dross deposited at the lower side of the cut edge needs to be removed. Relatively high heat input used during PAM causes wide HAZ coupled with significant change in metallurgical, mechanical properties besides developing residual stress. Hardenable steel mostly get hardened while precipitation hardened metals are softened.

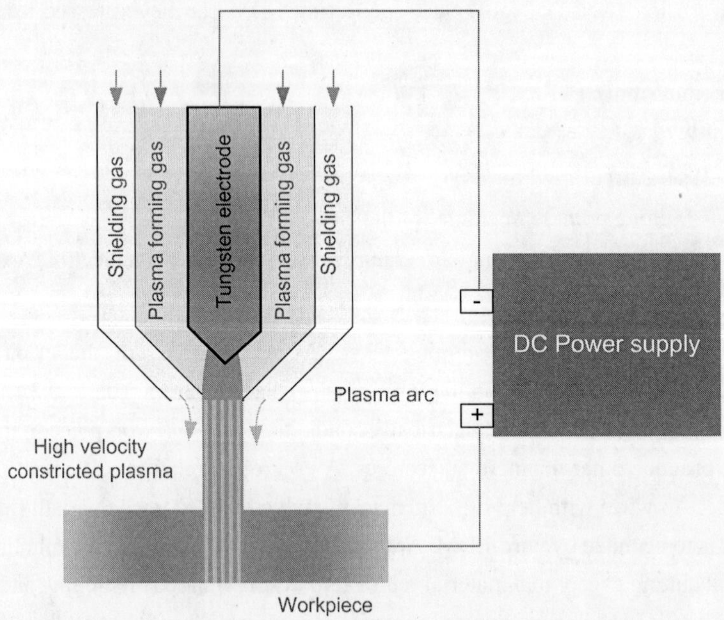

Fig. 4.24 Schematic showing plasma arc machining system.

All the factors related to plasma arc machining affecting heat input and ability to blow away molten metal determine the capability of plasma arc machining. Broadly, there are two types of factors related to PAM affecting cuttability namely arc and plasma. Arc related process parameters are current, power, speed, tungsten electrode, type of PAM machine (transferred / non-transferred arc plasma) while those related to plasma are plasma forming gas, nozzle design, stand-off distance, type of cover/shielding (argon, carbon dioxide, under-water environment). Relative importance of various PAM process parameters on material removal is shown in Fig. 4.25.

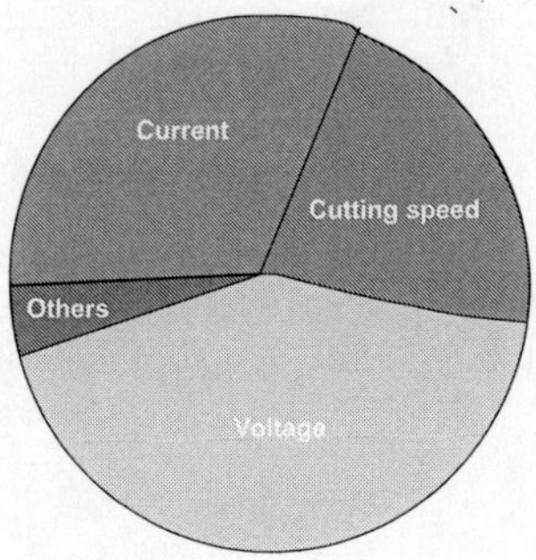

Fig. 4.25 Schematic showing relative effect of various PAM process parameters on material removal

Increase of arc power, and heat input (by increasing current, voltage, ionization potential of plasma forming gas and reducing travel speed) increases the penetration depth, MRR and ability to cut thick plates. However, current and stand-off distance should be optimized for the maximum MRR (Fig. 4.26).

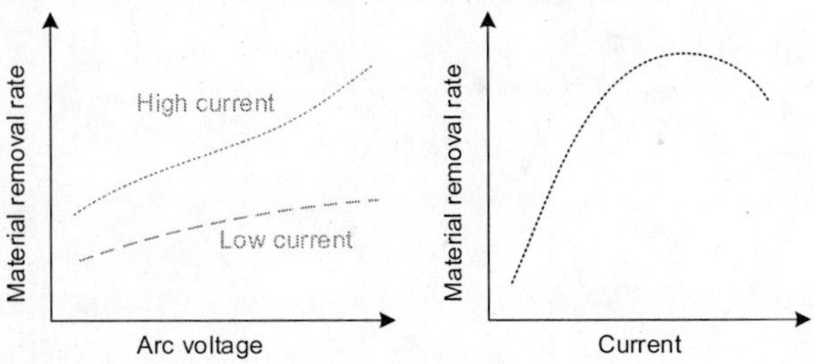

a) b)

Fig. 4.26 Schematic showing effect of various PAM process parameters on MRR surface variation with a) arc voltage with varying current and b) current.

Stand-off distance

It is the distance of nozzle from the work piece surface (5-10 mm). Increase in stand-off distance reduces the penetration, damage to the nozzle and increases width of cut (Fig. 4.27 a, b).

Cutting speed

There is direct relation between the metal thickness, arc power and cutting speed. Increase in cutting speed reduces the depth of penetration, increases drag of the melting front at the bottom and reduces width of cut (Fig. 4.27c). Optimum cutting speed can be obtained using energy balance based on the following relation:

$\eta \,.\, I.\, V = \rho \,.\, t.\, \Delta S \,.\, Vc$

Where

η is thermal efficiency plasma (% of heat transferred to work piece)

I is welding current (A)

V is the arc voltage (V)

ρ is the density of metal (kg/m^3)

t thickness of section being cut (m)

ΔS is the heat required for melting of unit volume of material (J/m^3)

Vc is the cutting speed m/s

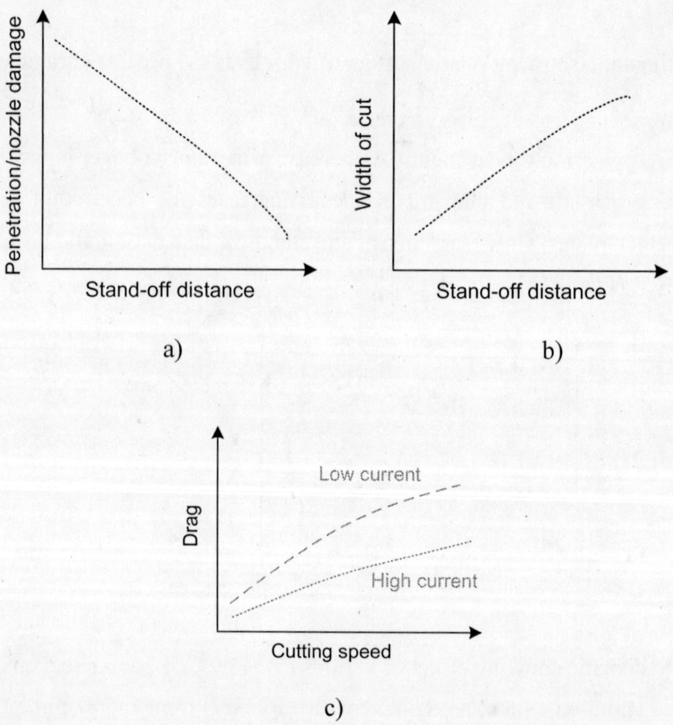

Fig. 4.27 Schematic showing effect of a) stand-off distance on penetration / nozzle damage and b) stand-off distance on width of cut and c) cutting speed on drag at bottom of cut edge obtained during PAM.

Plasma gas

Quality of machined surface (cut edge) and cutting speed depends on input process parameter (current, speed, voltage) apart from thermo-physical, and chemical properties of plasma forming gas. Individual gas or a mixture of gases (argon, hydrogen, nitrogen, oxygen and air) are commonly used as plasma forming gases. Hydrogen has high heat capacity at low temperature (3700°C). Due to high thermal conductivity of hydrogen, it effectively transfers heat to work piece surface hence hydrogen generated plasma produces higher cutting speed than other plasma forming gases. Therefore, hydrogen suits for cutting of thick sections and metal of higher thermal conductivity such as aluminium and copper. Use hydrogen-containing gases such ammonia (NH_3) is preferred over hydrogen due to economy, availability and no risk of explosion. Hydrogen plasma damages the thermal insulation of nozzle; therefore, it reduces the life of nozzle.

Argon is heavier and therfore it forms stable protective shield over the nozzle due to lower thermal conductivity. Type of gas and flow rate depends on the metal to be processed and section size. Oxygen in air plasma however causes oxidation of molten metal coupled possibility of exothermic reactions. Therefore, air plasma results in cutting speed about 1.5 to 2.5 times greater than the nitrogen plasma. Argon is expensive, low enthalpy, low arc voltage gas, hence it is preferred for machining of non-ferrous metal sensitive to the environment. The MRR and surface roughness / quality of cut edge are in general inversely related due to physical damage experienced by the workpiece material during thermal/chemical/mechanical machining as shown in Fig. 4.28.

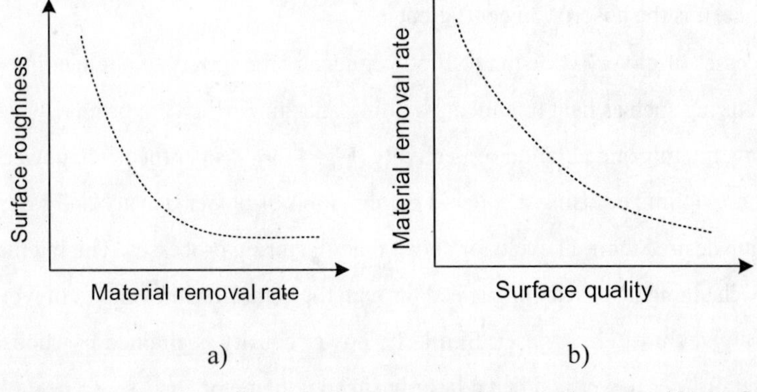

Fig. 4.28 Schematic showing effect of a) MRR on surface roughness and b) surface quality on MRR.

4.9 Laser Beam Machining

Laser and electron beam machining to a great extent work on the similar principle of ablation (evaporation) for controlled removal of the material for machining using extremely high power density (10^6 to 10^8 W /mm^2) beam directed over a very small area (few tens to hundreds of micrometres diameter). Laser (light amplification and stimulated emission of radiations) is a coherent beam of electro-magnetic radiations (wavelength in range of 0.1 to 70 μm); while for laser machining is performed using laser of 0.4 to 0.6 μm wavelength. Laser depending upon power (kW) and focused to a very small spot diameter (~40 to 200 μm) can result in very high-power density (10^6 to 10^8W/mm^2) without much divergence. Therefore, laser machining helps in creating fine micron size holes (up to 250 μm) and cutting narrow grooves and slots accurately. Laser machines are commonly named based on source of laser such as solid state laser using ruby crystal / Nd: YAG laser, gas laser (mixture of helium and neon, carbon dioxide). CO_2 laser is relatively high power than solid state lasers. Low power laser beams are used for marking on the metallic and non-metallic materials.

Heat generated by laser beam directed on the surface of workpiece depend on its absorption / reflection. Absorbed laser propagates into the crystals, then energy is gradually transferred to the lattice atoms in form of heat. Intensity of laser beam and its absorption decreases with increase in depth from the surface. In fact, most of the energy of the laser beam is absorbed by near the surface layer (0.01 μm) to generate heat and cause the melting/ablation of surface layers.

Laser Beam Intensity $I(d) = I_0 e^{-ud}$

Where $I(d)$ is the intensity of beam at the depth d from the surface, I_0 is the intensity of beam at the surface, u is the absorption coefficient

These processes offer very wide range of power density for variety of engineering applications in manufacturing such as heat treatment, welding, machine which are primarily based on solid state heating, melting and ablation respectively (Fig. 4.29). As per the need, power density and heat input are optimized using a suitable combination of power density and laser interaction time to attain desired thermal cycle for above manufacturing processes. The interaction time is realized by changing laser scanning speed through the controlled movement of workpiece with respect to a given position of laser. Similarly, power density is attained by choosing suitable type of laser or laser power and beam laser beam spot diameter.

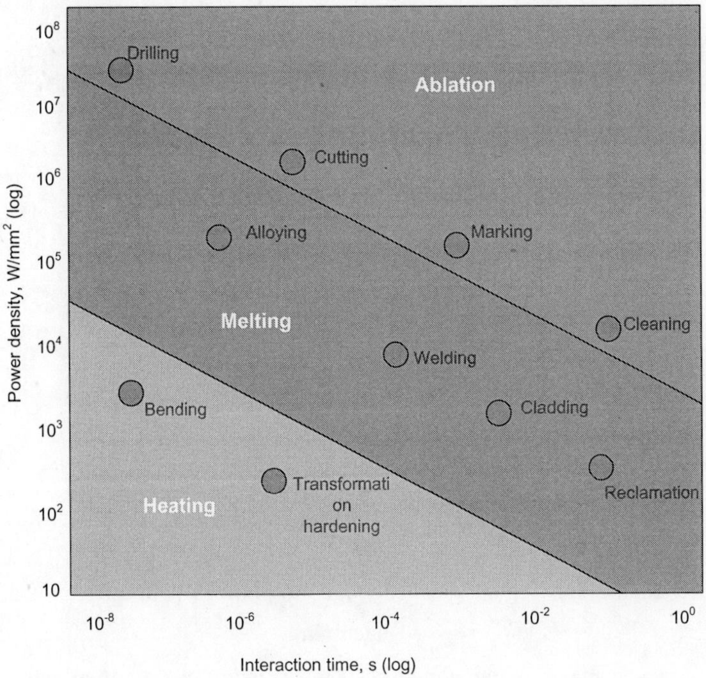

Fig. 4.29 Power density and laser interaction time relationship for various manufacturing processes including machining, welding and heat treatment.

The beam diameter, power, scanning speed (relative movement between workpiece and beam) affect the heat input and rate of material removal. Since the rate of delivery of energy due to high power density is very high therefore usually laser / electron beam scanning speed is very high compared to other processes like gas cutting, plasma arc cutting. Protection of the workpiece surface from atmospheric gases during laser beam machining using suitable shielding gas like argon, carbon dioxide improves surface finish and appearance. Unlike, electron beam machining, laser beam machining does not need vacuum. Laser beam (as per laser power, spot diameter, and laser-surface interaction time as per scanning speed) must deliver sufficient energy to raise the temperature of workpiece surface high enough to cause melting and evaporation (ablation) for material removal. Increasing laser power (kW), reducing spot diameter (μm) and reducing scanning speed increases the heat input (energy delivered/absorbed) which in turn increases the depth of penetration and material removal rate. The laser machining for best quality cut is expected to remove the material from the workpiece using ablation approach but practically melting and ablation in normal cutting both contribute appreciably. Melting of the metal in turn results in cut edge similar to the plasma machining but with the less severity in terms impurity/dross deposition and drag lines which in turn produce a smoother laser machined surface of better quality (Fig. 4.30).

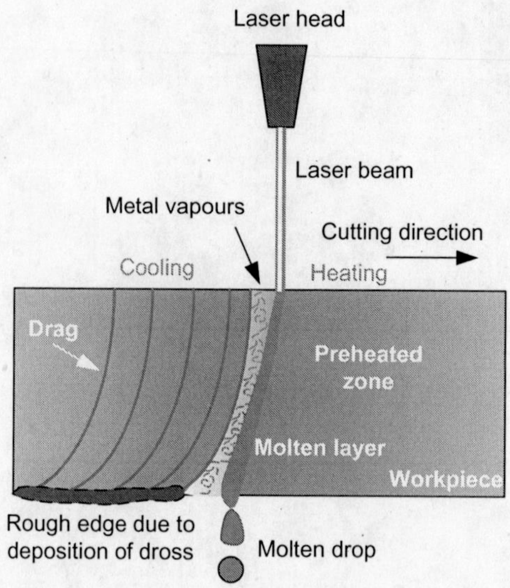

Fig. 4.30 Schematic showing a typical cut edge morphology with different features of laser machining.

Kerf width is very common parameters used as measured of quality of cut which indicates the width wherefrom material is removed during cutting processes. Laser / electron beam machining results in much lower kerf width than other processes like plasma cutting, flame cutting, and water jet cutting (Fig. 4.31).

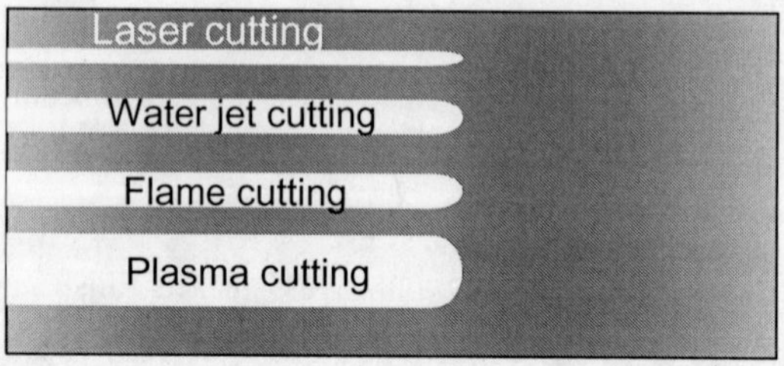

Fig. 4.31 Schematic showing a variation in kerf width in workpiece cut by different processes.

Increase of laser power and section thickness in general increases the kerf width due to increased width of zone wherefrom material is removed during laser cutting. Reducing laser interaction time by increasing cutting speed decreases the kerf with (Fig. 4.32). Variation in kerf width with laser power and scanning speed is mainly attributed to to change in energy delivered/ heat input affecting melting and ablation. Increase of heat input with increase of laser power and reducing scanning speed causes melting/ ablation of wider zone leading high kerf width.

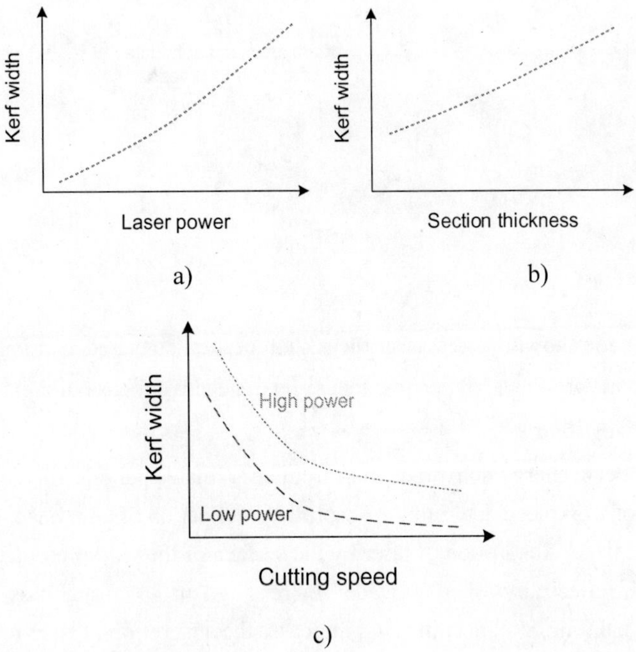

Fig. 4.32 Schematic showing effect process variation in process parameters on kerf width a) laser power, b) section thickness and c) cutting speed during laser machining.

The focusing of laser beam on the surface affects the desired power density, affecting material removal mechanisms, speed of cutting, heat / energy delivered per unit time. The position/location focus of laser beam with respect to the surface of workpiece can be zero, positive and negative. Focus of beam at the surface, above the surface and below surface results in zero, positive and negative focus respectively (Fig. 4.33). These factors in turn affect the quality of cut, cut edge morphology and kerf width as evident from the following schematic.

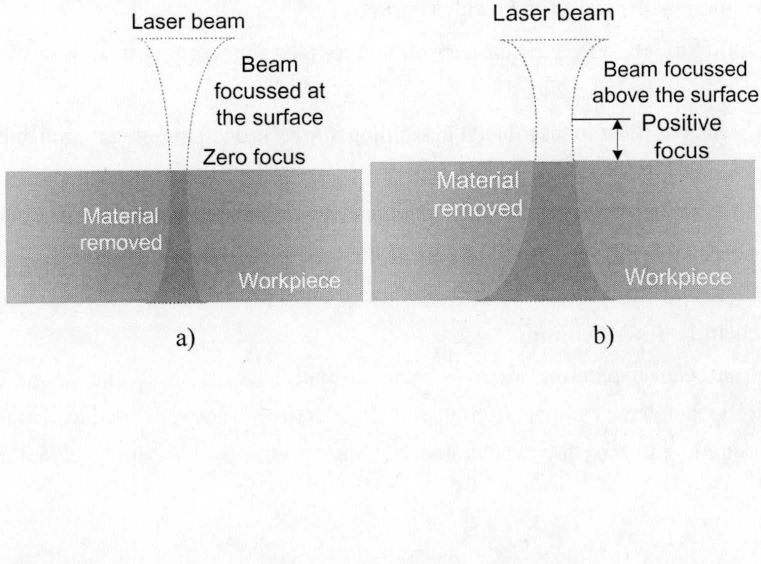

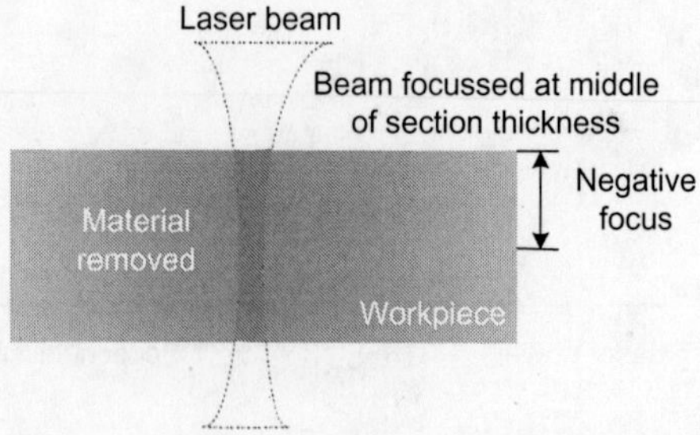

c)

Fig. 4.33 Schematic showing effect laser focus spot location on cut edge morphology including on kerf width a) zero focus, b) positive focus and c) negative focus during laser machining.

Laser beam absorption

However, laser beam energy delivered (apart from laser related parameters) depends on surface characteristics of workpiece determining absorption / reflection of laser beam directed over the surface of workpiece. Absorption of laser by the surface of the workpiece depends on surface roughness and reflectivity of workpiece. Increasing surface roughness and decreasing reflectivity (by painting, shot peening etc.) increases the absorption of laser for heat generation and melting/ablation. Laser beam can be directed on the workpiece continuously or in form of pulses. Laser machining uses pulse laser. The duration of laser pulse should be long enough to facilitate melting / ablation.

The application of laser machining includes drilling, cutting, piercing holes in very thin sheets e.g. making holes of 25 μm size in 25 μm thin brass foil. High thickness and high thermal conductivity and low melting point materials make laser machining difficult.

Advantages

- Low heat input during laser machining (as compared to other thermal energy based process like EDM, PAM) results in narrow heat affected zone which in turn also reduces the thermal distortion and residual stress.
- Cutting in any-odd position is possible provided the target surface is in direct line of sight from the laser gun.
- Absence of force in laser beam machining allows processing of very thin and very hard materials
- Very low heat input due to use of high power density refines grain structure of near surface layers due to rapid cooling of the recast layer and HAZ, which to some extent reduces the need of further strengthening treatment.

4.10 Electron Beam Machining

The electron beam machining involves removal material by melting and evaporation using intense heat generated by impact of high velocity electrons. Electrons produced at the cathode by thermo-ionic emission are accelerated to high velocity by applying accelerating voltage

(100kV) across cathode and anode. The beam of electrons of high velocity is passed through (electron focussing section) vacuum tube to ensure that beam retains kinetic energy (KE) in the electron gun. Impingement of high KE electron beam on to the workpiece generates heat (by converts the kinetic energy into thermal energy) and increases the temperature in a very short interval of time (Fig. 4.34).

Rapid and high rise in temperature of workpiece surface causes fusion and ablation / evaporation of metal from the work surface. The progressive effect of electron beam during the machining is shown in Fig. 4.35. The material is removed in controlled way to get the desired shape by appropriate relative movement between beam and workpiece (either beam is moved using magnetic coil or work piece is moved using CNC). In short, electrons are generated using electron gun using thermo-ionic emission followed by acceleration, focussing and directing over the surface of workpiece. In Electron beam machining is performed in vacuum environment for effective, and efficient machining. Electron beam machining in atmospheric conditions is not effective because interaction / impingement of electrons (in electron beam) with atmospheric gases reduces kinetic energy associated with electron beam and its ability to cut the materials. Low to high vacuum (10^{-2} to 10^{-5} Torr) is frequently used as per application. Net heat input used for electron beam machining by ablation is very low (in vacuum), therefore machined surface is very neat and clean with very limited effect on mechanical and metallurgical characteristics due to formation of thin heat affected zone.

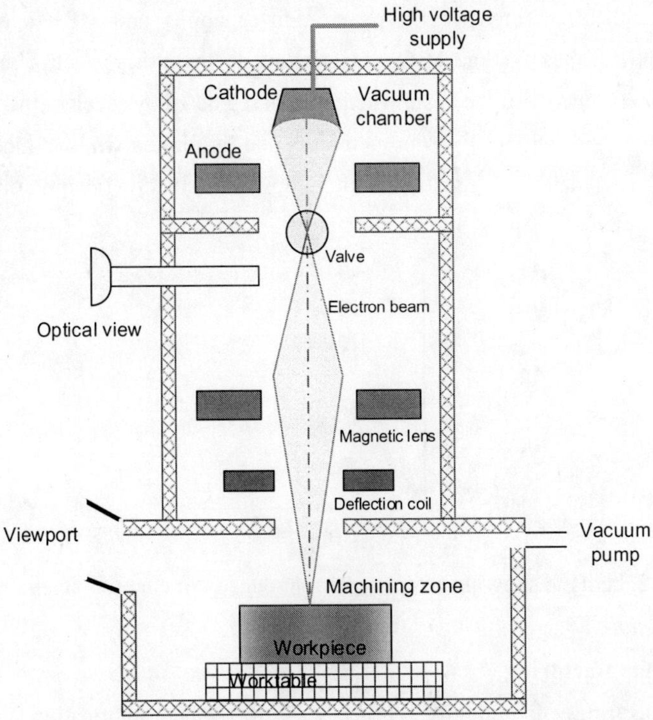

Fig. 4.34 Schematic showing electron beam machine system

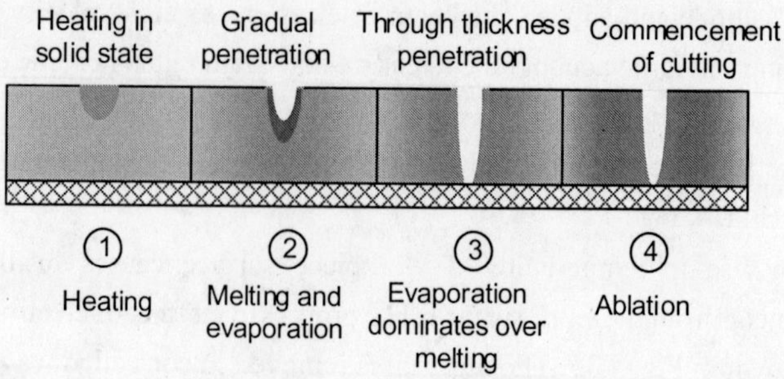

Fig. 4.35 Schematic showing progressive effective of electron beam during electron beam machining.

Power density of electron beam affects the MRR and heat input used for removing a given volume of materials. In general, power density and heat input are inversely related. Power density of electron beam directly determined by beam spot diameter. The beam spot diameter (20-50 μm) depends on beam current, accelerating voltage (affecting kinetic energy of electrons) and stand-off distance (electron gun to workpiece surface distance). Increasing accelerating voltage (50 kV to 150 kV) reduces the beam spot diameter which in turn increases the power density. Increasing power density increases the materials removal rate and speed of machining while increase of beam current and stand-off distance increases the beam spot size. Increasing beam current increases its penetration capability and MRR due to high power density and KE of beam (Fig. 4.36). Penetration depth during electron beam machining depends on kinetic energy of the beam which in turn regulated by accelerating voltage. During EBM at low power density (10^5 W/mm^2) molten pool is formed while at high power density ($10^7 - 10^8$ W/mm^2) material is predominantly removed by ablation (evaporation) and very less by melting.

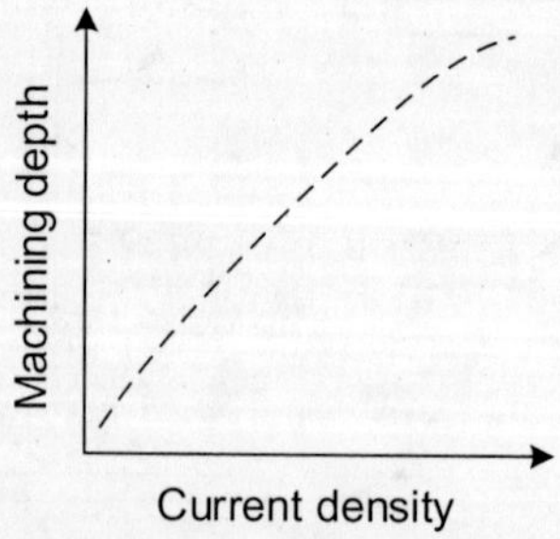

Fig. 4.36 Schematic showing effect of current density in electron beam machining on machining depth

4.11 Micro-manufacturing

Micro-manufacturing is family processes for the fabrication of micro-size feature/product/component using various mechanical/thermal/electrochemical manufacturing processes. Micro-manufacturing helps in making miniaturized products coupled with many advantages such as saving in material and energy consumption, light-weighting, enhanced sensitivity and favourable long terms economics due to low cost-to-performance ratio. The micro-manufactured products are smaller than 10 mm in size with close tolerance of less than $\pm$ 10 µm (ranging from 0.1 to 10 µm). Micro-parts are usually produced on a silicon wafer but these can be made of others materials as well depending upon processes used. Micro-manufacturing processes broadly fall in two categories a) bulk micro-manufacturing b) surface micro-manufacturing.

4.11.1 Bulk Micro-manufacturing

Bulk micro-manufacturing is a subtractive manufacturing process involving removal of material from the substrate to create desired 3-D geometrical features and structures. The material is removed by selective etching of silicon wafer. The etching process can be dry or wet. The wet etching dissolves the (unmasked) substrate material selectively (while other areas that are masked to avoid any removal of material) using suitable etchant / chemical solution for material removal. Dry etching relies on plasma for material removal to create the geometrical features. The material removal from unmasked areas by etching of substrate creates angled cavities/pits. The masking of substrate by suitable material" after (wafer surface) is done using photolithography. This approach is inexpensive, and suits for relatively simple geometrical micro-features. Sequential steps of bulk micro-manufacturing are shown in Fig. 4.37.

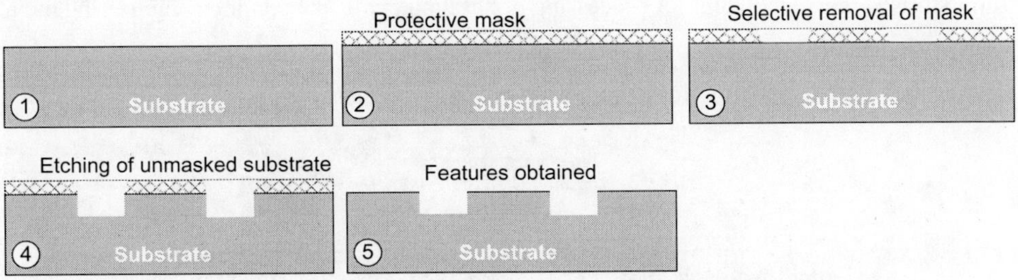

Fig. 4.37 Schematic showing sequential steps of bulk micro-manufacturing

4.11.2 Surface Micro-manufacturing

Surface micro-manufacturing is an additive process wherein layers are deposited over the substrate. A combination of steps like masking, depositing sacrificial layer (s), etching, depositing functional layer followed by removal of sacrificial layer. In other words, first apply sacrificial layer on substrate, then shape it with controlled material removal approach using etching, then develop functional/ structural layer over the processed sacrificial layer, lastly remove sacrificial layer, creating internal/hollow desired geometrical features on the substrate. Sequential steps of surface micro-manufacturing are shown in Fig. 4.38.

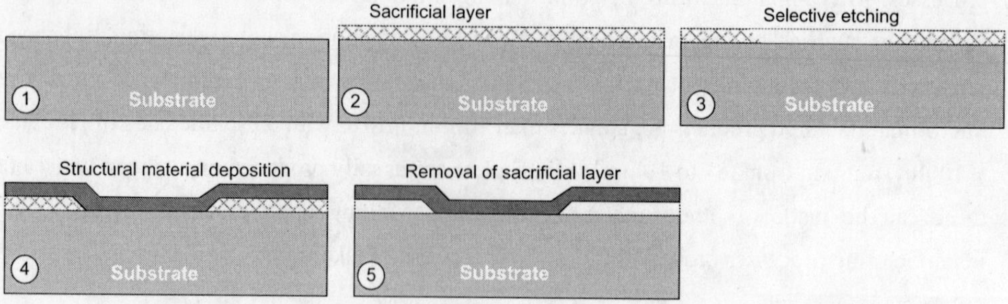

Fig. 4.38 Schematic showing sequential steps of surface micro-manufacturing.

4.11.3 Overview of micro-manufacturing

Micro-manufacturing can be additive (controlled layered deposition, micro-joining), subtractive (micro-machining by shearing using cutting tools, thermal cutting by melting / ablation by electric discharge, laser, electron beam machining, chemical/electrochemical (selective etching/dissolution to remove material), micro-forming and, micro/nano-finishing (lapping, polishing, abrasive flow finishing etc.). Schematic diagram shows classification of micro-manufacturing and respective processes (Fig. 4.39). A simple scaling down of conventional manufacturing processes does not help in micro-manufacturing due to challenges related to finish, dimensional control and close tolerance issues. The system required for micro-manufacturing must be robust and rigid (free from vibration / chatter etc.) to ensure desired finish, dimensional accuracy and tolerance. These processes are used to manufacture the miniaturised fine component for processing of hard materials like common engineering metals and alloy, glasses, silicon wafers and ceramic materials and used in the field of aerospace, electronics, computers, mobiles, automotive, robotics, medical etc.

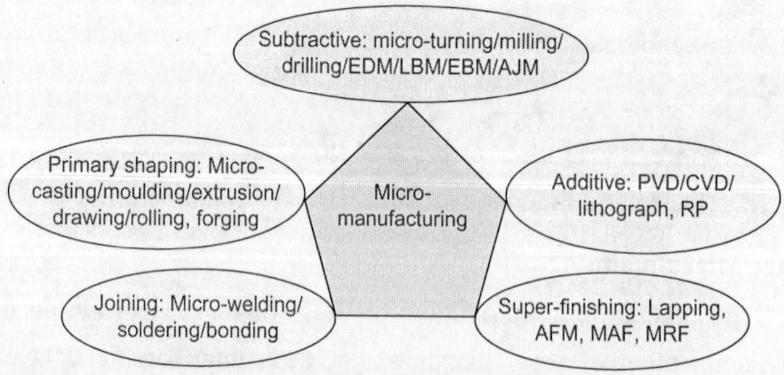

Fig. 4.39 Schematic showing classification of micro-manufacturing processes

The following section highlights few unconventional micro-machining processes along with their applications.

Mechanical micro-machining

- Micro-milling using tiny cutters to create complex geometries.

- Micro-turning using fine turning tool for producing miniature cylindrical parts.
- Micro drilling using very fine drill bits for creating highly precise, fine holes.
- Micro grinding uses fine abrasive particles for producing optical components, micro lenses.
- Micro ultrasonic Machining (Micro-USM) using fine tool for machining of materials like ceramics, glass, and hard metals for complex shapes and features in semiconductor and MEMS

Thermal micro-machining

- Micro electrical discharge machining (Micro-EDM) uses fine electrode for producing complex shapes with high aspect ratio e.g. micro-moulds, dies, and precision components.
- Micro laser beam machining (Micro-LBM) fine laser beam for machining of materials like metals, plastics, and ceramics especially in the semiconductor industry for circuit board production by creating micro-scale features with high aspect ratios.
- Micro electron beam machining (Micro-EBM) micron size spot diameter of electron beam for producing micro-sized features with complex geometries in the aerospace and medical industries for critical components.

Chemical and electrochemical micro machining

This category of micro-machining processes use chemical and electrochemical reactions for material removal, and provide distinct advantages in terms of precision and surface finish.

Chemical-micro-machining uses controlled chemical reactions for etching to produce fine features in micro-fabrication of metals, glass, and silicon.

Electrochemical-micro-machining (ECMM) uses anodic dissolution of workpiece in an electrolytic cell for precision machining to produce micro-components for applications in aerospace, medical, and automotive industries.

Hybrid micro-machining

Hybrid micro-machining involves a combination of different unconventional machining processes, to take the unique benefits of each method and enhance machining performance like electro-magnetic-abrasive finishing.

Assisted hybrid micro machining

Ultrasonic vibration and heat assisted micro-machining to enhance capabilities in terms of high MRR with reduced tool wear. This leads to cost-effective manufacturing.

Micro abrasive jet machining (Micro-AJM)

This process uses high-velocity abrasive particles for material erosion removal of brittle materials like glass and ceramics.

UNIT SUMMARY

This unit gives the concepts, and approaches, of making products of difficult to process materials using unconventional manufacturing and micro-manufacturing processes. Additionally, need of unconventional and micro-manufacturing processes has been presented. The principle, material removal mechanisms and important relevant process parameters of common unconventional manufacturing processes namely abrasive jet machining, water jet machining, ultrasonic machining, electrochemical machining, electric discharge machining, plasma arc machining, laser and electron beam machining have been explained using schematics. Further, influence of relevant process parameters of unconventional manufacturing processes on process performance characteristics such as MRR, and surface roughness has been described. Additionally, approaches of micro-manufacturing namely bulk and surface micro-manufacturing have been presented with sequential steps.

EXERCISE

Questions for self-assessment

1. Micro-manufacturing refers to making products of
    a. Micron-size
    b. Micron-size features
    c. Both micron size parts and features
    d. Only soft materials of micron size
2. Unconventional manufacturing processes in which material removal mechanism is ablation.
    a. Electro-chemical machining b. Plasma arc machining
    c. Laser beam machining d. All of these
3. Unconventional manufacturing process which produces minimum kerf width is
    a. Abrasive jet machining b. Laser beam machining
    c. Plasma arc machining d. All of these
4. Unconventional manufacturing process based on material removal by impact of abrasive is.
    a. Ultrasonic machining b. Laser beam machining
    c. Plasma arc machining d. All of these
5. The material removal in electrochemical machining governed by
    a. Newtons law b. Garry's law
    c. Archard's law d. Faradays law

6. Increase of normal load during an unconventional manufacturing process increases the MRR is
   a. Ultrasonic machining b. Abrasive jet machining
   c. Plasma arc machining d. All of these
7. Increase of current flow during unconventional manufacturing process increases the MRR is
   a. Electric discharge machining b. Plasma arc machining
   c. Electrochemical machining d. All of these
8. Recast layer on the machined surface is formed during.
   a. Abrasive jet machining b. Electric discharge machining
   c. Electrochemical machining d. All of these
9. Addition of abrasive in water jet machining results in
   a. Lower MRR
   b. Higher MRR
   c. Material removal remains unaffected.
   d. MRR first decreases then increases.
10. Unconventional manufacturing process which uses maximum power density
    a. Abrasive jet machining b. Electron beam machining
    c. Plasma arc machining d. Electric discharge machining

Answers of Multiple Choice Questions

Key for MCQ: 1 c, 2 c, 3 b, 4 a, 5 d, 6 a, 7 d, 8 b, 9 b, 10 b

Short and Long Answer Type Questions

1. What are conditions when unconventional manufacturing processes are selected over conventional processes?
2. What are two broad approaches of micro-manufacturing?
3. What is the principle of abrasive jet machining?
4. Explain the effect of abrasive jet machining process parameters on process performance characteristics such as cut edge feature, MRR and surface roughness?
5. Provide an overview of micro-manufacturing approaches and specific processes along with their applications.
6. What is the principle of water jet machining?
7. Explain the effect of water jet machining process parameters on process performance characteristics such as cut edge feature, MRR and surface roughness?

8. What is the principle of ultrasonic machining?
9. Explain the effect of ultrasonic machining process parameters on process performance characteristics such as cut edge feature, MRR and surface roughness?
10. What type of material is preferably processed by ultrasonic machining.
11. What are different components of electrochemical machining and explain their role in machining.
12. What is the principle of electric discharge machining?
13. Explain the effect of electric discharge machining process parameters on process performance characteristics such as cut edge feature, MRR and surface roughness?
14. What is the principle of plasma arc machining?
15. Explain the effect of plasma arc machining process parameters on process performance characteristics such as cut edge feature, MRR and surface roughness?
16. What is the principle of laser and electron beam machining?
17. Explain the effect of laser beam machining process parameters on process performance characteristics such as cut edge feature, MRR and surface roughness?
18. How do we select the power density and laser interaction time in laser material processing? Explain with the help of suitable schematic diagram.

KNOW MORE

Explore and identify the newer unconventional manufacturing process and micro-manufacturing process developed recently and industrial products / parts are made by these processes'. Try to visit relevant industries having unconventional manufacturing process and micro-manufacturing. Learn about recent progress and development around unconventional manufacturing process and micro-manufacturing process using information available in the public domain. Efforts may be made to learn and gain the expertise on them. Try establishing chronological development in the field of unconventional manufacturing process and micro-manufacturing process.

Scan me!

SUGGESTED RESOURCES FOR FURTHER READING/LEARNING

1. D K Dwivedi, Fundamentals of Metal Joining, Springer Nature, (2021)
2. S Kalpakjian, S R Schmid, Manufacturing Engineering and Technology, Pearson (2018)
3. M P Groover, Fundamentals of Modern Manufacturing, John Wiley and Sons, (2010)
4. D K Dwivedi, Dissimilar metal joining, Springer Nature (2024)
5. D K Dwivedi, Surface engineering, Springer Nature (2018)
6. A Ghosh, A K Malik, Manufacturing science, East-West Press (2010)
7. D K Dwivedi, Materials Engineering, AICTE, (2023)
8. D K Dwivedi, NPTEL Course "Joining Technologies for Metals": https://onlinecourses.nptel.ac.in/noc23_me130/preview
9. D K Dwivedi, NPTEL Course "Fundamentals of Manufacturing Processes" https://archive.nptel.ac.in/courses/112/107/112107219/

5 Additive Manufacturing Processes

Unit Specific / Learning Objective

The objective of this unit is to understand the following aspects

- To learn about the scope of additive manufacturing processes
- To introduce the concept, and capabilities of the additive manufacturing process
- To learn about the classification of additive manufacturing processes
- To develop understanding on principles and approaches of common additive manufacturing processes for manufacturing various products.
- To learn about additive manufacturing process suitable for polymer, metal, ceramic materials processing

Additionally, a few questions for self-assessment based on fundamentals have been included in this chapter. These questions are based on application, comprehension, analysis and synthesis. Suggested further reading and reference have been included for deep learners and readers.

Rationale

Manufacturing a complex geometry component made of a wide range of materials (polymer, metal, ceramics, composites) in limited volume is highly uneconomical and challenging by conventional manufacturing routes. Recent developments in additive manufacturing have revolutionized the ways component manufacturing is done in certain sectors like aerospace, automotive and electronics. Additive manufacturing has proven a very cost effective and useful for making complex parts and prototypes in product development stage. It is, therefore, important to familiarize and learn about this relatively new approach of manufacturing, where 3D components are developed using layer-by-layer deposition techniques. Learning and awareness about newer manufacturing technologies will equip mechanical/production/industrial engineers with the latest tools and techniques for efficient and cost-effective manufacturing of products for consumption by society.

Pre-Requisites

Physics: (Class XII)

Learning outcomes

U5-O1: Ability to understand approaches for making complex geometry products in low volume using additive manufacturing.

U5-O2: Ability to select appropriate additive manufacturing process as per material and size of component to be made.

U5-O3: Ability to make products of polymers, metals, and ceramics using additive manufacturing.

U5-O4: Ability to decide when additive manufacturing can be applied economically.

U5-O5: Ability to understand and anticipate possible issues and quality considering procedure adopted for additive manufacturing.

Unit-5: Outcomes	EXPECTED MAPPING WITH COURSE OUTCOMES (1- Weak Correlation; 2- Medium correlation; 3- Strong Correlation)					
	CO-1	CO-2	CO-3	CO-4	CO-5	CO-6
U5-O1	3	1	-	-	-	-
U5-O2	3	2	-	-	-	-
U5-O3	3	3	-	-	-	-
U5-O4	1	3	-	-	-	-
U5-O5	1	3	-	-	-	-

CO

1. Understand the different conventional and unconventional manufacturing methods employed for making different products
2. To motivate and challenge students to understand and develop an appreciation of the processes in correlation with material properties which change the shape, size and form of the raw materials into the desirable product.

5.1 Introduction

Additive manufacturing is a relatively new manufacturing process and is still in the development stage for a wide variety of materials. Currently, it offers limited capabilities to process only a few low melting temperature materials. The additive manufacturing technology has matured enough to process low melting temperature materials like polymers, and it is considered to be ready for industrial applications. Additive manufacturing makes complex design products by reducing material cost and production time (Fig. 5.1). Further, it allows manufacturing of high strength and low weight products using controlled porosity and infill density. These are important aspects for many industries, such as medical, automotive, and aerospace.

A lot of R&D is still needed in additive manufacturing for processing of high melting temperature materials for large-scale industrial production to manufacture common parts, and goods. Currently, the process is preferred to satisfy the demand for a variety of products in limited quantity made of low melting temperature materials like polymer (Fig. 5.2).

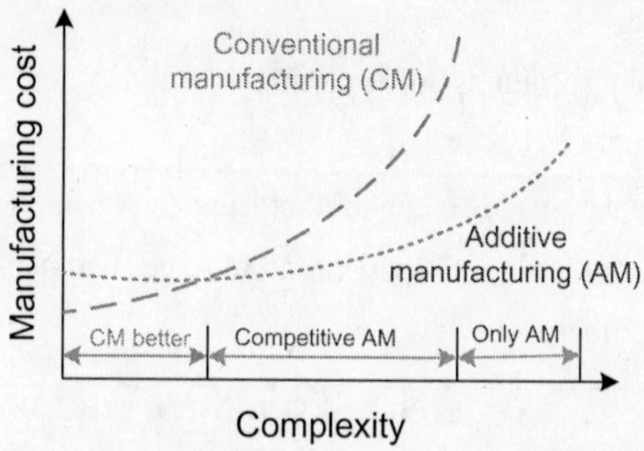

Fig. 5.1 Schematic showing the importance of conventional manufacturing and additive manufacturing with regard to manufacturing cost as a function of product design complexity

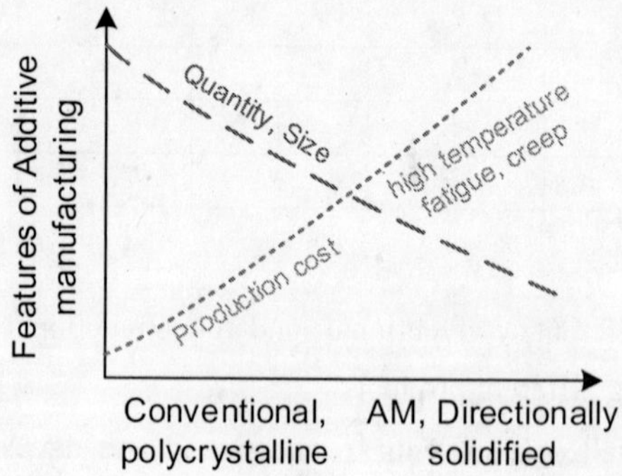

Fig. 5.2 Schematic showing the influence of conventional processed and additive manufactured products with the controlled structure on various manufacturing aspects (cost, size, quantity and mechanical properties)

Additive manufacturing is a generic name for a group of manufacturing processes which develop three-dimensional (3D) products using layer-by-layer (2D) deposition approach in a sequential manner. Additive manufacturing relies on the firmly bonding each layer (during deposition) with the previously deposited layer. The bond between two consecutive layers must be free from defects (void, pores, impurities, gases, cracks, inclusions). Further, the bond is developed through polymerization and curing in case of polymers, metallurgical interactions and diffusion in case of metals. The inter-layer bonding must be good and continuous for consistency and uniformity of the mechanical and other properties.

This technology was initially developed for low melting temperature polymeric materials only due to a) ease of melting, softening, forming and depositing and b) rapid curing (liquid to solid transformation) using suitable environments like heating, ultra-violet radiation, etc. Subsequently, the development of novel additive manufacturing processes like binder jetting, material jetting facilitated the development of 3D components of metals, ceramics, composites, sand, concrete, etc. However, metallic components are preferably developed using direct energy deposition, metal jetting, sheet lamination and laser/electron beam powder-bed additive manufacturing processes. Metallic components made by additive manufacturing have potential to offer better mechanical properties than conventional cast products due to better control over structure and its directionality in additive manufactured metallic components (Fig.5.3).

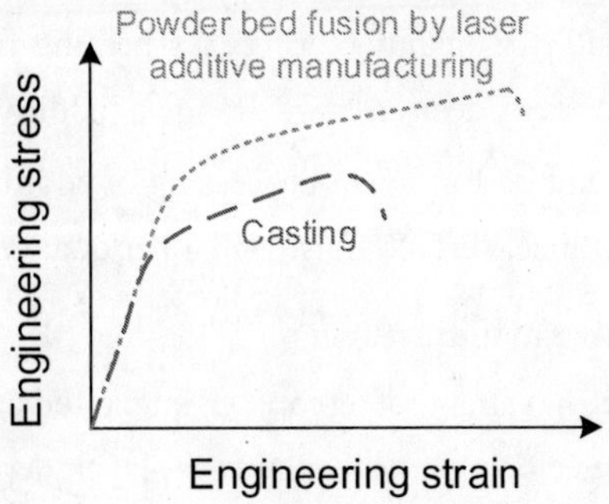

Fig. 5.3 Schematic showing relative mechanical behaviour of components made by conventional casting and additive manufacturing.

5.2 Steps in additive manufacturing

To manufacture a product using additive manufacturing approach irrespective of component material, size and shape the following steps are adopted:

- Development of a suitable 3D geometric model (CAD file) using software like CATIA, CAD, and FE. 3D camera systems are also used for developing geometrical model with help of existing products using reverse engineering.
- Convert the 3D geometric CAD file of the component to STL (Stereolithographic) file.
- Performing suitable slicing of STL file into the layers slicing determines how the material will be deposited layer-by-layer. Slicing can be unidirectional, bidirectional or multi-directional as per the complexity of the product. It determines the thickness of the layer to be deposited in each pass. The thickness of layer can be constant or variable in case of adaptable slicing. Thickness of layer affects the productivity and accuracy and, finishing of components especially on the curved surfaces. Thin layer deposition increases accuracy and surface finish but decreases productivity, as it increase number of passes needed to build up the product. In case of 3D metal printing, thickness affects the microstructure and mechanical properties also due to change in cooling conditions. That leads to variation in solidification structure and solid-state transformation in turn determines the final microstructure of the developed component (Fig. 5.4).

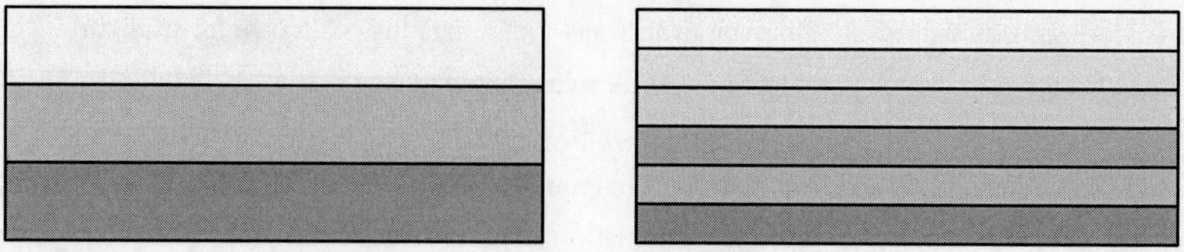

a) b)

Fig. 5.4 Schematic showing the effect of slice/layer thickness on the number of passes required

- The material is deposited (in 2D form) layer-by-layer to develop the (3D) component using suitable method of additive manufacturing. As per the material to be deposited, job complexity, and productivity desired a wide range of additive technologies could be used.
- Clean the component and perform post-processing of additively manufactured product to obtain the desired tolerance, surface finish and other quality characteristics, if required.

5.3 Requirement of additive manufacturing

Additive manufacturing is a variant of computer-integrated manufacturing with a unique approach to component development using layer-by-layer deposition of material. It needs relevant software and computer-integrated system with a suitable machine, which allows layer-by-layer material deposition in a controlled way.

Additive manufacturing (AM) starts with developing a geometrical CAD model of the prototype/product using CAD. The CAD files are then converted into STL file followed by developing sliced model files. These sliced model files provide inputs to the 3D printing machine to control the X, Y, and Z movements of heat source/feed material/ binder as per the additive manufacturing method. A material layer is built up to make a 2D surface of small thickness using X and Y movement of either heat source (laser, electron beam, ultraviolet, infrared) or material (polymer, metal, ceramic, composite in the form of solid/liquid/powder over a platform as per AM method (Table 5.1). Thereafter, the layer-by-layer deposition process is repeated until a 3D product of the desired shape and size is realized.

Table 5.1 Material, approach and additive manufacturing process

S. No.	Form of input material	Approach	Process
1	Solid	Sheet joining	Laminated objects
		Fusion and solidification	Direct energy deposition
2	Liquid	Polymerization	VAT polymerization Binder jetting
3	Powder	Fusion, Sintering, Extrusion	Extrusion Power bed fusion

The development of additive manufacturing processes has progressed significantly from the use of simple polymers to mixed polymers, metals, ceramics, composites, etc. Accordingly, advancement in additive manufacturing technologies resulted in many new variants of AM processes namely powder bed fusion, VAT polymerization, extrusion (FDM), material jetting, binder jetting, direct energy deposition methods (wire arc additive manufacturing (WAAM), laser and electron beam powder-based AM) and sheet lamination (adhesive, ultrasonic joining). These AM methods rely on sintering, fusion and curing (polymerization), melting and solidification, cutting and joining as per the material under process Table (5.1).

Additive manufacturing technologies can be grouped into the following categories a) sintering, b) melting and solidification and c) photo-polymerization/curing. Sintering is used to develop bonds between metals and polymeric powders using external heat supplied by a laser. Selective laser sintering develops bonds between thermoplastic powders. The heat generated by arc, plasma, laser and electron beam is used to melt high temperature metals in the form of wire, and powders followed by solidification to develop the product. One of the most used AM technologies is stereolithographic based on photo-polymerisation. Ultraviolet radiations are used for polymerization of photopolymer resin to create ceramic components (Table 5.2).

Table 5.2 Additive manufacturing process and basic approach

S. No.	Process	Basic approach
1	Binder jetting	A liquid binder is applied selectively to join materials in powder form followed by curing to obtain the desired shape through layer-by-layer deposition.
2	Directed energy deposition	An intense heat source is used for controlled melting of materials in wire/powder form followed by solidification to obtain the desired shape through by-layer deposition.
3	Material extrusion	Softened and viscus polymeric material is extruded through a nozzle and selectively applied to obtain the desired shape through layer-by-layer deposition.
4	Material jetting	Liquefied materials are applied in the form of droplets to obtain the desired shape through layer-by-layer.
5	Powder bed fusion	An intense heat source is used for the controlled melting of materials in a powder bed followed by solidification/sintering to obtain the desired shape through layer by layer development.
6	Sheet lamination	A thin sheet of material cut despite as per required geometry by laser followed by bonding using adhesive or solid-state joining to obtain the desired shape through layer-by layer development.
7	Vat photo-polymerization	Light-sensitive liquid resin in a vat is selectively cured/polymerised by UV radiations to obtain the desired shape through layer-by-layer development.

Layer thickness

The thickness of the layer (slice thickness) deposited in each pass significantly affects many aspects of products made by additive manufacturing namely dimensional accuracy, surface roughness, uniformity of intra/interlayer properties, the requirement of support structure during product development and most importantly, time to develop the product which in turn determines the productivity (Fig.5.5).

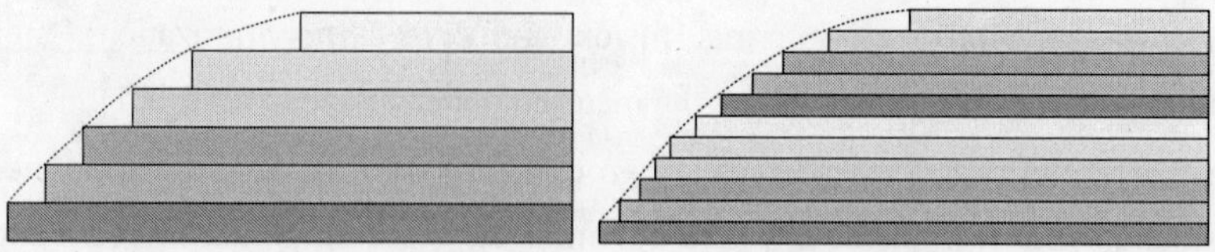

Fig. 5.5 Schematic showing the effect of slice/layer thickness on staircase effect on a curved surface and number of passes requirement

A thick layer deposited (for developing curved surfaces) in subsequent passes results in a step-like feature called the staircase effect. Deposition of material for developing additive manufacturing products using thin layer reduces the surface roughness, increases the dimensional accuracy, reduces the inter/intra layer heterogeneity, and reduces the need for internal support structures but increases the time required to develop the product thus adversely affecting the productivity (Fig. 5.6). Moreover, the thickness of layer deposited depends on multiple factors such net heat input, material fed per unit length as per AM process.

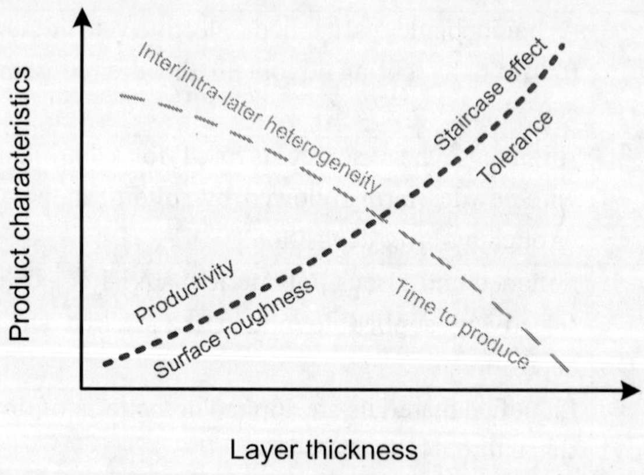

Fig. 5.6 Schematic showing the effect of slice/layer thickness on various product characteristics

Additive manufacturing technologies realize desired features such as controlled density and other characteristics by controlling print parameters, such as the number of layers, layer thickness, wall thickness, infill density, infill pattern, and pattern orientation. Infill density affects the modulus of elasticity and yield strength of components fabricated by additive manufacturing. Increasing infill density increases both the modulus of elasticity and yield strength of polymeric and metallic components (Fig. 5.7). Increasing number of layers beyond a critical number of layers (say 10 or 12 depending upon the material and print parameters) mechanical properties of the product becomes constant.

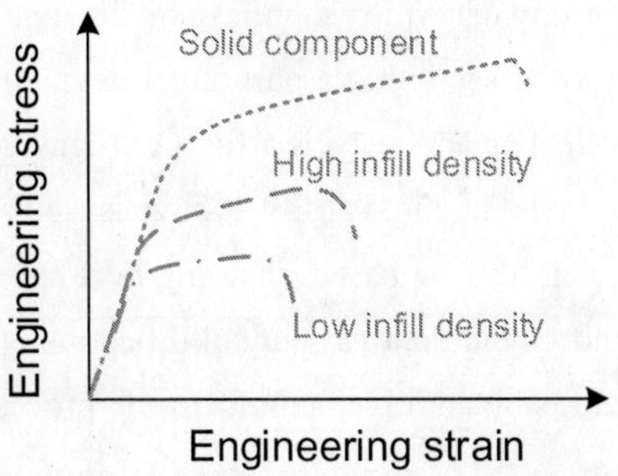

Fig. 5.7 Schematic showing the effect of infill density on mechanical behaviour of a component produced by additive manufacturing as compared to the solid component.

5.4.1 Powder bed fusion

The powder bed fusion additive manufacturing process is based on the melting and solidification of a layer of powder placed either over the build-up platform or already deposited layer. This process uses heat/radiation (from a suitable source) to melt a layer of powder along the well-defined path given by the sliced layer model file of the component. The desired heat for fusion/heating of powder can be provided by laser electron / electron beam or any other suirable heat source. The process is performed in a pre-heated chamber maintained either at low vacuum or inert environment to avoid oxidation of the molten material to minimize inclusion and porosity formation. The material (metals and polymer) is used in powder form for making products. The net heat input per unit length affects the depth up to which the powder layer (in the bed) melts and solidifies to build up a 2D layer. Increasing heat/radiation input per unit length (by increasing power of heat source, reducing travel speed) generally increases layer thickness developed in each pass. On successful application of the first layer over the build-up platform, the steps of spreading powder by blade/roller, melting and solidification are repeated. However, before initiating the next round of pass/layer deposition build-up platform is lowered by a distance equal to the thickness of earlier deposited layer. The product building platform is lowered successively after each pass with the progress of product development (Fig. 5.8). On completion of deposition of one layer along a path as per part geometry, another layer of powder applied (either over entire or partial area on earlier deposited layer) with help of a roller/blade followed by application of heat to cause melting and then curing/solidification. These steps of powder spreading, heat application and solidification are repeated until part of the desired 3D geometry is developed.

As the process goes on, the height of the product increases with an increasing number of layers while the roller/blade and heat source remain at the same level. Therefore, the build up platform is lowered accordingly with a height equal to the build-up layer thickness in each pass. A hopper is used as storage for powder which supplies powder material for spreading. Un-melted powder provides support for the section of a part under development during the process. Un-melted powder is later collected and recycled for use. This process is primarily used for polymers, which can be melted and cured easily. Above is true for powder bed fusion applied for metals. This approach can also be based on using heat for sintering and curing only for making 3D products instead of the melting and solidification approach. The following are a few variants of powder bed fusion additive manufacturing processes.

- Selective Laser Melting (SLM): involves melting of powders and solidification
- Selective Laser Sintering (SLS): involves bonding of powder particles through sintering
- Electron Beam Melting (EBM): involves melting of powders and solidification
- Direct Metal Laser Sintering (DMLS): involves metallurgical bonding of metallic powder particles through sintering

The powder bed fusion process is a little slow and takes a long time to develop a product with a typical layer thickness of around 100 µm.

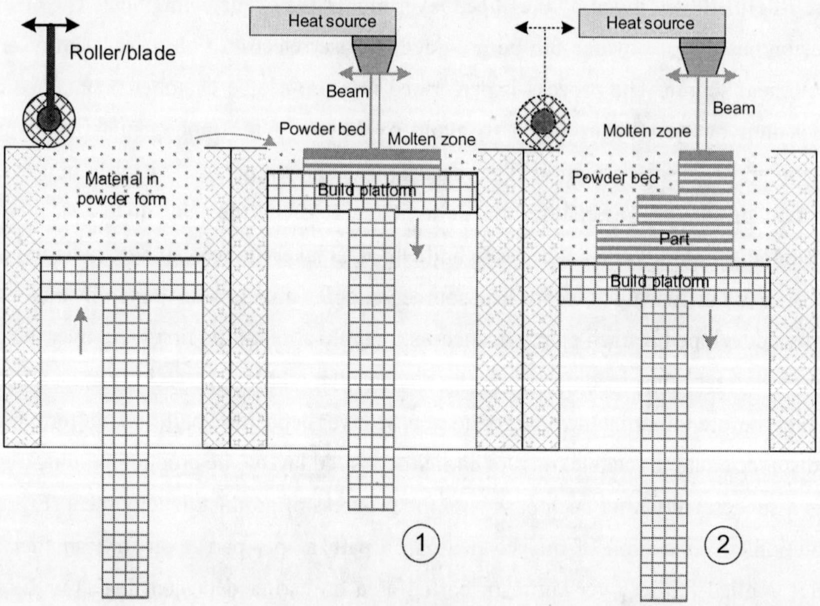

Fig. 5.8 Schematic showing stages of making products by powder-bed fusion additive manufacturing

5.4.2 Binder jetting

The binder jetting process is somewhat like the powder bed-fusion process. Binder jetting uses two types of materials, namely a) build-up / product material in powder form and b) binder.

This innovative process is used for manufacturing products of polymeric, metallic, ceramic, and composite materials as it allows the development of products with a combination of different materials and colours in different layers/sections as per need. However, the strength of the product developed by this process is very limited as inter-layer bonding occurs due to low-strength binder/adhesive only.

In this process, first, the material in powder form sprayed/sprinkled over the build-up platform and then a jet of binder is applied along a well-defined path given by the sliced layer model file of the component. The amount of binder applied per unit length determines the thickness of the layer developed in a single pass and followed by curing using a suitable heat/radiation source to speed up product development. Increasing the amount of binder per unit length in general, increases the thickness of the layer developed. On completion of deposition of one layer (thickness 8-20 μm), another layer of powder is applied (either over entire/partial area of the earlier deposited layer) with the help of a roller/blade followed by binder jetting and curing (Fig. 5.9). With the progress of the process, height of product increases with an increasing number of layers while roller/blade and heat source remain at the same level. Therefore, the platform is lowered accordingly with a height equal to the build-up layer thickness in each pass. The steps of powder application, binder jetting, and curing are repeated until part of the desired geometry is developed. Un-melted powders provide support for section under-development during the process. Un-melted powder is later collected and recycled for use.

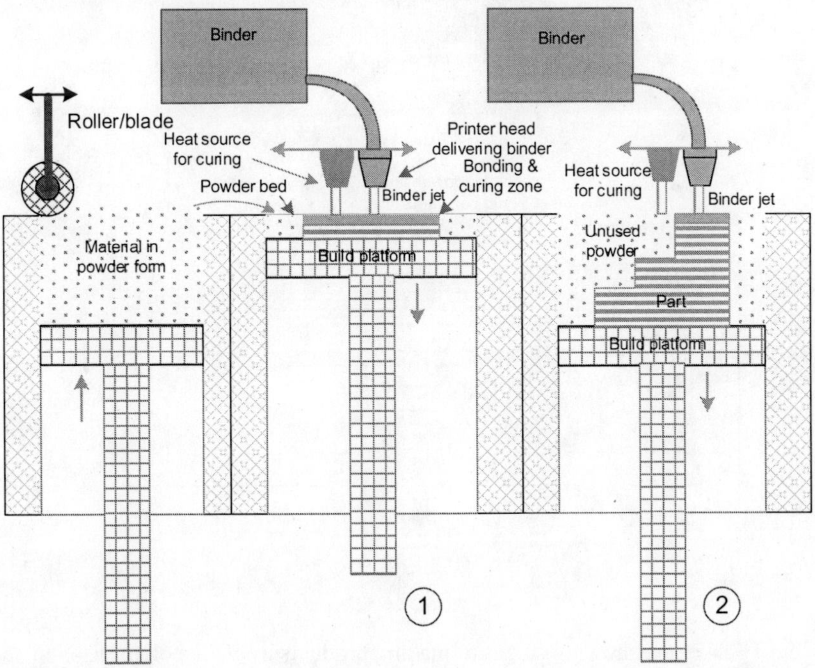

Fig. 5.9 Schematic showing stages of making products by binder jetting additive manufacturing

5.4.3 VAT Polymerization

The VAT polymerization process uses a VAT of liquid polymer for 3D printing additive manufacturing. VAT refers to the tub containing the liquid photopolymer resin. An ultraviolet beam is directed on to the photosensitive liquid resin to cause the polymerization, which converts liquid into solid for building up a 2D layer of polymer. Polymerization involves chemical reactions where molecules (monomers) combine to form long chainlike or cross-linked networks of molecules to form a solid polymer layer during additive manufacturing. The path traced by UV light determines the shape of a 2D layer developed. The build-up platform (on which the product is developed) is lowered gradually so that fresh photosensitive liquid resin can spread and cover the already cured/polymerized/solidified polymer layer. A roller/blade movement (like powder bed fusion process) over the build-up / earlier developed layer across the length of the component ensures uniformity of thickness of liquid resin (for further polymerization in subsequent passes). Another layer of liquid polymer is then exposed to UV radiation for further polymerization of the second layer (Fig. 5.10). The platform height is lowered again by the distance equal to the thickness of layer built in each pass. The same process is repeated until the desired product is realised. There are two main limitations of the process, a) process is suitable for photo/UV sensitive resins only and b) the process needs the development of support structures (which are later removed) for making the product due to weak polymeric material. This is similar to the support needed in case of powder bed fusion process or binder jetting process.

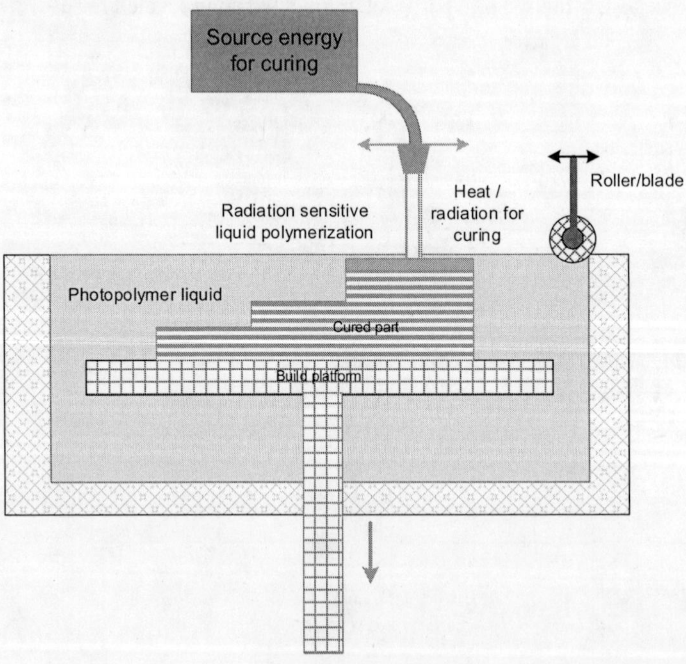

Fig. 5.10 Schematic showing stages of making products by VAT polymerization additive manufacturing

5.4.4 Material jetting

The material jetting is mainly used for low melting temperature materials like polymers (Polypropylene, HDPE, PS, PMMA, PC, ABS, HIPS, EDP) and waxes. The material jetting process applies the material in the form of fine "droplets on demand" or in continuous jet form followed by rapid solidification/curing using ultraviolet rays as per the material (Fig.5.11). Droplets directed at the desired position/ target location on the platform or already deposited layer using appropriate controls like thermal/piezoelectric actuators. Like other additive manufacturing processes, the model /prototype is developed by material jetting using a layer-by-layer approach. The first layer deposited (~16 to 20 μm) on the platform as per the cross-section of the component to be developed. Subsequent layers are deposited over the already-developed layer. Each time a layer is deposited the platform is lowered. The process allows the fabrication of high accuracy components using multi-material/colour combinations in different layers. However, the process is limited to polymers and waxes.

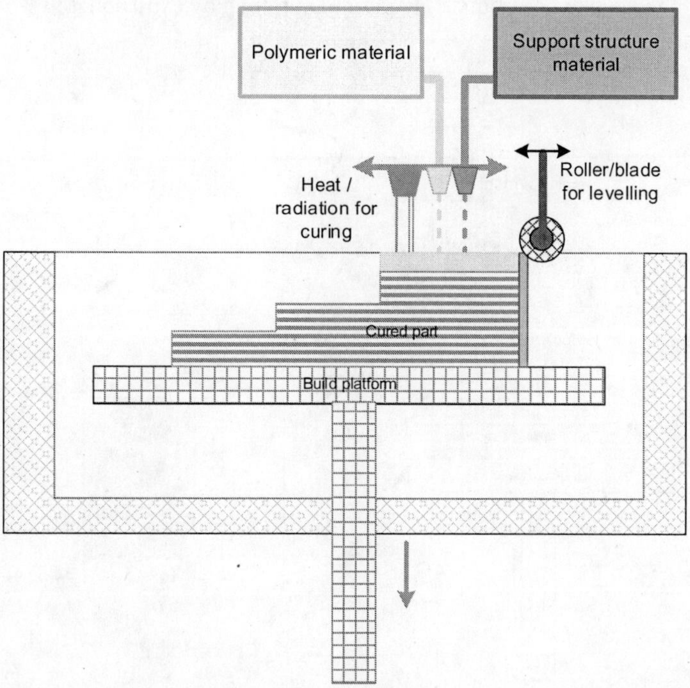

Fig. 5.11 Schematic showing the approach of making product by material jetting additive manufacturing

5.4.5 Extrusion (Fusion Deposition Modelling)

The extrusion process of additive manufacturing is somewhat similar to that of material jetting with the difference that the material during extrusion process is heated for melting/softening followed by extrusion through a nozzle. While, in material jetting, the material is applied in the form of droplets. The material for extrusion can be used in the form of powder and wire depending on the type of extruder used a) plunger type (powder), b) filament type (wire) and c) screw type (powder and wire). The wire is kept in the spool and then it is fed to the extruder and nozzle for extrusion. External heating is used suitably for softening and melting of polymers. The extruded material is deposited (in the form of a continuous stream) over the platform along the path traced by the nozzle with the help of controller as per the cross-section of the product to be manufactured (Fig. 5.12). The path traced by nozzle (horizontally) is controlled by a mechanised system getting inputs from the sliced model data. Subsequent layers deposited over the earlier deposited layers help to build up the 3D product. The platform over which 3D printing is done moved up /down with the progress of the process. The inter-layer bonding in the extrusion process depends on the inter-mixing of the new layer and already deposited layer. Further, the inter-layer bonding can be adjusted by controlling extrusion temperature and chemistry. The dimensional accuracy of products manufactured by extrusion process is limited due to use of thick layer for 3D printing by extrusion.

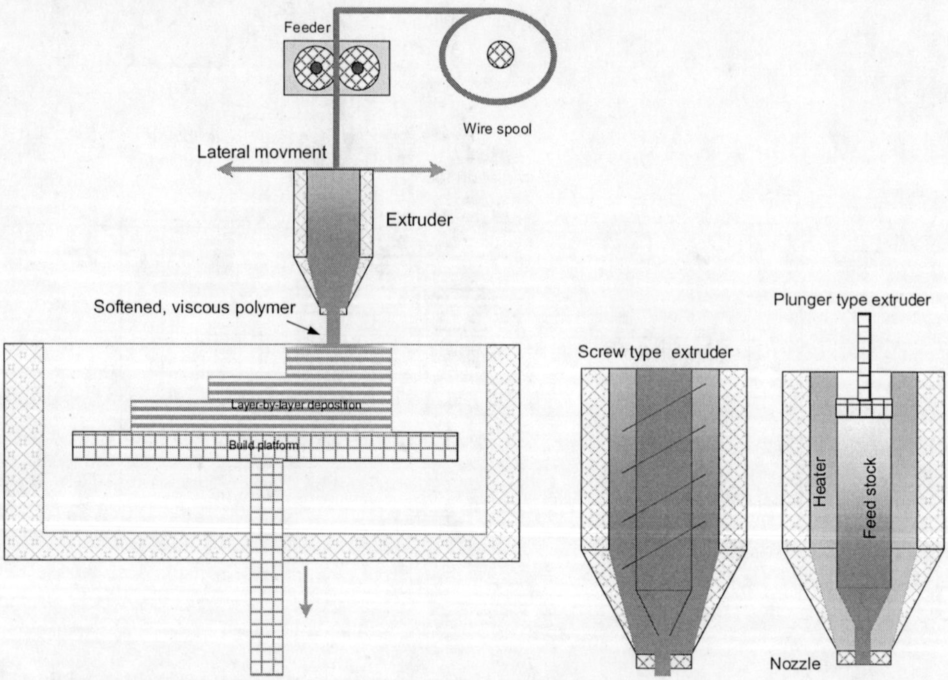

Fig. 5.12 Schematic showing the approach of making product by extrusion additive manufacturing

Metal additive manufacturing (MAM) is mainly limited to powder fusion and direct energy deposition approaches. A relatively new technique called bounded metal deposition is an extrusion-based additive manufacturing for making low-volume prototypes / products (economically) made of stainless steel, copper, and titanium. These metals in powder form are mixed with wax and binder to produce rods, which are fed into the extruder. In extruder, these rods are fused, softened and extruded to form 3D metal parts during additive manufacturing. Thereafter, the de-binding process is applied to the 3D printed part (having low strength) to remove binder followed by sintering to impart the desired strength and densification. The process is applied in 3 stages, namely, infill structure, side wall, and top/bottom wall (Fig. 5.13).

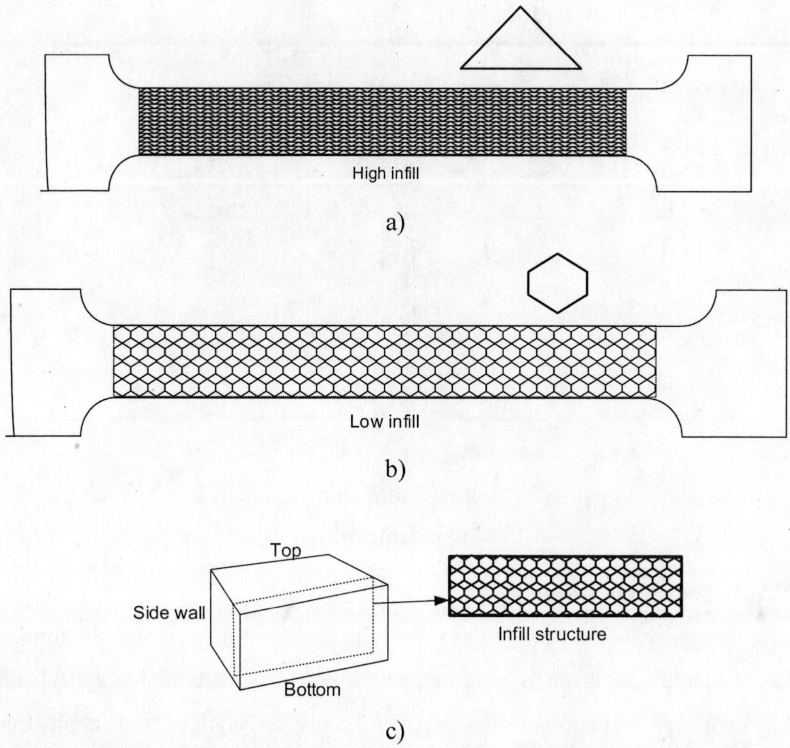

Fig. 5.13 Schematic showing a) high infill structure, b) low infill structure and c) approach of bonded metal deposition (BMD) an extrusion-based additive manufacturing

5.4.6 Sheet lamination

The sheet lamination process is also known as laminated object manufacturing. This process primarily uses sheets of material (metal, paper/ polymer) cut into the desired cross-section using laser cutting /shearing from stock. Then sheets are stacked one over other and joined using suitable approaches like ultrasonic welding, laser welding, and adhesive joining (Fig. 5.14). Metallic sheets (aluminium, copper, stainless steel and titanium) and polymer are joined by ultrasonic welding and; friction stir welding. While adhesive joining is used for making paper laminated objects. The process allows the development of composite material products using laminated sheets of different materials. To realize the final size, shape and accuracy, the laminated sheet object is machined using a suitable machining process.

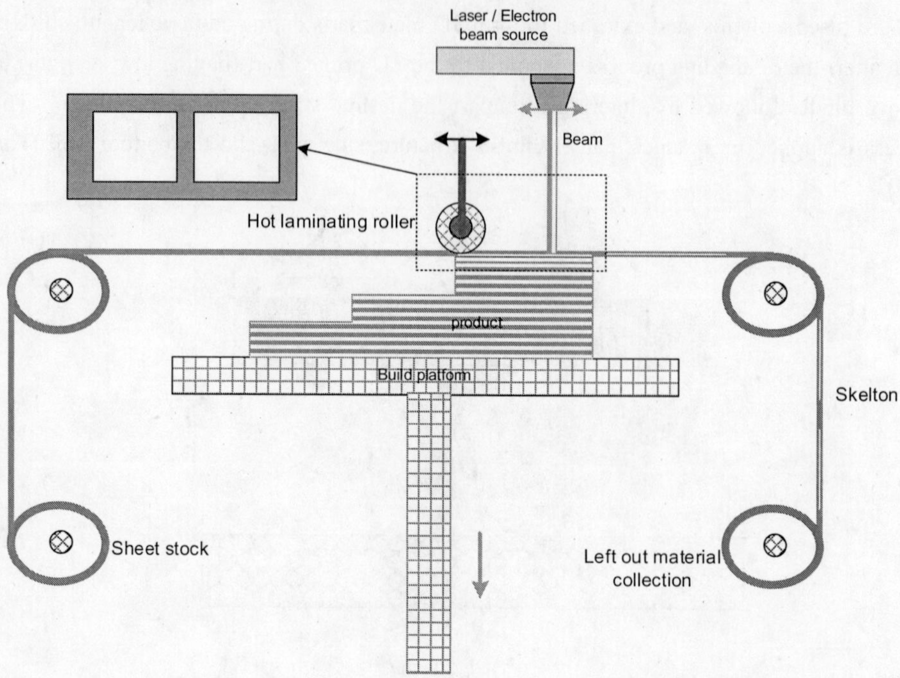

Fig. 5.14 Schematic showing the approach of making products by sheet lamination additive manufacturing

5.4.7 Direct energy deposition

The direct energy deposition process involves the fusion of material (in the form of powder and wire) for building a layer to either develop a new product/model or repair the damaged one. The energy for the fusion of material (metal, polymer, composite) is applied in the form of a laser, electron beam, plasma and arc as per the process (Fig. 5.15). The degree of control needed for additive manufacturing using a direct energy deposition process is very high. The energy (in the form of laser/electron beam/ plasma/arc) and consumable material (of which product is to be made) are both fed, controlled and manipulated using a 4 or 5 axes robotic arm to ensure deposition of the material at the target location. Melting of material makes it sensitive to interact with other chemical species (impurities present in the form of hydrocarbons, and atmospheric gases). Chemical interaction of the material with gases and impurities promotes defects like pores, inclusions and cracks. Therefore, it is important that material at high temperature (or in a molten state) is protected from environmental gases by providing a controlled environment through suitable a) vacuum and b) inert gases / inactive gases as per the material. The electron beam assisted direct energy deposition process needs vacuum for effective and efficient operation and protection from atmospheric gases.

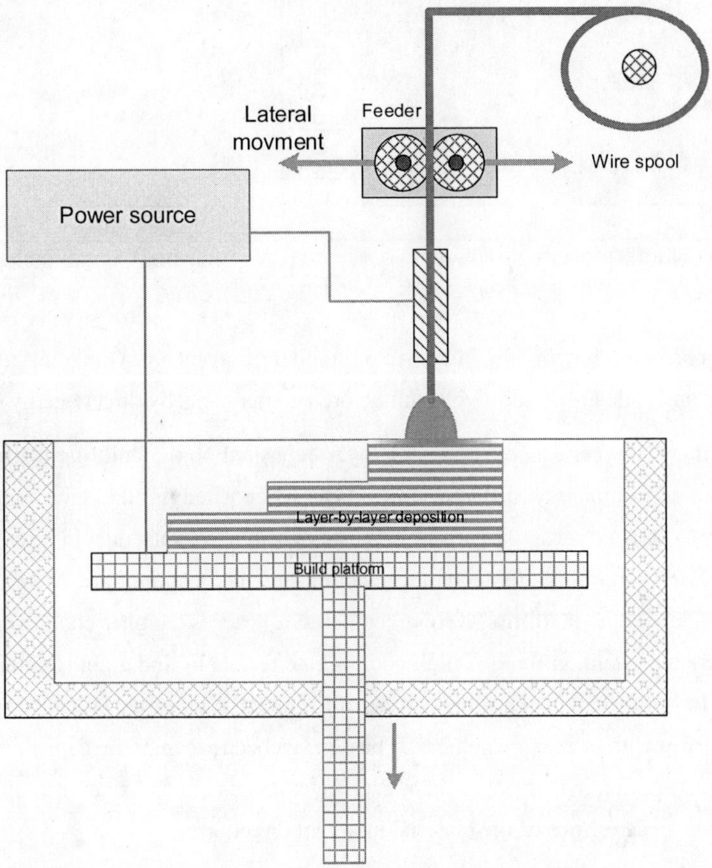

Fig. 5.15 Schematic showing the approach of making product by direct energy deposition additive manufacturing

In general, the thermal cycle and re-melting of the material during deposition of the material layer in subsequent passes by the direct energy deposition process, significantly affects the chemical composition, microstructure and mechanical properties of the metal 3D printed parts (Fig. 5.16). Material is deposited at high temperature over the earlier deposited layer, experiences varying thermal cycles (heating rate, high temperature retention and cooling rate). These two aspects, a) repeated melting and b) imposition of multiple thermal cycles, significantly determine the final microstructure and mechanical properties of the fabricated component.

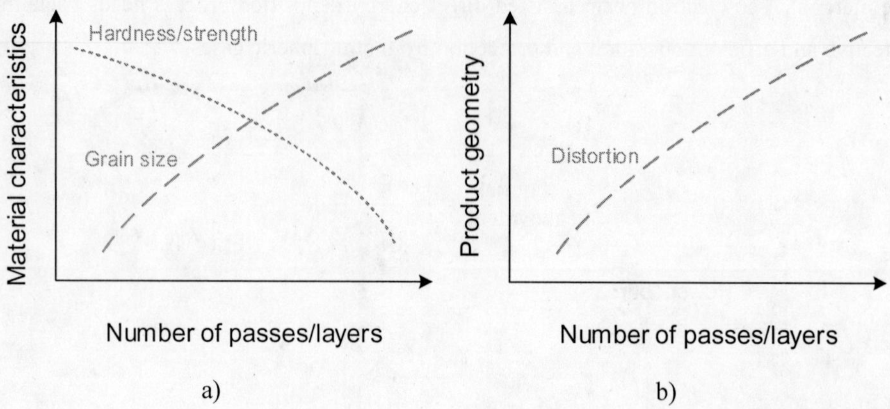

Fig. 5.16 Schematic showing the influence of number of layers on a) materials properties and b) distortion tendency of additive manufactured components by direct energy deposition

The thermal cycle experienced by the first layer deposited on the build-up platform (at room temperature) is completely different from layers deposited in the later stages (at high temperature). This is particularly true for heat-sensitive metals due to exposure to high temperature, long/short high temperature retention time and cooling rate. Material deposition on the low temperature platform (at room temperature) causes a higher cooling rate and lower high temperature retention time. A high cooling rate results in fine grain structure and higher hardness and yield strength. The temperature of the already deposited layer during subsequent passes increases with increasing number of passes/layers due to material deposition. Therefore, a continuous variation in thermal cycle of each layer causes gradual change in mechanical and dimensional characteristics of the material in height direction.

UNIT SUMMARY

This unit gives the concepts, approaches, and requirements of making products using additive manufacturing. The sequential steps have been present in a generic manner for different additive manufacturing processes. Principles, and methodology adopted for common additive manufacturing processes, namely powder bed fusion, extrusion, direct energy deposition, sheet lamination, material jetting and binder jetting have been presented for better understanding. The significance of layer thickness on the quality of the product has been elaborated. Additionally, efforts have been made to explain the influence of a number of passes on structure and quality aspects of metallic components made by direct energy deposition approach.

EXERCISE

Questions for self-assessment

1. Additive manufacturing is preferred to make products of

    a. Simple shape　　b. High volume in number
    c. Complex shape　　d. All of these

2. Additive manufacturing for making large components relative to conventional die-casting is

    a. Fast　　b. Economical
    c. Ineffective　　d. Preferred

3. Layer thickness deposited in one pass during additive manufacturing affects

    a. Production time　　b. Dimensional accuracy
    c. Surface finish　　d. All of these

4. The additive manufacturing process based on solid-state joining is

    a. Powder bed fusion　　b. Extrusion
    c. Sheet lamination　　d. Direct energy deposition

5. Powder is used as input raw material in case of

    a. Sheet lamination　　b. Filament type extrusion
    c. VAT polymerization　　d. Plunger type extrusion

6. An additive manufacturing process in which photo-sensitive liquid resin is

    a. Sheet lamination　　b. Extrusion
    c. VAT polymerization　　d. Direct energy deposition

7. An additive manufacturing process used for high temperature metals like steel is

    a. Materials jetting　　b. Extrusion
    c. VAT polymerization　　d. Direct energy deposition

8. An additive manufacturing process used for making multi-material/colour products of polymers is

    a. Materials jetting　　b. Extrusion
    c. VAT polymerization　　d. Powder bed fusion

9. The build-up platform during the additive manufacturing process (like powder bed fusion, material jetting) after each pass is

    a. Lowered randomly
    b. Lowered by height double of layer thickness deposited
    c. Lowered by height same as layer thickness deposited
    d. All of these

10. Step that determines the thickness of a layer deposited during additive manufacturing, like powder bed fusion is
    a. Geometry modeling b. Slicing of STL file
    c. Amount of raw materials supplied d. All of these

Answers to Multiple Choice Questions

Key for MCQ: 1 c, 2 c, 3 d, 4 c, 5 d, 6 c, 7 d, 8 a, 9 c, 10 b

Short and Long Answer Type Questions

1. What is polymerization in the additive manufacturing of polymers?
2. What is the general approach to making 3D components using additive manufacturing?
3. What are the sequential steps of making products by additive manufacturing?
4. What is the significance of layer thickness in the productivity and quality of the products made using additive manufacturing?
5. When is the additive manufacturing process preferred over the conventional manufacturing processes to make the 3D components?
6. Enlist the materials that can be used to make the 3D components through additive manufacturing.
7. Briefly describe the general approaches to making 3D components using common additive manufacturing processes.
8. What are the typical applications of additive manufacturing?
9. Explain the importance of layer thickness on accuracy and surface roughness of the components made by additive manufacturing.
10. Enlist the standard powder bed fusion-based additive manufacturing processes.
11. Describe the general approach of making 3D products using the following additive manufacturing processes with the help of a suitable schematic.
    a. Powder bed fusion
    b. Material jetting
    c. Binder setting
    d. VAT polymerisation
    e. Extrusion
    f. Sheet lamination
    g. Direct energy deposition

12. What is the effect of the number of layers to be used for developing a 3D product of metal using direct energy deposition manufacturing on quality characteristics?
13. Compare the material-getting and binder-jetting processes in terms of their capabilities.
14. What is the significance of sintering in the powder bed fusion process?
15. What is the significance of the post-processing of products made by sheet lamination additive manufacturing?

KNOW MORE

Explore the additive manufacturing penetration in industries to make goods of common use. Try to visit a modern manufacturing rapid prototyping and additive manufacturing lab/industry to find out how real components are manufactured by additive manufacturing. A lot of information about progress and development around additive manufacturing is available in the public domain. Efforts may be made to learn and gain the expertise.

Scan me!

SUGGESTED RESOURCES FOR FURTHER READING/LEARNING

1. M P Grover, "Fundamentals of Modern Manufacturing", John Wiley & Sons, (2010)
2. D K Dwivedi, Materials Engineering, AICTE, (2023)
3. D K Dwivedi, NPTEL Course "Fundamentals of Manufacturing Processes" https://archive.nptel.ac.in/courses/112/107/112107219/
4. https://www.appliedengineering.com/blog/2021/1/22/7-types-of-additive-manufacturing
5. https://www.intechopen.com/chapters/50453#
6. https://www.lboro.ac.uk/research/amrg/about/the7categoriesofadditivemanufacturing/materialjetting/
7. https://www.youtube.com/watch?v=2LumoE9KjoY

6 Joining and Fastening Processes

Unit Specific / Learning Objective

The objective of this unit is to understand the following aspects

- To learn about various approaches of material joining
- To introduce the concept of fusion, solid-liquid, solid state and adhesive joining processes
- To understand the importance of heat input and weld protection in fusion welding
- To develop an understanding on the principles and approaches of common joining processes like arc welding, brazing/soldering, adhesive joining, and forge, friction and friction stir welding
- To learn about the suitability of joining processes for similar and dissimilar metal joining, considering their compatibility in respect of metallurgical / mechanical properties

Additionally, a few questions for self-assessment based on fundamentals have been included in this chapter. These questions are based on application, comprehension, analysis and synthesis. Suggested further reading and reference have been included for deep learners and readers.

Rationale

The manufacturing of the components is realised using a wide range of conventional and unconventional manufacturing processes. However, most conventional (casting, machining and forming) and unconventional machining processes are limited to manufacturing of relatively simple shapes and small to moderate size components. The fabrication of very complex and extremely large size components and systems invariably requires joining of relatively simple and small to moderate size components to achieve the desired size and shape. In the current manufacturing scenario, joining is an inevitable process to manufacture goods and systems made of either single material or multiple material components. Joining of single material components to achieve the desired size and shape is relatively easier than the joining of multi material components due to the difference in their mechanical, physical and metallurgical characteristics. It is therefore, important to learn techniques suitable for joining similar and dissimilar materials. The fusion welding processes are extensively used for joining similar materials with great ease, while the joining dissimilar materials by fusion welding requires extra care and many precautions about controlled heat input, weld pool protection and careful filler metal selection. Therefore, it is important to learn about joining processes (brazing, soldering, adhesive joining, and solid state joining) suitable for dissimilar material combinations. Learning and awareness about joining technologies will equip mechanical/production/industrial engineers with the latest tools and techniques for efficient and cost-effective manufacturing of products for consumption by society.

Pre-Requisites

Physics: Materials engineering

Learning outcomes

U6-O1: Ability to understand approaches for making complex geometry products of single/multi-materials using fusion welding, adhesive and solid state joining

U6-O2: Ability to select appropriate joining processes as per the material of components to be joined.

U6-O3: Ability to select suitable process parameters of fusion welding processes for developing a sound weld joint.

U6-O4: Ability to understand the way joint characteristics are affected by heat input and weld pool protection associated with different arc welding processes.

U6-O5: Ability to apply arc welding, brazing and soldering, adhesive joining and solid-state joining processes for developing joints.

Unit-6: Outcomes	**EXPECTED MAPPING WITH COURSE OUTCOMES** (1- Weak Correlation; 2- Medium correlation; 3- Strong Correlation)					
	CO-1	**CO-2**	**CO-3**	**CO-4**	**CO-5**	**CO-6**
U6-O1	3	3	-	-	-	-
U6-O2	3	3	-	-	-	-
U6-O3	3	2	-	-	-	-
U6-O4	3	3	-	-	-	-
U6-O5	3	3	-	-	-	-

CO

1. Understand the different conventional and unconventional manufacturing methods employed for making different products
2. To motivate and challenge students to understand and develop an appreciation of the processes in correlation with material properties which change the shape, size and form of the raw materials into the desirable product.

6.1 Introduction

The joining of materials is inevitable in the current manufacturing scenario to obtain the desired size, shape, and complex geometries of one or multi-material parts. The joining, depending upon the material compatibility of the components can be realized through various approaches such as mechanical interlocking, fusion of faying surfaces, plastic deformation, and chemical and metallurgical interactions. The material combination incompatible due to large differences in mechanical, physical, chemical and metallurgical characteristics is joined using approaches like mechanical interlocking (nut-bolts, rivets, etc.), plastic deformation (friction and friction stir welding), diffusion bonding, chemical (adhesive bonding), and metallurgical interactions (soldering and brazing) based processes which do not involve melting, inter-mixing and dilution of parent materials (Fig. 6.1).

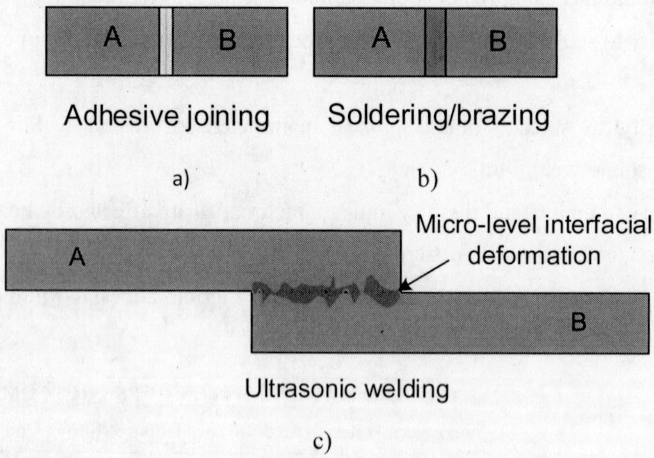

Fig. 6.1 Schematic diagram showing a few processes of joining without fusion

Still, these processes are sometimes preferred for the joining of similar material due to economic reasons, ease of joining and requirement of high reliability for critical applications like the use of nuts/bolts, and rivets for fabrication of bridge structures and aircraft components. Chemical and metallurgical interaction based joining processes offer joint strength significantly lower than respective parent materials. Therefore, therefore, these are preferred for the development of non-load-carrying (non-structural) joints.

Similar material combinations are relatively easier to join by fusion based processes like arc welding (shielded metal welding, gas metal arc welding, plasma arc welding and gas tungsten arc welding), gas, laser and electron beam welding. Power density and weld pool protection approach (during welding) for each fusion-welding process are different. Therefore, heat affected zone, soundness and mechanical performance of their weld joints also vary significantly. Optimum heat input and effective weld pool protection during fusion welding, in general, results in a sound (defect free) weld joint with high mechanical performance and limited heat affected zone. Conversely, too high or low heat input results in poor or defective joints (lack of fusion, penetration). Further, fusion-welding processes invariably develop a region adjacent to the weld where changes in mechanical and metallurgical characteristics are observed due to thermal (heating and cooling) cycle imposed during welding. This region, which is affected by welding heat, is called a heat-affected zone (HAZ). The HAZ generally deteriorates the mechanical performance and corrosion resistance of the weld joint. Fusion weld joints always exhibit wider HAZ, than solid state joining processes. The HAZ can be minimized by reducing net heat input (KJ/mm) for welding or imposing external cooling of the region of parent metal adjacent to the weld metal (Fig. 6.2).

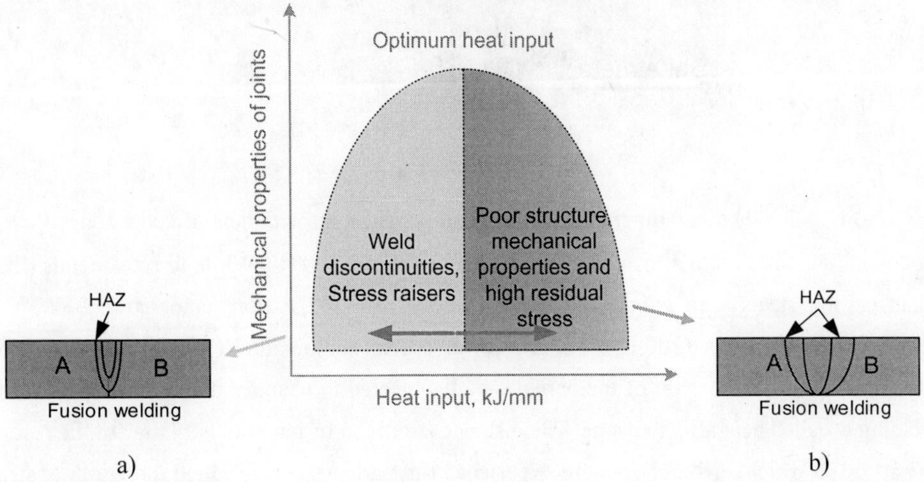

Fig. 6.2 Schematic diagram showing the effect of heat input on fusion weld joint properties a) low and b) high heat input

Poor weld pool protection from the atmospheric gases leads to porosity, and inclusion in the weld metal. Therefore, molten metal should be protected from air to ensure fabrication of sound weld metal. The fusion welding processes are very common in fabrication industries due to easy, cheaper, fast and without much capital investment. The fundamentals, approaches, and process parameters of common arc welding processes, adhesive joining, brazing & soldering, and solid-state joining process have been presented.

6.2 Fusion welding processes

The fusion welding processes use heat (from suitable heat sources such as gas flame, arc, plasma, laser, and electron beam) for melting the faying surfaces of the component to be joined. Subsequently, loss of heat from the weld pool (to base metal/backing plate and air) causes solidification of the molten weld pool, which in turn leads to metallic continuity between components to produce a weld joint. A part of heat applied for melting the faying surface of metallic component dissipated to the underlying un-melted parent metal due to thermal conductivity, causing many changes in mechanical and metallurgical characteristics of parent metals in the form of heat-affected zone (Fig. 6.3). Metal in vicinity of weld metal if heated above a certain critical temperature experiences such changes in mechanical and metallurgical characteristics. The critical temperature above which changes occur depends on the parent metal composition and its condition (work hardened, heat-treated, tempered).

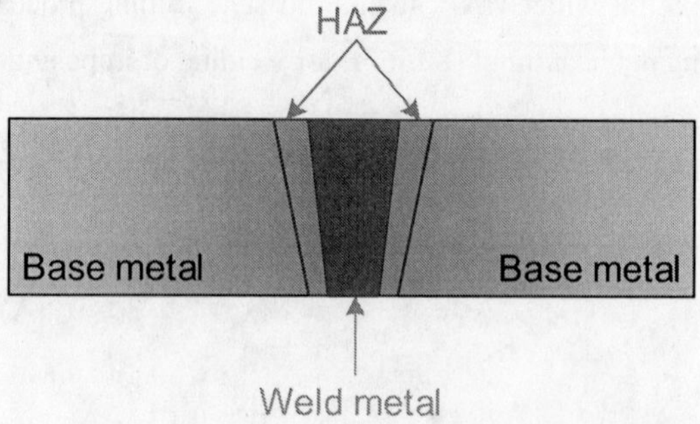

Fig. 6.3 Schematic diagram showing fusion weld joint with heat-affected zone

For example, aluminium alloys experience changes above 150 °C. While ferrous metals (like plain carbon steels) can experience change above recrystallization temperature (400 °C), tempering temperature, (300-650°C), and lower critical temperature (730 °C) as per parent metal condition. The region of the parent metal subjected to changes due to heat applied for welding is called heat affected zone. The distance (from the fusion boundary toward the parent metal) up to which such changes are experienced in parent metal is called the width of heat affected zone. The heat input must be kept as low as possible for developing a sound weld joint to minimize the heat-affected zone.

Heat input for welding is calculated differently than heat being generated by heat source, as the heat source is continuously moving during the fusion welding. Therefore, the term "net heat input" is a better indicator of heat input as it is obtained from the ratio of heat supplied to parent metal per unit time (kJ or W) to the speed of heat source (mm/min or mm/s). The fusion welding processes (arc, gas, laser & electron) generate and supply heat differently.

Additionally, the net heat input required for developing a sound fusion-weld joint depends on the power density of the heat source used for welding. Higher the power density of the heat source lower is the net heat input required for welding as it takes less time to supply the desired amount of heat (latent heat) for melting, so less heat is dissipated to the underlying base metal (Fig. 6.4). Reduction in net heat input decreases the size/ area of weld metal, width of heat affected zone, residual stresses and chances of distortion. Therefore, high power density fusion welding processes (laser / electron beam welding) offer better quality weld joints than gas and arc welding processes.

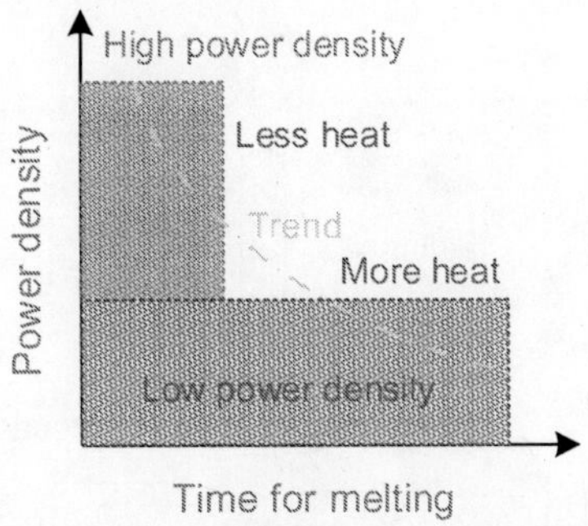

Fig. 6.4 Schematic diagram showing the effect of power density on time delivery of desired heat for melting base metal during fusion welding.

The arc welding process generates heat as per arc voltage (V) and welding current (I) used for welding. While, gas welding generates heat by exothermic reactions as per the type of fuel and oxygen pressure and fuel gas to oxygen ratio. It is relatively easier to control heat generation and provide controlled net heat input during arc welding simply by adjusting the welding current and welding speed (S). Arc voltage is usually fixed and is set as per the requirement of the electrode for developing the stable arc.

6.3 Arc welding

The arc welding processes use heat generated by a stable welding arc for melting the faying surfaces of components (to be joined), followed by solidification of the molten weld pool to produce a weld joint. Power is supplied by a suitable welding power source, which is capable to deliver high current at low voltage (Fig. 6.5). The welding power source can supply DC or AC depending on the type of welding process, and electrode, need of heat generation and arc stability. Heat generation by welding arc primarily depends on arc voltage (V) and welding current (I). The travel speed of the welding arc (S) during welding determines the net heat input ($\eta VI/S$) for a given arc power (VI). η is the thermal efficiency of the arc, which can vary from 40-99% as per the arc welding process. For example, submerged arc welding offers arc efficiency > 90% while TIG and MIG welding offer thermal efficiency of arc about 60-70% and 80-85%, respectively. Melting of thin section components needs lesser net heat input than thick ones. An appropriate combination of welding current (I) and welding speed (S) is established for the desired heat input to get through thickness penetration weld joint in single pass welding for moderate thick section component (5-25 mm). Theoretical calculation of arc power and net heat input using different arc welding process parameters is given in Table 6.1.

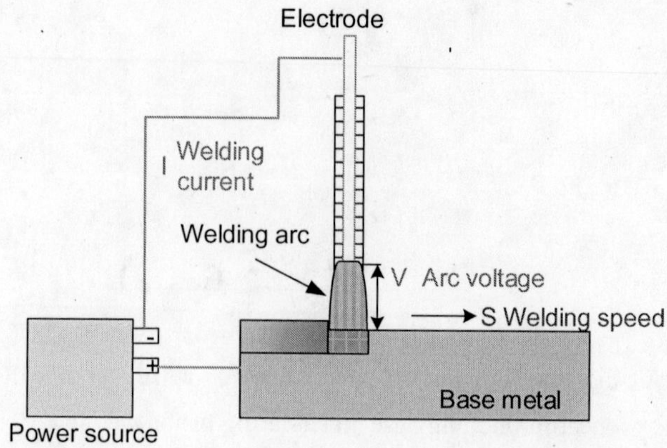

Fig. 6.5 Schematic diagram showing a typical setup of arc welding process for fusion welding.

Table 6.1 Arc power, heat generation and net heat input (assuming 100% arc efficiency)

S. No.	Welding current, I	Arc voltage, V	Welding speed, S in mm/min	Arc power (VI) or Heat generated, kJ	Net heat input
1	120	12	100	120 X 12: 1440 J 1440/1000: 1.44 kJ	(120X12X60)/1000X100 =0.86 kJ/mm
2	250	20	150	250 X 20: 5000 J 5000/1000: 5.0 kJ	(250X20X60)/1000X150 =2.0 kJ/mm
3	500	30	200	500 X 30: 15000 J 15000/1000: 15 kJ	(500X30X60)/1000X200 =4.5 kJ/mm

The filler metal (a consumable electrode or external filler wire) may or may not be used during arc welding processes. The fusion welding processes involving the melting of faying surfaces only (without the use of filler metal) followed by solidification of the weld metal are called autogenous welding. Welding thin sections by gas tungsten arc welding, gas welding and laser beam welding are classified as autogenous welding processes. The consumable arc welding processes such as shielded metal arc welding (SMAW), metal inert gas welding (MIGW), flux cored arc welding (FCAW) use filler metal. The filler metal can be either a matching type (similar to base metal in terms of composition and properties) or completely different as per the requirement of weld metal properties (high toughness, corrosion resistance, etc.).

Three common arc-welding processes in our scope of the course are:

- Shielded metal arc welding SMAW also known as manual metal arc welding, MMAW
- Gas metal arc welding GMAW also known as metal inert gas welding MIGW
- Gas tungsten arc welding GTAW also known as tungsten inert gas welding TIGW

The first two processes, namely SMAW and GMAW, are consumable arc welding processes. Consumable electrode in these processes performs two functions: a) developing a welding arc between electrode and parent metals and b) melting of electrode (using heat produced by welding arc) feeds the molten filler metal and fill the gap between the parent metals. The third arc welding process. namely GTAW, uses a non-consumable tungsten electrode. This electrode helps establish welding arc between the electrode and parent metal only to apply heat for welding. Filler metal in GTAW, if required, can be fed separately as filler wire as per need for joining of thick sections (> 5mm) only.

6.4 Welding Arc

Welding arc involves flow of current (electrons and ions) across the electrode and parent metal through electrical conducting gap between them. The presence of electrons and ions makes it electrically conducting, In the presence of a sufficient potential difference between the electrode and parent metal, the current starts to flow, resulting in welding arc (Fig. 6.6).

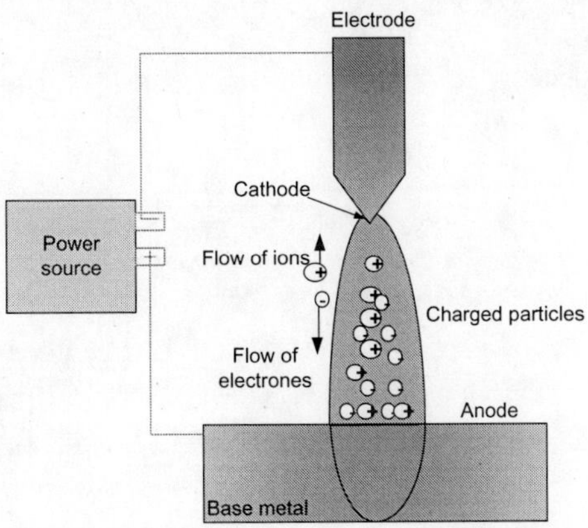

Fig. 6.6 Schematic diagram showing mechanism of welding arc in an arc welding process. Sustained heat generation and emission of electrons maintain the heat balance, and charge particle density in the arc zone to ensure continuity of current flow and produce a stable welding arc.

6.5 Arc initiation

Two methods are commonly used for starting/ igniting a welding arc, namely touch start and field start. In the touch arc initiation method, a welding electrode (connected to the power supply) is touched with the patent metal (at a location where welding is to be started). Then after a fraction of a second, it is slightly withdrawn (moved away) to establish the gap between the two to initiate the welding arc. The steps of the touch start method are schematically shown in Fig. 6.7. Touching and withdrawing of the electrode generates first short-circuiting (heat generation) then the creation of an electrically conducting gap (between electrode and parent metal) due to thermo-ionic emission of electrons and ionization of metal vapours generated due to short circuiting. In the presence of a sufficient potential difference between the electrode and parent metal, welding current starts to flow through the electrical conducting gap (arc gap). The distance between the electrode tip and parent metal is termed as arc length. The touch start method is commonly used in welding processes like SMAW, GTAW, etc.

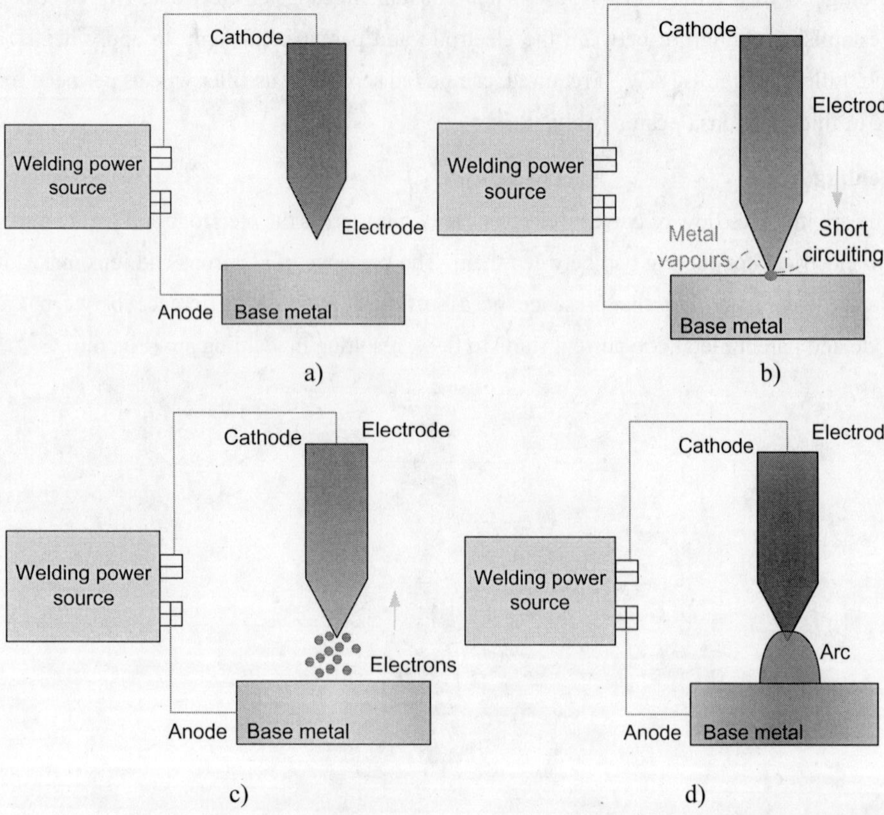

Fig. 6.7 Schematic diagram showing four steps of welding arc initiation by touch start method a) connect electrode and base metal to the power source, b) touch the parent metal for short-circuiting, c) withdraw electrode and d) establish welding arc.

In the field start method, a very high potential difference (10^7 V) is established between the electrode and parent metal using a special power supply called a high frequency (HF) unit. High potential difference develops a strong electro-magnetic field to facilitate emission of electrons from electrode. The emission of electrons (in enough density) in gap between the electrode and parent metal makes it electrical conducting to facilitate the flow of current and initiate a welding arc. Once the arc is initiated, the normal welding power supply comes into action and the HF unit supply is withdrawn. The steps of the field start method are schematically shown in Fig. 6.8. The field start method is preferred for the automatic welding process and all those arc welding processes where direct touching of the electrode to parent metal is not preferred (like GMAW, PAW, and GTAW, etc.) due to inclusion defect formation tendency.

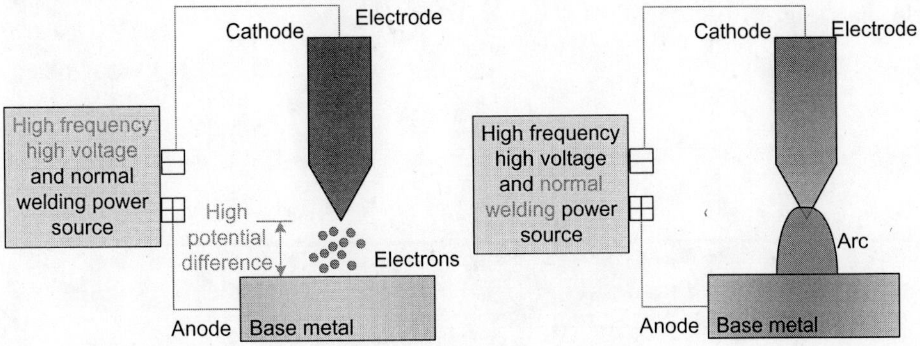

Fig. 6.8 Schematic diagram showing four steps of welding arc initiation by touch start method a) impose high potential difference using HF unit across the electrode and base metal, and b) establish welding arc.

6.6 Heat input and protection of weld

The quality of the weld joint produced by each of these arc welding processes differs primarily due to a) net heat input and b) protection of welding pool during welding. The power density of each arc welding process is different (GTAW>GMAW>SMAW). High power density lowers the net heat input (Fig. 6.9). High heat input reduces the quality of weld joint due to the formation of wide HAZ, coarse grain structure and increased thermal damage in the form of residual stress and distortion.

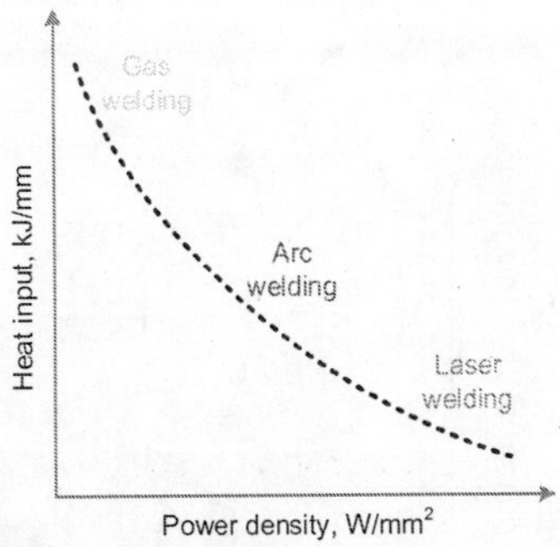

Fig. 6.9 Schematic diagram showing the effect of power density on heat input for fusion welding.

The presence of atmospheric gases around the weld arc and molten metal increases the tendency of formation of weld defects like porosity and inclusions. At high temperature, these gases act in two ways: a) dissolution of gases at high temperature in molten metal promotes porosity due to rapid cooling of weld metal during solidification and b) chemical reaction between the gases and molten metal promotes the formation of oxides and nitrides as inclusions. These defects break the metallic continuity and act as a site of stress concentration, which in turn decrease the load carrying capacity, and mechanical performance of the fusion weld joints (Fig. 6.10).

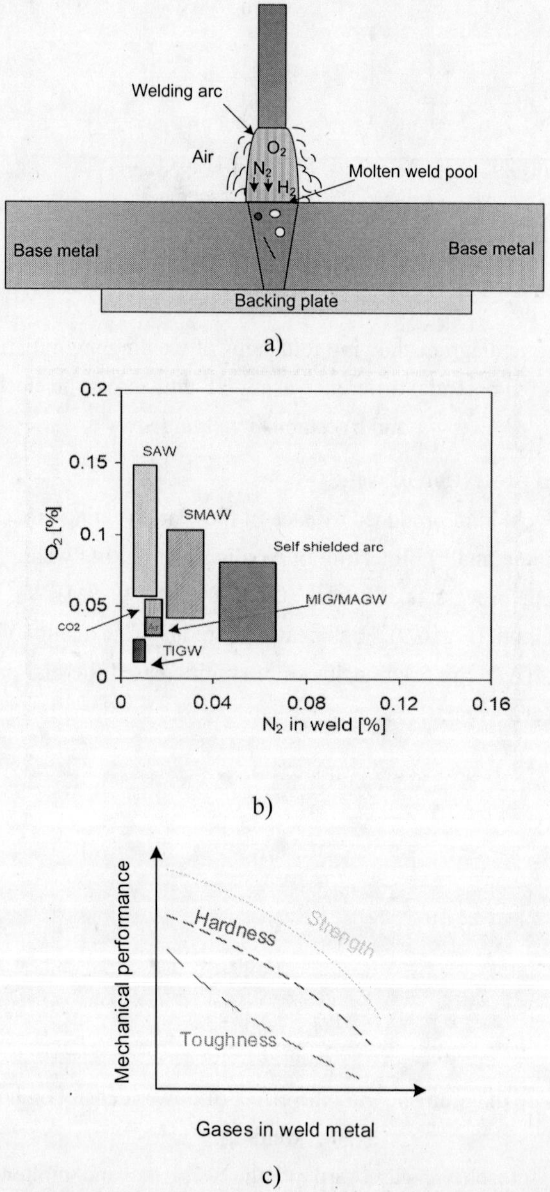

Fig. 6.10 Schematic diagram showing a) a typical gaseous environment in and around the welding arc, b) gaseous found in weld produced by different arc welding processes, and c) the effect of gases in weld metal on mechanical performance.

Further, the approach of shielding the molten welding pool is also different in the case of SMAW, GMAW and GTAW (Table 6.2). SMAW involves the formation of a weak inactive gas shroud/cover of inactive gas (CO_2) around the welding arc/ pool by thermal decomposition of electrode coating through arc heat, which provides weak shielding to the weld pool. GMAW uses the formation of a firm inactive / inert gas cover of inert gas (Ar/He) or inactive gas like (CO_2) around the welding arc with the help of a jet of shielding gas coming out of the nozzle. The jet provides effective shielding. GTAW uses the formation of a firm inert gas cover only around the welding arc using a jet of inert shielding gas (Ar/ He) coming out of the nozzle. It provides the most effective shielding due to a) use of inert gases only and b) short arc length and it results in the best quality fusion welding joint amongst these three processes due to a) use of inert gases only and b) short arc length. The protection of the weld pool is relatively poor and net heat input is higher for SMAW and GMAW than GTAW. Therefore, the quality of sound GTAW joints is far better than SMAW and GMAW joints.

$$Net\ heat\ input\ H_{net}(\frac{KJ}{mm}) = \frac{V\ (Volts) \times I(Ampere)}{S\ (m/min) \times 1000}$$

Where I is the welding current (ampere), V arc voltage (volt), welding speed (m/min), net heat input (kJ/mm).

Table 6.2 Technological aspects of arc welding process

S. No.	Welding process	Filler	Shielding	Quality	Net heat input
1	SMAW	Flux coated electrode	Thermal decomposition of flux	Moderate	High
2	GMAW	Bare electrode	Inactive or inert gas jet shielding	Good	Moderate to high
3	GTAW	Optional	Inert gas	High quality	Low

6.7 Arc characteristics

Arc characteristics show the variation in arc voltage as a function of welding current due to varying conditions generated during welding within the welding arc with respect to heat, temperature, charge particle density and arc shape (Fig. 6.11). The Increase of welding current increases heat generation, arc diameter and temperature within the arc, which in turn increases the charge particle density. Increased charge particle density reduces electrical resistance for the flow of current. These factors in turn reduce the voltage across the arc gap leading to dropping characteristics. Further, the increase of current increases the heat, and temperature but at the same time, the increase of arc diameter also increases the loss of heat and charge particles from the arc surface. These opposite effects lead to a balance of heat/ charge particle generation / loss causing no change in voltage with an increase of current resulting in flat characteristics. Further, a higher current distorts the shape of arc by bulging, leading to much greater surface area of the arc, and causing much more loss of heat and charge particles from the arc surface. This causes an increase in voltage with current, leading to rising characteristics.

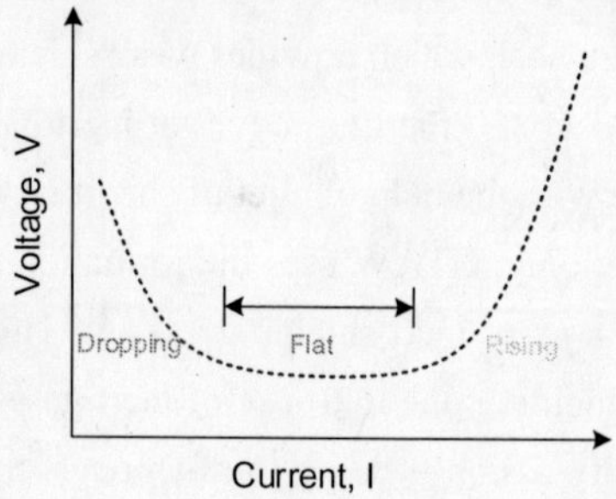

Fig. 6.11 Schematic diagram showing arc characteristics

6.8 Welding power source

Arc welding power source delivers a low voltage and high current supply to establish a welding arc. The power source can supply AC or DC as per the need of the process and electrode. Arc welding using DC provides a more stable and smoother arc than AC. That is due to continuous variation in the magnitude and direction of the flow of current / voltage during AC welding. The welding power sources are also classified based on the delivered current and voltage relationship with arc length during arc welding. Constant current and constant voltage are the two most common types of welding power sources. The intersection of welding power characteristics with arc characteristics is called the operating point. The operating point shows the actual current and voltage at a given arc length.

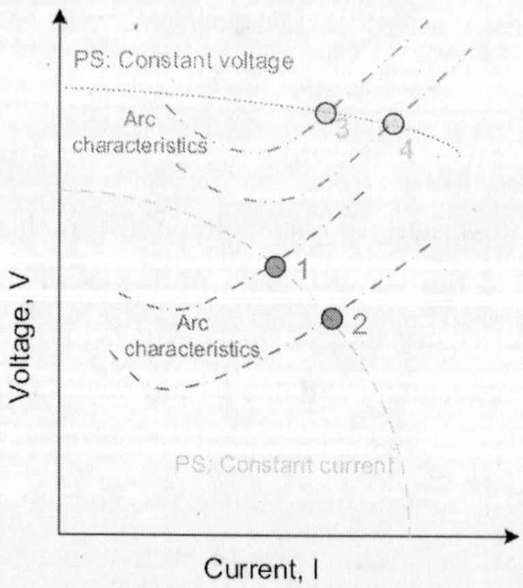

Fig. 6.12 Schematic diagram showing welding power and arc characteristics for constant current and constant voltage type of power sources.

Welding current largely remains constant even with minor variation of arc length during welding in case of the constant current power source e.g. a little a decrease of arc length from operating point 1 to 2. A constant voltage power source causes a very large increase in welding current with a decrease in arc length from operating point 3 to 4 (Fig. 6.12).

6.9 Electrode Polarity

The polarity of electrode continuously changes during AC welding in every half cycle. While, in the case of DC welding, polarity depends on connections of power source made to the electrode and parent metal. Two types of polarity are used in DC welding i.e., direct current straight polarity (direct current electrode negative DCEN) and direct current reverse polarity (direct current electrode positive DCEP). The DC electrode negative polarity is invariably preferred for shielding metal arc welding, gas tungsten arc welding and plasma arc welding. While DCEP polarity is used in case of fine-diameter electrode during gas metal arc welding and submerged arc welding to get a high deposition rate and self regulating arc. Electrode polarity in DC arc welding affects three aspects: a) arc stability, b) heat generation and c) weld metal cleaning (Fig. 6.13).

Welding electrodes for SMAW and GTAW are designed to act as cathode for easy emission of electrons to obtain easy arc initiation and good arc stability during DC welding. Therefore, DCEN polarity is preferably used in these processes unless the application is very unique e.g. requirement of cleaning action of weld pool. GMAW process uses uncoated electrodes of metal mostly similar to the parent metal. Therefore, DCEP helps in achieving higher melting rate and greater deposition rate.

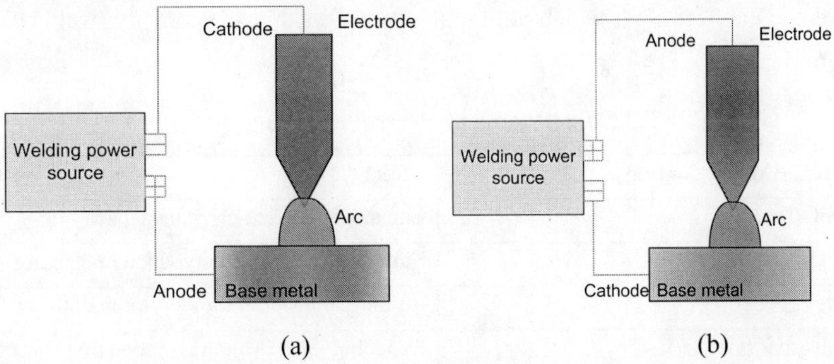

Fig. 6.13 Schematic diagram showing the effect of electrode polarity during DC welding (a) DCEN and (b) DCEP. Also mark the figures as (a) and (b).

The heat generated (VI) by AC welding arc is almost the same both at the parent metal and electrode sides. However, heat generation by DC welding on the parent metal and electrode side heavily depends on the electrode polarity. Two-third of DC welding arc heat is generated on the anode side and the remaining one-third on the cathode side. Therefore, GTAW invariably uses DCEN for longer electrode life except during GTAW for Al welding to produce a clean weld using DCEP/AC. Applying DCEP during GTAW makes the workpiece cathode, which helps in loosening and removing the alumina oxide layer formed over molten weld pool during welding, resulting in cleaner weld metal.

6.10 Fusion welding processes

6.10.1 Shielded Metal Arc Welding

Shielded metal arc welding (SMAW) uses heat generated by arc established between a consumable electrode and parent metal for melting faying surfaces to produce a weld joint (Fig. 6.14). The consumable electrode of SMAW has a coating of flux over the core wire. The coating of flux performs many functions such as easy arc initiation and arc stabilization, providing inactive shielding gas shroud for protection of the weld pool, adding alloying elements, adjusting the viscosity of slag favourably to support weld pool in odd position welding, removing impurities by forming slag and increasing deposition rate by mixing metal powers with flux.

Electrode coating thickness in SMAW is characterized by a parameter called coating factor, which is the ratio of diameter of electrode including coating and diameter of core wire. Three types of electrode coatings are the most common, namely rutile, acidic and basic. Common constitutes of flux coating in SMAW electrodes and their function are listed in **Table 6.3.** Combustion of coating provides protection to the weld pool. Melting of core wire provides the desired filler metal to fill the gap/groove for producing weld metal. Welding arc movement in SMAW is controlled manually. Therefore, fluctuations in welding speed and heat input-linked penetration are common. Variation in welding speed (for given arc voltage V and welding current I) affects the net heat input which in turn affects the weld bead geometry (weld bead width and penetration).

Table 6.3 Constituents in electrode coating

S. No.	Constituent SMAW coating	Effect
1	Quartz (SiO_2)	Enhancing current-carrying capacity
2	Rutile (TiO_2)	Enhancing slag viscosity, good re-striking
3	Magnetite (Fe_3O_4)	Refining transfer of droplets through the arc
4	Calcareous spar ($CaCO_3$)	Reducing arc voltage, producing inactive shielding gas, slag formation
5	Fluorspar (CaF_2)	Increasing slag viscosity of basic electrodes, decreases ionization
6	Calcareous- fluorspar (K_2O Al_2O_3 $6SiO_2$)	Improving arc stability by easy ionization
7	Ferro-manganese and Ferro-silicon	Acting as de-oxidant
8	Cellulose	Producing inactive shielding gas
9	Potassium Sodium Silicate (K_2SiO_3 / Na_2SiO_3)	Acting as a bonding agent

Welding current in SMAW usually varies from 50-600 A and arc voltage ranges from 30-100 V. Welding current selection depends on net heat input desired based on a) section thickness to be welded in a single pass and b) electrode diameter (diameter of core wire). The thick section needs higher net heat input for deeper penetration, which is realised using high welding current and a little lower the welding speed. However, the maximum current that an electrode can handle depends on electrode diameter, i.e., diameter of the core wire). In general welding current varies from 4 to 5 times the electrode diameter.

Further, protection to the weld pool provided by inactive gases shroud formed due to the thermal decomposition of electrode coating. The protection in SMAW is very poor. The poor weld pool protection allows entry of atmospheric gases in the weld zone/pool leading to an increased possibility of weld defects formation in the form of porosity, and inclusions due to dissolution, interaction and reactions of atmospheric gases with molten weld metal.

The most common welding power source for SMAW is a welding transformer. The transformer is very cost effective, portable and easy to maintain. However, it provides AC. DCEN is the preferred polarity for easy arc initiation and maintenance during SMAW. Constant current power sources are invariably used for SMAW as they deliver largely constant welding current during welding. The ability to deliver almost constant current during SMAW by constant current welding power source ensures consistent penetration and uniform weld bead geometry due to constancy of heat generation (VI) as shown in Fig. 6.12. SMAW is the most common arc welding process used for general welding applications in workshops and industries.

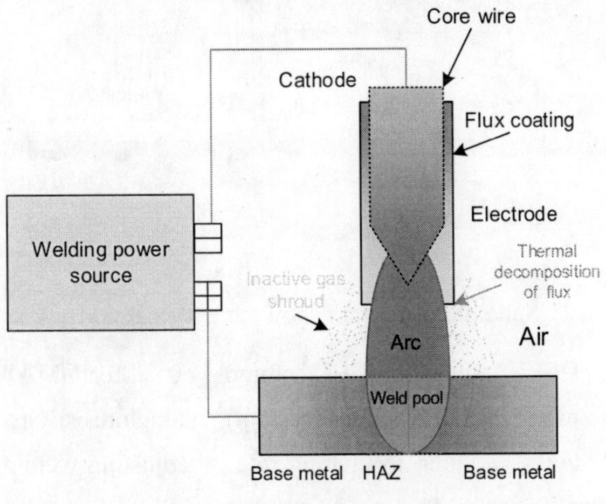

Fig. 6.14 Schematic diagram showing a typical SMAW system.

6.10.2 Gas metal arc welding

Gas metal arc welding (GMAW) is one of the most commercially used welding processes for developing good quality welding joints at a reasonably high deposition rate and moderate cost per unit length of weld. Similar to SMAW, GMAW also uses heat generated by an arc established between a consumable electrode and parent metal for melting the faying surfaces of base metals to be joined (Fig. 6.15). The protection to the weld pool (from atmospheric gases) in GMAW is provided by a shroud formed by a jet of inert / inactive shielding gas as per the metal system and quality requirements. Since the approach to protect the weld pool in GMAW is more effective than the SMAW, quality of the GMAW joint is better than that of the SMAW joint in terms of oxygen and nitrogen content in the weld metal. These gases in weld metal otherwise led to the formation of weld defects like porosity and inclusions. Inert gases like Ar, He and mixtures of Ar + He are used for high quality weld joints. While, mixtures of Ar + $CO_2/O_2/H_2$ and inactive gas like CO_2 are commonly used during GMAW for welding commercial quality weld joints of ferrous metals.

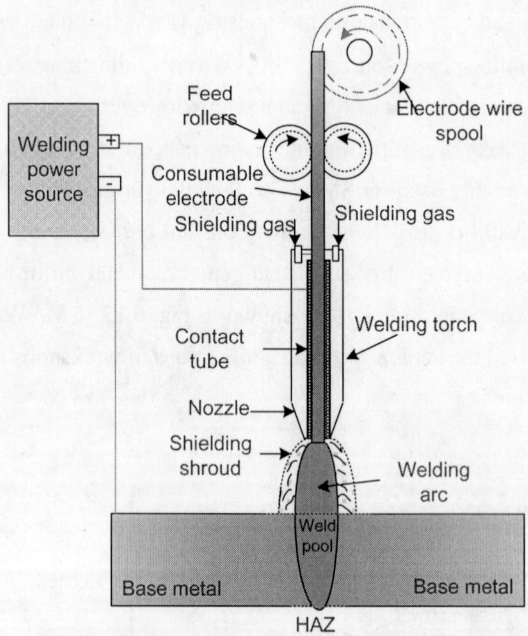

Fig. 6.15 Schematic diagram showing a typical GMAW system.

A constant voltage (DCEP) power source is commonly used for GMAW to realize the self-regulating arc while using a small diameter (~1 mm) and high resistivity electrode (steels). A self-regulating arc allows variation in melting rate by adjusting welding current in case of constant voltage power source and by sensing the arc gap. Self-regulating arc helps to maintain arc length. A fluctuation in melting rate due to any reason during welding (using constant feed rate of electrode) alters the arc gap. For example, a reduction in the arc gap increases the welding current (with constant voltage power source), which in turn increases melting rate to maintain the arc gap and reverse happens with an increase of the arc gap (Fig. 6.12). A constant current power source is used in case of a large diameter (> 3-4 mm) or low resistivity electrode (aluminium).

GMAW process uses two groups of wire feed systems which are classified based on a) speed of filler and b) type of force used to feed electrode. Based on spool of wire, there are two types of feed system, namely constant speed and variable speed wire feed system (Fig.6.16). Additionally, the wire feed system is also classified based on the type of force: a) pull type of wire feed, b) push type and c) pull-push both. The force applied depends on the location where rollers are installed to feed the wire.

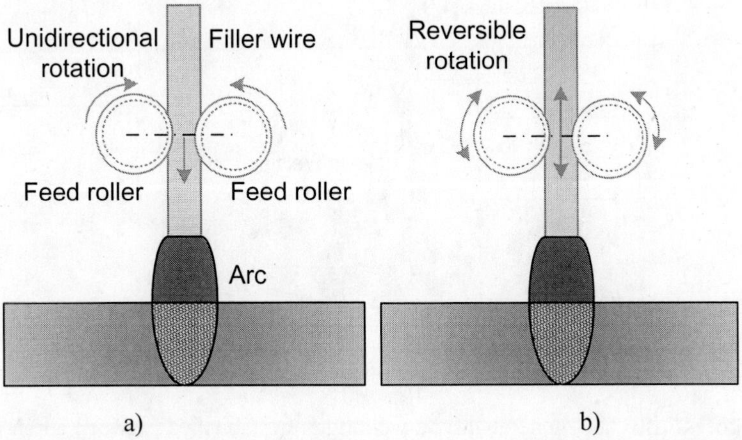

Fig. 6.16 Schematic for wire feed system a) constant speed and b) variable speed feed system

It is important to maintain the arc length during GMAW for consistency in weld quality and characteristics. In case of large diameter electrodes, melting rate does not respond that fast to the change in welding current. Therefore, a variable speed electrode feed system is used to maintain the arc gap. Under such welding conditions, self-regulating arc mechanism does not work to maintain the arc length. A variable speed feed system senses the arc gap and fluctuation in the arc gap due to any reason, is corrected by changing the electrode feed rate to maintain the arc length. Constant speed wire feed system is used with constant voltage power source while using small diameter electrode to realize the self regulating arc.

6.10.3 Gas tungsten arc welding

Gas tungsten arc welding (GTAW) is one of the most important welding processes for developing high quality welding joints to satisfy stringent quality requirements for fabrication of components related to nuclear reactors, aerospace, spacecraft, and pressure vessel sectors. The penetration and deposition rate (if the filler is used) obtained by GTAW is relatively low due to the inherent low heat input nature of this process. The low heat input and very good protection of the weld pool are the two most attractive features of GTAW resulting in high quality weld joints.

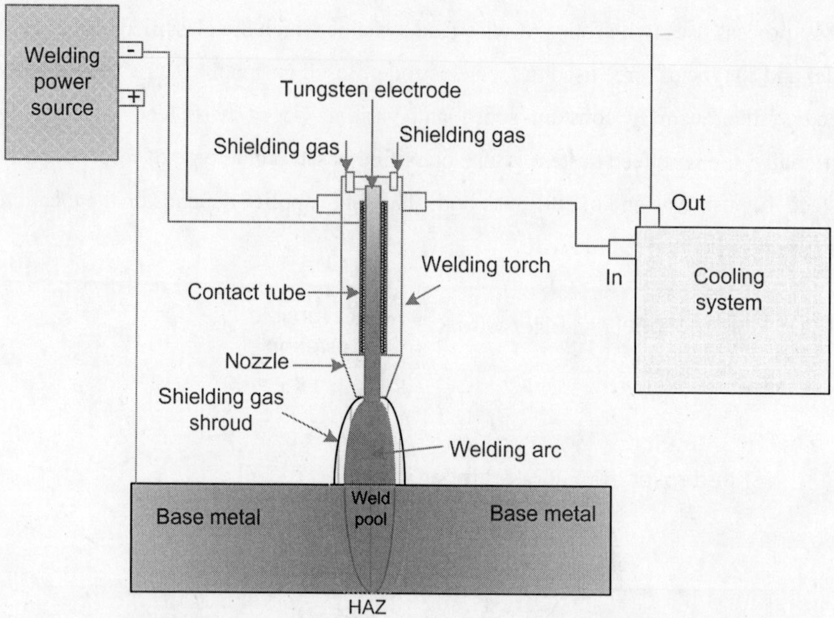

Fig. 6.17 Schematic diagram showing a typical GTAW system

GTAW process uses heat generated by a welding arc established between a non-consumable tungsten electrode and parent metal to melt the faying surfaces. The protection to the weld pool (from atmospheric gases) is provided by a jet of inert gases like Ar, He, or their mixture as shielding gas (Fig. 6.17). A combination of short arc length, non-consumable tungsten electrode and inert shield gas protection provides very effective protection to the weld pool which in turn results in the cleanest weld metal amongst all arc welding processes (Fig. 6.10b). Low heat input obtained through GTAW provides shallow penetration, which facilitates the welding of thin sheets (< 3 to 4 mm) in a single pass of welding.

GTAW machine is rated based on the maximum welding current 200 A, 300 A, 400 A, etc. Low current welding torches are air cooled as these torches can handle heat generated without much-thermal damage. However, high current rating GTAW systems are water cooled for longer life and good performance.

Single pass welding of thin sheets is usually autogenous, involving just melting of faying surfaces followed by solidification to develop weld joints. To weld thicker sections, the edges of the components are prepared in the form of single or double U, V, J bevel grooves as per thickness and requirements of quality in terms of residual stress and distortion. Thereafter, first tagging is done to ensure the correct position of two components. Then, the root pass welding performed using low heat input, followed by the multi-pass welding are performed until the groove is filled in. Multi-pass welding needs a supply of filler metal in the arc zone. A suitable combination of filler wires can be fed either manually or with the help of a wire feeder (Fig. 6.18). A constant current (DCEN) power source is commonly used for GTAW to facilitate constancy of current due to fluctuations in arc length in manually controlled torch. Application of DCEP or AC is preferred only for welding aluminium alloys to obtain better cleaning action. However, more heat generation (using DCRP) on tungsten electrode side causes faster thermal degradation/erosion of the electrode. Tungsten electrodes coated by thorium or zirconium increase the current carrying capacity of the electrode compared to pure tungsten electrodes.

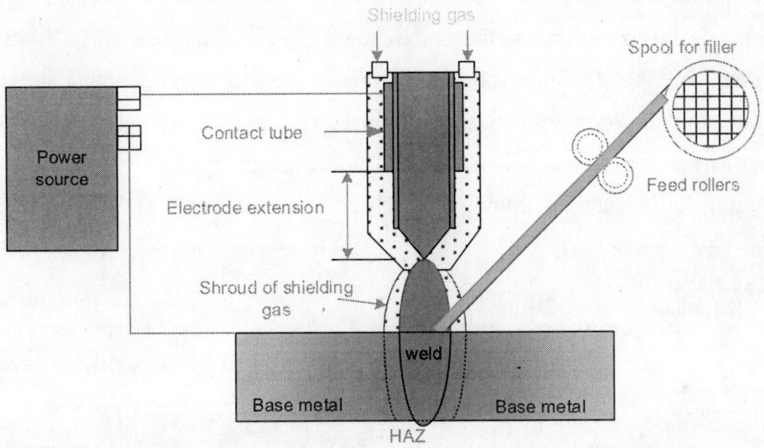

Fig. 6.18 Schematic diagram showing a typical GTAW with external filler wire feeding

6.11 Brazing and soldering

Brazing and soldering are two different processes but work on a similar approach. These are classified as solid/liquid metal joining processes for developing lap joint. The parent metals are heated to a high temperature (as per the filler metal to be used) using suitable heat source in a solid state without causing any melting. A low melting point filler (brazing/soldering metal) is melted when placed over the components to be joined. Heating of parent metal/filler can be realized using a suitable external heat source like gas flame, induction, resistance heating, etc. Application of a suitable flux on the parent metals at the joint interface (before applying filler) leads to cleaning of surfaces, improving fluidity and spread-ability in the closely control gap. The gap between the sheet/parent metals during brazing / soldering is called clearance. Clearance is controlled carefully to realize good bonding and spreading of filler through capillary action. The molten filler metal spreads at the interface between the components by capillary action.

The general approach for brazing and soldering to develop a joint is the same, wherein low melting temperature metal is melted using a suitable heat source (resistance heating, induction heating, gap flame, frictional heating, molten bath, etc.) as shown in Fig. 6.19. The molten filler spreads in the closely controlled gap (between the parent metals called clearance from 0.025 to 0.25 mm) by capillary action. To realize good capillary action and distribution of filler metal, clearance should be closely controlled. Applying flux during brazing/soldering removes the impurities from the surfaces and improves the fluidity and spread-ability of molten filler metal over the entire bonding/overlap area. Spreading of the molten filler metal due to capillary action is significantly governed by the cleanliness and roughness of parent metals, fluidity of molten metal and clearance (Fig. 6.20). Clearance affects capillary pressure and spreading of filler metal at the interface, which in turn affects joint strength based on the bonding ratio. The bonding ratio is the bonded area to the total joint area. Smooth and clean surfaces result in good brazing and soldering. The flux (borax) commonly used for brazing and soldering must be removed to avoid the corrosion tendency of joints. Various types of joints (braze / solder) are developed as per the desired orientation and arrangement of sheets. A few common joint configurations for butt and lap joining of sheets are shown in Fig. 6.21.

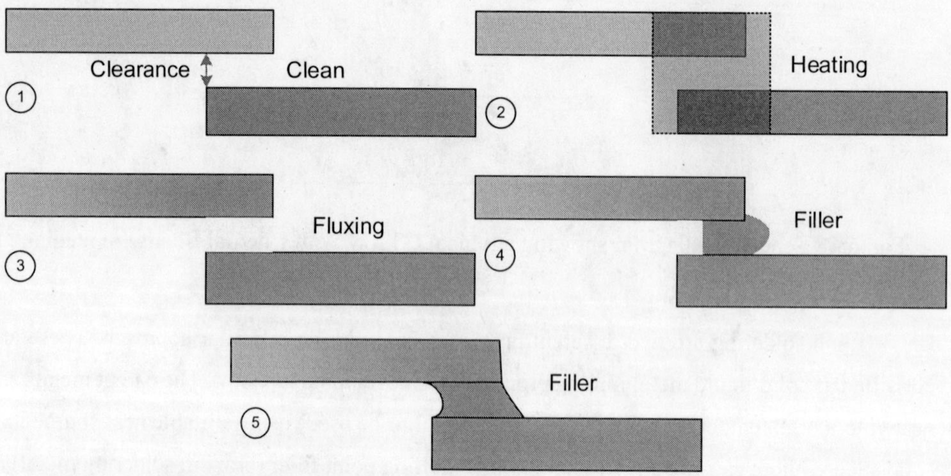

Fig. 6.19 Schematic diagram showing sequential steps of brazing/soldering process

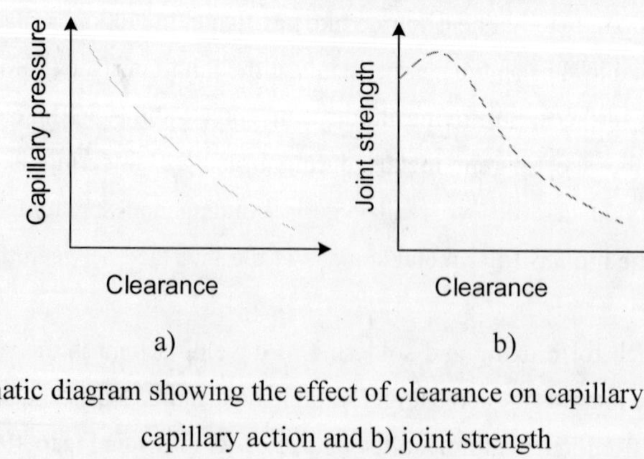

Fig. 6.20 Schematic diagram showing the effect of clearance on capillary pressure controlling capillary action and b) joint strength

The joint in brazing and soldering is formed due to metallurgical interaction between the molten filler metal and parent metal. These filler metals (brazing/soldering metal) usually differ significantly from the parent metals (in composition). Therefore, the interaction between the molten filler metal and solid surface parent metals develops an intermetallic compound (IMC). The mechanical properties of IMC formed at interfaces of the parent metals, apart from filler metal itself, determine the strength of brazed/soldered joint. For example, the brazing of steel and aluminium using Al-Si filler forms two different types of IMCs on each side and filler metal (Al-Si) as shown in Fig.6.22.

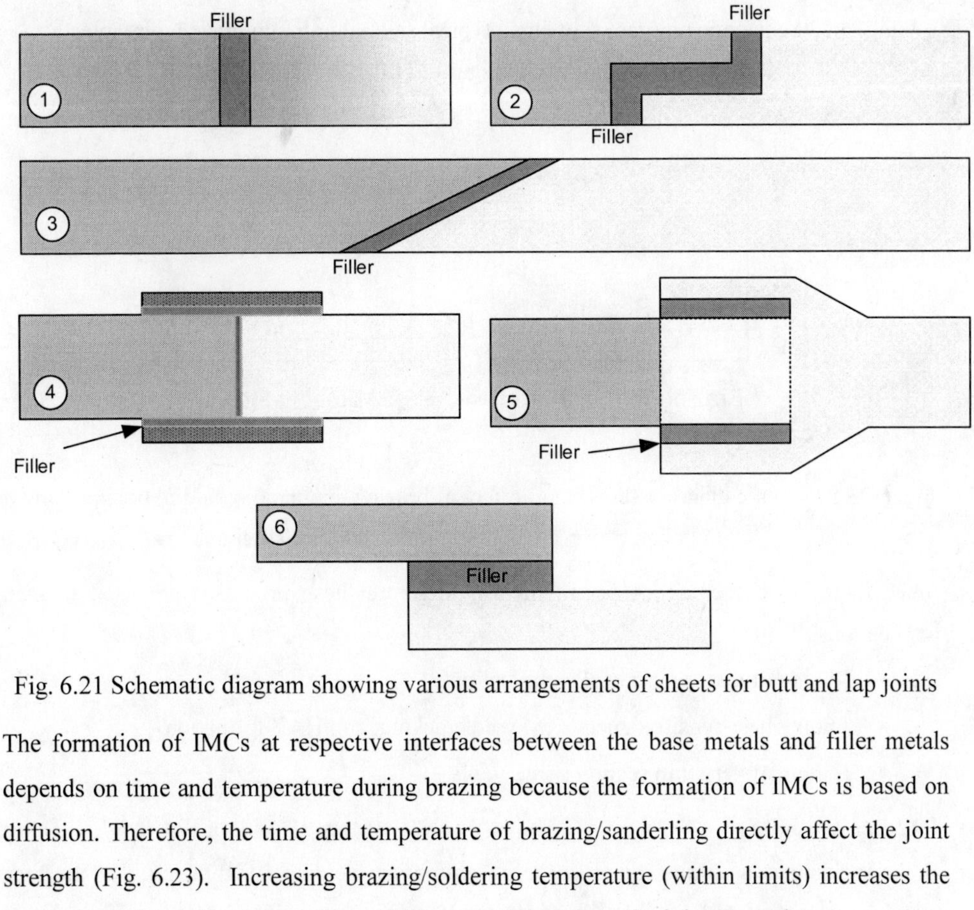

Fig. 6.21 Schematic diagram showing various arrangements of sheets for butt and lap joints

The formation of IMCs at respective interfaces between the base metals and filler metals depends on time and temperature during brazing because the formation of IMCs is based on diffusion. Therefore, the time and temperature of brazing/sanderling directly affect the joint strength (Fig. 6.23). Increasing brazing/soldering temperature (within limits) increases the boding ratio due to better spreading of filler, which increases the joint strength.

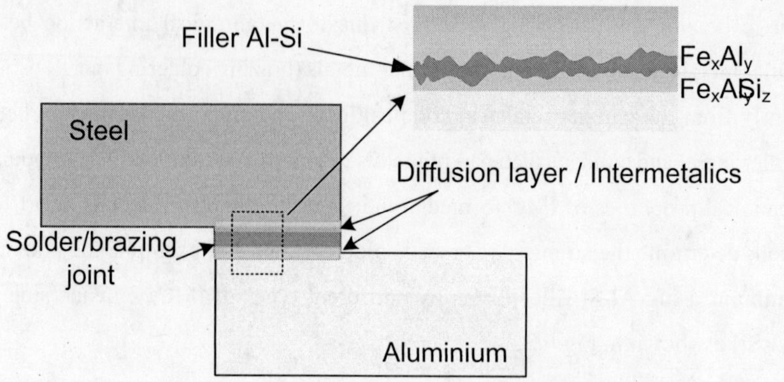

Fig. 6.22 Schematic diagram showing a typical steel-aluminium brazed joint interface morphology with regard to filler and IMCs

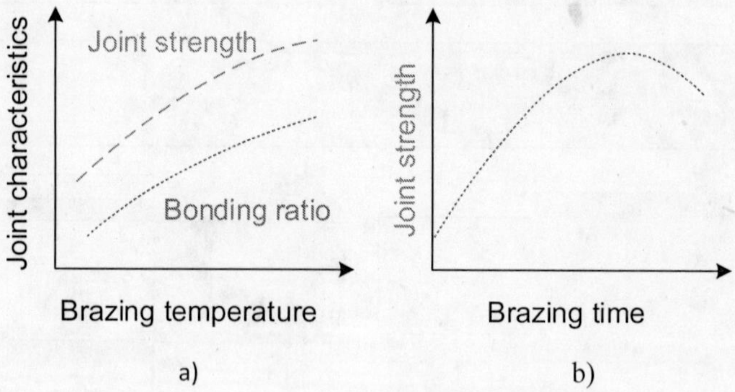

Fig. 6.23 Schematic diagram showing a) effect of brazing temperature and b) brazing time on joint characteristics (bonding ratio and joint strength)

Since there is no melting of parent metals, therefore these processes are used in many applications.

- Joining of dissimilar metal combinations
- Joining heat-sensitive metals to avoid cracking, and HAZ formation
- Joining of very thin section sheet, wires

6.12 Braze welding

Braze welding is a unique joining process combining welding and brazing. For the braze welding, edge (groove) preparation of relatively thick components in butt configuration is carried out. Then groove is filled-in by brazing process without capillary action. There is no melting of faying surfaces of base metals in braze welding. The mechanical performance of braze weld joint (apart from soundness) solely depends on the characteristics of brazing materials and IMCs formed at the respective interfaces (Fig. 6.24).

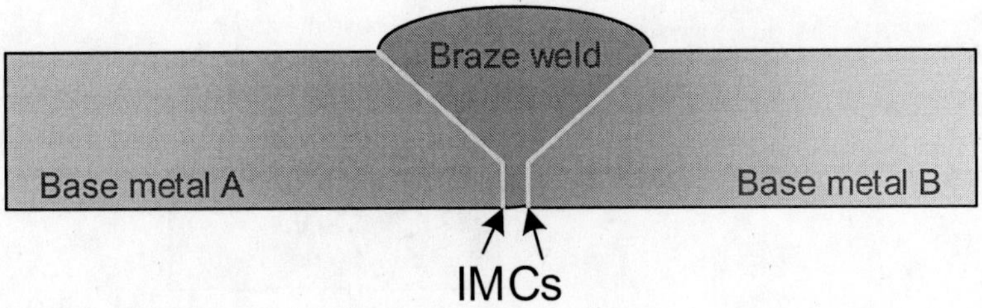

Fig. 6.24 Schematic diagram showing braze welding joint

6.13 Adhesive bonding

Adhesive bonding is based on the approach of chemical interaction between adhesive and parent metals to develop a bond. Adhesive bonding is invariably used to develop lap joints due to large overlap / area requirement to get reasonably good strength. Overlap available in the case of butt joints configuration is very limited. Therefore, adhesive joints in butt configuration offer very poor bond stength hence these are not preferred. Overlap length is the main design aspect of adhesive joining apart from the placement of sheet and additional coversheet.

Adhesive joining involves three main steps: a) surface preparation (cleaning, degreasing, etc.) and roughening for high bond strength, b) applying adhesive at the interface in between adherends and c) curing of adhesive to impart the desired joint strength. These steps are presented schematically in Fig. 6.25.

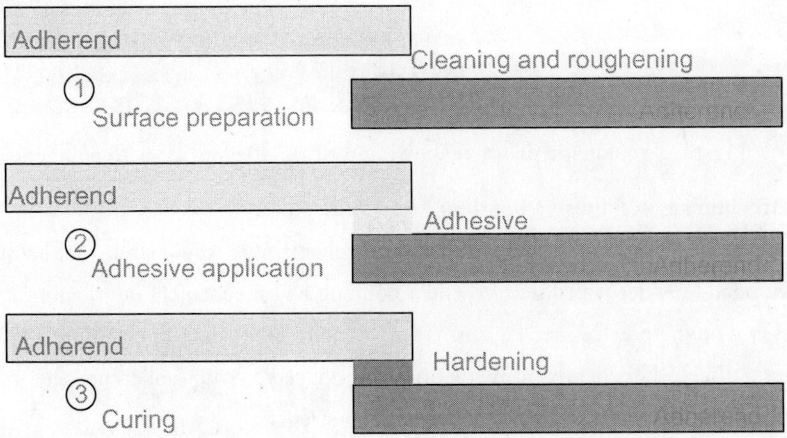

Fig. 6.25 Schematic diagram showing steps of adhesive joining

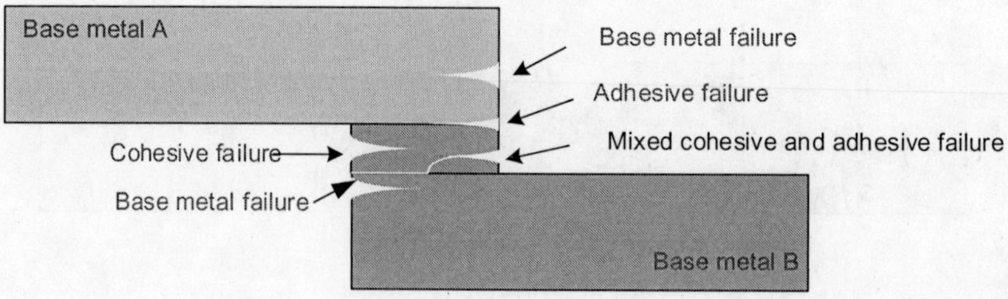

Fig. 6.26 Schematic diagram showing various possible failure location in adhesive bonding

The failure of an adhesive bond, can occur from any of the four locations, namely base metal failure, cohesive failure, adhesive failure or mix of cohesive and adhesive failure as shown in Fig. 6.26. Location of failure of adhesive bond suggests the weak zone/link on which attention should be given to improve the bond strength. The following are a few conditions to obtain a good adhesive joint.

- Wetting of faying surfaces with adhesive as per surface energy of adherend with respect to adhesive (Fig. 6.27)
- Interaction of adhesive with faying surfaces
- Clean surfaces of adherend free from impurities and gaseous packets / bubble
- Proper joint design.

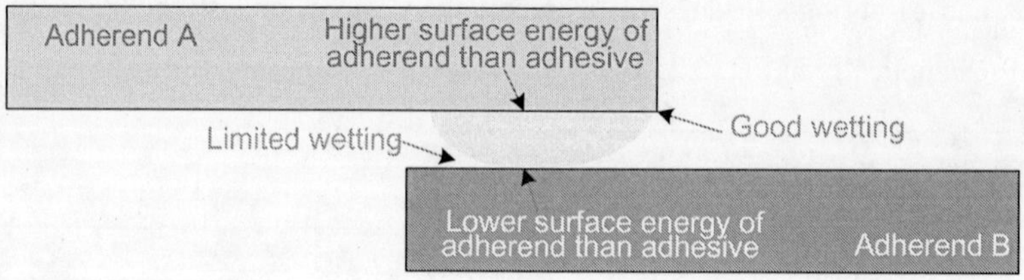

Fig. 6.27 Schematic diagram showing wetting of adhesive with adherend

6.13.1 Mechanism of adhesive bonding

There are multiple hypotheses regarding the mechanism(s) responsible for the strength of adhesive bond (Vander wall force, covalent bonding and mechanical interlocking). Clarity is still missing on the precise mechanism. However, surface treatment, cleanliness, and surface roughness affect the chemical interactions of adhesive with adherend and mechanical interlocking which in turn affect the adhesive joint strength.

6.13.2 Adhesive

The adhesive is a mixture of suitable polymers (thermo-setting, thermo-plastic), resins/hardeners, elastomers, and filler. These ingredients facilitate easy adhesive joining coupled with desired mechanical performance. The resin and hardener allow hardening and strength of the adhesive joint. Elastomer provides resilience and plastic strain capacity. Filler helps to realize other desired characteristics like electrical/thermal conductivity/resistivity, etc. Adhesives based on thermo-setting resins offer higher strength and low ductility than those of thermo-plastic adhesive. Therefore, thermo-setting polymer-based adhesives are used for structural adhesive joining applications.

6.13.3 Adhesive joint strength

The strength of adhesive joint is determined by the type of adhesive, type and amount of elastomer/fillers, and overlap length and curing condition of the adhesive joint. Curing is a hardening process of adhesive joint, which is temperature and time dependent. Curing of thermoplastic adhesive joint occurs through a reversible process with the change of phase from liquid to solid transformation without any chemical reactions. While curing of thermo-setting adhesive joint occurs through irreversible process coupled with chemical reactions involving long chain & cross-linking polymerization. Cross-linking polymerization in thermo-setting polymers results in higher bond strength than long-chains only in thermo-plastics.

Curing of adhesive joint at high temperature occurs in a few minutes, while at room temperature it takes longer. The maximum adhesive joint strength is achieved by optimizing cutting temperature and time (Fig. 6.28). Both under and over curing reduce the strength of adhesive joint due to a) lack of polymerization and b) thermal decomposition of polymers, respectively.

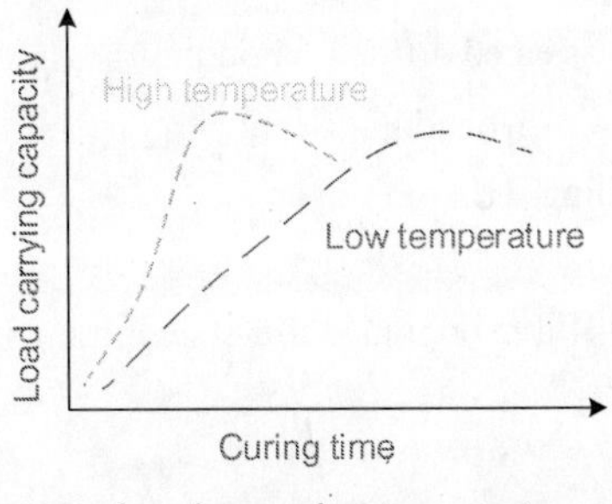

Fig. 6.28 Schematic diagram showing curing temperature and time on strength of the adhesive bond

6.14 Solid state joining process

The solid-state joining (SSJ) processes develop a joint between two components in a solid state without any (or very negligible) melting of faying surfaces under improper joining conditions. Solid state joining processes, unlike the fusion welding process, work at very low heat input. Therefore, these are found suitable for joining of dissimilar material, very heat sensitive metals, and metals with large incompatibility (variations in physical, chemical, mechanical and metallurgical properties).

These (solid-state) joints can be developed using bonding / joining mechanisms like diffusion, metallurgical reactions, plastic deformation and mechanical interlocking (with / without application of external heat). The surface of components to be joined must be free from impurities like oxides, oil, paint, etc. to develop a good metallurgical joint in a solid state joining to ensure perfect metallic intimacy. Solid state joining invariably involves macro/micro-scale plastic deformation. Therefore, high ductility and low yield strength are preferred in at least one metal of the combination to facilitate easy joining. Further, heating of metallic components (during SSJ) either due to in-situ phenomena like friction, impact, or external heating (using gas flame, induction, or resistance heating), reduces the yield strength and increases the ductility. Softened metals make the solid state joining easier and faster. Solid state-joining processes are classified based on various technological aspects.

- Macro-deformation of faying surfaces of components to be joined
  - Forge welding
  - Friction welding
  - Friction stir welding
- Micro-deformation at interfaces of components to be joined
  - Ultrasonic welding
  - Explosive welding
  - Roll bonding
- Diffusion across the surface of components to be joined
  - Conventional diffusion bonding
  - Pulse pressure assisted diffusion bonding
  - Modified surface diffusion bonding
  - Diffusion bonding with interlayer
  - Diffusion brazing

The following section presents three popular solid-state joining process namely forge welding, FSW & FW.

6.14.1 Forging welding

The forging welding is a macro-plastic deformation based joining process. Metallic components are heated using a suitable method (coal fired furnace, induction heating, resistance heating) to temperature (0.4 to 0.6 Tm) high enough for softening and inducing ductility. The heating temperature depends on the metal and is usually above the recrystallization temperature. The steel components are heated to an austenitic state (more than the lower critical temperature). Thereafter, suitable flux is applied on the heated faying surfaces of components (to be joined) for removing impurities and oxides. These components are placed in the proper position followed by controlled plastic deformation through mechanized/manually operated hammers. The components may be manipulated suitably between the hammer blows to achieve the desired plastic deformation for mechanical interlocking and metallurgical bonding. A metallurgical joint formed after forging welding leaves no distinct interface between two forge-welded components. The steps of forge welding are shown using schematic diagrams in Fig.6.29.

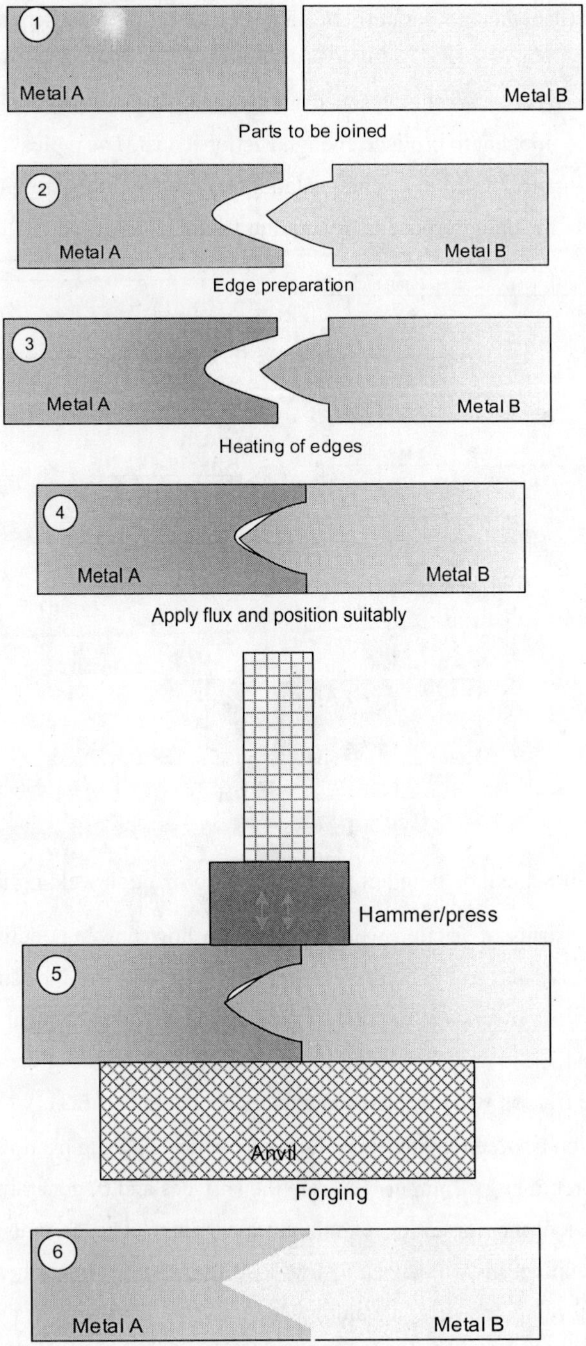

Fig. 6.29 Schematic diagram showing steps of forge welding

6.14.2 Friction welding

The friction welding process uses frictional heat generated under in-situ conditions during welding to increase the temperature of faying surfaces and soften metallic components followed by forging action to develop a friction weld joint. One component is held stationary while the other one is rotated at high speed and gradually brought in contact under normal load with stationary component to produce enough frictional heat. The typical friction welding steps are shown in Fig. 6.30. Many other rotational combinations are possible between the components with the main purpose of generating frictional heat.

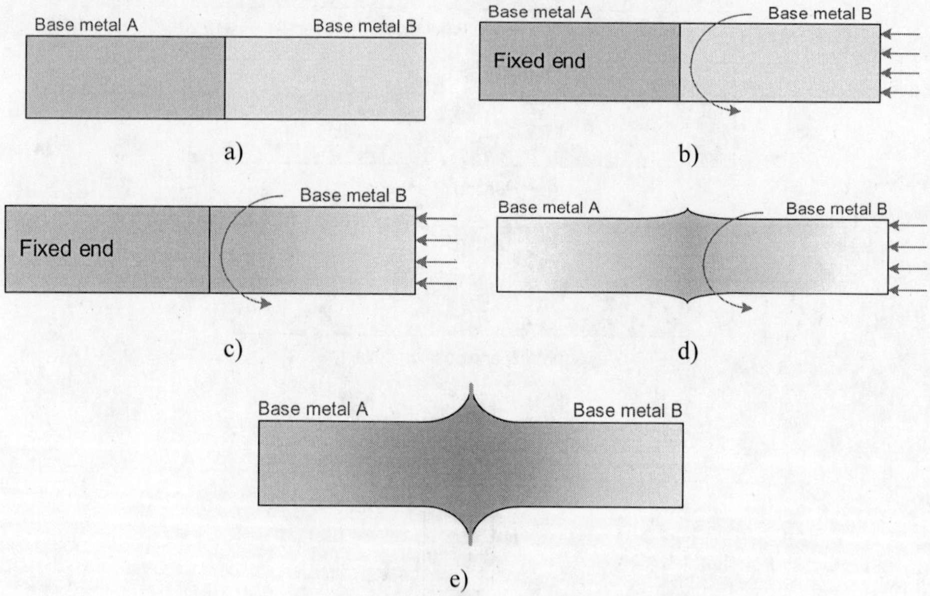

Fig. 6.30 Schematic diagram showing steps of friction welding from a) to e)

There are two variants of friction welding based on how power is delivered for joining: a) constant speed drive and b) inertia drive. Approach-wise both are the same, but they differ in terms of delivery of power as a function of time during welding. Typical variation in pressure (force), rotational speed and shortening of component length during the constant speed drive and inertia drive friction welding is schematically shown in Fig. 6.31.

The rubbing action between faying surfaces of components during friction welding contributes in two ways: a) removing all impurities from the surfaces and b) generating frictional heat for softening, diffusion and formation of metallurgical joint. The normal load on the rotation components is applied in two stages: a) low load to cause frictional heating followed by b) application of forging load (high value) which causes upsetting. As soon as the desired temperature at the rubbing surfaces (interface) is achieved, normal pressure is increased (during constant speed drive friction welding) to cause upset forging. Upsetting brings two components close to each other at the atomic level, leading to the development of metallurgical bonds by forming new grains across the interface through diffusion. However, normal load varies only in the case of constant speed drive friction welding and not during inertia welding.

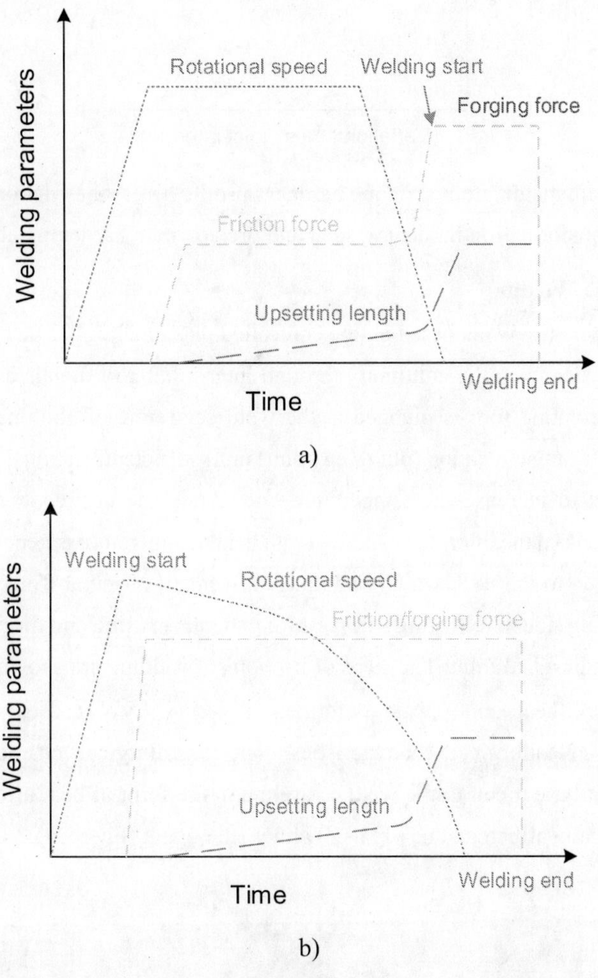

Fig. 6.31 Schematic diagram showing variations in process parameters during a) constant speed drive and b) inertia drive friction welding

Thermo-mechanical exposure of steel components during friction welding results in the hardening of joint interface due to the transformation of soft phases like ferrite, pearlite into bainite and martensite. While reverse happens in the form of softening during friction welding of precipitation hardening metal due to reversion (loss/dissolution) of precipitates and coarsening of grains and over-tempering e.g. in case of quenched and tempered (Q & T) steel). A typical hardness profiles of transformation hardening steel and precipitation hardening aluminium alloy friction weld joint is shown in Fig. 6.32.

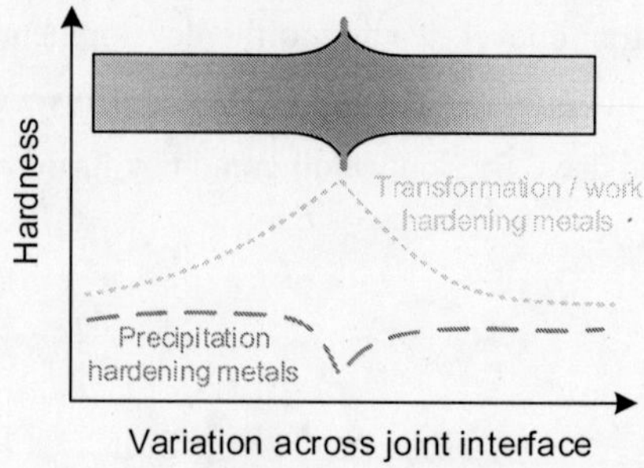

Fig. 6.32 Schematic diagram showing hardness profile across the friction welding joint interface of transformation hardening steel and precipitation hardening aluminium alloy.

6.15 Friction Stir Welding

Friction stir welding (FSW) is based on the controlled plastic deformation of two components to be joined to realize metallic continuity through inter-mixing of metals using a consumable rotation tool. A rotating tool is plunged at the weld centreline of abutting components and continued to rotate at one location (plunging point) until sufficient frictional and deformational heat is generated to increase the temperature and obtain the desired thermal softening of metallic components at the interface. Once enough heat / temperature is generated, translational movement is given to the tool, which facilitates movement of metal from front side to back side (and advancing side to retreating side) resulting in inter-mixing and forging action of metal to produce a metallurgical joint. The steps of friction stir welding are shown in Fig. 6.33.

A combination of heat and plastic deformation during FSW causes many changes in mechanical and metallurgical characteristics. The metallurgical characteristics vary on approaching from base metal to the weld centreline in the form of heat affected zone (HAZ), thermo-mechanically affected zone (TMAZ) and weld nugget (Fig.6.34).

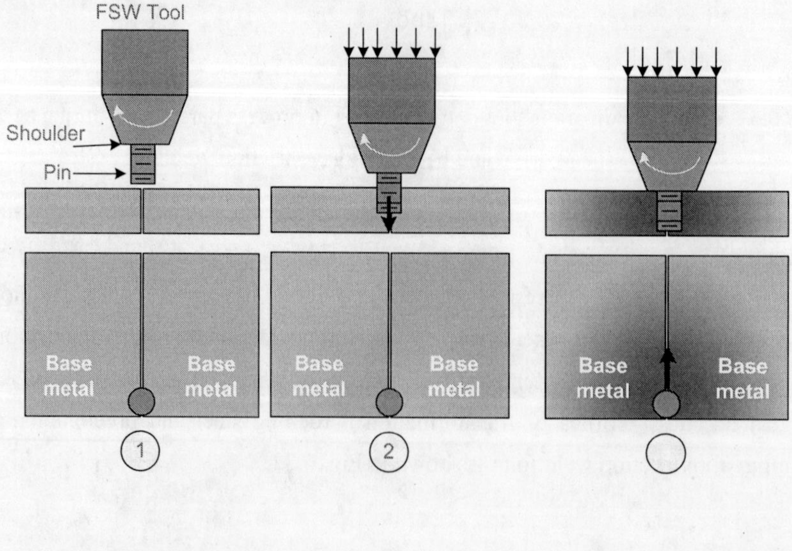

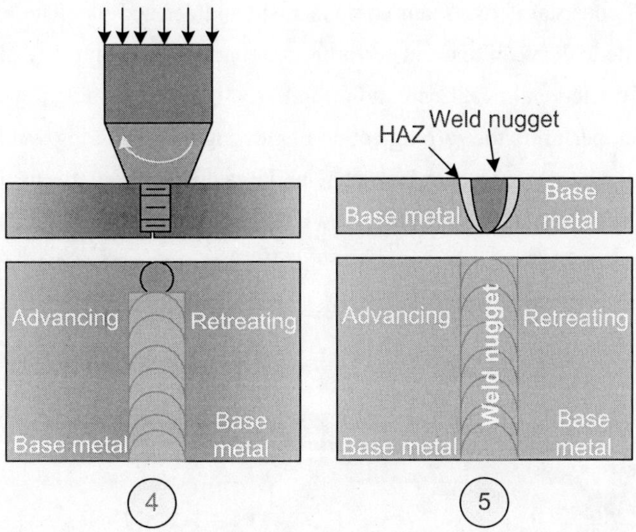

Fig. 6.33 Schematic diagram showing sequential steps of friction stir welding 1) Tool rotation, 2) Plunging, 3) Dwelling, 4) Traversing and 5) Weld completion.

HAZ, in general, shows grain coarsening, coupled with reversion, over tempering, averaging in case of precipitation hardening metals and transformation hardening in case of steel and other hardenable metals. TMAZ in FSW joints is a zone formed due to the combined effect of heat and plastic deformation. This zone is relatively thinner than the weld nugget and HAZ. The weld nugget is a very interesting and important zone determining joint properties. A combination of heat and high strain rate plastic deformation in weld nugget during FSW causes dynamic recrystallization, resulting in significant grain refinement. However, the plastic deformation-based work hardening of metal in the weld nugget zone primarily depends on the work hardening behaviour of the parent metal. More prominent work hardening is observed in low stacking fault energy metals like steel, stainless steel, super alloys, etc., than high stacking fault energy metals like aluminium and magnesium alloys. Like friction welding, FSW joints also exhibit similar trend of hardness/ strength variation for transformation and precipitation hardening metals (Fig. 6.32).

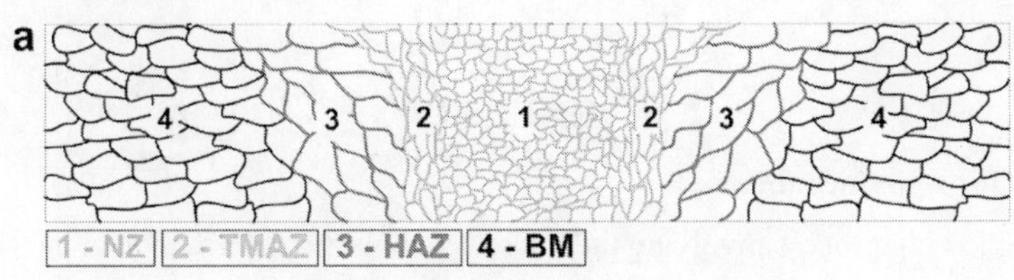

Fig. 6.34 Schematic diagram showing variation in microstructural features across the friction stir weld joint

The FSW tool consists of two main components: shoulder and pin. The tool pin penetrates parent metals along the weld line and performs two functions: a) controlled plastic deformation of metal and b) frictional heat generation. Similarly, the tool shoulder, apart from frictional heat generation, performs the forging action of flowing metals during welding. The FSW of different metals like steel and aluminium having large difference in mechanical, metallurgical and physical properties is little difficult. The FSW tool pin in case of similar metal joining is plunged and traversed along the weld centreline. While, in the case of dissimilar metal joining, the tool pin axis is off set towards the soft metal like aluminium (Fig.6.35)

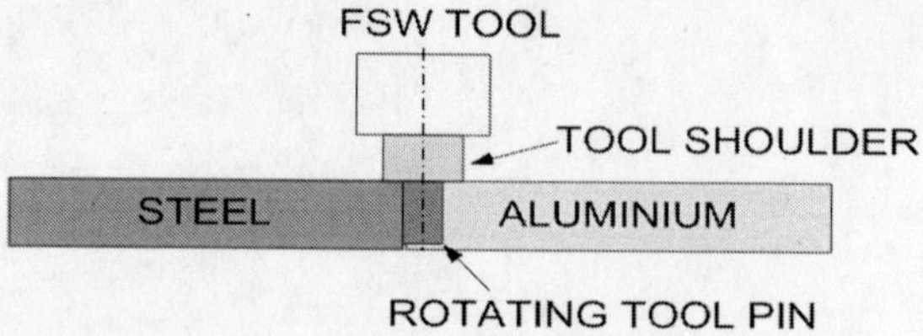

Fig. 6.35 Schematic diagram showing the FSW tool and its placement during steel-aluminium joining by the friction stir welding

FSW process parameters, namely tool rotational speed, translational/ traverse speed, normal load, tool geometry (tool and shoulder diameter, and tool pin length) affect the frictional heat generation, net heat input and plastic deformation. Therefore, FSW parameters affect the soundness, mechanical and metallurgical characteristics of FSW joints.

UNIT SUMMARY

The fusion welding process, solid-liquid joining processes, adhesive and solid state joining processes have been presented. The effect of power density associated with fusion welding processes on the heat input and the joint characteristics have been described considering the physics of the welding process. Fundamentals related to the physics of welding arc have also been presented. The joining processes such as shielded metal arc welding, gas metal arc welding, tungsten inert gas welding, brazing and soldering, adhesive joining, forge welding friction welding, and friction stir welding have been discussed.

EXERCISE

Questions for self-assessment

1. The joining process involving the micro-level plastic deformation at the joint interface is

    a. Gas welding b. Arc welding
    c. Ultrasonic welding d. Forge welding

2. The welding process which develops the metallurgical joint across the metallic components
   a. Fusion welding
   b. Brazing
   c. Friction stir welding
   d. All of these
3. The heat input for the fusion welding must be
   a. Maximum
   b. Minimum
   c. Optimum
   d. All of these
4. The increase of heat input during the fusion welding increases
   a. Width of heat-affected zone
   b. The cross-sectional area of the weld
   c. Average grain size
   d. All of these
5. Heat-affected zone in a fusion weld joint experiences change in
   a. Density
   b. Composition
   c. Microstructure
   d. All of these
6. The net heat input during the arc welding depends on
   a. Welding current
   b. Electrode size
   c. Welding environment
   d. All of these
7. For a given welding current and arc voltage, during arc welding, an increase in welding speed
   a. Increases heat affected zone
   b. Decreases heat input
   c. Increases heat input
   d. Increases thermal efficiency of the welding arc
8. The heat dissipated to the underlying base metal during the fusion welding
   a. Increases with the increase of power density of the process
   b. Decreases with the increase of power density of the process
   c. Remains unaffected by the power density of the process
   d. All of these
9. The time to melt the faying surfaces of the base metals during arc welding increases with
   a. Decrease in power density
   b. Increase in welding speed
   c. Increasing the flow rate of the shielding gas
   d. All of these

10. The thermal efficiency of the welding arc is maximum for

    a. Plasma arc welding
    b. Tungsten inert gas welding
    c. Submerged arc welding
    d. Metal inert gas welding

11. The autogenous welding process uses

    a. Matching filler
    b. Over-matching filler
    c. Under-matching filler
    d. No filler

12. A very high potential difference across the electrode and the base metal is established to initiate the welding arc by

    a. Touch start method
    b. Field start method
    c. Carbon block method
    d. All of these

13. Almost equal amount of the heat is generated, on the anode and cathode side during the arc welding when using

    a. Alternative current
    b. Direct current straight polarity
    c. Direct current reverse polarity
    d. All of these

14. The heat input supplied for a fusion welding process is minimal in case of

    a. Gas welding
    b. Arc welding
    c. Laser welding
    d. Plasma welding

15. The cleanest weld in terms of oxygen and nitrogen content in the weld metal is produced by

    a. Shielded metal arc welding
    b. Gas metal arc welding
    c. Tungsten inert gas welding
    d. Gas welding

16. In general, oxygen content in the welded metal affects the mechanical strength adversely due to

    a. Formation of new phases
    b. Formation of defects in the form of inclusions and porosity
    c. Formation of the large weld zone
    d. All of these

17. Self-regulating arc during constant voltage power source used for gas metal arc welding is produced when

    a. Filler wire diameter is small
    b. Filler wire diameter is large
    c. Filler wire is long
    d. All of these

18. A solid-state joining process which forms thermo-mechanically affected zone in weld joints is

    a. Friction welding
    b. Forge welding

c. Friction stir welding d. All of these

19. The arc welding process, which uses the consumable electrode, is

a. SMAW b. GMAW

c. SAW d. All of these

20. The strength of an adhesive joint depends on

a. Type of adhesive b. Overlap length

c. Curing d. All of these

Answers to Multiple Choice Questions

Key for MCQ: 1 c, 2 d, 3 c, 4 d, 5 c, 6 a, 7 b, 8 b, 9 a, 10 c, 11 d, 12 b, 13 a, 14 c, 15 c, 16 b, 17 a, 18 c, 19 d, 20 d

Short and Long Answer Type Questions

1. Why should the heat input for the fusion welding be optimum?
2. What is the heat-affected zone in a fusion weld joint?
3. What are the factors affecting the formation of heat-affected zones in an arc weld joint?
4. How to calculate the net heat input in the arc welding process?
5. What is the effect of the power density of a welding process on the net heat input for fusion welding?
6. What is a welding arc?
7. Describe the methods for starting a welding arc using the suitable diagram.
8. Why should the weld pool be protected from atmospheric gases during fusion welding?
9. Explain the approaches to protecting the weld pool in common arc-welding processes.
10. Explain the arc characteristic using a suitable schematic diagram.
11. Classify the different types of power sources used for arc welding.
12. Explain the constant current and constant voltage type of power sources concerning the variation in arc length during the welding.
13. What are the different types of electrode polarities used in arc welding?
14. Explain the effect of electrode polarity on arc welding concerning heat input and arc stability.
15. What is the principle of the shielded metal arc welding process?
16. Why does the SMAW process offer a moderate-quality weld joint?
17. Compare the shielded metal arc and gas metal arc welding processes.
18. What is a self-regulating arc?
19. Describe the role of the electrode wire feed system in controlling the arc length.

20. What is the principle of the gas tungsten arc welding process?
21. Why does the gas tungsten arc welding process offer the cleanest weld metal among the arc welding processes?
22. What are sequential steps used in brazing and soldering?
23. What are the typical applications of brazing and soldering processes?
24. What is the importance of clearance brazing and soldering processes?
25. How do the brazing conditions, like brazing temperature and time, affect the joint characteristics?
26. Compare the brazing and braze welding processes.
27. Explain the sequential steps of adhesive joining.
28. What is the importance of curing in adhesive joining?
29. Explain the different factors affecting the strength of adhesive joints.
30. What is the importance of solid-state joining for developing dissimilar metal joints?
31. What is the principle of the friction welding process?
32. Compare the constant speed drive and inertia drive type of friction welding processes.
33. How do friction and friction stir welding affect the joint characteristics of precipitation and the transformation of hardenable metals?
34. Explain the sequential steps of the friction stir welding process using a suitable diagram.

Numerical Problems

1. Two steel plates of 5 mm thickness are joined using shielded metal arc welding process at welding speed of 120 mm per minute, welding current of 200 ampere and arc voltage of 35 Volt. Considering the thermal efficiency of the shielded metal arc welding process 90%, calculate the net heat input in kJ/mm and cross-sectional area of the weld in mm^2. Assume the heat required to melt unit volume of the steel is 2 J per mm^3.
2. GMAW of 25 thick plates performed using 600 amperes welding current and 30 arc voltage. Assume, arc efficiency is 100% and heat required to melt unit volume of the steel is 1.5 J per mm^3. Process produces weld metal at the rate of 150 mm cube per minute. Calculate the welding speed and net heat input used for the welding.

KNOW MORE

Explore the new joining processes and their penetration in Indian industries to make goods of common use. Try to visit a heavy engineering industry like BHEL and pressure vessel manufacturing companies to find out how real components are manufactured by joining. A lot of information about progress and development in welding, joining, and hybrid joining technologies for similar and dissimilar materials joining are available in the public domain. Efforts may be made to learn and gain expertise.

Scan me!

SUGGESTED RESOURCES FOR FURTHER READING/LEARNING

1. D K Dwivedi, Fundamentals of Metal Joining, Springer Nature, (2021)
2. S Kalpakjian, S R Schmid, Manufacturing Engineering and Technology, Pearson (2018)
3. M P Groover, Fundamentals of Modern Manufacturing, John Wiley and Sons, (2010)
4. A Ghosh, A K Malik, Manufacturing science, East-West Press (2010)
5. D K Dwivedi, Materials Engineering, AICTE, (2023)
6. D K Dwivedi, NPTEL Course "Joining Technologies for Metals": https://onlinecourses.nptel.ac.in/noc23_me130/preview
7. D K Dwivedi, NPTEL Course "Fundamentals of Manufacturing Processes" https://archive.nptel.ac.in/courses/112/107/112107219/
8. Ravi Shankar, Dheerendra Kumar Dwivedi, Activating flux tungsten inert gas welding for enhanced weld penetration, Journal of Manufacturing Processes, 22 (2016) 211-228
9. Gaurav Sharma, Dheerendra Kumar Dwivedi, Microstructure and mechanical properties of dissimilar steel joints developed using Friction Stir Welding, International Journal of Advanced Manufacturing Technology, 88, (2017) 1299-1307
10. A Kulkarni, DK Dwivedi, M Vasudevan, Novel functionally graded joint between P91 steel-AISI 316L SS, Welding Journal, 100 (August 2021), 269-280

7 Mathematical Models for Manufacturing Processes

Unit Specific / Learning Objective

The objective of this unit is to understand the following aspects

- To learn important mathematical models related to thermo-mechanical aspects of casting, forming and machining processes
- To learn the concept of designing a gating system for casting process
- To learn about the mechanics of bulk metal forming process
- To develop an understanding on the mechanics of chip formation, power consumption, and tool life
- To enable engineers to make decisions for efficient, economical and effective manufacturing using casting, forming and machining

Additionally, a few questions for self-assessment based on fundamentals have been included in this chapter. These questions are based on application, comprehension, analysis and synthesis. Suggested further reading and reference have been included for deep learners and readers.

Rationale

The scope of the manufacturing processes is extremely wide with reference to the fabrication of different components by material removal, material addition or material deformation. Materials are processed by different means ranging from heat transfer for melting and solidification of the molten metal during the casting, application of the forces to facilitate the desired plastic deformation by bulk deformation approaches like rolling, forging, extrusion, and wire drawing, to the controlled shearing of the metal for removing it from the bulk material to obtain the desired size, shape, surface finish, and tolerance by machining processes. Therefore, it is important to understand the mathematical models showing the relationship between the various process parameters, process mechanics, process physics on the time to manufacture the product, forces and power requirement, and productivity. Learning and awareness about mathematical models related to manufacturing processes will equip mechanical/production/industrial engineers for efficient and cost-effective manufacturing of products.

Pre-Requisites

Physics: (Class XII)

Learning outcomes

U7-O1: Ability to design gating system and riser for manufacturing sound casting.

U7-O2: Ability to determine force and power consumption for bulk deformation during common forming processes like rolling, forging, extrusion and wire drawing.

U7-O3: Ability to calculate the cutting forces, shear angle, shear stress and strain during machining of metals.

U7-O4: Ability to estimate tool life for varying cutting conditions.

U7-O5: Ability to develop suitable procedures for efficient and economical casting, forming and machining.

Unit-7: Outcomes	EXPECTED MAPPING WITH COURSE OUTCOMES (1- Weak Correlation; 2- Medium correlation; 3- Strong Correlation)					
	CO-1	CO-2	CO-3	CO-4	CO-5	CO-6
U7-O1	2	3	-	-	-	-
U7-O2	2	3	-	-	-	-
U7-O3	2	3	-	-	-	-
U7-O4	2	3	-	-	-	-
U7-O5	2	3	-	-	-	-

CO

1. Understand the different conventional and unconventional manufacturing methods employed for making different products.
2. To motivate and challenge students to understand and develop an appreciation of the processes in correlation with material properties which change the shape, size and form of the raw materials into the desirable product.

7.1 Importance of mathematical models in casting

An important characteristic of metal casting is the flow of molten metal and heat. The entire gating system is designed to ensure smooth molten metal flow through the gating system and efficient heat transfer during the molten metal flow in the gating system, including the riser and mould cavity, and facilitating the production of sound and defect-free castings. However, the design of the gating system deals with the conflicting requirements of the (high/low) molten flow rate, and therefore, the flow rate of the molten metal in the gating system is optimised. Theoretically, it is ideal to fill the mould cavity in the minimum possible time (using a very high flow rate) to realise a high production rate and almost simultaneous solidification in the different zones and parts of the casting. However, a high flow rate causes turbulence in the molten metal when flowing through the gating system and its part. Turbulent molten flow increases the tendency of a) erosion of the parts of the gating system and walls of the sand mould, b) air entrapment in the mould cavity, and c) interaction of the molten metal with atmospheric gases leading to the formation of inclusions and gaseous defects. Therefore, the molten metal must maintain as much laminar flow as possible in both the gating system and the mould cavity. The laminar flow can be achieved by ensuring the low velocity of molten metal flowing through the gating system, which is expected to increase the time needed to fill the mould cavity.

Similarly, heat flow from the molten metal should also be considered while designing the gating system and its part. The heat transfer rate from the molten metal should be such that it allows enough time to fill the mould cavity before the commencement of the solidification of the molten metal to avoid defects like cold shut and mis-run. Heat transfer is crucial in the design of the riser to ensure that the solidification of the molten metal in the riser occurs only after solidification of the molten metal in the mould cavity. To achieve the proper temperature gradient in the mould cavity during the solidification of the molten metal, suitable chills and chaplets are used to realise the directional solidification and avoid shrinkage defects in the casting. The following section discusses the fundamental principles of the molten metal flow that are useful for designing gating system components.

7.2 Gating System and Design

A typical gating system used for casting is shown in Fig. 7.1. The molten metal is fed into the pouring basin. A slow pouring rate of the molten metal increases the mould filling time, which in turn increases the tendency of casting defects (misrun, cold shut, etc.) due to early commencement of solidification before filling of the mould. To some extent, these issues can be mitigated by using high superheat melt. However, high superheat increases gas pick tendency due to high solubility of gases leading to defects such as gas holes and porosity. On the other hand, fast pouring of the metal tends to erode the mould walls, cause turbulence, form dross, and damage mould in the form of cuts and wash. Therefore, molten metal must be poured in mould at an optimal velocity. An effective gating system is designed to distribute the molten metal into the mould cavity at an optimum rate to avoid defective casting due to excessive temperature loss, turbulence, and entrapment of gases and inclusions. The gating system includes all the pathways through which the molten metal flows into the mould cavity. These include the pouring basin, sprue, runner, gate, and riser.

- **Pouring Basin:** Directs the molten metal from the crucible to the sprue.
- **Sprue:** A vertical tapered channel that feeds the molten metal to the runner.

- **Choke:** Smallest cross-sectional area of the gating system before in-gate usually at the sprue base.
- **Runner:** A channel with a large cross-section that carries the molten metal from the sprue to the mould cavity through the in-gate.
- **Gate:** Connects the runner to the mould cavity.
- **Riser:** Serves as a reservoir to feed molten metal during solidification to compensate for shrinkage of the molten metal due to liquid to solid phase transformation.

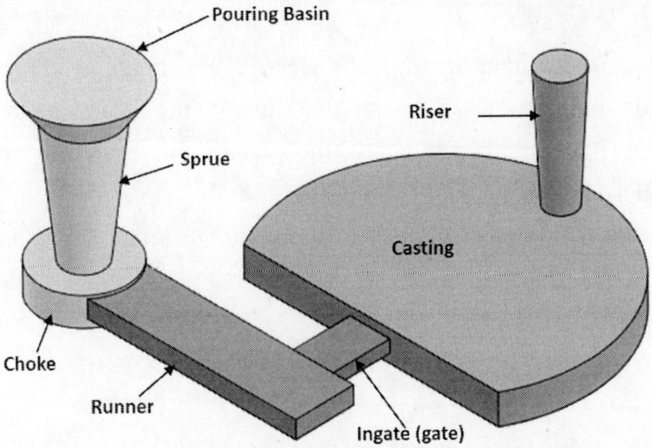

Fig. 7.1 Schematic diagram showing a typical gating system for casting

A well-designed gating system aims to produce defect-free and high yield casting by realizing the following.

- **Smooth flow of the molten metal by** avoiding sudden/sharp turns in the gating system. The smooth flow of molten metal into the mould cavity prevents turbulence, air aspiration, and erosion of the gating system and mould.
- **Proper Filling Rate:** The mould cavity should be filled before the commencement of solidification of the molten metal while avoiding casting defects like misrun.
- **Avoid Turbulence:** Molten metal should flow into the mould without turbulence to avoid air-pick, air-metal interaction leading to oxidation in case of reactive metals.
- **Filter Impurities:** Prevent slag, impurities, and gases from entering the mould to avoid defects.
- **Economics and Practical:** The gating system should be cost-effective, easy to implement, and easy to remove after solidification.

7.3 Principles of Fluid Flow in Gating Design

Two key principles govern fluid flow in gating design: a) the law of mass continuity and b) Bernoulli's theorem. These principles, however, find limited direct applicability due to varying temperature of the molten metal, and changing fluid properties such as surface tension and viscosity.

7.3.1 Law of Mass Continuity

The volume flow rate remains constant for incompressible liquids in a closed system. This can be expressed as:

$$Q = A_1 v_1 = A_2 v_2 \tag{1}$$

where, A is the cross-sectional area, v is the average velocity of the liquid, and Q is the volume flow rate (m^3/s). Subscripts 1 and 2 denote different points in the system. The flow rate must be constant throughout (at different points) the system.

7.3.2 Bernoulli's Theorem

Derived from the conservation of energy, Bernoulli's theorem relates the pressure, velocity, and height of the fluid, including frictional losses in a filled system. The simplified equation for incompressible flow is:

$$\frac{P}{\rho g} + \frac{v^2}{2g} + h = constant \tag{2}$$

where, P is the pressure, v is the velocity of the liquid, ρ is the liquid's density, g is gravitational acceleration, and h is the height above a reference level.

To maintain energy conservation at any point including frictional losses, the system follows the equation given for the two different points:

$$\frac{P_1}{\rho g} + \frac{{v_1}^2}{2g} + h_1 = \frac{P_2}{\rho g} + \frac{{v_2}^2}{2g} + h_2 + f \tag{3}$$

The above equation must be satisfied, where subscripts 1 and 2 denote two different points in the system, and f accounts for frictional losses, including those from liquid-mould wall interactions and turbulence.

7.4 Sprue design

A sprue guides the molten metal to the runner. Through the runner, molten metal flows into the mould cavity via an in-gate. The molten metal flows under pressure through sprue, runner and in-gate. Air aspiration (air suction through porous sand mould walls) occurs if pressure during the flow of molten metal through these elements drops below atmospheric pressure. Air entered into gating system due to low pressure, air interacts with molten metal in two ways a) dissolution in melt, b)chemical reactions causing inclusion and porosity. Therefore, air aspiration in the gating system should be minimized by using a tapered sprue (large cross-section area at the top and narrow at the bottom). The tapered sprue design ensures that pressure does not drop below the atmospheric level. Mass continuity and Bernoulli's equation are applied to design the sprue (Fig. 7.2 (a)).

Applying the Eq. (3) between points 2 and 3 in Fig. 7.2, we get

$$\frac{P_2}{\rho g} + \frac{{v_2}^2}{2g} + h_2 = \frac{P_3}{\rho g} + \frac{{v_3}^2}{2g} + f \tag{4}$$

Here, P and v are the pressure and velocity of the liquid metal at points 2 and 3. Assuming a) atmospheric pressure at the bottom of sprue (gauge pressure P_3=0), b) equal velocities of the molten metal at these two points of interest (v_2=v_3), and c) no frictional losses (f=0). Let us take the case of cylindrical sprue design.

On solving, we get $P_2 = -\rho g h_2$, indicating a negative pressure, suggesting the straight cylindrical shape sprue design (solid line) is unacceptable due to air aspiration tendency (Fig. 7.2).

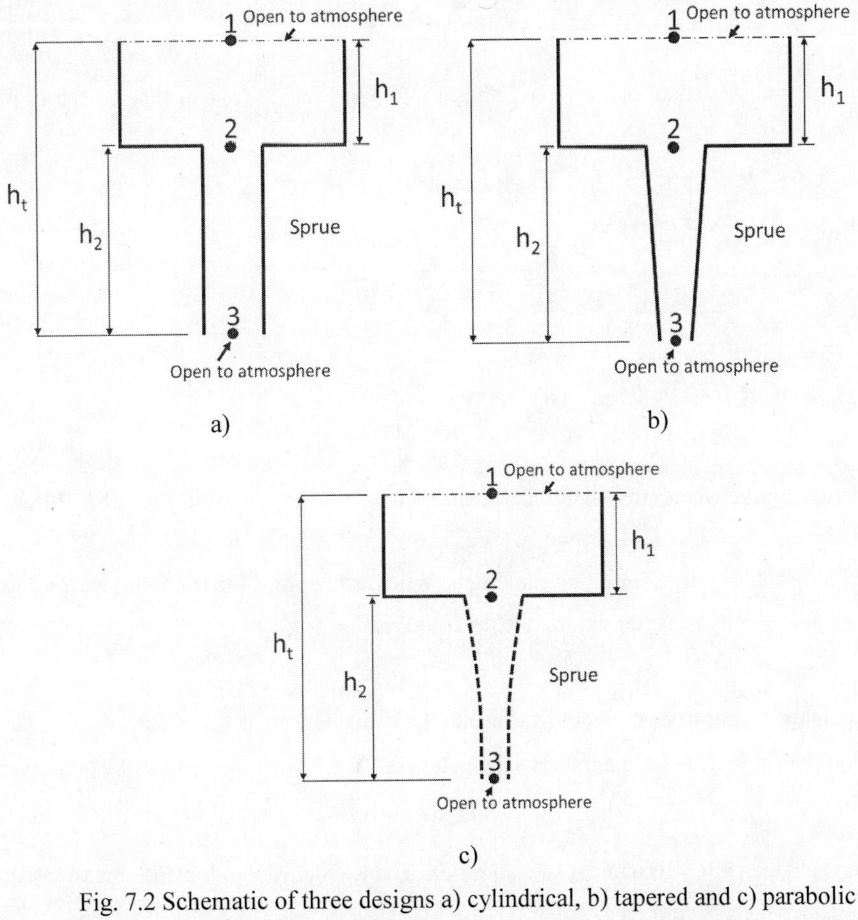

Fig. 7.2 Schematic of three designs a) cylindrical, b) tapered and c) parabolic

To avoid negative pressure at point 3, the sprue should have a tapered (Fig. 7.2(b)). The ideal profile can be determined by assuming that pressures at the top and bottom of the (P_2=P_3) sprue are equal. Then we get

$$\frac{v_2{}^2}{2g} + h_2 = \frac{v_3{}^2}{2g} \tag{5}$$

From the mass continuity equation Eq. (1):

$$v_2 = \frac{A_3 V_3}{A_2} = X v_3 \tag{6}$$

Considering $X = \frac{A_3}{A_2}$

Using Eq. (5) and (6), we get

$$\frac{X^2 v_3{}^2}{2g} + h_2 = \frac{v_3{}^2}{2g}$$

Or

$$X^2 = 1 - \frac{2gh_2}{v_3^2} \tag{7}$$

Applying Bernoulli's equation between points 1 and 3 in Fig. 7.2 (c) (for tapered sprue) with $P_1 = P_3$ and $v_1 = 0$, we get

$$v_3{}^2 = 2gh_t$$

Substituting this in Eq. (7), we get

$$X^2 = 1 - \frac{h_2}{h_t} = \frac{h_1}{h_t}$$

or

$$X = \frac{A_3}{A_2} = \sqrt{\frac{h_1}{h_t}} \tag{8}$$

The relationship between cross-sectional area and height at any point in the sprue follows a parabolic geometry. The ideal sprue profile, shown with dotted lines in Fig. 7.2, ensures constant atmospheric pressure along its length. When accounting for frictional losses due to viscosity, the velocity of metal exiting the gate is given by:

$$v_3 = c\sqrt{2gh_t} \tag{9}$$

where, h_t is the height from the liquid surface to the sprue bottom, and c is the friction factor. If the liquid level reaches height x above the gates (see Fig 7.4(b)), the gate exit velocity is:

$$v_3 = c\sqrt{2g(h_t - x)} \tag{10}$$

Turbulence in the gating system causes aspiration. The Reynolds number (Re), measures fluid flow characteristics, is defined as:

$$Re = \frac{\rho v D}{\mu} \tag{11}$$

where, ρ is density, μ is viscosity, v is velocity, and D is the channel diameter. In gating systems, Re ranges from 200 to 2000 for laminar flow. Values between 2000 and 20000 indicate mixed flow, and above 20000 have severe turbulence, leading to dross formation (Fig. 7.3). Minimizing turbulence reduces air aspiration, and air-melt interaction, which in turn helps in reducing dross and casting defects.

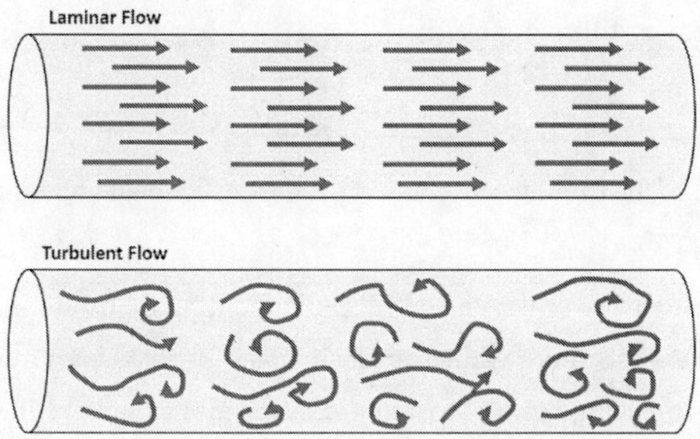

Fig. 7.3 Schematics for laminar and turbulent flows

7.5 Gating design

Three gating systems are very common (i) top gating, (ii) bottom gating, and (iii) horizontal gating. Top gating and bottom gating designs are shown in Fig. 7.4.

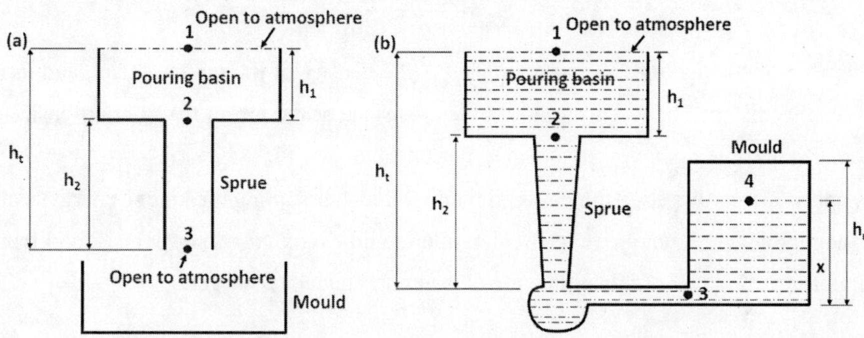

Fig. 7.4 Types of gating (a) top gating, and (b) bottom gating

7.5.1 Top gating

In the top gating, the molten metal fed vertically from the top to fill the mould, with atmospheric pressure at the bottom of the gate. The top gating design suits when the liquid needs to be introduced vertically. However, vertical feeding from the top promotes a tendency of splashing and oxidation.

Apply Bernoulli's equation between points 1 and 3 in Fig. 7.4 (a) and assuming P_1 = P_3= atmospheric pressure, v_1=0 (with a stagnant top layer of the molten metal) and neglecting frictional losses, we get:

$$h_t = \frac{{v_3}^2}{2g} \tag{12}$$

$$\text{or, } v_3 = \sqrt{2gh_t}$$

where, v_3 is the molten metal velocity at the gate (now referred to as v_g), and g is the gravitation acceleration.

Hence, the mould cavity filling time t_f is:

$$t_f = \frac{V}{A_g v_3} \tag{13}$$

where, V is volume of the mould cavity and A_g is cross-sectional area of the in-gate.

7.5.2 Bottom gating

In case of bottom gating, the molten metal fills the mould cavity from the bottom which avoids splashing and oxidation. Bottom gating design is ideal for reducing turbulence and oxidation by filling mould cavity using bottom-up approach. The molten metal velocity at the gate varies with the static head of the molten metal.

Applying Bernoulli's equation between points 1 and 3 in Fig. 7.4(b). Assuming that the (gauge) pressure at point 1 is zero, as it is open to the atmosphere, v_1=0 (with a stagnant top layer of the molten metal) and neglecting frictional losses, we get:

$$h_t = \frac{P_3}{\rho g} + \frac{{v_3}^2}{2g} \tag{14}$$

where, P_3 is the gauge pressure at point 3, ρ is the density of the molten metal, and h_t is the total height (distance between the liquid metal-surface at the top in the pouring basin to the bottom of the sprue), which is assumed to be constant.

Now apply Bernoulli's equation between points 3 and 4, assuming the kinetic energy is almost lost (negligible) as the molten metal enters the mould cavity (v_3=0) at point 3, and that $v_4$is negligible (as top layer of the molten metal is almost stagnant), we get:

$$P_3 = \rho g x \tag{15}$$

where, P_3 is the gauge pressure at point 3 and ρ is density of molten metal and x is total height between bottom gate centreline to the top surface of the molten metal in the mould.

From Eq. 14 and 15, the molten metal velocity v_3 at the bottom gate obtained as

$$h_t = x + \frac{{v_3}^2}{2g} \tag{16}$$

$$v_3 = \sqrt{2g(h_t - x)}$$

Eq. 16 shows the molten metal velocity at the bottom gate that depends on the static head of the molten metal in the mould. Thus, the time taken to fill the mould cavity (t_f) can be calculated by integrating the Eq. 18. Let the metal rise in the mould by a height dx over a time interval dt; A_g and A_m represent the cross-sectional areas of the gate and the mould, respectively. Here $v_g = v_3$ Then

$$A_m dx = A_g v_g dt \tag{17}$$

Using Eq. 16 and 17, we get

$$\frac{dx}{\sqrt{2g(h_t - x)}} = \frac{A_g}{A_m} dt$$

or

$$\frac{dx}{\sqrt{2g}\sqrt{(h_t - x)}} = \frac{A_g}{A_m} dt \tag{18}$$

Integrate the equation between t=0, x= 0; and t= t_f, x= h_m, we get

$$\frac{1}{\sqrt{2g}} \int_0^{h_m} \frac{dx}{\sqrt{(h_t - x)}} = \frac{A_g}{A_m} \int_0^{t_f} dt$$

$$t_f = \frac{A_m}{A_g} \frac{1}{\sqrt{2g}} 2(\sqrt{h_t} - \sqrt{h_t - h_m}) \tag{19}$$

If there is a riser in the gating system for metal casting then additional filling time for riser should also be considered. The open riser is filled up to the sprue height. Use the cross-sectional area of riser and height (in place of mould area) of riser for calculation of filling time.

$$t_{f(riser)} = \frac{\sqrt{2}A_r}{A_g} \sqrt{\frac{h_t}{g}} \tag{20}$$

7.5.3 Horizontal Gating

Horizontal gating uses horizontal channels to distribute molten metal with minimal turbulence. The design of horizontal gating incorporates extra need-based sections for improved distribution to keep the flow of molten metal smooth.

7.6 Pouring Time

The pouring time of steel cannot be compared to that of cast iron due to differences in heat transfer, fluidity, viscosity, surface tension, and solidification time. Further, non-ferrous metals need longer pouring times to produce defect-free products.

The mass, and the surface area to volume ratio of the castings affect the pouring time. Here, mass refers to the mass of the casting. The mass of the metal in the gating system is not considered unless it is the same as the mass of the casting. The following are a few standard empirical approaches for calculating pouring time for different casting metals.

Grey cast iron (Mass < 450 kg)

Time to completely fill the mould, $t = K(1.41 + \frac{T}{14.59})\sqrt{W}$ s (21) where, $K = \frac{\text{Fluidity of iron in inches}}{40}$

T is the average sectional thickness, mm

W is the mass of casting in kg

Grey cast iron (Mass > 450 kg)

Pouring time, $t = K(1.236 + \frac{T}{16.65})\sqrt[3]{W} s$ (22)

Cast Steel

Pouring time, t = (2.4335-0.3953 log W) $\sqrt{W}$ s (23)

Shell moulded ductile iron (vertical pouring)

Pouring time, t = $K_1\sqrt{W}$ s (24)

where, K_1 is 2.080 for thinner sections and 2.970 for heavier sections.

Copper alloy

Pouring time, t = $K_2\sqrt[3]{W}$ s (25)

K_2 is the constant given by –

Tin bronze: 2.80

Brass: 1.90

Top gating: 1.30

Bottom gating: 1.80

Table 1 provides the pouring rates for different casting alloys governed by the above-mentioned equations.

Table 1: Pouring rates

		Metals		
	Weight of casting (kg)	**Steel**	**Pig iron**	**Aluminium alloys**
Pouring rates (kg/s)	**Up to 10**	1.20 – 1.40	1.10	0.25 – 0.30
	10 – 50	1.90 – 2.50	1.50 – 2.00	0.50 – 0.70
	50 – 100	4.00 – 5.00	3.00 – 4.00	1.00 – 1.30
	100 – 500	4.50 – 7.00	3.50 – 6.00	1.20 – 2.00

7.7 Choke Area

The optimised pouring time will be beneficial only if the main control area (choke area), responsible for the controlled flow of the molten metal into the mould cavity, is designed properly. The functionality of this choke area is to control the flow of molten metal to fill the mould within the specified pouring time. The choke area is typically located around the bottom of the sprue. The choke area calculated using Bernoulli's principle is expressed as

$$A = \frac{W}{dtC\sqrt{2gH}} \tag{26}$$

where, A is the choke area, mm^2

t is the pouring time in s

H is the effective metal head in mm

d is the molten metal's mass density expressed in kg/mm^3

g is the acceleration caused by gravity, mm/s^2

C is the efficiency factor

The castings' dimensions and the gating system determine the sprue's effective height (H) as given by the following equations. Schematic representation of p, h, and c for different types of castings is shown in Fig. 7.5.

Top gating system, $H = h$ (27)

Bottom gating system, $H = h - \frac{c}{2}$ (28)

Parting gating system, $H = h - \frac{p^2}{2c}$ (29)

where, p is the height of the mould cavity in the cope, c is the overall height of the mould cavity, and h is the height of the sprue.

The efficiency factor of the gating system has different values across different sections of the gating elements. Ideally, a circular-shape cross-section is preferred for a higher efficiency coefficient. That is because lower surface area-to-volume ratio for the circular cross-section helps to reduce heat loss and minimize frictional energy loss, thereby increasing casting yield. The overall efficiency of the gating system can be calculated by Eq. (30). The loss coefficient values are depicted in Table 2 and efficiency factors are given in Table 3.

$$C = \frac{1}{\sqrt{1 + k_1 \frac{A}{{A_1}^2} + k_2 \frac{A^2}{{A_2}^2} + \cdots}} \tag{30}$$

where, K_1, K_2, … are the loss coefficients occurring for direction changes, and A_1, A_2, … are the areas changing downstream of metal flow, and A is the choke area.

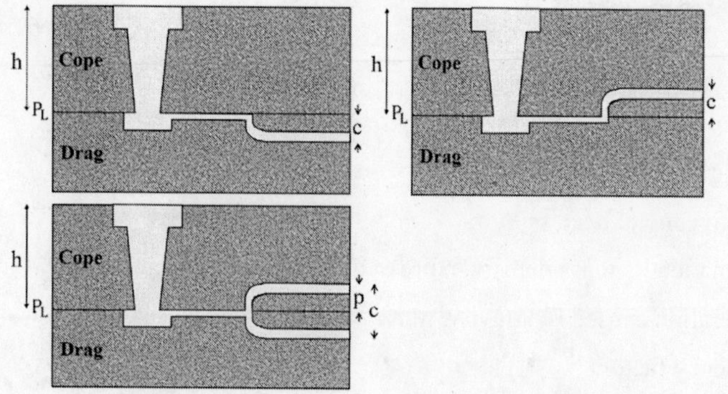

Fig. 7.5 Schematic representation of h, p and c for different types of castings

Table 2: Numerical values of the Loss coefficient

Gate element	Sharp	Round
25% cross-sectional area reduction from runner to in-gates	2.00	0.50
Bend of sprue into a runner	2.00	1.00
Junction perpendicular to runner	4.0 – 6.0	-
Right angle bends in runner:		
Square cross-section	2.00	1.50
Round cross-section	1.50	1.00
Molten metal movement from pouring cup to sprue	0.75	0.20
Runner choke when choke area is nearly $\frac{1}{3}$ of runner area plus bend of sprue into runner	13.00	-

Table 3: Efficiency factors

Type of system	Tapered choked sprue	Straight sprue runner choke
One runner entering the in-gates	0.90	0.73
Two runners with multiple in-gates in the perpendicular direction (90º bend)	0.85	0.70
Two runners with multiple in-gates (no bend)	0.90	0.73

7.8 Gating ratio

The gating ratio refers to the ratios of the cross-sectional area of the sprue, runner, and in-gates. The notations consist of the sprue, runner, and in-gate areas. The location of the choke area plays a significant role in determining the type of gating system. Gating systems classified based on the size of the choke area are:

- Non-pressurized gating system
- Pressurized gating system

7.8.1 Non-pressurised gating system

In the non-pressurized gating system, the choke area is typically positioned at the lower end of the sprue base. Consequently, the combined area of the runner and in-gate is larger than the size of the sprue base. This minimizes the occurrence of flaws caused by turbulence. This type of gating system is particularly beneficial for aluminium and magnesium alloys. The common gating ratios of a non-pressurized gating system are in the ratio of

Sprue: Runner: in-gate: 1: 4: 4

The major disadvantages of the non-pressurized gating system are as follows:

- Some parts of the gating system may permit partial air aspiration. A tapered sprue helps in reducing air aspiration.
- Conversely, the big cross-sectional area of runners and in-gates decreases the yield of casting process as a large amount of metals gets solidified in runners, and in-gates which needs to be removed and recycled.

7.8.2 Pressurised gating system

In the pressurized gating system, the in-gate cross-sectional area is the smallest. This causes backpressure throughout the gating system, reducing turbulent flow and the tendency of air aspiration. These types of gating systems are preferred for ferrous castings. An example of this type of gating system is:

Sprue: Runner: in-gate: 1: 2: 1

The design of the runner system should minimize sharp corners and sudden changes in cross-section to reduce turbulence and gas related defects. Traditional trapezoidal-shape runner sections help in reducing turbulence. A common practice is to locate the runner in the cope and the in-gate in the drag to trap slag and impurities and restrict their entry into the mould cavity to minimize inclusions in the casting. However, placement of the runners in the drag and the in-gates in the cope is recommended for aluminium alloy castings. This arrangement restricts the heavier dross (density 3.99 g/cm^3) compared to aluminium (density 2.70 g/cm^3) at the in-gate and supplies clean molten aluminium to the mould.

Table 4: Common gating ratios used in foundry for different metals

Metal	Gating ratio
Aluminium	1:3:3
	1:4:4
Magnesium	1:2:2
	1:4:4
Brass	1:2.88:4.8
Copper	2:8:1
	3:9:1
Grey cast iron	2:1.5:1
	2:3:1
Malleable iron	1:2:9.5
	1.5:1:2.5
	2:1:4.9
Steel	1:1:7
	1:2:1
	1:2:1.5

7.9 In-gate Design

The in-gate design and its placement play an important role in producing a metal casting. In-gate design affects three aspects: a) ease of removal of in-gate and runner from the final casting after the solidification, b) avoid damage to sand mould wall, and c) reducing air aspiration tendency to produce sound casting. The width-to-depth ratio of in-gate kept around 4, which facilitates the ease of removal of the casting by cutting. The following suggestions are worth noting in order to finalise the location of the in-gates (Fig. 7.6).

- In-gate positioned in such a way that molten metal stream does not strike mould walls and other features, to avoid any possibility of damage by erosion and impact.
- Position the in-gates, preferably along the longitudinal axis of the mould wall.
- Position in-gates away from chills and core prints.
- The cross-sectional area of the in-gates should be smaller than the thinnest section of the casting, which allows the in-gates to solidify first thereby reducing the possibility of air aspiration and isolating the casting.

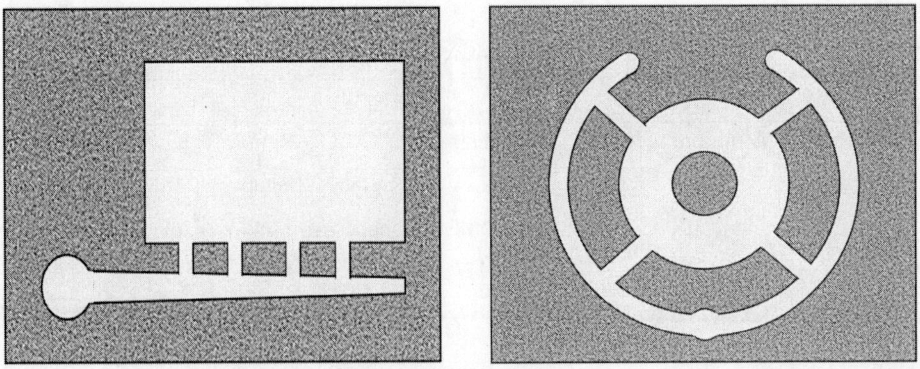

a) b)

Fig. 7.6 Schematic of multiple in-gates designs for uniform flow through all the gates for various types of castings: a) flat, rectangular and b) hollow, cylinder

7.10 Casting Yield

The casting yield is a measure of the efficiency of a casting process related to material utilization and energy. A ratio of the actual weight of (the metal used) casting to the total weight of the metal poured into the mold. The actual weight of casting is usually lesser than the total quantity of metal fed into the mold during casting due to wastages in the form of a) casting rejected due to defects, and b) metal solidified in the gating system (sprue, runner, in-gate, riser) needs to be removed from the casting and recycled. Thus, the term "casting yield" is defined mathematically as:

$$\text{Casting yield} = \frac{\text{m}}{\text{M}} \text{ X } 100 \tag{31}$$

where, m is the actual casting mass of the solidified product, and M is the total mass of the metal poured into the mould.

The above equation suggests that even if there is no defective casting, yield will always be less than 100% due to the solidification of metal in the gating system other than mould. Therefore, an optimal design of a gating system for high casting yield, should allow the minimum volume of the molten metal left to solidify in the gating system (pouring basin, sprue, runner, in-gate, riser) while ensuring production of sound casting. High casting yield improves the economics of the foundry. However, casting yield depends on many factors, such as the type of metal, and the complexity of the design (Fig. 7.7). A complex design casting needs more runner, in-gates and risers to produce a sound casting. The increase of gating system size, and number eventually reduces the casting yield. Metals with high shrinkage offer lower casting yield, as they need large size riser. Similarly, products with simple geometry offer higher casting yield than those of complex designs. The casting yield for a few common metals is shown in Table 5.

Table 5: Casting yields

Casting Description	**Materials**						
	Aluminium	Steels			Simple shape and massive	Cast iron	
		Small pieces	Heavy machinery parts	Simple shapes		Small pieces	Heavy machinery parts
Yield range (%)	22 to 45	35 to 45	55 to 65	75 to 85	85 to 95	45 to 55	65 to 75

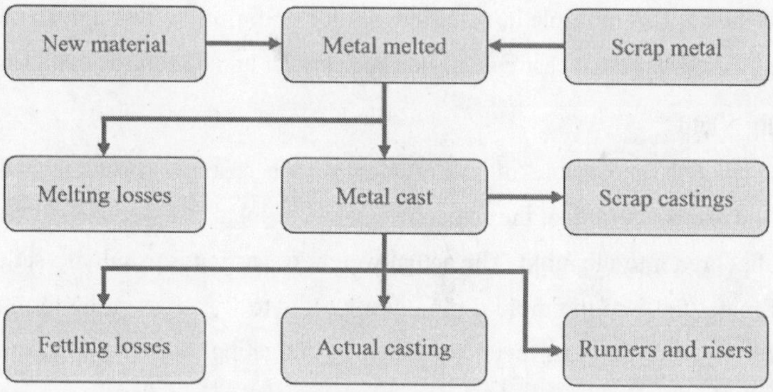

Fig. 7.7 Utilisation of the metal in the foundry

7.11 Solidification and Cooling of Metals

A fundamental understanding of solidification of the molten metal is crucial for manufacturing sound and defect-free castings. Heat dissipation from the molten metal immediately after pouring reduces the temperature gradually until the commencement of the solidification. The time for solidification affects the solidification rate as per cooling rate. High cooling rate reduces the solidification time of casting, which in turn increases the gas and inclusion entrapment tendency. However, the cooling rate varies with time across the sections of casting. The cooling rate affects the microstructure, phases and grain structure of the casting. Higher the cooling rate, finer the grain size. Cooling rate, therefore, affects the chemical homogeneity, soundness of casting, and mechanical and metallurgical characteristics. Many metals, like steel, show solid-state transformation during cooling after solidification which affects the crystal structure, microstructure and mechanical properties of the casting. Fast cooling in case of hardenable ferrous metals like high carbon steel and cast iron increases embrittlement and cracking tendency. These factors significantly affect the overall quality of the castings. Factors affecting casting characteristics include the metal of casting, metallurgical transformation, cooling rate imposed during the solidification as per mould characteristics, the surface area to volume ratio of the casting, and the mould design. Cooling curve of the casting indicates variation in temperature as a function of time during solidification and cooling to room temperature (Fig. 7.8).

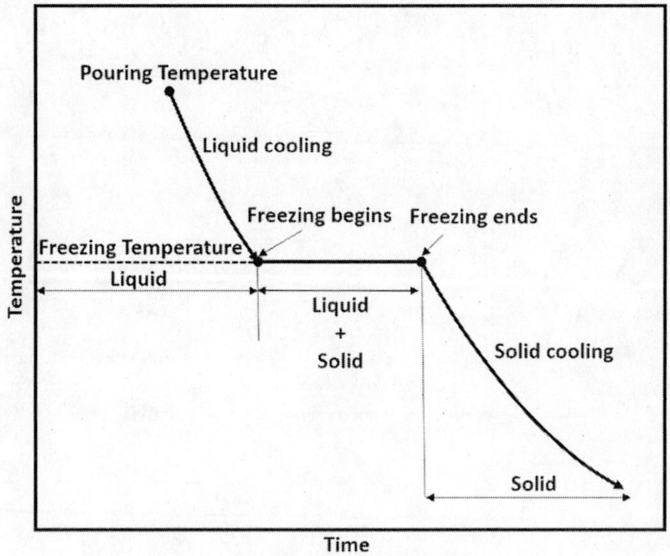

Fig. 7.8 Solidification of pure metals

7.11.1 Pure Metals

Pure metals like aluminium (which melts at 660°C) have a fixed melting temperature and solidification (from beginning to the end) completes at the same constant temperature (Fig. 7.8). On pouring the molten metal into a mould cavity, cooling starts immediately. So, the molten metal temperature drops gradually up to freezing temperature. The solidification progresses with the loss of latent heat while the temperature of melt remains constant. During solidification, the solid-liquid interface moves from the mould walls towards the centre. The solid-liquid metal interface may proceed from all directions, ending at the centre of the casting. However, the pattern of solidification may leave casting defects in the region, which solidifies at last, called hot spot. Therefore, directional solidification helps to minimize defects in center of casting as solidification progresses from one end to another causing defects at one end of the casting instead of the centre. Defective region at the end allows easy removal / repair as per severity and need. Once the molten metal in the mould has cooled and solidified, the metal in the mould cavity is called the casting. The high cooling rate imposed during green sand mould / die-casting produces fine randomly oriented equiaxed grains adjacent to the mould wall, followed by long columnar grains growing perpendicular to the mould wall (Fig. 7.9).

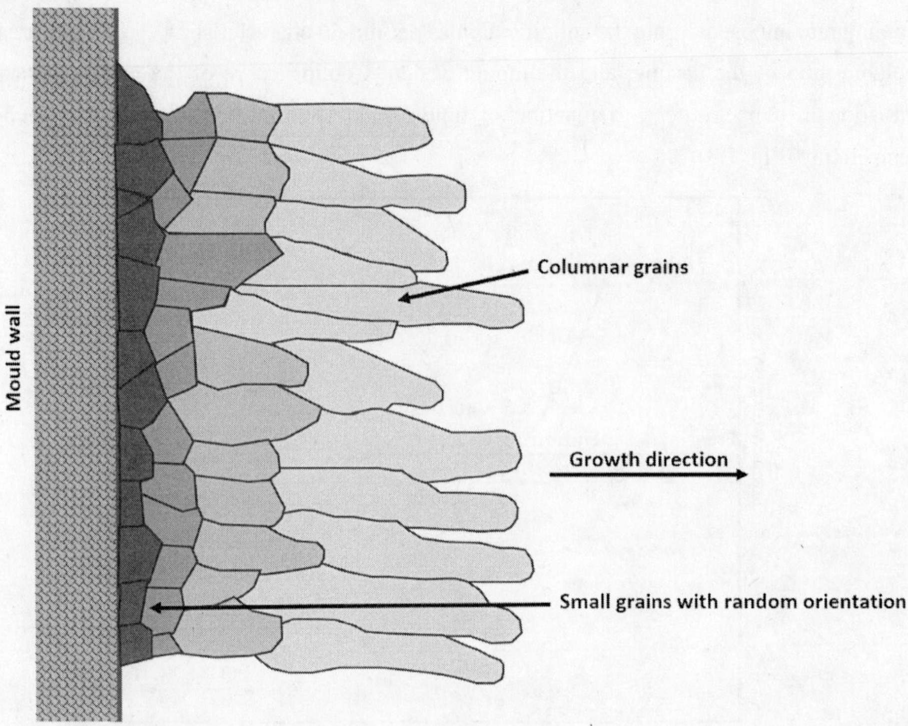

Fig. 7.9 Schematic diagram showing the development of grain structure during solidification

7.11.2 Alloys

An alloy (except eutectic alloy) solidifies over a range of temperatures (Fig. 7.10). The commencement of solidification occurs as molten metal temperature goes below the liquidus temperature. The molten metal temperature continuously decreases with progress of liquid to solid phase transformation until the solidus temperature. Solidification of alloy between liquidus and solidus temperature shows co-existence of both liquid and solid phases. This state is called a mushy zone with solid columnar dendrites and liquid metal in between the dendrite arms (Fig. 7.10.). The temperature difference between the liquidus and solidus temperature is known as the solidification temperature range. The solidification temperature range is zero for pure metals and eutectic alloys. The direction of grain growth in an alloy depends on variation in local composition, variation in solidus temperature with composition during the solidification and thermal properties of the mould determining the cooling rate.

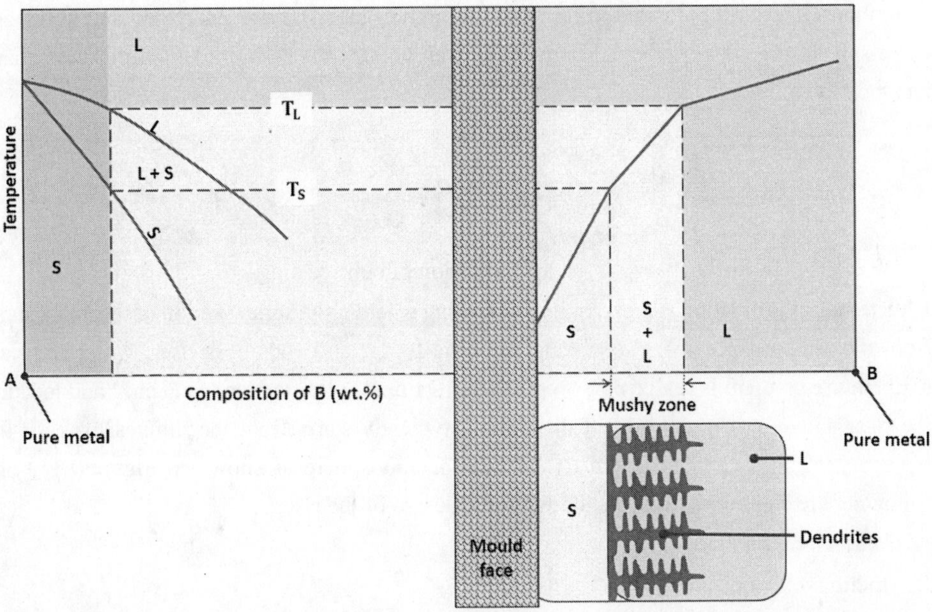

Fig. 7.10 Schematic of the selected part of the phase diagram of an alloy and dendrite formation

A slow cooling rate produces a coarse structure due to the long solidification time, allowing the grain to grow significantly during solidification. Additionally, a low cooling rate leads to a high growth rate and low nucleation rate promoting coarse grain structure. Higher cooling rate on the other hand, produces a finer structure due to short solidification time and high nucleation rate coupled with low growth rate. Further, an extremely high cooling rate (like rapid solidification casting processes) can lead to an amorphous structure due to the quenching effect. The grain size and crystal structure affect the mechanical properties of castings. Fine grain structure, in general, improves the mechanical properties. Further, fined grains reduce micro-porosity and cracking tendencies during solidification due to better distribution of impurities and low melting point phases along too many grain boundaries compared to coarse grain structure. Inconsistent grain size and distribution of alloying elements encourage anisotropic properties in the casting.

7.12 Riser Design

Riser design in metal casting is critical for developing defect-free casting. The riser feeds the molten metal to the mould cavity (in terminal stage of solidification) for compensating shrinkage caused by liquid to solid phase transformation. Riser acts as reservoirs of the molten metal to feed the melt as per need during the solidification. Designing of the riser needs information like type of metal and the complexity of the casting. A complex design of cast product geometry and high thermal expansion coefficient metal increases the number and size of the riser in terms of the volume of molten metal to be fed to the mould cavity. The riser continuously feeds the desired volume of the molten metal to prevent voids and shrinkage defects in casting. The practical design of the riser includes the selection of optimal size, shape and location of riser.

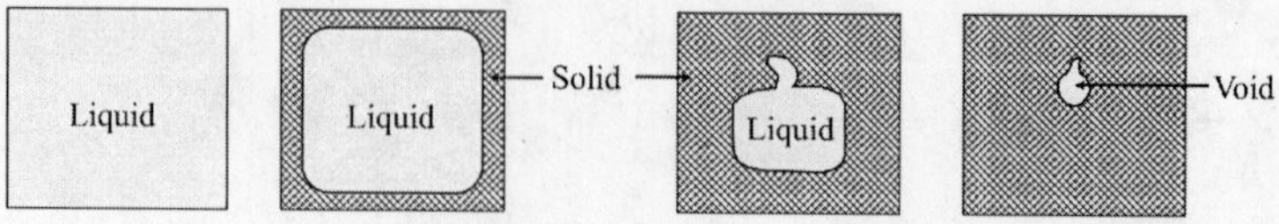

Fig. 7.11 Solidification of cube casting

Directional solidification is preferred in the casting wherein the solidification of the metal starts from the remotest point of the casting from the feeder and ends near riser. An appropriate temperature gradient is realized to obtain the directional solidification using chill and locating the riser suitably. The cooling of the casting typically starts from the thinnest part, or the boundary of the casting exposed to the sand or atmosphere as shown in Figure 7.11. The following are commonly used methods for the design of the riser.

A. Caine's Method

B. Modulus Method

C. Naval Research Laboratory Method

7.12.1 Caine's Method

The cooling characteristics during solidification of the molten metal depend on the surface area to volume ratio of the casting. The heat loss from the molten metal to the mould wall primarily depends on the surface area of the casting exposed to the surrounding mould surface, while the net heat content by the molten in the mould depends on casting volume. Large surface area increases the rate of heat loss to the mould causing higher cooling. Large casting volume increases the amount of heat to be dissipated through the mould wall to complete the solidification. Conversely, increasing the casting volume increases the solidification time for a given mould. High surface area to volume ratio results in a high cooling rate and short solidification time. For the effective functioning of the riser, it is important that the riser should be not solidified before the complete solidification of molten metal in the mould cavity. Similar to the casting, the cooling characteristics of the riser also depend on the surface area to volume ratio.

Chvorinov rule shows a relationship between solidification time and volume-to-surface area ratio. The square of the volume-to-surface area ratio determines the solidification time for a casting.

$$t_s = k\left(\frac{V}{S}\right)^2 \qquad (32)$$

where, t_s is the solidification time (s), V is the casting volume, S is the surface area, and k is the mould constant that depends on the metal of casting pouring temperature, and mould thermal characteristics.

The 'freezing ratio,' X, is defined as the ratio of the cooling characteristics of the casting to that of the riser.

$$X = \frac{\left(\frac{S}{V}\right)_{casting}}{\left(\frac{S}{V}\right)_{riser}} \tag{33}$$

The design of the riser should be such that it feeds the molten metal to mould and solidifies at the last. Therefore, the freezing ratio (X) should be greater than unity.

Mathematically, a sphere has the minimum ratio of surface area to volume. Spherical shape riser is unsuitable (for riser design) due to difficulty in making for use. Additionally, the hottest metal in the spherical riser is found at the centre, which further complicates feeding of the molten metal to the mould. A cylinder shape riser is therefore most popular choice for riser design due to its ease of moulding riser and favourable freezing ratio.

Based on the principle of Chvorinov, Caine developed a relationship for the freezing ratio:

$$X = \frac{a}{Y - b} + c \tag{34}$$

where, Y is the ratio of "volume of riser to volume of casting", and a, b, and c are the constants depending on the casting metal.

Constants for a few common metals are listed in Table 6. Caine identified a relationship between "ratio of volume of riser to volume of casting" and the freezing ratio for developing shrinkage free casting as shown in Fig. 7.12.

Table 6: Caine's equation constants

Casting metal	Steel	Brass, cast iron	Silicon bronze	Aluminium bronze	Aluminium	Grey cast iron
a	0.10	0.04	0.24	0.24	0.10	0.33
b	0.03	0.017	0.017	0.017	0.06	0.03
c	1.00	1.00	1.00	1.00	1.08	1.00

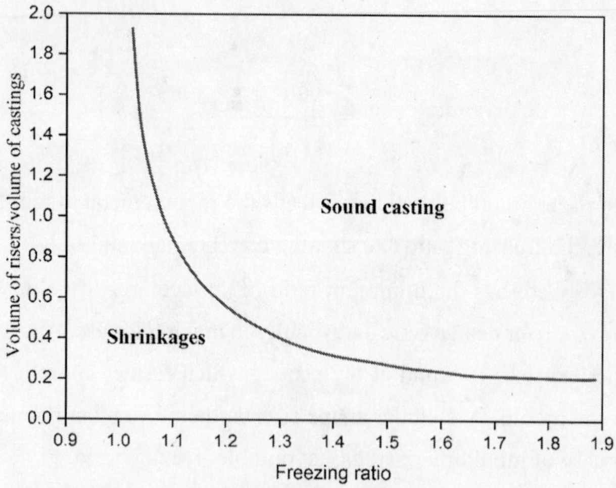

Fig. 7.12 Caine relationship showing condition for developing sound casting

7.12.2 Modulus method

The modulus is the ratio of the volume of the casting to its surface area and the same definition is applicable for the riser as well. Conversely, modulus is the inverse of the cooling characteristic. It has been established that if the riser's modulus is greater than the casting's modulus with a factor of 1.2, then the riser satisfactorily feeds the molten metal to mould during the solidification. Consider a cylindrical shape riser with equal height (h) and diameter (D).

Volume of the cylinder (V) $= \frac{\pi D^2}{4} \times h = \frac{\pi D^3}{4}$ (if h = D).

Surface area of the riser considering only the top end as the bottom end assumed to be opening in the mould.

Surface area (S) $= \frac{\pi D^2}{4} + \pi D^2$

The modulus of riser (M_r)$= \frac{V}{S} = 0.2$ D

If modulus of the riser (M_r) is taken 1.2 times the modulus of casting (M_c)

$M_r = 0.2\,D = 1.2\,M_c$

This suggests that the diameter of the riser is six time the modulus of casting (M_c). The modulus method offers a riser design having a direct relationship with the modulus of the casting, thus preventing the trial-and-error approach of Caine's method. However, this method does not consider the quantity of metal to be fed to compensate for the shrinkage.

To consider the volume of molten metal for compensating shrinkage of the casting, the equation is adjusted: $D^3 - 5.46\,M_c.\,D^2 - 0.05093\,V_c = 0$

where, V_c is the volume of the casting.

The volume of component can be neglected in the case of thick castings or castings with a small surface area compared to their volume. However, the volume component becomes significant in the case of thin section castings, such as plates and sheets. For these cases, a **ranginess factor R** is used to define the casting type.

$$R = \frac{\text{The modulus of a cube having the same volume of casting}}{\text{Modulus of casting}}$$

Table 7: Modulus of a few common geometrical shapes

Casting shape	Casting shape	Modulus, M_c
Plate	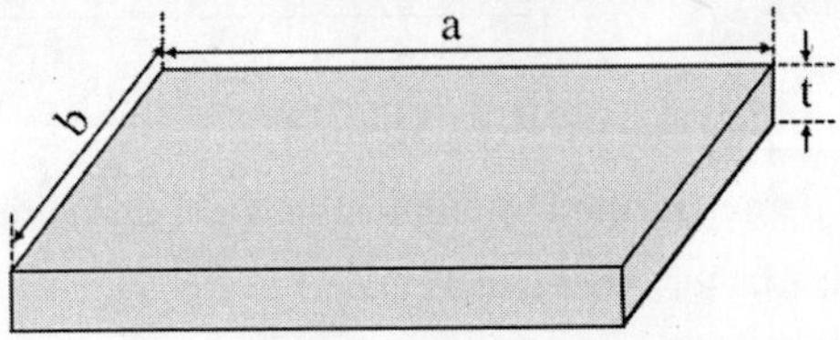	0.5 t (a < 5t)
Long bar	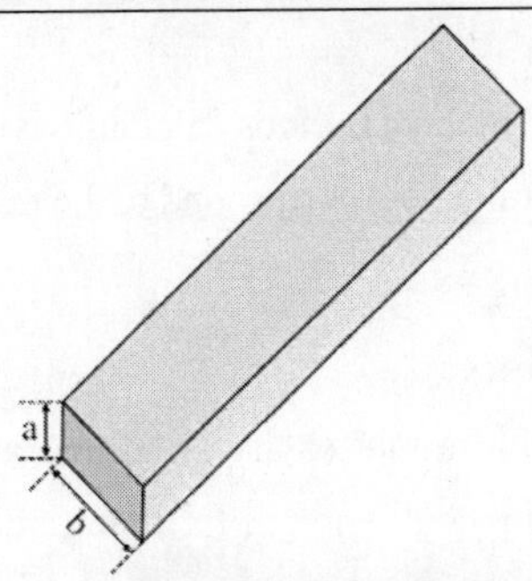	$\frac{ab}{2(a+b)}$
Cube	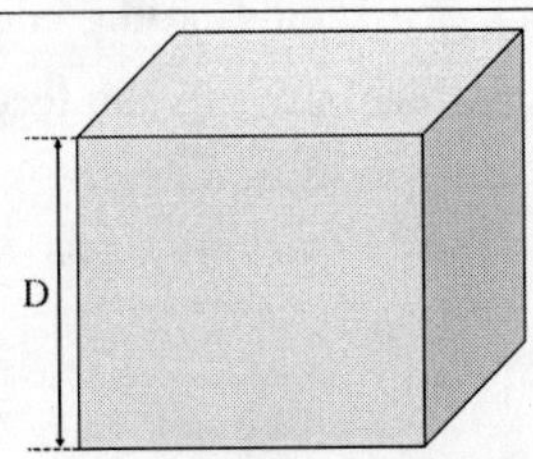	$\frac{D}{6}$
Cylinder	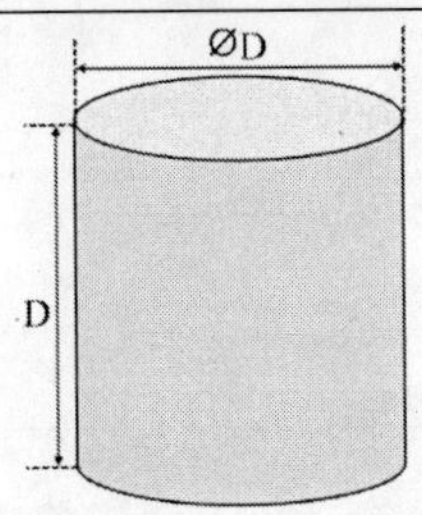	$\frac{D}{6}$

Sphere	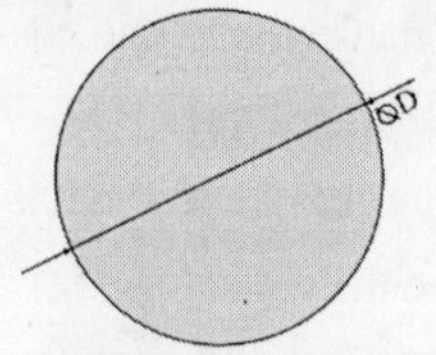	$\frac{D}{6}$
Hollow cylinder	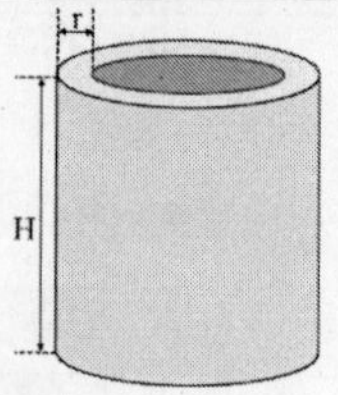	$\frac{rH}{2(r+H)}$

7.12.3 Naval Research Laboratory (NRL) Method

This method simplifies Caine's method by eliminating the freezing ratio and introducing a term "shape factor". The shape factor is defined as under:

$$Shape\ factor = \frac{Length+Width}{Thickness}$$

The NRL methodology simplifies the laborious calculations of the surface area and volume of casting. The length, width, and thickness correspond to the maximum dimensions of the casting sections (Fig. 7.13 and 7.14).

7.12.3.1 Connection to the Risers

The connection of the riser with mould cavity is termed as neck. The neck size should be optimised. The neck size is kept small enough for ease removal of the riser from the casting after solidification. On the contrary, it should be big enough to avoid solidification of the molten metal in the neck section, which prevents the feeding of metal from the riser to the cavity.

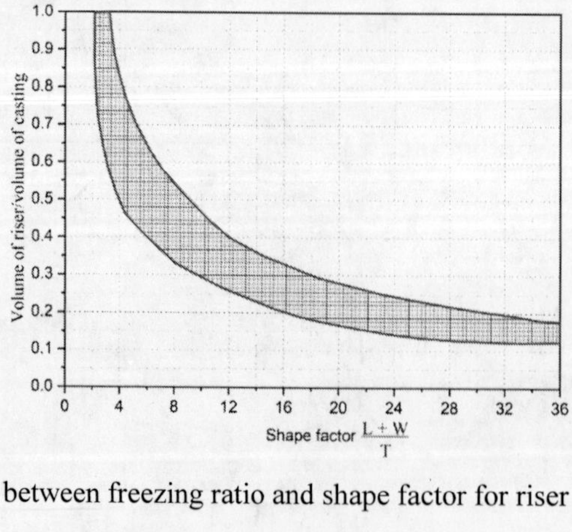

Fig. 7.13 Relationship between freezing ratio and shape factor for riser volume selection

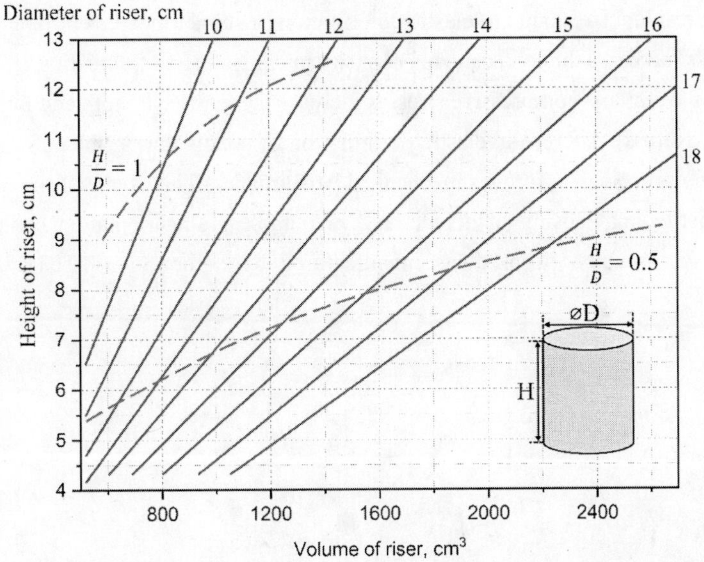

Fig. 7.14 Selection chart for riser dimensions based upon NRL method

7.13 Chills

The chills are metallic objects with higher heat-absorbing capability than sand moulds. They act as localized cooling zones to provide the desired temperature gradient for realizing the directional solidification in the casting. Two types of chills are used: a) external chills and b) internal chills. External chills are placed in the moulding sand near the mould wall to provide localized cooling. External chills can be made of any suitable metal, and these do not become the part of the casting. Internal chills are made of matching or the same metal as casting metal and these are placed in the mould cavity itself. Size and cleanliness of internal chills are crucial for producing sound casting because skin of chills melts by heat of molten metal and becomes an integral part of the casting.

7.14 Bulk Deformation Metal Forming Process

Plastic deformation of a metal is a prerequisite for bulk metal deformation manufacturing processes. The deformation of metal begins with elastic deformation followed by plastic deformation above the yield stress. The stress required to cause the elastic deformation of a specific value is governed by Hook's law up to the elastic limit. Application of further higher level of stress above the yield point/ strength results in plastic deformation.

The elastic deformation is recovered completely on the removal of load and regains the original size and shape. The elastic deformation is important in manufacturing processes with reference to two aspects: a) residual stresses and b) spring back effect (Fig.7.15). Many deformation-based manufacturing processes (contouring rolling, burnishing, shot peening, etc.) develop compressive residual stress due to elastic deformation of sub-surface layers. The compressive residual stress increases the load carrying capacity under static and fluctuating tensile stresses. Conversely, the residual compressive stresses increase the tensile strength and fatigue strength (under tensile stress). Therefore, elastic deformation of metals during the deformation-based manufacturing processes, improves mechanical performance. This is one of the reasons along with work hardening, closing of defects and favourable grain orientation behind the good mechanical performance of products manufactured by deformation-based manufacturing processes.

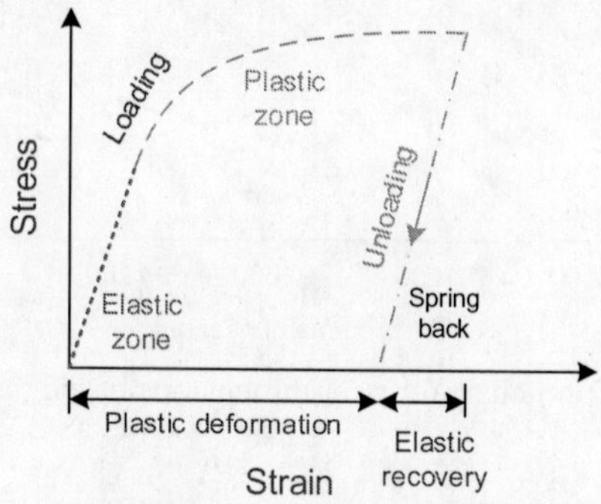

Fig. 7.15 Schematic stress-strain diagram showing elastic recovery on unloading causing spring back

Similarly, manufacturing of products using plastic deformation-based processes produces the desired shape of the product, through the elastic and the plastic deformation. On removal of the load applied during the manufacturing, the elastic deformation disappears resulting in change of size and shape. This undesirable change in shape and size makes it difficult to realise the product of the desired geometry and tolerance. This phenomenon (occurring due to the elastic recovery) is called spring back effect.

7.15 Plastic deformation and yield criteria

The stress required to cause the elastic deformation (specific elastic strain) can be obtained using a true stress-strain diagram simply by drawing a vertical line from the point of the desired elastic strain. The intersection of the vertical line with the stress-strain curve gives the amount of stress required to cause the given elastic strain. The stress-strain diagram for metals like carbon and alloy steel clearly shows the yield point indicating the minimum stress required for the commencement of the plastic deformation in a given metal condition. However, many FCC metals (Al, Cu, austenitic stainless steel, etc.) alloys do not show specific yield point. In those cases, off-set yield point (0.002%) stress is obtained. The stress corresponding to the yield point is the flow stress to be applied to realise the plastic deformation in a metal without any work-hardening effect. It is important to note that a given amount of plastic deformation (in terms of plastic strain) can be obtained by applying a specified value of external stress. However, the commencement of the plastic deformation strengthens the metal due to work hardening, thereby increasing the stress required to cause further plastic deformation. Therefore, it becomes essential to consider the work-hardening behaviour of the metal in plastic deformation-based manufacturing processes to determine the required force/stress for manufacturing.

The flow stress (σ) needed to realize a given plastic strain (ε) of a metal (having work hardening exponent (n) is obtained using the following relation:

$$\sigma = X\varepsilon^n$$

where, X is the material related constant accounting for strength and is also commonly denoted as K.

The work hardening behaviour is observed during plastic deformation of metal below recrystallization temperature mainly under cold working conditions only.

Since work hardening and stress requirements continuously increase during plastic deformation, therefore flow stress used in manufacturing (to realize a given plastic strain) is considered as the "average flow stress". The flow stress continuously increases from the commencement of the plastic deformation beyond the yield point till the specified plastic strain.

The average flow stress (σ_{av}) needed to realize a given plastic strain (ε) of a metal (having work hardening exponent (n) is obtained using the following relation:

$$\sigma_{av} = X\varepsilon^n /1+n$$

where, X is the material related constant accounting for strength and is also commonly denoted as K, n is work hardening exponent and ε is the true strain.

Under hot working conditions, the yield strength is reduced due to recovery and recrystallization and the work hardening behaviour is almost absent. Therefore, plastic deformation of metal under hot working conditions is relatively easier and less power consuming.

The effect of temperature, strain, strain rate, and recrystallization on flow stress can be expressed in the following form:

$$\sigma = \frac{2}{3(1-m)^{\frac{1}{2}}} X\varepsilon^n \epsilon^m \exp(-\beta T)$$

X is material related constant accounting for strength, ε in true strain, n is the strain hardening exponent, ϵ is strain rate, m is strain rate sensitivity exponent, β is material constant, and T is temperature.

Work done in deformation / per unit volume (W): (stress x strain) = (stress x area) x (strain x original length) = Force x Deformation

$$W = \frac{X\varepsilon^{n+1}}{1+n} = \sigma_{av}.\varepsilon$$

These fundamentals are applicable for linear/unidirectional true stress / strain conditions. However, in actual manufacturing scenario, the metals are frequently subjected to two and three dimensional stresses. Therefore, under such conditions, plastic deformation criteria need consideration of theories of ductile failure of metals like Maximum Shear Stress (Tresca theory), and Maximum Distortion Energy Theory (Von Misses Criteria). Yielding under bi/tri-axial stress conditions uses a combination of the principal stresses. A few empirical relationships have been developed to understand the yielding behaviour of metals under combined stress conditions.

7.15.1 Maximum Shear Stress (Tresca) Theory

As per the maximum shear stress theory, the failure (by plastic deformation or yielding) of a mechanical component made of ductile material (subjected to uniaxial, biaxial or tri-axial loading) occurs when the maximum shear stress at a point in the material exceeds the value equivalent to the maximum shear stress developed in the standard specimen during the tensile test. As we know the specimen during the tensile test is subjected to a uniaxial condition of stress (σ_2 & $\sigma_3 = 0$) while maximum principal stress ($\sigma_1 = S_{yt}$).

As a result, the maximum shear equals 50% of the difference between the maximum and minimum principal stresses. Therefore, the maximum shear stress in a simple tensile test specimen is half of the yield strength of metal in a tensile test. Therefore, the deformation condition according to maximum shear stress theory is:

$$\text{Absolute } T_{max} = (S_{ys})_{TT} \ or = S_{yt}/2$$

where, S_{ys} is yield strength in shear under tri-axial stress-state, which is unknown and S_{yt} is the yield strength in the tension test.

A Hexagon graphically illustrates stress distribution, indicating that the material will attain its elastic limit once the stresses (σ_1 and σ_2) exceed this area (Fig. 7.16). Further, the maximum distortion-strain energy approach evaluates the yielding condition better than the Tresca theory.

Step 1: Determine the three principal stresses (σ_1, σ_2, and σ_3) from the tri-axial stress system using principal stress equations or Mohr's circle method.

Step 2: Find out the maximum (σ_1) and the minimum (σ_3) principal stresses

Step 3: Determine the value of the maximum shear stress $\tau_{max}=(\sigma_1 - \sigma_3)/2$.

Step 4: Find out the allowable stress value of the material; allowable stress = σ_{sy}/N or $\sigma_y/2N$ as mentioned above (N=Factor of safety)

Step 5: Compare the value calculated in Step 3 with the allowable value found in Step 4. If the value at Step 3 is less than the allowable value at Step 4, then the design is safe as per the maximum shear stress theory.

For the plastic deformation, the maximum shear stress $(\tau_{max.})_{TT}$ induced at a point in a metal during the tensile loading should be more than allowable shear stress $(\tau_{allowable})$ while considering the factor of safety (*F*) as shown in Fig. 7.16.

$\tau_{allowable} = (\tau_{max.})_{TT} / F = (S_{ys})_{TT}/F = S_{yt}/2.F$

Absolute $\tau_{max.} \leq (S_{ys})_{TT}/F = S_{yt}/2.F$

Uniaxial stress state

Absolute $\tau_{max.} \leq S_{yt}/2.F$

Biaxial stress state (σ_3=0)

Higher of [*absolute value of* $\sigma_1/2$, $(\sigma_1-\sigma_2)/2] \leq S_{yt}/2.F$

The absolute value of $\sigma_1 \leq S_{yt}/F$ when σ_1 and σ_2 are similar in nature

The absolute value of $(\sigma_1-\sigma_2)] \leq S_{yt}/F$ or when σ_1 and σ_2 are different in nature

Tri-axial stress state

Higher of [absolute value of $(\sigma_1-\sigma_2)/2$, $(\sigma_2-\sigma_3)/2$, $(\sigma_3-\sigma_1)/2] \leq S_{yt}/2.F$ or

Higher of [absolute value of $(\sigma_1-\sigma_2)$, $(\sigma_2-\sigma_3)$, $(\sigma_3-\sigma_1)] \leq S_{yt}/F$

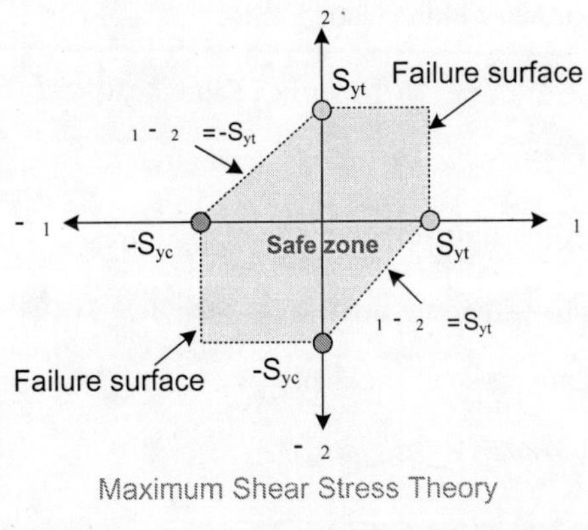

Fig. 7.16 Schematic diagram shows deformation zone (beyond failure surface) considering two normal stresses as per Maximum Shear Stress Theory.

7.15.2 Maximum Distortion Energy Theory (Von Mises)

As per the maximum distortion energy theory, plastic deformation or yielding of ductile material (subjected to uniaxial, biaxial or tri-axial loading) occurs when the maximum distortion energy per unit volume is greater than distortion energy per unit volume at the yield point during the tensile test. As we know the specimen during the tensile test is subjected to a uniaxial condition of stress (σ_2 & σ_3 = 0) while maximum principal stress ($\sigma_1 = S_{yt}$). Therefore, the maximum distortion energy per unit volume for plastic deformation should be more than the distortion energy per unit volume at the yield point during the tensile test (Fig. 7.17).

Total strain energy / unit = (Volumetric strain energy / volume) + (Distortion energy / volume)

Distortion energy / volume = (Total strain energy / unit) - (Volumetric strain energy / volume)

Total strain energy / volume (within elastic limit): area under elastic curve: $\frac{1}{2}\, stress\ (\sigma) strain\ (\varepsilon)$

For tri-axial stress state

Total strain energy / volume (within elastic limit): $\frac{1}{2}\sigma_1.\varepsilon_1 + \frac{1}{2}\sigma_2.\varepsilon_2 + \frac{1}{2}\sigma_3.\varepsilon_3$

Since $\varepsilon_1 = \frac{1}{E}[\sigma_1 - \mu(\sigma_2 + \sigma_3)]$,

$\varepsilon_2 = \frac{1}{E}[\sigma_2 - \mu(\sigma_1 + \sigma_3)]$,

$\varepsilon_3 = \frac{1}{E}[\sigma_3 - \mu(\sigma_1 + \sigma_2)]$

Therefore, total strain energy / volume (within elastic limit): $\frac{1}{2}\sigma_1.\varepsilon_1 + \frac{1}{2}\sigma_2.\varepsilon_2 + \frac{1}{2}\sigma_3.\varepsilon_3$ can be written as under by substituting values of respective strains

Total strain energy / volume (within elastic limit)

$= \frac{1}{2}\sigma_1.\frac{1}{E}[\sigma_1 - \mu(\sigma_2 + \sigma_3)] + \frac{1}{2}\sigma_2.\frac{1}{E}[\sigma_2 - \mu(\sigma_1 + \sigma_3)], + \frac{1}{2}\sigma_3.\frac{1}{E}[\sigma_3 - \mu(\sigma_1 + \sigma_2)]$

$= \frac{1}{2E}[\sigma_1^2 + \sigma_2^2 + \sigma_3^2 - 2\mu(\sigma_1.\sigma_2 + \sigma_2.\sigma_3 + \sigma_3.\sigma_1)]$

Volumetric strain energy per unit volume = $\frac{1}{2}$ Average stress × volume strain

$= \frac{1}{2}[(\sigma_1 + \sigma_2 + \sigma_3)/3] \times [\frac{1-2\mu}{E}(\sigma_1 + \sigma_2 + \sigma_3)] = [\frac{1-2\mu}{6E}(\sigma_1 + \sigma_2 + \sigma_3)^2]$

Distortion energy / volume = (Total strain energy / unit) - (Volumetric strain energy / volume)

$= \frac{1}{2E}[\sigma_1^2 + \sigma_2^2 + \sigma_3^2 - 2\mu(\sigma_1.\sigma_2 + \sigma_2.\sigma_3 + \sigma_3.\sigma_1)] - [\frac{1-2\mu}{6E}(\sigma_1 + \sigma_2 + \sigma_3)^2]$

$= [\frac{1+\mu}{6E}[(\sigma_1 - \sigma_2)^2 + (\sigma_2 - \sigma_3)^2 + (\sigma_3 - \sigma_1)^2]$

Distortion energy per unit volume in metal at yield point during tensile test can be obtained using $\sigma_1 = S_{yt}/F$, $\sigma_2 = \sigma_3 = 0$

Distortion energy per unit volume at the yield point during the tensile test= $\frac{1+\mu}{3E}(\sigma_1)^2 = [\frac{1+\mu}{3E}(S_{yt}/F)^2]$

For plastic deformation, the distortion energy/volume under tri-axial stress state $\leq$ Distortion energy per unit volume at yield point during tensile test

$[\frac{1+\mu}{6E}[(\sigma_1 - \sigma_2)^2 + (\sigma_2 - \sigma_3)^2 + (\sigma_3 - \sigma_1)^2] \leq [\frac{1+\mu}{3E}(S_{yt}/F)^2]$

For deformation, the distortion energy / volume under biaxial stress state (σ_3=0) $\leq$ Distortion energy per unit volume at yield point during tensile test

$$[\frac{1+\mu}{6E}\ [(\sigma_1 - \sigma_2)^2 + (\sigma_2 - \sigma_3)^2 + (\sigma_3 - \sigma_1)^2] \leq [\frac{1+\mu}{3E}\ (S_{yt}/F)^2]$$

Conversely, $[\sigma_1^2 - \sigma_2^2 + \sigma_1.\sigma_2] \leq (S_{yt}/F)^2$

The theory works effectively for ductile material but not under hydrostatic stress state. A comparison of maximum distortion energy and maximum shear stress theories is shown in Fig. 7.18.

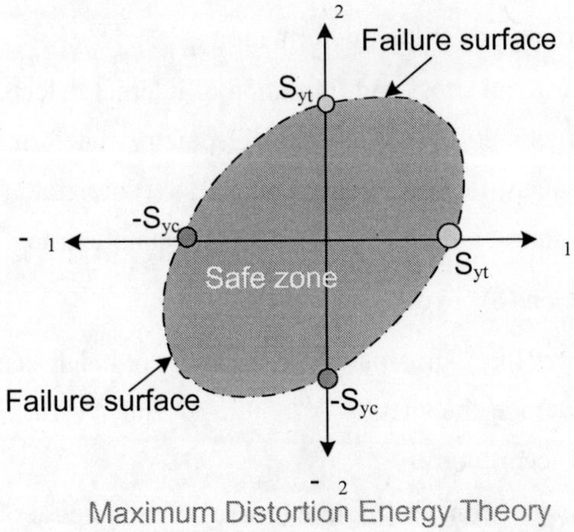

Fig. 7.17 Schematic diagram shows the deformation zone (beyond the failure surface) considering two normal stresses as per Maximum Distortion Energy Theory.

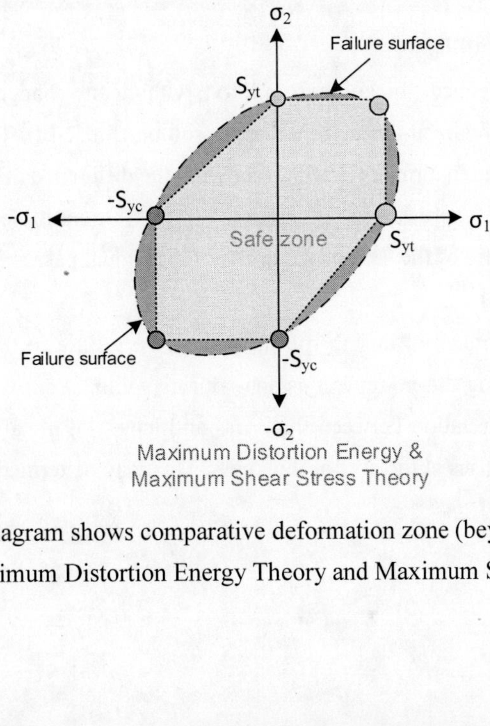

Fig. 7.18 Schematic diagram shows comparative deformation zone (beyond failure surface) corresponding to Maximum Distortion Energy Theory and Maximum Shear Stress Theory.

7.16 Work needed during bulk deformation

The bulk deformation based manufacturing processes use closed or open dies to force metal to flow. Metal flows in a controlled way in case of open die. While, the flowing metal fills the cavity in case of closed dies. The work to be done for bulk deformation is affected not just by mechanical properties and work hardening behaviour under deformation conditions but also by friction and geometry of the product resulting from the deformed zone. An effective lubrication reduces the frictional work. However, additional/redundant work needed for deformation during manufacturing significantly varies with the geometry of the deformation zone, which in turn affects the force required for bulk deformation.

The development of residual stress and formation of internal defects during bulk deformation are also influenced by geometry of deformation. Geometry of deformation is measured in terms of Delta (δ), which is quantified as a ratio of thickness (t) or height (h) to contact length (l) of the deformation zone during bulk deformation based manufacturing.

Geometry of deformation (δ) = $\frac{t}{l}$ or $\frac{h}{l}$

Manufacturing processes like extrusion where thickness or height/length changes significantly during processing, Average thickness $t = (t_1 + t_2)/2$ and Average contact length $l = (t_1 + t_2)/2Sin\alpha$ are obtained accordingly.

This equation suggests that contact length increases with increase of die angle. So increasing the geometry of deformation (δ), increases the redundant strain, which in turn increases redundant work. Redundant strain (λ) is a function of δ and expressed $\lambda = 1 + \delta/4$ for plane strain deformation.

7.17 Mechanics of rolling

The rolling process reduces thickness from t_1 to t_2 without any change in the width of slab. The desired thickness is realized through multi-pass rolling (Fig.7.19). The extent of reduction in thickness is quantified in terms of draft (d) showing the difference of initial and final thickness (t_1 - t_2). It can also be expressed in reduction (r %) = d/t_1. In multiple pass rolling, reduction is obtained from the ratio of the sum of the drafts of individual passes (d_1+ d_2+ d_3+ d_4+ d_4..) and original thickness (t_1).

There is no loss of material during rolling (except very little in the form of chipping off). Therefore, considering the volume constancy during rolling from entry to exit, a continuous variation and direct relation between thickness and length of metal being rolled is observed wherein length increases at the cost of thickness. This may be termed as spreading.

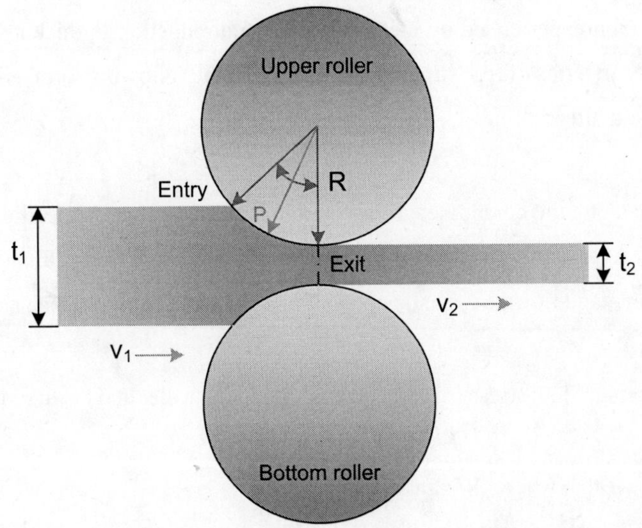

Fig. 7.19 Schematic diagram showing important parameters at entry, exit and contact interface

$$t_1 w_1 l_1 = t_2 w_2 l_2 \text{ where, } (w_1 = w_2). \text{ So, } t_1 / t_2 = l_2 / l_1 \text{ (where } l_2 >> l_1)$$

Taking volume constancy from entry to exit, flow rates of the metal must remain constant before and after the rolling. Therefore, the velocities before and after can be related as follows:

Cross-sectional area x velocity of metal before rolling = Cross-sectional area x velocity of metal before rolling

$$t_1 w_1 v_1 = t_2 w_2 v_2$$

where, v_1 and v_2 are the velocity of the metal at the entry and exit during rolling.

Since $w_1 = w_2$, continuous reduction in thickness (t_1 to t_2) during rolling will cause an increase in velocity (v_1 to v_2) of metal. The velocity of metal initially at the entry in rolling stand is lower than roller surface velocity while that is higher than roller surface at the exit. Two velocities (of metal and roller surfaces) are the same at the neutral plane. The difference in velocity of a) metal at the exit after rolling (v_2) and b) that of roller surface (v_r) is called slip (s) and is given by $s = (v_2 - v_r)/ v_r$

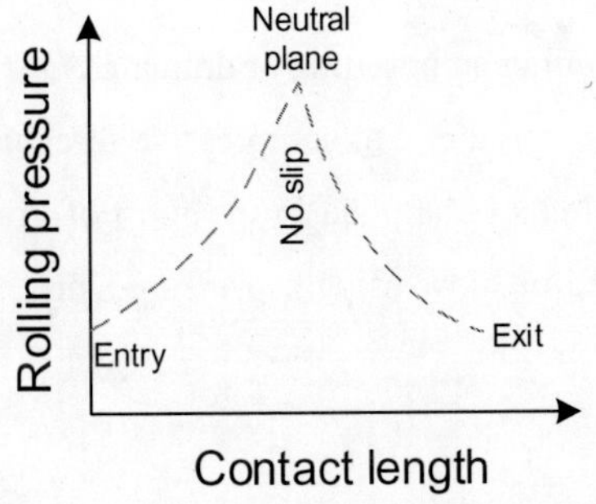

Fig. 7.20 Schematic diagram showing pressure variation along the contact length from entry to exit

Plastic deformation experienced by metal resulting in a reduction in thickness of slab during rolling measured in terms of true strain and expressed in the following form using the thickness of slab before and after rolling:

$$\varepsilon = \ln t_1/t_2$$

Actual pressure along the contact length varies and is maximum at the neutral plane with zero slip (Fig. 7.20). Average force required for plastic deformation during rolling is obtained from the product of average flow stress and contact area between rollers and slab as given below:

$$F_r = \sigma_{av}.w.l$$

where, σ_{av} is average flow stress (MPa), and w width of the roller and l is the roller-slab contact length expressed by:

$l = R(t_1 - t_2)^{0.5}$ (where, R is radius of rollers).

Rolling force (F_r) and roller-slab contact length (l) affect the torque required to rotate rollers for rolling. The torque (T) for each roller is expressed:

$$T = F_r . l/2$$

The power (P) needed for rotating each roller is obtained from the torque (T) and angular velocity (ω). Angular velocity ($\omega = 2\pi N$) primarily depends on the rotational speed (rpm) of the roller.

Power needed for each roller $P = T.\omega = 2\pi.N.T$

$$= 2\pi.N.F_r.l/2 = \pi.N.F_r.l$$

As rolling is performed by a set of two rollers,

power required for rolling = $2.\pi.N.F_r.l$

where, P = power (J/s or W); N = rotational speed, 1/s (rev/sec); F_r = rolling force, N; and l = contact length, m.

7.18 Mechanics of forging

The forging process follows either an upsetting or drawing out approach for changing of cross-section and length of stock material due to compressive force using open or closed dies (Fig. 7.21). The compressive load can be applied in the form of gradually increasing pressure or suddenly applied impact load or blow using a pressure / machine forging and drop forging respectively.

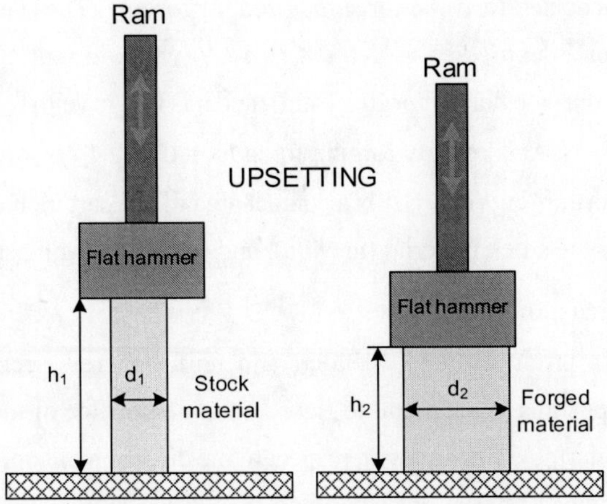

Fig. 7.21 Schematic diagram showing upset forging with change of dimensions in terms of height and diameter

Compressive stress is obtained using the area of dies in contact with stock material and applied load. While, true strain is calculated from the change in height / thickness of stock due to compressive load during forming using the following expression:

True strain $\varepsilon = \ln h_1 / h_2$

where, h_1 is the initial height / thickness and h_i is the instantaneous height/thickness of the stock material during forging (mm), and h_2 is the final thickness / height of stock resulting in the maximum true strain in one stroke of punch during forging.

The force required for forging (like the rolling process) is obtained from flow stress and contact area of the die being used to apply compression load for upsetting/drawing out:

$$F_f = \sigma_{av}.A$$

where, F_f is compressive force for forging (N); A is area through which compressive load is applied on the stock material (mm^2); and σ_{av} is average flow stress (MPa) for a given strain during forging.

Forging involves continuous deformation of metal in the form of upsetting / drawing out leading to dynamic strain due to plastic deformation. Continuously increasing plastic strain increases the flow stress required for further deformation due to work hardening except in perfectly plastic materials or during hot working (having zero strain-hardening exponent n).

In case of hot working, flow stress becomes equal to the yield strength of stock metal as per forming temperature. The forging force under cold working conditions (or when work hardening takes place) continuously increases till the completion of forging in each stroke as increasing strain causes work hardening continuously. Further, the area of contact of stock metal with die and flow stress is maximum at the end of the stroke. Like rolling, friction and geometry of the product also affect the force required for forging. These are considered using a shape factor C_f which is expressed as $\boldsymbol{1 + 0.4\ (\mu\ l / h)}$ where μ is friction coefficient, l is contact length with die surface during forging (mm), and h is height (mm) of stock at an instant.

$$\text{Accordingly forging force } F_r = C_f.\sigma_{av}.A$$

where, F_r is the force for forging (in N), A is a contact area of the part including flash (in mm^2), σ_{av} is the flow stress of the stock material (in MPa), and C_f is the forging shape factor.

7.19 Mechanics of extrusion

The extrusion process produces long, slender, and uniform cross-section products using compressive force by pushing stock metal to flow through an orifice of the die. The direction of movement of metal during extrusion with respect to the direction of compressive force leads to two types of extrusion: a) direct extrusion and b) indirect extrusion. Force for extrusion depends on the plastic behavior of metal as per flow stress (depending on the temperature and speed of extrusion) and friction at the metal-extrusion chamber interfacial contact (Fig. 7.22).

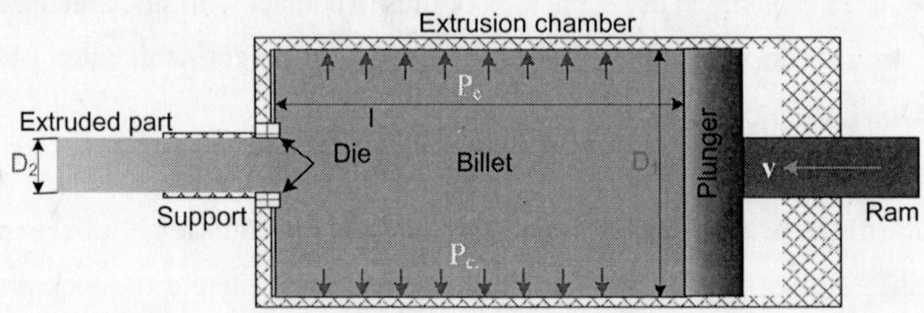

Fig. 7.22 Schematic diagram showing direct extrusion with change of dimensions in terms of diameter and contact length

Moreover, metal-extrusion chamber interfacial friction is absent during indirect extrusion. While suitable lubricants (between stock metal and extrusion chamber interface) are used to reduce friction during direct extrusion. The friction force must be overcome before the commencement of any extrusion. Reduction in cross-section due to extrusion is measured in terms of extrusion ratio. This is also known as the reduction ratio (R_{ex}) and is expressed as follows:

$$\text{Extrusion ratio, } R_{ex} = A_1 / A_2$$

where, A_1 is the initial cross-sectional area of the billet (in mm^2), and A_2 is the cross-sectional area of the component after extrusion (in mm^2).

The extrusion ratio R_{ex} gives the true strain due to extrusion while neglecting the influence of friction and redundant work, if any.

$$\text{True strain in extrusion } \varepsilon = \ln R_{ex} = \ln (A_1 / A_2)$$

Compressive stress / pressure P_{ex} to be applied using ram for extrusion (under ideal conditions i.e. no friction or redundant work) is calculated as follows:

$$P_{ex} = \sigma_{av}.ln\ R_{ex}$$

where, σ_{av} is the average flow stress due to deformation (in MPa) = $X\varepsilon^n / 1+n$

(However, n will be negligible for hot extrusion)

One of several empirical equations to obtain true strain and the corresponding ram pressure during extrusion is as follows:

$$\text{Instantaneous true strain } \varepsilon_x = a + b\ ln\ R_{ex}$$

where, a and b are empirical constants depending on the extrusion die angle. Typical value a is 0.8 while b ranges from 1.2 to 1.5.

These constants (a and b) increase with the extrusion die angle. The ram pressure to perform indirect extrusion (as there is no major frictional effect) can be estimated based on Johnson's extrusion strain formula as follows:

$$P_{ex} = \sigma_{av}.\varepsilon_x$$

where, σ_{av} is calculated based on ideal strain, rather than extrusion strain.

The effect of friction in direct extrusion is accounted using the following expression to quantify the pressure required to overcome interfacial friction. Additional pressure needed × cross-sectional area = frictional force ×area of contact = normal load ×coefficient of friction ×interfacial frictional contact area

$$P_f.\pi D_1^2/4 = \mu.P_c.\pi D_1 l$$

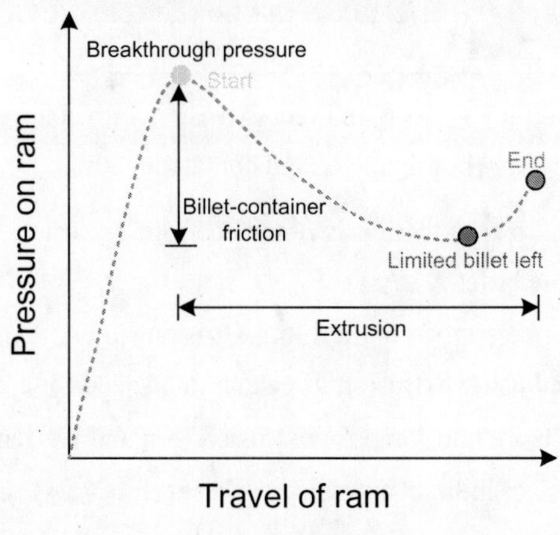

Fig. 7.23 Schematic diagram showing variation extrusion pressure for direct extrusion with the travel of ram

where, P_f is extra pressure needed to deal with billet- container interfacial friction (in MPa), $\pi D_1^2/4$ billet cross-section before extrusion (in mm^2), μ is billet-container interfacial friction coefficient, P_c is pressure exerted by billet on the container wall during extrusion (in MPa), and $\pi D_1 l$ = area of the interface between billet and container wall (in mm^2).

In case of metal-container surface sticking, friction stress shall be approximately equal to the shear force required to cause flow (as per the shear yield strength of the billet) under extrusion conditions (Fig. 7.23).

$$\mu . P_c . \pi D_1 l = \sigma_s . \pi D_1 l$$

where, σ_s is shear strength (in MPa) of the billet.

Assuming shear strength (σ_s) is half of the yield strength of the metal (σ_y), then additional pressure (P_f) to overcome friction becomes

$$P_f = \sigma_y (2l/D_1)$$

Pressure to be applied on ram for direct extrusion:

$$P_{de} = \sigma_y (\varepsilon_x + 2l/D_1)$$

where, the term $2l/D_1$ accounts for the additional pressure due to billet-container interfacial friction, l is the length of metal yet to be extruded, and D_1 is the initial billet diameter.

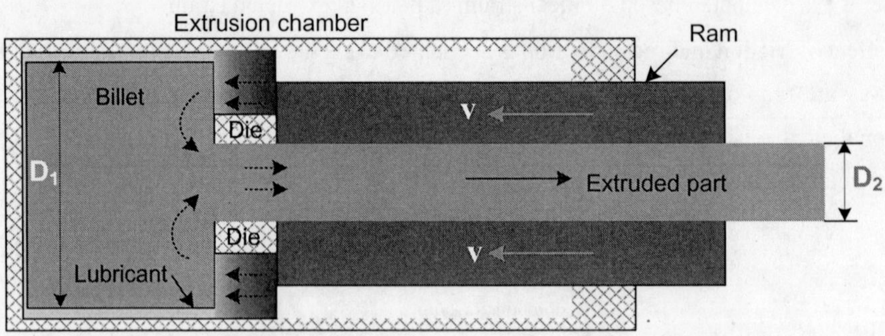

Fig. 7.24 Schematic diagram showing indirect extrusion with change of dimensions in terms of diameter and contact length

Force (F_{ex}) for direct/indirect extrusion is obtained from extrusion pressure (P_{ex}) and initial cross-sectional area of the billet A_1: $F_{ex} = P_{ex} . A_1$

where, F_{ex} is the force to be applied on ram for extrusion (in N), then power (P_w) required for extrusion can be obtained using extrusion force and ram speed for extrusion $P = F_{ex} . v$

where, P is power (J/s), F_{ex} = ram force for extrusion (N); and v = ram speed (m/s).

The friction factor in case of indirect extrusion is absent (Fig. 7.24). The influence of the shape of the product on the extrusion pressure is accounted by considering the shape factor of the die. The die shape factor considers the extrusion pressure needed for a given cross-section to that of round cross-section of the identical cross-sectional area. Die shape factor for extrusion is given by

$C_{ex} = 0.98 + 0.02 \, (C_M/C_R)^{2.25}$

where, C_{ex} = die shape factor; C_M = perimeter of cross-section of the given component to be extruded (in mm); and C_R = perimeter of a circular cross-section of the same area (in mm).

Extrusion pressure for other than circular cross-sections considering die shape factors can be obtained as follows:

$$\text{Indirect extrusion } P = C_{ex}.\sigma_{av}.\varepsilon_x$$

$$\text{Direct extrusion } P = C_{ex}.\sigma_{av}(\varepsilon_x + 2l/D_1)$$

where, P is extrusion pressure (in MPa), C_{ex} is the shape factor.

A comparative variation of extrusion pressure with the travel of ram is shown in Fig. 7.25. High maximum extrusion pressure for direct extrusion than indirect extrusion is attributed to friction condition difference.

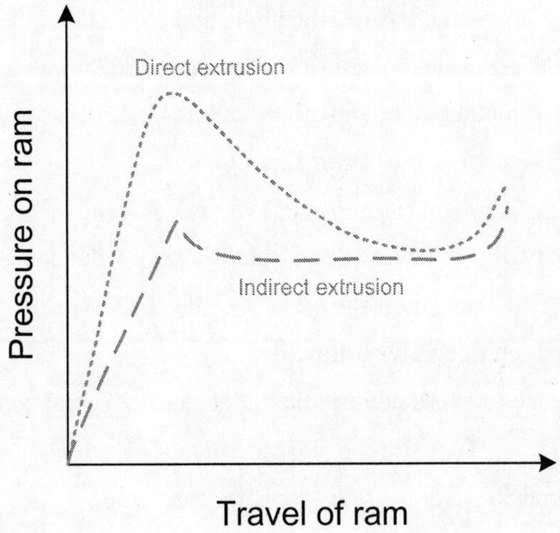

Fig. 7.25 Variation of extrusion pressure for direct and indirect extrusion with travel of ram

7.20 Mechanics of wire drawing

The wire drawing is similar to the extrusion in terms of approach involving reduction in cross-section of metal by passing large diameter metal through the die. However, two processes differ with respect to actual stress, leading to the change in cross-section. Tensile load is applied on the bar to cause plastic flow of the metal for wire drawing, which indirectly applies compressive load while metal passes through the die (Fig. 7.26). While extrusion exclusively uses compressive load only. Change in cross-section in wire drawing is expressed in terms of % reduction in area:

$$\text{Reduction in cross-section area in wire drawing } R_{wd} = (A_1 - A_2)/A_1$$

where, A_1 is the initial cross-sectional area of bar (in mm^2); and A_2 = cross-sectional area of metal after wire drawing (in mm^2).

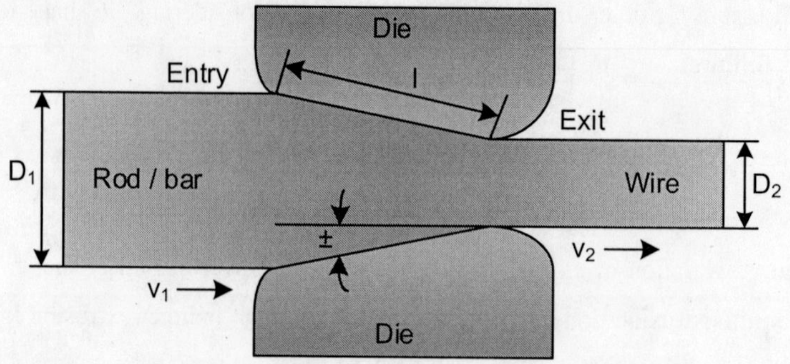

Fig. 7.26 Schematic diagram showing wire drawing with change of dimensions in terms of diameter, besides die angle and contact length

In the case of large-diameter stock metals, it is called a bar/rod drawing. The difference in size between the diameter of metal before and after the drawing process is called a draft.

$$Draft\ D = D_1 - D_2$$

where, D_1 initial size of bar / rod (in mm); and D_2 = size of the metal after drawing (in mm). True strain for wire drawing (assuming negligible friction / redundant work,) is obtained from

$$\text{True strain } \varepsilon = ln\ A_1/\ A_2 = ln\ (1/(1- R_{wd}))$$

where, R_{wd} is the reduction due to wire drawing.

Further, the stress needed to cause deformation under such an ideal condition is expressed

$$\text{True stress } \sigma = \sigma_{av}.\varepsilon = \sigma_{av}.ln\ (A_1/\ A_2)$$

where, $\sigma_{av} = \mathbf{X}\varepsilon^n$ / 1+n is the average flow stress for true strain.

A typical empirical equation for stress for wire drawing is given below.

$$\text{Stress for wire drawing } \sigma_{wd} = \sigma_{av}\ (1 + \mu/tan\ \alpha)\varphi(ln\ A_1/A_1)$$

where, σ_{WD} wire drawing stress (MPa), μ metal-die interfacial friction coefficient, α is the die angle (half-angle), and factor φ factor accounts for inhomogeneous deformation considering geometry aspect affecting redundant work.

$$\varphi = 0.88 + 0.12(D_{av}/l)$$

where, D is the average size (in mm) of metal obtained from $(D_1 + D_2)/2$ and l metal-die contact length (in mm) during wire drawing calculated using $(D_1 - D_2)/2sin\alpha$

Accordingly, wire-drawing force is obtained using a cross-sectional area of wire and stress for drawing.

$$\text{Force for wire drawing } F\ (in\ N)= A_2.\sigma_{wd} = A_2.\sigma_{av}\ (1 + \mu/tan\ \alpha)\varphi(ln\ A_1/A_1)$$

Similarly, power (J) for wire drawing is calculated using force for wire drawing and velocity of the metal (m/s) at the exit after drawing workpiece: $F.v$

In hot working conditions, the work hardening is neglected. So, $\sigma_{av} = \sigma_y$ (because n = 0),

$$\sigma_{wd} = \sigma_y\ ln\ (A_1/\ A_2) = \sigma_y\ ln\ (A_1/\ A_2) = \sigma_y\ ln\ (1/(1-R_{wd})) = \sigma_y$$

$$ln(1/(1-r)) = 1$$

This gives a condition for maximum possible reduction, r_{max}: 0.632 (theoretical maximum limit) $A_o/A_f = e = 2.7183$

Practically, in a single pass, wire-drawing allows a maximum reduction of 0.5. While that is 0.3 in case of multiple-stage wire drawing.

7.21 Machining

Machining is a manufacturing process where material is removed from the bulk materials in a controlled way mostly by shearing mechanism to obtain the desired size, shape and other desired dimension characteristics such as flatness, straightness, taperness, finish and tolerance. The machining is broadly categorised as orthogonal and oblique cutting depending on the orientation/inclination of the cutting edge with respect to the direction of cutting.

The orthogonal cutting uses cutting edge normal to the direction of cutting. The material removed in the form of chips flows perpendicular to the cutting edge on the rake face of the tool. Cutting forces generated during orthogonal machining act in two directions only. The inclination of the cutting edge with respect to the cutting direction affects cutting performance significantly in terms of cutting forces, tool temperature, and tool life. These aspects have been described in detail in Section 3.4 of Unit 3.

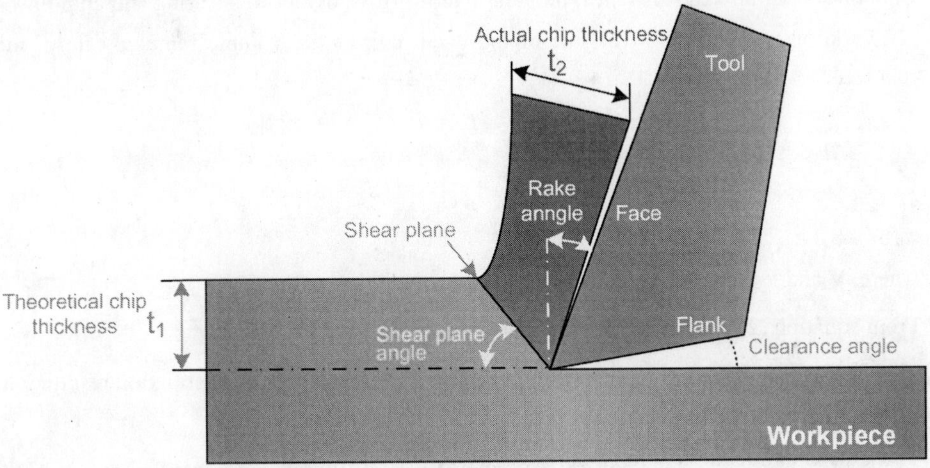

Fig. 7.27 Tool-workpiece interaction with various cutting angles and planes

7.22 Geometry of chip formation (orthogonal cutting)

A simplified diagram of chip formation (continuous chips) is shown in Figure 7.27. The uncut chip thickness t_1 (corresponding to feed during turning and depth of cut during shaping) is deformed to produce chip thickness t_2 (Fig. 7.27). The material being removed during machining experiences two velocities, namely, chip sliding velocity (Vc) on the rake face and shear velocity (Vs) along the shear plane, respectively as shown in Fig 7.31. The chip thickness ratio (r) is a dimensionless parameter in machining and is expressed as a ratio of the uncut chip thickness (t_1) to the chip thickness (t_2)

$r = \frac{t_1}{t_2}$................. (1)

where, t_2 = Chip thickness (in mm), and t_1 = Uncut chip thickness (in mm)

The chip thickness ratio is an important parameter in machining which affects tool temperatures, wear and tool life, cutting forces, power consumption, surface finish and quality of machined surfaces. High chip thickness ratio indicates the formation of thick chip generating high cutting force, and power consumption, high tool wear rate and low tool life. These conditions also promote rough surfaces with poor tolerance. Conversely, low chip thickness ratio produces thin chip leading to improved tool life and surface finish. Assume the density of workpiece metal is constant during the cutting operation. In orthogonal cutting, width of cut (b) becomes equal to the width of the chip (b) and considering the volume of the theoretical uncut chip equals the volume of metal removed.

Volume of the uncut chip = Volume of metal removed

$$\rho \times l_1 \times b \times t_1 = \rho \times l_2 \times b \times t_2$$

or $r = \frac{t_1}{t_2} = \frac{l_2}{l_1}$ ....(2)

where, $l_1 = initial\ uncut\ length\ of\ chip$ and $l_2 = final\ cut\ length\ of\ chip$

Chip thickness ratio can also be expressed in terms of velocities of shearing and chip flow.

As we know, volume removal rate of the uncut chip = the volume removal rate of metal removed.

$$\rho \times V \times b \times t_1 = \rho \times V_c \times b \times t_2$$

or $r = \frac{t_1}{t_2} = \frac{V_c}{V}$ ....(3)

∴ ($b_1 = b_2$).

where, V and V_c are cutting velocity and chip velocity respectively.

From equation (2) and (3) we have, $r = \frac{t_1}{t_2} = \frac{V_c}{V} = \frac{l_2}{l_1}$

Shearing leads to greater thickness of the chip after removal due to deformation resulting in $t_2 > t_1$. Therefore, r is always less than 1.

Thus, the chip thickness ratio is represented as,

$r = \frac{t_1}{t_2} = \frac{l_2}{l_1} = \frac{V_c}{V} = \frac{\sin\emptyset}{\cos(\emptyset - \alpha)} = \frac{1}{\gamma}$........................(4)

where, γ is chip reduction ratio and φ, α are shear angle and rake angle respectively.

7.23 Cutting force analysis

Cutting force analysis during orthogonal cutting is presented in the following section with the help of Merchant Theory. The cutting forces acting in the machining zone are depicted using the ***Merchant force circle*** in Fig. 7.28.

- Shear force (Fs) is the resistance to shear of the metal during chip formation acts along the shear plane.
- Force (Fn) is a backup force on the chip provided by the workpiece and acts in the normal direction to the shear plane.
- Normal force (N) acts on the chip and is normal to the rake face of the tool.
- Friction force (F) is frictional resistance offered by the tool to the chip flow.
- Cutting force (Fc) is the main cutting force and acts horizontally on the cutting edge
- Thrust force (Ft) is feed force and acts vertically on the cutting edge

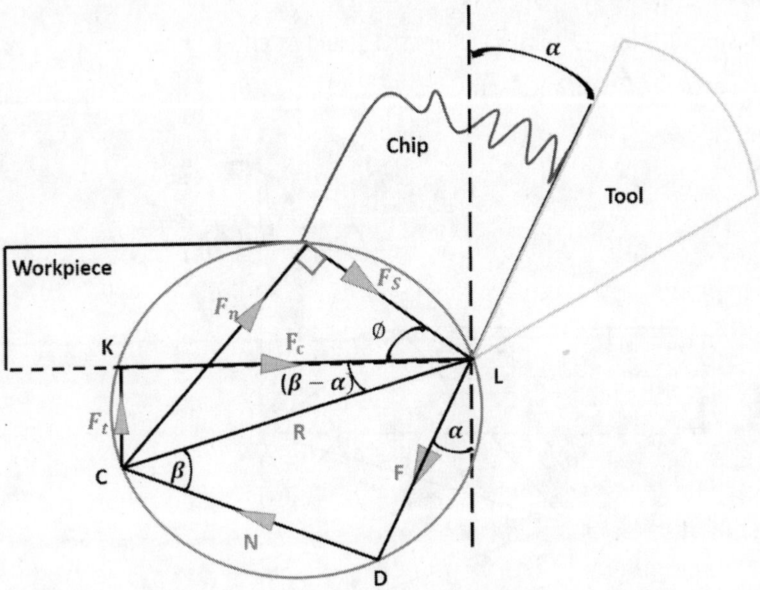

Fig. 7.28 Merchant circle diagram

Merchant theory is based on the following assumptions:

- The work material behaves like an ideal plastic material.
- Minimum energy principle is employed.
- Shear strength τ_s and friction angle β are constant and unaffected by shear angle Ø.

Limitations Merchant theory are:

- It is only applicable to orthogonal cutting.
- The F/N ratio indicates the apparent coefficient of friction, not the actual coefficient of friction.
- The hypothesis relies on single shear plane theory.

7.23.1 Determination of tool plane forces (F and N)

The diameter of the merchant circle gives the resultant force (R). On drawing a line KE perpendicular to LD and CG perpendicular to KE in the merchant circle diagram (Fig. 7.29), the following is obtained.

F = DL = EL + DE

F = $F_c \cos(90 - \alpha)$ + CG $\quad$ *as* DE=CG

F = $F_c \cos(90 - \alpha) + F_t \cos(\alpha)$ using ΔKEL and ΔCGK

So, F = $F_c \sin(\alpha) + F_t \cos(\alpha)$.......................(5)

Also, N = DC = EG = EK – GK

Or N = $F_c \sin(90 - \alpha)\ - F_t \sin(\alpha)$ using ΔKEL and ΔCGK

So N = $F_c \cos(\alpha) - F_t \sin(\alpha)$..................................(6)

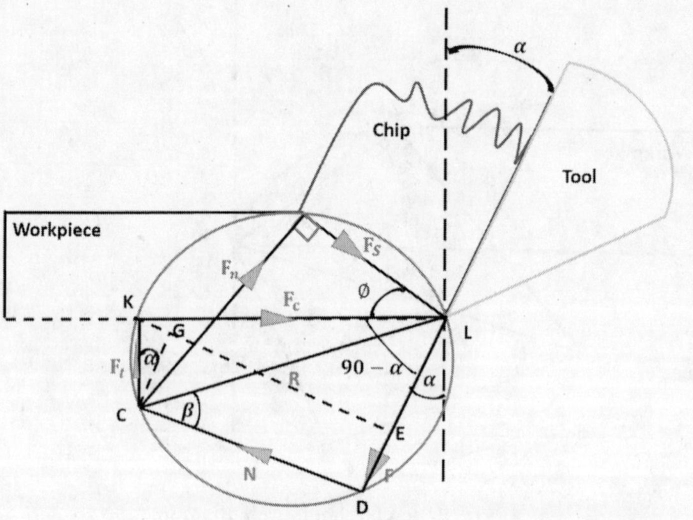

Fig. 7.29 Merchant circle diagram used for determination of tool plane forces

7.23.2 Calculation of coefficient of friction and friction angle (μ and tanβ)

The coefficient of friction is the ratio of friction force and normal force.

$$\mu = \frac{F}{N}$$

Or

$$\mu = \frac{F}{N} = \frac{F_c \sin(\alpha) + F_t \cos(\alpha)}{F_c \cos(\alpha) - F_t \sin(\alpha)}$$

and

$$tan\beta = \mu = \frac{F}{N} \text{...........(7)}$$

7.23.3 Determination of shear plane forces (Fs and Fn)

On drawing a line HK perpendicular to NL and PK perpendicular to NC in the merchant circle diagram (Fig. 7.30), the following is obtained:

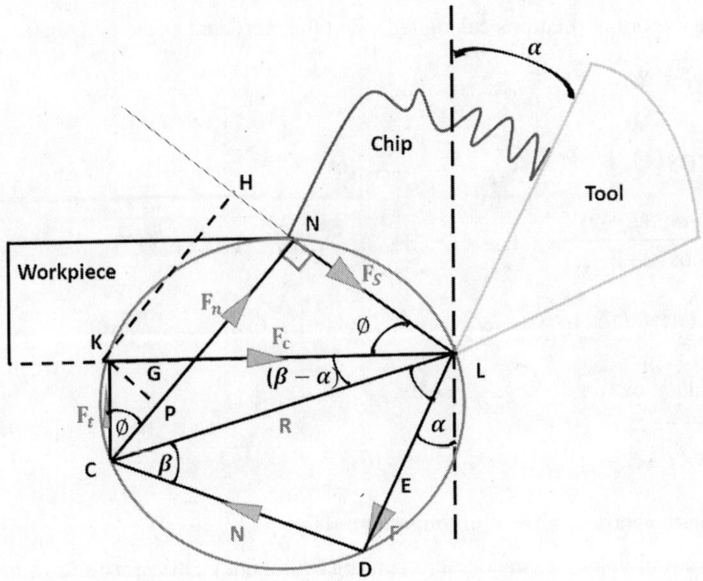

Fig. 7.30 Merchant circle diagram used for determination of shear plane forces

$F_s = NL = LH - NH$

$F_s = F_c\cos(\emptyset) - PK$ $\quad$ *as* NH = PK using ΔLKH and ΔCGK

$F_s = F_c\cos(\emptyset) - F_t\sin(\emptyset)$.. (8)

Also, $F_n = CN = PN + CP$

$F_n = KH + CP$ $\quad$ *as* PN = KH using Δ LKH and ΔCGK

$F_n = F_c\sin(\emptyset) + F_t\sin(\emptyset)$.. (9)

7.23.4 Calculation of Shear and normal stress (τs and σn)

Shear plane area (A_s), as shown in Fig 7.27, is given by

$A_s = \frac{b \times t_1}{\sin\emptyset}$..................... (10)

where, b = width of cut, t_1 = uncut chip thickness and Ø is the shear plane angle.

So, the Average shear stress (τ_s):

$$\tau_s = \frac{F_s}{A_s} = \frac{F_c\sec(\beta-\alpha)\cos(\emptyset+\beta-\alpha)}{\frac{bt_1}{\sin\emptyset}}$$

$\tau_s = \frac{F_c\sec(\beta-\alpha)\cos(\emptyset+\beta-\alpha)\sin\emptyset}{bt_1}$......................... (11)

Also, the normal stress (σ_n) on the shear plane

$$\sigma_n = \frac{F_n}{A_s} = \frac{F_c \sin(\emptyset) + F_t \sin(\emptyset)}{\frac{bt_1}{sin\emptyset}} \text{ .... (12)}$$

Some of the important relations calculated using the merchant circle diagram are:

(i) $\frac{F_c}{R} = \cos(\beta - \alpha)$..(13)

(ii) $\frac{F_s}{R} = \cos(\emptyset + \beta - \alpha)$..(14)

(iii) $\frac{F_c}{F_s} = \frac{\cos(\beta-\alpha)}{\cos(\emptyset+\beta-\alpha)}$..(15)

(iv) $\frac{F_n}{F_s} = \tan((\emptyset + \beta - \alpha)$..(16)

(v) The resultant cutting force is given by,

$R = \sqrt{F_c^{\,2} + F_t^{\,2}}$ .... (17)

7.23.5 Velocity relationships in orthogonal cutting

The three types of velocities encountered during orthogonal cutting are shown in Fig.7.31.

- **Cutting velocity (V):** The velocity of the tool with respect to the workpiece and it is directed along the cutting surface (turning, shaping).
- **Shear velocity (V_s):** The velocity of the chip with respect to the workpiece and is directed towards the shear plane.
- **Chip velocity (V_c):** The velocity of the chip with respect to the tool and is directed along the tool face.

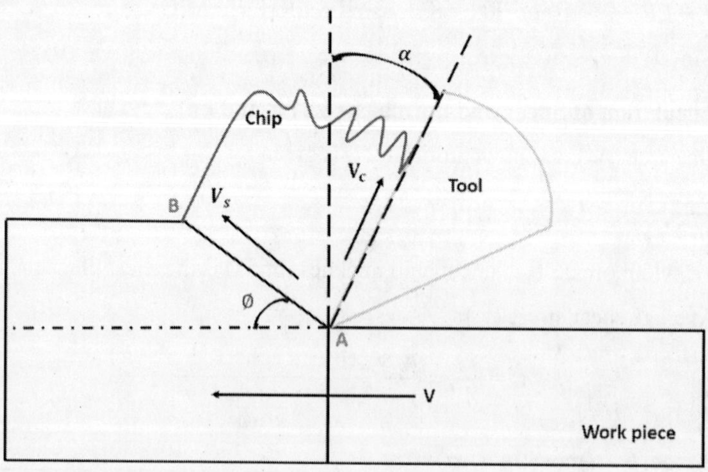

Fig. 7.31 Cutting, shear and chip velocity represented using velocity triangle

Assuming equilibrium, all the velocities will form a polygon, which can be represented using a velocity triangle vector diagram as shown in Fig. 7.32.

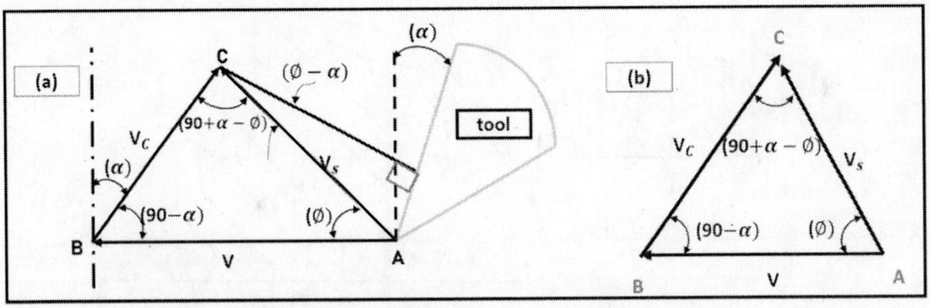

Fig. 7.32 (a) Detailed diagram showing velocities with tool (b) Velocity triangle

Apply the sine rule in the given velocity triangle ABC and we have

$$\frac{V}{\sin(90+\alpha-\emptyset)}=\frac{V_c}{\sin\emptyset}=\frac{V_s}{\sin(90-\alpha)} \quad \ldots\ldots\ldots\ldots\ldots\ldots (18)$$

Determination of V_c:

Using equation (18), we have,

$$\frac{V}{\sin(90+\alpha-\emptyset)}=\frac{V_c}{\sin\emptyset}$$

$$V_c=\frac{V\,sin\emptyset}{\cos(\alpha-\emptyset)}=\frac{V\,sin\emptyset}{\cos(\emptyset-\alpha)}\ldots\ldots\ldots\ldots\ldots\ldots\ldots\ldots\ldots\ldots (19)$$

In terms of chip thickness ratio, it is represented as,

$V_c = V\times r$..............................(20)

Determination of V_s:

Using equation (18), we have,

$$\frac{V}{\sin(90+\alpha-\emptyset)}=\frac{V_s}{\sin(90-\alpha)}$$

$$V_s=\frac{V\cos(\alpha)}{\cos(\emptyset-\alpha)}\ldots\ldots\ldots\ldots\ldots\ldots (21)$$

In terms of chip thickness ratio, it is represented as,

$\vec{V_s}=\vec{V}+\vec{V_c}$ (Using velocity triangle)

$V_s = V + V.r$

$V_s = V(1+r)$..............................(22)

7.24 Shear strain and shear strain rate

Cutting shear strain (ε) is the deformation per unit length of two mutually orthogonal sides. Considering Piispanen's model of card analogy, a chip is considered as a card or plate-like element of thickness Δl which is displaced through distance B relative to each other during machining (Fig. 7.33).

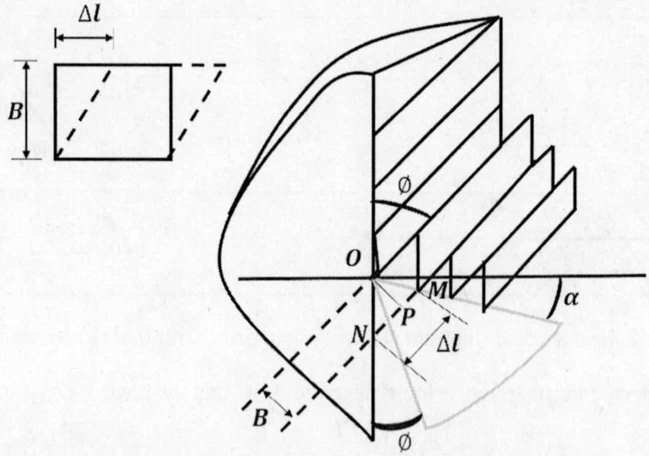

Fig. 7.33 Enlarged view of shear zone for shear strain

From the Fig. 7.33,

$$\angle POM = 90 - (90 - \emptyset) - \alpha = (\emptyset - \alpha)$$

Shear strain is calculated using,

$$(\varepsilon) = \frac{\Delta l}{B} = \frac{\text{NM}}{\text{OP}} = \frac{\text{NP+PM}}{\text{OP}} = \frac{\text{NP}}{\text{OP}} + \frac{\text{PM}}{\text{OP}}$$

Or $\varepsilon = \cot\emptyset + \tan\,(\emptyset - \alpha)$

Or

$$\varepsilon = \frac{\cos\emptyset}{\sin\emptyset} + \frac{\sin(\emptyset - \alpha)}{\cos(\emptyset - \alpha)} = \frac{\cos\emptyset\cos(\emptyset - \alpha) + sin\emptyset\sin(\emptyset - \alpha)}{\cos(\emptyset - \alpha)sin\emptyset}$$

Or

$$\varepsilon = \frac{\cos(\emptyset - \emptyset + \alpha)}{\cos(\emptyset - \alpha)sin\emptyset}$$

Or

$$\varepsilon = \frac{\cos(\alpha)}{\cos(\emptyset - \alpha)sin\emptyset}$$

Shear Strain rate is the rate of shear strain i.e. flow rate

$$\dot{\varepsilon} = \frac{d\varepsilon}{dt} = \frac{V_s}{thickness\ of\ shear\ zone\ (t_s)}$$

7.25 Determination of shear angle

The shear angle (∅) can be obtained in terms of t_1, t_2 and α using chip thickness ratio and back rake angle. The shear plane angle (∅) can be computed using Fig. 7.34.

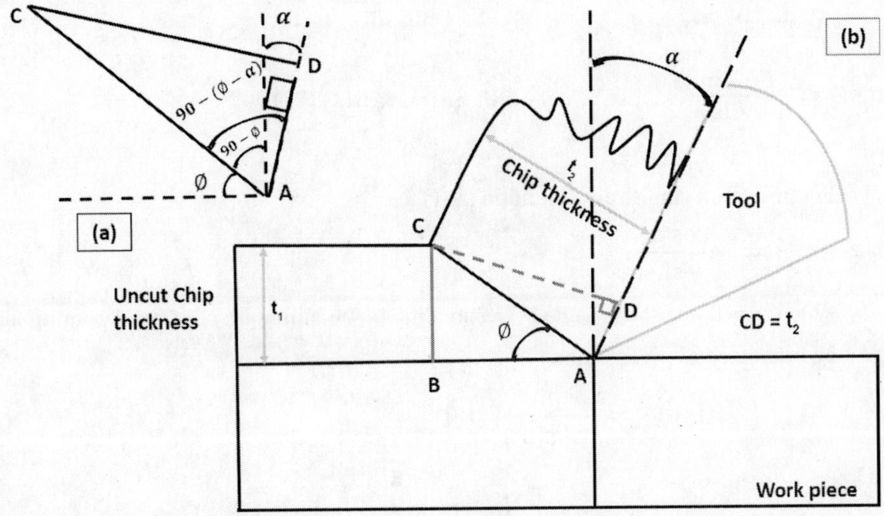

Fig. 7.34 Enlarged view of shear zone for shear angle

From $\Delta ABC,\ sin\emptyset = \frac{BC}{AC} = \frac{t_1}{AC}$

Or $AC = \frac{t_1}{sin\emptyset}$ ....(4)

Also from $\Delta ACD,\ \sin(90 - (\emptyset - \alpha)) = \frac{CD}{AC} = \frac{t_2}{AC}$

Or $\cos(\emptyset - \alpha) = \frac{t_2}{AC}$

Or $AC = \frac{t_2}{\cos(\emptyset - \alpha)}$ ....(5)

From equations (4) and (5), we have

$$\frac{t_1}{sin\emptyset} = \frac{t_2}{\cos(\emptyset - \alpha)}$$

Or $\frac{t_1}{t_2} = \frac{sin\emptyset}{\cos(\emptyset - \alpha)}$

Thus, $\mathbf{r} = \frac{\mathbf{t_1}}{\mathbf{t_2}} = \frac{\mathbf{sin\emptyset}}{\mathbf{\cos(\emptyset - \alpha)}}$

Now rearranging and expanding $\cos(\emptyset - \alpha)$ term, we have,

$r \cos(\emptyset - \alpha) = \sin\emptyset$

$r(\cos\emptyset.\cos\alpha + \sin\emptyset.\sin\alpha) = \sin\emptyset$

divide both sides by $\sin\emptyset$, we have

$r(\cot\emptyset.\cos\alpha + \sin\alpha) = 1$

r cot $\emptyset$.cos α = 1 – rsin α

$\cot \emptyset = \frac{1 - r\sin\alpha}{r\cos\alpha}$

or $\tan\emptyset = \frac{r\cos\alpha}{1 - r\sin\alpha}$ ....(23)

Note:

1- For minimum chip strain condition (r=1)

$$\tan\emptyset = \frac{\cos\alpha}{1 - \sin\alpha}$$

2- When $\alpha = 0$, the shear angle corresponding to the minimum chip strain condition can be calculated as given below,

$$\tan\emptyset = \frac{1}{1 - \sin 0} = 1$$

Or

$$\boxed{\emptyset = \frac{\pi}{4}}$$

7.26 Metal removal rate (MRR)

The material removal rate during machining shows the volume of metal removed in unit time (mm^3/min or mm^3/sec). It helps in determining the time required to remove the specific quantity of material from the workpiece. An optimum MRR reduces the machining cost using suitable cutting tool material with proper geometry and robust support. The MMR is expressed as

Metal removal rate or MRR = $t \times f \times V$......................(24)

where, t - Depth of cut (in mm), f - Feed (in mm / rev) and V - Cutting speed (in mm / sec).

7.27 Total work done in machining

In orthogonal machining, the total work done (W_T) can be calculated by

W_T = work done during cutting + work done in shear + work done against friction

Or $W_T = F_C V + F_s V_s + F V_C$.................................(25)

where,

- W_T = Total work done (in J)
- Fc = Cutting force (in N)
- V = Cutting velocity (in m/s)
- F_s = Shear force (in N)
- V_s = Shear velocity (in m/s)
- F = Friction force (in N)
- V_C = Chip velocity (in m/s)

This equation represents the energy required to remove a unit volume of material using a cutting force (Fc), shear force (F_s) and friction force (F).

7.28 Shear angle relationships

Many attempts have been made to establish a relationship between the rake angle (α) and friction angle (β) and the shear plane angle (∅). Several ideas have been put up to try and figure out how these are related and used in optimizing the economics of machining. The following present a few common theories in this regard.

7.28.1 Ernst-Merchant theory

Ernst-Merchant theory is based on the minimal energy criterion to derive said relationship. It considers that shearing during the machining occurs along a plane that requires the minimum energy for shearing. The following assumptions are made

a) Cutting is orthogonal.

b) Shear strength of work piece along the shear plane is independent of the amount of compressive (normal) stress acting on it.

c) Chips are continuous without built-up edges.

d) Energy of the chip elements separation is disregarded, and the plane where shearing deformation occurs is determined by the minimum energy criterion.

Except shear plane angle (∅), all other parameters may be assumed to remain constant during the machining process (provided no strain hardening occurs). If the derivative of average shear stress relative to ∅ is equal to zero, it would provide the minimal energy condition.

Average shear stress(τ_s) is given as,

$$\tau_s = \frac{F_s}{A_s} = \frac{F_c \sec(\beta - \alpha)\cos(\emptyset + \beta - \alpha)}{\frac{bt}{sin\emptyset}}$$

$$\tau_s = \frac{F_c \sec(\beta - \alpha)\cos(\emptyset + \beta - \alpha) sin\emptyset}{bt}$$

For maximum shear stress $\frac{\partial \tau_s}{\partial \emptyset} = 0 \quad (as\ \beta\ and\ \alpha\ are\ constant\ for\ a\ case)$

$$\therefore \cos(\emptyset + \beta - \alpha)\, cos\emptyset - \sin(\emptyset + \beta - \alpha)\, sin\emptyset = 0$$

$$\tan(\emptyset + \beta - \alpha) = cot\emptyset = \tan(90 - \emptyset)$$

$$\emptyset = \frac{\pi}{4} + \frac{\alpha}{2} - \frac{\beta}{2} \quad \text{.......................................(26)}$$

where, $\emptyset$, β and α are shear angle, friction angle and rake angle, respectively.

7.28.2 Modified Ernst-Merchant theory

The original theory was developed for synthetic plastic materials, but it was inadequate for metals. The Modified Ernst-Merchant theory was developed considering behaviour of metals in machining processes. The modified theory considers the effect of strain hardening, thermal softening, and tool-chip interface friction, which are significant in the machining of metals. Accordingly, shear stress is expressed as

$$\tau_s = \tau_o + k\,\sigma_n$$

where, k is machining constant, $\tau_o = constant\ depends\ on\ machining\ conditions$ and $\sigma_n = normal\ shear\ stress$.

Therefore,

$$\tau_s = \tau_o + k\,(\frac{F_n}{A_s})$$

$$\tau_s = \tau_o + k\left(\frac{F_s \tan(\emptyset + \beta - \alpha)}{A_s}\right) = \tau_o + k\,(\tau_s \tan(\emptyset + \beta - \alpha))$$

On rearranging, we have

$$\tau_s = \frac{\tau_o}{1 - k\tan(\emptyset + \beta - \alpha)}$$

Now, according to minimal energy condition, the derivative of average shear stress relative to shear angle is equal to zero i.e.

$$\frac{\partial \tau_s}{\partial \emptyset} = 0 \ \ (as\ \beta\ and\ \alpha\ are\ constant\ for\ a\ case)$$

On differentiating, we have,

$$\cot(2\emptyset + \beta - \alpha) = k$$

$2\emptyset + \beta - \alpha = cot^{-1}(k)$....................(27)

where, for the particular material, "k" is determined by the slope of the shear strength vs. compressive stress curve. The term "k" can also refer to the machining constant.

7.28.3 Lee and Shaffer theory

Lee and Shaffer proposed an alternative method to determine the shear plane angle analytically in 1949 with assumptions that (a) the metal during machining acts like a perfect plastic and doesn't stiffen under stress, (b) the direction of the maximal shear stress coincides with the shear plane, and (c) deformation happens on a thin-shear plane. Using the above assumptions and slip line field theory, the following relationship was given.

$\emptyset = \frac{\pi}{4} + \alpha - \beta$....................(28)

7.29 Tool life

For metal machining, tool life can be expressed based on multiple parameters such as:

- Cutting edges (e.g., teeth on a milling cutter)
- Parts produced (e.g., number of work pieces machined)
- Machining time (e.g., hours, minutes)

- Cutting distance (e.g., meters, feet)
- Spindle rotation (e.g., RPM x time)

The following aspects help in identifying the degradation of tool life during machining include:

1. Surface roughness increases
2. Heat dissipation decreases
3. Material removal rate decreases
4. Machining accuracy decreases
5. Machine vibration increases
6. Tool chip interface temperature increases

Taylor's equation (based on Flank Wear) is given as and shown schematically in Fig. 7.35. This equation shows the relation between cutting speed and tool life.

$VT^n = C$......... (29)

where, V = cutting speed (in m/min)

T = Time (in min)

n = exponent depends on tool material

C = constant based on tool and work and cutting condition.

Also, Equation (29) can be expressed as $V_1T_1^n = V_2T_2^n = C$....... (30)

On taking log on both sides, we have

$\log V_1 + n \log T_1 = \log V_2 + n \log T_2$

$$n = \frac{\log V_1 - \log V_2}{\log T_2 - \log T_1} \text{......................(31)}$$

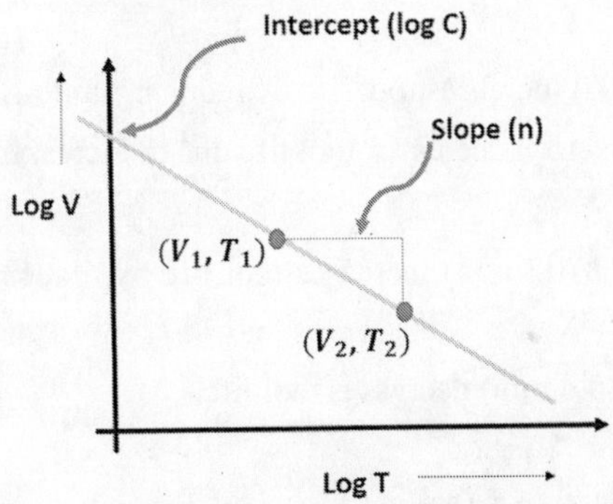

Fig. 7.35 Plot between log value of cutting speed and Tool life.

The values listed below might be used for 'n'.

1- for HSS tool: n = 0.1 to 0.15

2- for carbide tool: n = 0.2 to 0.4

3- for ceramic tool: n = 0.4 to 0.6

Further, the Extended or Modified Taylor's equation is given as

$VT^n f^{n1} d^{n2} = C$........................ (32)

where, V = cutting speed (in m/min)

T = Time (in min)

n, n_1, n_2 = exponent depends on tool material

C = constant based on tool and work and cutting condition.

d = depth of cut and

f = feed rate

The above expression can also be written as,

$$T = \frac{C^{1/n}}{V^{1/n} \times f^{1/n1} \times d^{1/n2}} \text{.....................} (33)$$

Also, From the experimental findings, we have

$$\frac{1}{n} > \frac{1}{n1} > \frac{1}{n2}$$

i.e. tool life is primarily influenced by cutting speed, while feed and depth of cut following closely behind.

Effects of various parameters on tool life are as follows:

(A) Effect of type of cutting employed: Continuous (contact) cutting results in an increase in tool life whereas intermittent (contact) cutting adversely affects tool life.

(B) Effect of tool material: With the increase in the hot hardness of material, the tool life increases.

(C) Effect of tool geometry: Tool geometry significantly impacts tool life in machining processes. Effect of various tool geometry parameter on tool life is given below:

1. Cutting Edge Angle:

- Positive angle (20-30°) increases tool life by reducing cutting forces and heat generation.
- Negative angle (-5 to -10°) decreases tool life due to increased forces and heat.

2. Nose Radius:

- Larger nose radii (0.8-1.2 mm) increases tool life by reducing stress concentrations and heat generation.
- Smaller nose radii (<0.4 mm) decreases tool life.

3. Clearance Angle:

- Adequate clearance angle (5-10°) prevents rubbing with the workpiece and increases tool life.
- Insufficient clearance angle increases to tool wear and reduces life.

4. Rake Angle:

- Positive rake angle (5-10°) increases tool life by reducing cutting forces and heat generation.

- Negative rake angle (-5 to -10°) decreases tool life in HSS tool but increases life in case of ceramics and CBN.

5. Tool Edge Sharpness:

- Sharpness (<0.1 mm edge radius) increases tool life by reducing cutting forces and heat generation but weakens cutting edge.

- Dull tools (>0.1 mm edge radius) decreases tool life.

6. Chip Breaker Geometry:

- Effective chip breakers improve tool life by reducing chip accumulation and heat generation.

Optimizing tool geometry can significantly improve tool life by reducing cutting forces, heat generation, and wear. However, the ideal geometry varies depending on the machining operation, workpiece and tool material.

(D) Effect of cutting Fluid: The effect of cutting fluid on tool life is expressed using the Schaubroch equation, i.e.

(a) In terms of concentration of cutting fluid:

$$T = \frac{T_o}{(1+\alpha(C-C_o))} \text{.............................} (34)$$

where,

T = tool life with cutting fluid

T_o = tool life without cutting fluid

α = coefficient of effectiveness of cutting fluid (dependent on fluid and material)

C = concentration of cutting fluid

C_o= minimum effective concentration of cutting fluid

This equation describes how the tool life increases with the use of cutting fluid, depending on the fluid's effectiveness and concentration.

The Schaubroch equation shows that:

- Without cutting fluid (C=0), tool life is T_o.
- With cutting fluid, tool life increases as concentration increases.
- There is a minimum effective concentration (C_o) below which the fluid has no effect
- The coefficient α represents the fluid's effectiveness in improving tool life.

Note that this equation is simple and actual tool life may vary depending on many factors, including cutting conditions, tool material, and workpiece material.

(b) In terms of Temperature of cutting fluid:

The Schaubroch equation can also be expressed in terms of tool-chip interface temperature (t_i) as:

$$T = \frac{T_o}{(1+\beta(t_i-t_o))} \text{...................................} (35)$$

where,

T = tool life with cutting fluid

T_o= tool life without cutting fluid

β = coefficient related to the effectiveness of cutting fluid in reducing tool-chip interface temperature

t_i = tool-chip interface temperature with cutting fluid

t_o = tool-chip interface temperature without cutting fluid (reference temperature)

This equation shows that:

- Tool life increases as the tool-chip interface temperature decreases.
- The cutting fluid's effectiveness (β) reduces the interface temperature, leading to longer tool life.
- The reference temperature (t_o) represents the maximum interface temperature without cutting fluid.

This version of the Schaubroch equation highlights the importance of tool-chip interface temperature in determining tool life and the influence of cutting fluids on temperature and tool performance.

7.30 Machinability

It is defined as the ease with which any material can be machined.

The factors affecting machinability are:

(1) Surface finish: The higher the surface finish, the better the machinability achieved.

(2) Tool life: Higher tool life results in better machinability.

(3) Material removal criteria: large volume material removal denotes better machinability.

(4) Machinability rating index: The machinability rating index measures how easily a material can be machined.

Machinability rating index:

It is expressed as the ratio of the cutting speed for 60 minutes tool life for a test material to the cutting speed for 60 minutes tool life for machining of a standard material.

$$\text{Machinability rating index (MRI)} = \frac{V_{60}^{T}}{V_{60}^{s}} \quad \text{.........................} \quad (36)$$

where, V_{60}^{T} = cutting speed for 60 minute tool life of a test material and

V_{60}^{s} = cutting speed for 60 minute tool life for machining of a standard material

Important note: cutting steel is used as standard reference material in the calculation of the machinability rating index.

UNIT SUMMARY

This unit presents the mathematical models related to the design of the gating system and the design of riser considering the size and shape of castings. The mechanics of bulk metal forming processes like rolling, forging, extrusion, and wire drawing have been presented to estimate the forces. The mechanics of chip formation have been explained with the help of merchant theory for orthogonal cutting to determine cutting force, shear stress and shear strain, tool wear. Important aspects of tool life have been presented for ease of understanding the process physics and take effective decisions for higher productivity.

EXERCISE

Questions for self-assessment

1. The merchant theory is related with
   a. Bulk metal deformation
   b. Sheet metal shearing
   c. Riser design
   d. Metal cutting
2. Shear plane angle during the orthogonal cutting is primarily affected by
   a. Rake angle
   b. Clearance angle
   c. Cutting edge angle
   d. Nose geometry
3. The cutting speed and tool life relationship is given by
   a. Molar's equation
   b. Taylor's equation
   c. Beyer's equation
   d. Merchant's equation
4. The type of flow desired in the gating system is
   a. Laminar flow
   b. Turbulent flow
   c. Biaxial flow
   d. All of these depend upon the design of casting
5. The average flow stress during the bulk metal forming is affected by
   a. Type of metal
   b. Work hardening exponent
   c. True strain
   d. All of these
6. The maximum flow rate of the molten metal in the gating system depends on
   a. Pouring basin
   b. Sprue base
   c. In-gate
   d. Choke area
7. The pouring time for manufacturing a sound casting depends on
   a. Microstructure of metal
   b. Density of metal
   c. Fluidity of metal
   d. All of these

8. The maximum draft for rolling of a metal depends on

    a. Roller diameter
    b. Metal-roller interface friction
    c. Lubrication during rolling
    d. All of these

9. The maximum reduction in area that can be achieved by the wire drawing process in one pass depends on

    a. Pressure applied
    b. Roller diameter
    c. Die angle
    d. Type of stress applied

10. The relationship between the pressure and contact length during the rolling from entry to exit is correctly expressed as

    a. Pressure remains constant
    b. Pressure gradually decreases
    c. Pressure gradually increases
    d. Pressure first increases and then decreases

Ans. 1d, 2a, 3b. 4a, 5d, 6d, 7c, 8d, 9c, 10d

Short and long questions

1. What is the importance of the type flow of the molten metal during the casting for developing the sound products?
2. What is the significance of the law of mass continuity in the design of the sprue of a gating system?
3. Explain the importance of Bernoulli's theorem in the gating system design to avoid air aspiration and turbulent flow.
4. What are the different types of in-gate design approaches?
5. Establish the pouring time required for filling the mould cavity with the top and bottom in-gate designs.
6. What is the importance of the pouring time in developing the sound castings?
7. Elaborate on the common models available to determine the pouring time for different metals and casting sizes.
8. What is the choke area in design of the gating system?
9. What is the significance of the gating ratio in the development of sound castings. Elaborate on the pressurised and non-pressurised grating systems.
10. What do you understand from the yield of casting? Explain the different strategies for increasing the yield of the casting process.
11. What is the importance of directional solidification In the development of sound casting?

12. Describe the following methods of riser design: a) Caines method, b) Modulus method, c) Naval research laboratory method
13. Explain the significance of elastic and plastic deformation in manufacturing by forming processes.
14. Using a suitable schematic diagram, explain the springback phenomenon in metal forming processes and its effect on the tolerance of manufactured products.
15. Explain flow stress for metals in annealed and deformed conditions using suitable mathematical expressions.
16. What is the relevance of Tresca theory and Von Mises theory in bulk metal deformation for forming processes?
17. Explain the slip in the rolling process.
18. Using fundamentals, establish the equation for the force required in the rolling of metals.
19. How to determine the force required in forging affected by part geometries? Explain the rationale behind the difference in the extrusion pressure required for direct and indirect extraction processes.
20. Why does the extrusion pressure change with the travel of ram during direct and indirect the extrusion?
21. What is the importance of die design in the wire drawing process?
22. How does the die design affect the stress required for wire drawing?
23. What is the effect of chip thickness ratio in metal cutting?
24. Describe the merchant force circle diagram for orthogonal cutting used for determining the cutting forces during the machining.
25. What is the metal removal rate in machining and how the metal removal rate can be expressed mathematically?
26. What are the factors that constitute total work for machining?
27. Explain different theories proposed for expressing the relationship between the tool rake angle, friction angle during the machining and shear plane angle.
28. Explain the Taylor's tool life equation.
29. Describe the various factors affecting the tool life like tool geometry, cutting fluid application during the machining and temperature of the cutting tool during the machining.
30. Define the machinability rating index using a suitable mathematical expression.

Solved Numerical Problems

7.1 In a gating system design, a down sprue with a height of 18 cm has a diameter of 2 cm at its top end. If the molten metal in the pouring basin is maintained at a height of 6 cm, determine the diameter (in cm) of the sprue at the bottom to avoid aspiration.

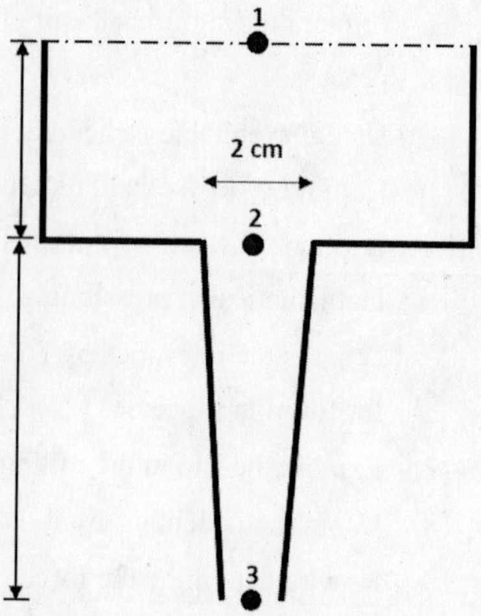

Solution: Given: $h_1 = 6$ cm and $h_2 = 18$ cm

To avoid aspiration

$$\frac{A_3}{A_2} = \sqrt{\frac{h_1}{h_1+h_2}}$$

where, A_2, and A_3 are cross-sectional area at top and bottom of sprue, respectively. h_1 and h_2 are the height of pouring cup and sprue, respectively.

$$A_2 = \frac{\pi d_2^2}{4}, A_3 = \frac{\pi d_3^2}{4} \text{ So, } \frac{A_3}{A_2} = \frac{d_3^2}{d_2^2}$$

$$\frac{d_3^2}{d_2^2} = \sqrt{\frac{h_1}{h_1+h_2}}, \text{ or } \frac{d_3^2}{2^2} = \sqrt{\frac{6}{6+18}}, \text{ So } \boldsymbol{d_3 = 1.41 \text{ cm}}$$

7.2. In a top gating design, sprue feeds the molten metal to fill a mould with dimensions 50 cm × 25 cm × 15 cm. Calculate the mould filling time for a given gate cross-sectional area of 5 cm^2 for the gating system as shown in the figure.

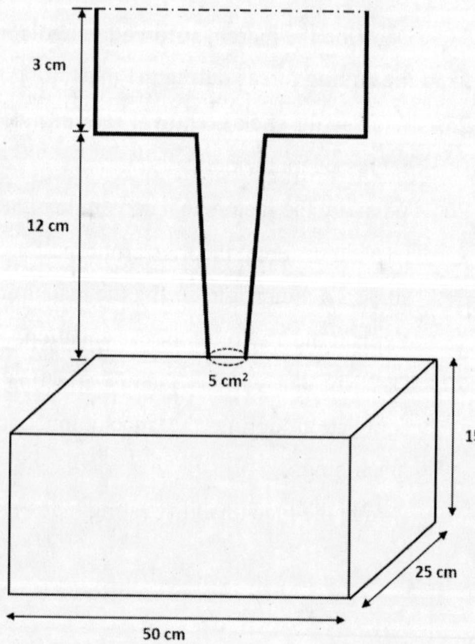

Solution: Given: Area of gate (A_g) = 5 cm^2

$h_t = 12 + 3 = 15$ cm

The volume of mould (V) = 50 cm × 25 cm × 15 cm

So, Velocity at the bottom of sprue (v)

$= \sqrt{2gh_t} = \sqrt{2 \times 981 \times 15} = 171.55$ cm/s

Mould filling time (t_f) $= \frac{V}{A_g v} = \frac{50 \times 25 \times 15}{5 \times 171.55}$

= 21.85 s.

7.3 Determine the pouring time of a 361 kg grey cast iron casting having an average section thickness of 23.20 mm. Assume that iron has a fluidity of 30 inches.

Solution: Using, the formula for grey cast iron with a mass less than 450 kg,

Pouring time, $t = K(1.41 + \frac{T}{14.59})\sqrt{W}$ s

where K $= \frac{Fluidity\ of\ iron\ in\ inches}{40} = \frac{30}{40} = 0.75$

$t = 0.75(1.41 + \frac{23.20}{14.59})\sqrt{361}$

t = 42.75 s

7.4 Determine the optimum pouring time for casting of cast iron with an average section thickness of 62.67 mm and mass of 512 kg. Consider cast iron's fluidity of 35 inches. Estimate pouring time by taking equation of grey cast iron and steel both.

Solution: Using, the formula for grey cast iron with a mass more than 450 kg,

Pouring time, $t = K\left(1.236 + \frac{T}{16.65}\right)\sqrt[3]{W}$s

where K $= \frac{\text{Fluidity of iron in inches}}{40} = \frac{35}{40} = 0.875$

$t = 0.875\left(1.236 + \frac{62.67}{16.65}\right)\sqrt[3]{512}$

t = 35 s (Grey cast iron)

Using the formula for **steel castings,**

Pouring time, t = *(2.4335-0.3953 log W)* $\sqrt{W}$ *s*

t = *(2.4335-0.3953 log 512)* $\sqrt{512}$

t = 30.83 s (Steel)

7.5 Melted metal is poured through a gate with a height of 'h' and a cross-sectional area of 'A' into a mould of 100 mm × 90 mm × 20 mm. It takes t_1 to fill the mould. At this point, the height has quadrupled, and the cross-sectional area has doubled. The equivalent filling time is t_2. The ratio of t_2 to t_1 is

(a) 1

(b) 2

(c) 0.5

(d) 0.25

Solution: $t_1 = (V) / (A \times \sqrt{2gh})$

Now for t_2, we have $h_2 = 4$ h, $A_2 = 2A$

$t_2 = (V) / [(2A) \times \sqrt{2g \times 4h}]$

So $t_2 / t_1 = 0.25$

Answer: (d) 0.25

7.6 A bottom gating system with a sprue height of 1250 mm and total mould cavity height of 500 mm is used for casting a 500 kg steel product. The molten metal density and efficiency factor are given as 7.2×10^{-6} kg/mm^3 and 0.90, respectively. Assume the acceleration due to gravity 9.81×10^3 mm/s^3 and pouring time equation for steel casting-

Solution: t = (2.4335-0.3953 log W) √ (W) s. Determine the following parameters.

(a) Pouring time (t)

(b) Effective metal head (H)

(c) Choke area (A)

(a) Using the formula, t = (2.4335-0.3953 log W) √ (W) s

t = *(2.4335-0.3953 log 500) √500)*

t = 30.55 s

(b) Effective metal head for bottom gating system,

$$H = h - \frac{c}{2} = 1250 - \frac{500}{2}$$

H = 1000 mm

(c) Choke area, $A = \frac{W}{dtC\sqrt{2gH}}$

$$A = \frac{500}{7.2\times10^{-6}\times30.55\times0.90\times\sqrt{2\times9.81\times10^3\times1000}} = 570.21\ mm^2$$

A = 570.21 mm^2

7.7 A magnesium cube of dimension 150 mm is produced using casting without a riser. The complete cube is moulded in the top gate of a flask filled with green sand. The height of the cope flask is 150 mm. The molten metal was poured from 50 mm height than cope height. The gating ratio is 1:2:2, with tapered sprue. Determine the time (in seconds) needed to fill the mould cavity using 350 mm^2 in-gate area while neglecting energy losses. Assume the acceleration due to gravity 9.81×10^3 **mm/s^2.**

Solution: Pouring time = Volume/ flow rate = V/Q

V = Volume of mould = 150 × 150 × 150 mm^3 = 3.375 × 10^6 mm^3

Here, the gating ratio indicates that the sprue area is equal to half of the gate area.

Therefore, area of sprue = 350/2 = 175 mm

Q = Flow rate = *(175)* × $\sqrt{2\times9.81\times1000\times(150+50)}$ mm^3/s = 3.526 × 10^5 mm^3/s

Pouring time (t) = *V/Q*

t = *(3.375 × 10^6)/ (3.526 × 10^5)*

t = 9.57 s

7.8 A steel cylinder with a diameter of 165 mm and a height of 220 mm is manufactured through casting without using a riser. Using a top gating configuration, the cylinder is fully formed inside the drag of a green sand flask. The height of the cope is 250 mm, and the metal pouring is done from a height of 75 mm above the cope. The gating ratio is 1:2:1, with tapered sprue. Using a 300 mm^2 in-gate area, calculate the time (in seconds) required to fill the mould cavity without accounting for energy losses. Assume that the gravitational acceleration is 9.81×10^3 mm/s^2.

(a) 14.16

(b) 7.08

(c) 12.42

(d) 6.21

Solution: Pouring time = V/Q .... (1)

V = Volume of mould = $[(\pi \times 165^2)/4] \times 220$ $mm^3 = 4.704 \times 10^6$ mm^3

Q = Flow rate = $(300) \times \sqrt{2 \times 9.81 \times 1000 \times (250 + 75)}$ $mm^3/sec = 7.575 \times 10^5$ mm^3/s

Here area of sprue is same as the gate area, according to the provided gating ratio (1:2:1).

Putting all values in equation (1) - Pouring time (t) = V/Q

t = $(4.704 \times 10^6)/(7.575 \times 10^5)$

t = 6.21 s

7.9 A horizontally cast steel slab measuring 30 x 20 x 5 cm made with a side riser. The riser is cylindrical in shape and has the same height and diameter. Given a diameter (D) of 15.0 cm, the freezing ratio of the mould is

(a) 0.8

(b) 1.25

(c) 0.625

(d) 1.6

Solution: Freezing ratio (F.R.) = $(A_c / V_c) / (A_r / V_r)$

V_c = Casting volume = $30\times20\times5$ cm^3 =

A_c = Casting area = $2\times[(30\times20)+(20\times5)+(5\times30)]$ cm^2

A_r = Area of riser = $[2\times(\pi D^2/4)]+(\pi D^2)$, Here L = D

where D = Cylinder's diameter, L = Cylinder's height

V_r = Riser's volume = $(\pi D^3/4)$, since L = D

By using the equation of freezing ratio, we get that F.R. = (8D/ 75) = (8×15.0/75) = 8/5

F. R. = 1.6

7.10 Using the modulus approach, determine the height (mm) of a riser for casting of a cylindrical shape having diameter of 100 mm and height of 50 mm. Ignore the cooling due to the bottom surface of the cylindrical riser.

Solution: Modulus = Volume / Surface area

The surface area of the riser = $\frac{\pi D^2}{4} + \pi D^2$ [neglecting the bottom surface area and d = h]

The volume of the riser = $\frac{\pi D^3}{4}$

So, Modulus, $(V_r / A_r) = \frac{D}{5}$

Similarly, the Modulus of casting is $(V_c / A_c) = \dfrac{\frac{\pi D^2}{4}}{\pi Dh + 2 \times \frac{\pi D^2}{4}} = 12.5$

$M_r = 1.2\ M_c = 1.2 \times 12.5 = 15$

So, $\frac{D}{5} = 15$, D = h = 15 x 5 = 75 mm, **h = 75 mm**

7.11 A side riser with equal height and diameter is used for a steel casting with dimensions of 50 cm x 30 cm x 10 cm. The shape factor and the ratio of the riser's volume to the casting volume are given below. Calculate the riser's diameter (cm).

Shape factor	2	4	6	8	10	12
V_r / V_c	1	0.75	0.60	0.55	0.45	0.30

Solution: According to NRL method, shape factor = $\frac{L+W}{T} = \frac{50+30}{10} = 8$,

Now, from the table, the $\frac{Vr}{Vc} = 0.55$

Volume of casting = L x W x T = 50 x 30 x 10 = 15000 cm^3

The volume of riser = $\frac{\Pi d^2 x\, h}{4} = \frac{\Pi d^3}{4}$ (d = h)

So, V_r = 0.55 x 50 x 30 x 10 = 8250 cm^3

And the diameter of the riser is $\{ \frac{\Pi d^3}{4} = 8250 \}$

d = 21.90 cm.

7.12 Casting's shape factor can be determined using the Naval Research method as

(a) (L+t)/W

(b) (2L+W)/t

(c) (2W+L)/t

(d) (L+W)/t

where, L, W, and t are the length, width, and thickness of casting, respectively.

Answer: (d) (L+W)/t

7.13 In a two-high rolling mill, a 200 mm wide by 20 mm thick plate has to be reduced to 15 mm thick in a single pass. The roll moves at 30 metres per minute with a 600 mm radius. The strain hardening exponent of the work material is 0.22 and its coefficient related to strength is 260 MPa. To complete this action, find the (a) roll force, (b) roll torque, and (c) power needed.

(a) Draft d = 20 - 15 = 5 mm,

Contact length L = (600 x 5) $^{.5}$ = 54.77 mm

True strain ε = ln(20/15) = ln 1.25 = 0.288

Average flow stress = 260(0.288)$^{0.22}$/1.22 = 162.06 MPa

Rolling force F = 162.06(200)(40) = **1,296,480 N**

(b) Torque T = 0.5(1,296,480) (54.77 x 10^{-3}) = **35,504.10 N-m**

(c) N = (30 m/min)/(2π x 0.600) = 7.96 rev/min = 0.132 rev/s

Power P = 2π (0.132)(1,296,480)(54.77 x 10^{-3}) = 58,892.82 N-m/s = **58,892.82 W**

7.14 A hot rolling mill with 500 mm diameter rolls can exert up to 1,750,000 N of force. The mill may produce up to 100 horsepower. The objective is to lower a 40 mm plate's thickness by as much as possible in a single pass. The plate's initial width is 250 mm. The work material has a strain hardening exponent of zero and coefficient related to material strength is 140 MPa on heating for rolling. Ascertain the operation's (a) maximum draft, (b) related true strain, and (c) maximum roll speed.

Solution: (a) Assumption: The maximum possible draft is determined by the force capability of the rolling mill and not by the coefficient of friction between the rolls and the work.

Draft d = 40 - t_f

Contact length L = (250d)$^{0.5}$

Average flow stress = 140(ε)^0 /1.0 = 140 MPa

Force F = 140(250) (250d) $^{0.5}$ = 1,750,000 (the limiting force of the rolling mill)

(250d) $^{0.5}$ = 1,750,000/35,000 = 50

250 d = 2500

d = 2500/250 = **10mm**

(b) True strain ε = ln(40/t_2)

t_2 = t_o -d = 40 - 10 = 30mm

ε = ln(40/30) = ln 1.333 = **0.287**

(c) Given maximum possible power HP = 100 hp = 100 x 746 W = 74600 W

Contact length L = (250 x 10)$^{0.5}$ = 50mm

P = 2πN(1,750,000)(50) = 549,778,714.38N

549,778,714.38N = 74600

N = 0.000135 rev/sec = 0.0081 rev/min

v_r = 2πRN = 2π(250)(0.0081) = **12.72 mm/min**

7.15 A two-high rolling mill is to be used to reduce the thickness of a plate from 25 mm to 20 mm in a single pass. The width of the plate is 240 mm. The roll moves at a speed of 40 m/min and has a radius of 500 mm. The work material's strain hardening exponent is 0.2 and coefficient related to material strength is 260 MPa. Compute the following: Roll force, roll torque, and the power needed to complete the task.

Solution: (a) Draft d = 25 - 20 = 10 mm,

Contact length L = $(500 \times 5)^{.5}$ = 50 mm

True strain ε = ln(25/20) = ln 1.25 = 0.223

Average flow stress = $260(0.223)^{0.2}/1.2$ = 160.49 MPa

Rolling force F = 160.49 (240)(50) = **1,925,880 N**

(b) Torque T = $0.5(1,925,880)(50 \times 10^{-3})$ = **48,147 N-m**

(c) N = (40 m/min)/(2π x 0.500) = 12.73 rev/min = 0.212 rev/s

Power P = $2\pi(0.212)(1,925,880)(50 \times 10^{-3})$ = 128,267 N-m/s = **128,267 W**

7.16 Warm upset forging is applied to a cylindrical item in an open die. The first measurements are 50 mm in height and 55 mm in diameter. The height is lowered to 35 mm after forging. At the die-work interface, the coefficient of friction is 0.25. A strain hardening exponent of 0.15 and a coefficient related to material strength is 500 MPa. Define the work material's flow curve. Determine the force needed to perform the operation at the following points in time: (a) 35 mm, (b) 45 mm, and (c) when the yield point is achieved (yield at strain = 0.002).

Solution: (a) V = $\pi D^2 L/4 = \pi(55)^2(50)/4$ = 118,791.47 mm^3

Given ε = 0.002,

Flow stress = $500(0.002)^{0.15}$ = 196.85 MPa, and h = 50 - 50(0.002) = 49.9 mm

A = V/h = 118,791.47 /49.9= 2380.59 mm^2

Shape factor C_f= 1 + 0.4(0.25)(55)/49.9 = 1.11

F = 1.11(196.85)(2380.59) = **520,167.25 N**

(b) Given h = 45, ε = ln(50/45) = ln 1.143 = 0.1054

Flow stress = $500(0.1054)^{0.15}$ = 356.78 MPa

V = 118,791.47 mm3

from part (a) above.

At h = 45, A = V/h = 118,791.47 /45 = 2639.81 mm2

For corresponding D

A = $\pi D^2/4$

D = $(2639.81*4/\pi)^{0.5}$ = 57.98 mm

C_f= 1 + 0.4(0.25)(57.98)/45 = 1.129

F = 1.129(356.78)(2639.81) = **1,063,327.66 N**

(c) Given h = 35, ε = ln(50/35) = ln 1.6 = 0.3567

Flow stress = $500(0.3567)^{0.15}$ = 428.37 MPa

V = 118,791.47 mm^3

from part (a) above.

At h = 35, A = V/h = 118,791.47/35 = 3394.04 mm^2

For corresponding D

$A = \pi D^2/4$

$D = (3394.04*4/\pi)^{0.5}$ = 65.74 mm

$C_f = 1 + 0.4(0.25)(65.74)/35 = 1.187$

F = 1.187(428.37)(3394.04) = **271,880.22 N**

7.17 An open die is used to perform a hot upset forging procedure. The workpiece's initial dimensions are 20 mm diameter and 45 mm height. The component is squeezed till 40 mm in diameter. The work metal yields at 100 MPa with a strain hardening exponent (n) of 0 at the higher temperature. At the die-work interface, there is a 0.3 coefficient of friction. Ascertain (a) the part's end height and (b) the highest force needed to complete the operation.

Solution: (a) $V = \pi D_1^2 h_1/4 = \pi(20)^2(45)/4$ = 14,137.17 mm^3

$A_2 = \pi D_2^2/4 = \pi(40)^2/4$ = 1256.64 mm^2

$h_2 = V/A_2$ = 14,137.17 /1256.64 = **11.25 mm**

(b) $\varepsilon = \ln(45/11.25) = \ln 4 = 1.3863$

Flow stress= $100(1.3863)^0$ = 100 MPa

Force is maximum at largest area value,

A_2 = 1256.64 mm^2

D = $(4 \times 1256.64/\pi)^{0.5}$ = 40 mm

$C_f = 1 + 0.4(0.3)(45/11.25) = 1.48$

F = 1.48(100)(1256.64) = **185,982.72 N**

7.18 Indirect backward extrusion is used to reduce a cylindrical billet measuring 125 mm in length and 60 mm in diameter to 30 mm in diameter. 90° is the established die angle. Given the work metal's flow curve with a strength coefficient of 1000 MPa and a strain hardening exponent of 0.15, and using the Johnson equation parameters a=0.8 and b=1.4, compute the following: (a) extrusion ratio, (b) true strain (for homogeneous deformation), (c) extrusion strain, (d) ram pressure, and (e) ram force.

Solution: (a) Extrusion ratio $R_{ex} = A_1/A_2 = D_1^2/D_2^2 = (60)^2/(30)^2 = \mathbf{4}$

(b) True strain $\varepsilon = \ln R_{ex} = \ln 4 =$ **1.386**

(c) $\varepsilon_x = a + b \ln R_{ex} = 0.8 + 1.4(1.386) =$ **2.740**

(d) Average flow stress = $1000(1.386)^{0.15}/1.15$ = 913.20 MPa

Pressure = 913.20 (2.740) = **2502.17 MPa**

(e) $A_1 = \pi D_1^2/4 = \pi(60)^2/4 = 2827.43$ mm2

F = 2502.17 (2827.43) = **7,074,710.52 N**

7.19 Direct extrusion is used to create an L-shaped structural section from an aluminium billet with a starting diameter of 90 mm and a length of 300 mm. The dimensions of the cross-section are shown below. The flow curve parameters for the aluminium alloy are X = 260MPa and n = 0.15. Calculate the following given that the operation's die angle is 90° and the Johnson strain equation constants are a=0.8 and b=1.5: (a) Extrusion ratio, (b) shape factor, (c) length of the extruded section, and (d) maximum force needed to move the ram forward at the beginning of extrusion, assuming that the butt is still in the container after the ram stroke (e.g., 25 mm).

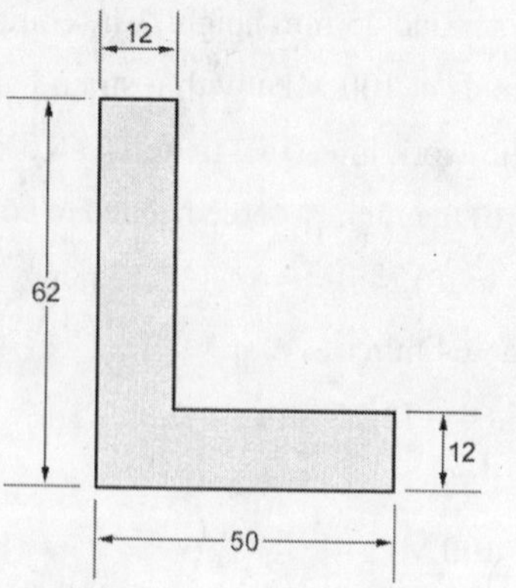

Solution: (a) Extrusion ratio $R_{ex} = A_1/A_2$

$A_1 = \pi(90)^2/4 = 6361.73$ mm^2

$A_2 = 2 \times (12 \times 50) = 1200$ mm^2

Extrusion ratio = 6361.73 /1200= **5.301**

(b) To determine the die shape factor, we need to determine the perimeter of a circle whose area is equal to that of the extruded cross-section, A = 1200 mm^2.

The radius of the circle is $R = (1200/\pi)^{0.5} = 19.54$ mm, $C_c = 2\pi(19.54) = 122.8$ mm.

The perimeter of the extruded cross-section $C_x = 62 + 50 + 12 + 38 + 50 + 12 = 224$ mm

Shape factor = $0.98 + 0.02(224/122.8)^{2.25}$ = **1.057**

(c) Total original volume $V = 0.25\pi(90)^2(300) = 1{,}908{,}517.54$ mm^3

The final volume consists of two sections: (1) butt, and (2) extrudate.

The butt volume $V_1 = 0.25\pi(90)^2\,(25) = 159{,}043.13$ mm^3.

The extrudate has a cross-sectional area $A_2 = 1200$ mm^2

Its volume $V_2 = LA_2 = 1{,}908{,}517.54 - 159{,}043.13 = 1{,}749{,}474.37$ mm3

Thus, length L = 1,749,474.37/1200 = **1457.89 mm**

(d) $\varepsilon = \ln 5.301 = 1.667$

$\varepsilon_x = 0.8 + 1.5(1.667) = 3.3$

Average flow stress= $260(1.667)^{0.15}/1.15 = 244.09$ MPa

Maximum ram force occurs at the beginning of the stroke when L is maximum at L = 300 mm

P = shape factor. Average flow stress ($\varepsilon_x + 2L/D_1$) = 1.057(244.09)(3.3 + 2(300)/90) = 2571.43 MPa

$F = PA_1 = 2571.43\ (6361.73) =$ **16,358,743.37 N**

7.20 A die with a 2.6 mm hole is used to draw a spool of wire that has a starting diameter of 3 mm. At the work-die contact, the die's coefficient of friction is 0.11, and its entrance angle is 16 degrees. The work metal has a strain hardening coefficient of 0.2 and coefficient X of material is 500 MPa. There is no temperature restriction during the drawing process. Ascertain the necessary draw force, draw stress, and area reduction for the operation.

Solution: (a) $r = (A_1 - A_2)/A_1$

$A_1 = 0.25\pi(3)^2 = 7.07\ mm^2$

$A_2 = 0.25\pi(2.6)^2 = 5.31\ mm^2$

Reduction area R_{ex} = (7.07 – 5.31)/ 7.07 = **0.249**

(b) Draw stress σ_d:

$\varepsilon = \ln(7.07/5.31) = \ln 1.331 = 0.286$

Average flow stress = $500(0.286)^{0.2}/1.2 = 324.39$ MPa

$\varphi = 0.88 + 0.12(D/l)$

$D = 0.5(3 + 2.6) = 2.80$

Contant length $l = 0.5(3 - 2.6)/\sin 16 = 0.726$

$\varphi = 0.88 + 0.12(2.80/0.726) = 1.34$

σ_d = average stress$(1 + \mu/\tan\alpha)\varphi(\ln A_1/A_2)$ = 324.39 (1 + 0.11/tan 16)(1.34)(0.286) = **172.01 MPa**

(c) Draw force F:

$F = A_2\sigma_d = 5.31\ (172.01) =$ **913.37 N**

7.21 A 20 mm draft is used to draw a bar stock with a starting diameter of 100 mm. The work-die interface has a 0.1 coefficient of friction, and the draw die has an entry angle 18°. The metal has a yield stress of 150 MPa, which is considered fully plastic behaviour. If the exit velocity is 2.0 m/min, find the following: (a) area reduction, (b) draw stress, (c) draw force necessary for the operation and (d) power required to complete this operation.

Solution: (a) Reduction area = $(A_1 - A_2)/A_1$

$A_1 = 0.25\pi(100)^2 = 7853.98\ mm^2$

$D_2 = D_1 - d = 100 - 20 = 80$ mm,

$A_2 = 0.25\pi(80)^2 = 5026.55\ mm^2$

Reduction area = (7853.98 - 5026.55)/ 7853.98 = **0.359**

(b) Draw stress σ_d:

$\varepsilon = \ln(7853.98 / 5026.55) = \ln 1.562 = 0.446$

Flow stress = X = 150 MPa

$\varphi = 0.88 + 0.12(D/L_c)$

D = 0.5(100 + 80) = 90 mm

Contact length l = 0.5(100 - 80)/sin 18 = 32.36 mm

$\varphi = 0.88 + 0.12(90/32.36) = 1.214$

σ_d = average flow stress $(1 + \mu/\tan\alpha)\varphi(\ln A_1/A_2)$ = 150(1 + 0.1/tan 18)(1.214)(0.446) = **106.21 MPa**

(c) F = $A_2\ \sigma_d$ = 5026.55 (106.21) = **533,869.88 N**

(d) P = 533,869.88 (2 m/min) = 1,067,739.76 N-m/min = 17,795.66 N-m/s = 17,795.66 W = **23.85 hp**

7.22 With a tool rake angle of 20°, carbon steel is processed at a 400 m/min cutting speed. Both uncut chip and cut chip are 0.4 mm wide and 1.6 mm thick. If the work material's shear stress is 400 N/mm^2 and the average coefficient of friction between the tool and the chip is 0.5. Calculate (i) the shear angle during machining and (ii) the thrust and cutting component of force.

Solution: Friction angle is calculated using the coefficient of friction $\mu = 0.5$

So, $\tan\beta = \mu = 0.5$

Or $\beta = 26.56°$

Using Ernst merchant theory

$$\emptyset = \frac{\pi}{4} + \frac{\alpha}{2} - \frac{\beta}{2}$$

$$\emptyset = 45 + \frac{20}{2} - \frac{26.56}{2} = 41.72°$$

Now, $F_c = 2 \times \tau_s \times b \times t \times \cot\emptyset = 2 \times 400 \times 1.6 \times 0.4 \times \cot 41.72$

Or $F_c = 574.63$ N

$$\frac{F_t}{F_c} = \tan(\beta - \alpha)$$

$$\frac{F_t}{574.63} = \tan(26.56 - 20)$$

$F_t = 66.08$ N

7.23 During an orthogonal cutting, the given findings were noted; depth of cut 0.25 mm, Cutting velocity: 40 m/min, width of cut: 5 mm, cutting force component normal to cutting velocity vector = 150 N, rake angle = 20°, and cutting force parallel to the cutting vector = 1250 N. Determine resultant cutting force and friction angle.

Solution: As we know, the average coefficient of friction between the tool and the chip is calculated as,

$$\mu = \frac{F_c \sin(\alpha) + F_t \cos(\alpha)}{F_c \cos(\alpha) - F_t \sin(\alpha)} = \frac{1250 \sin(20) + 150\cos(20)}{1250 \cos(20) - 150 \sin(20)}$$

$\mu = 0.503$

Also, $\tan\beta = \mu = 0.503$

Or $\beta = 26.72°$

The resultant cutting force is given by,

$$R = \sqrt{{F_c}^2 + {F_t}^2} = \sqrt{1250^2 + 150^2} = 1258.96N$$

7.24 At a cutting speed of 5 m/s, the depth of cut in orthogonal cutting is 0.75 mm. For a chip thickness of 0.75 mm, the chip velocity is?

Solution: Velocity of chip = $V \times r$

$$= \frac{\text{depth of cut}}{\text{chip thickness}} \times V = \frac{0.75}{0.75} \times 5 = 5 \text{ m/s} \qquad [V = \text{chip velocity}]$$

7.25 During orthogonal cutting, the shear angle is 45°, cutting tool rake angle is 20°, and the cutting velocity is 25 m/min. Determine the chip's velocity along the tool face under the specified machining conditions.

Solution: $V_c = \frac{V \sin\emptyset}{\cos(\emptyset - \alpha)} = \frac{25 \times \sin 45}{\cos 25} = 19.50 \text{ m/min}$

7.26 In a machining process, the chip thickness ratio is 0.6 and the rake angle of the tool is 20°.What is the shear strain value?

Solution: $\tan\emptyset = \frac{r \cos\alpha}{1 - r \sin\alpha} = \frac{0.6 \times \cos 20}{1 - 0.6 \times \sin 20} = 0.708$

Or $\emptyset = 35.30°$

$\therefore$ shear strain(ε)is given as,

$\varepsilon = \cot\emptyset + \tan(\emptyset - \alpha) = \cot 35.30 + \tan 15.30 = 1.69$

7.27 During an orthogonal machining process, the following findings were noted; uncut thickness is 0.6 mm, cutting speed is 10 m/min, rake angle is 25°, width of cut is 10 mm, chip thickness is 0.9 mm, thrust force is 250 N and the cutting force is 1400 N. Calculate the shear strain and shear angle.

Solution: From Merchant's theory, the shear strain and shear angle values are

$$r = \frac{t_1}{t_2} = \frac{0.6}{0.9} = 0.67$$

$$\therefore \tan\phi = \frac{r\cos\alpha}{1 - r\sin\alpha} = \frac{0.67 \times \cos 25}{1 - 0.67 \times \sin 25} = 0.845$$

$$\text{or } \phi = 40.20°$$

Now, shear strain (ε) $= \cot\phi + \tan(\phi - \alpha) = \cot 40.20 + \tan 15.2$

Or $\varepsilon = 1.45$

7.28 The chip thickness and the uncut thickness in an orthogonal machining operation are equal to 0.75 mm. Calculate the shear plane angle if the tool rake angle is 0°.

Solution: The chip thickness ratio is calculated as,

$$\boxed{r = \frac{t_1}{t_2} = \frac{0.75}{0.75} = 1}$$

also

$$\therefore \tan\phi = \frac{r\cos\alpha}{1 - r\sin\alpha} = \frac{1\cos 0}{1 - \sin 0} = 1$$

Or $\phi = 45°$

7.29 The cutting velocity of 60 m/min is used with an uncoated carbide tool used for the orthogonal turning of a 120 mm diameter low carbon steel bar . The depth of cut is 2 mm, and the feed rate is 0.12 mm/rev. The resultant chip thickness is 0.36 mm. When the major cutting edge angle is 90° and the orthogonal rake angle is zero, the shear angle in degrees equals to?

Solution: Uncut chip thickness(t_1)= f× sinϕ $= 0.12 \times \sin 90 = 0.12$

Given, $t_2 = 0.36$

So, chip thickness ratio is calculated as;

$$r = \frac{t_1}{t_2} = \frac{0.12}{0.36} = 0.33$$

Also

$$\therefore \tan\phi = \frac{r\cos\alpha}{1 - r\sin\alpha} = \frac{0.33\cos 0}{1 - 0.33\sin 0} = 0.33$$

Or $\phi = 18.26°$

7.30 During orthogonal machining, a cutting tool with a cutting speed of 300 m/min and a feed rate of 0.2 mm/rev is used. If the machining process lasts for 10 minutes, and the width and depth of cut are 5 mm and 2 mm, respectively, calculate the Metal Removal Rate (MRR) in cubic millimetres per minute (mm³/min).

Solution: Given Data:

- Feed rate (f) = 0.2 mm/rev (feed rate per revolution)
- Cutting speed (V) = 300 m/min
- Machining time (t) = 10 minutes

- Depth of cut = 2 mm
- Width of cut= 5 mm

Metal Removal Rate (MRR) is given by the formula:

MRR = feed × depth of cut × cutting speed

MRR = 0.2 × 2 × 300000

MRR = 120000 mm³/min

7.31 A 50 mm diameter steel bar is turned at a feed rate of 0.35 mm/rev and a cut depth of 8 mm. The workpiece rotates at 60 revolutions per minute (RPM). Determine the material removal rate in mm^3/s.

Solution: MRR is calculated using feed, depth of cut and cutting velocity during machining. Therefore,

MRR = f ×d ×V =(0.35)(8)× $\left(\frac{\pi\times50\times60}{60}\right)$ = 439.6 mm /s

7.32 On a lathe, the orthogonal machining concept is used to turn a cylinder. The rake angle is 20°. It is found that the shear angle is 30°. Using Earnest and Merchant theory, the coefficient of friction at the chip tool contact is?

Solution: Ernest Merchant Theory

$$\emptyset = \frac{\pi}{4} + \frac{\alpha}{2} - \frac{\beta}{2}$$

where, $\emptyset$, β and α are shear angle, friction angle and rake angle, respectively.

$$30 = 45 + \frac{20}{2} - \frac{\beta}{2}$$

or $\beta = 50°$

therefore, $\mu = tan\beta = 1.19$

7.33 The tool's rake angle in an orthogonal cutting operation is 10°, and the friction angle is 30°. By applying Merchant's shear angle relationship, the shear angle value will be?

Solution: Ernest Merchant Theory

$$\emptyset = \frac{\pi}{4} + \frac{\alpha}{2} - \frac{\beta}{2}$$

where, Ø, β and α are shear angle, friction angle and rake angle, respectively.

or

$$\emptyset = 45 + \frac{10}{2} - \frac{30}{2}$$

or $\emptyset = 35°$

7.34 The turning process is performed using an HSS tool. When turning at a 30 m/min speed, the tool has a one-hour lifespan. Doubling the cutting speed will result in a reduction of the tool life to 2.0 minutes. Find a suitable RPM speed for turning a 300 mm diameter workpiece in 60 minutes.

Solution: Given: $V_1 = 30$ m/min; $T_1 = 1$ hr = 60 min, $V_2 = 2V_1$, $T_2 = 2$ min, $T_3 = 60$ min,

Using Taylor tool life equation, we have

$$V_1T_1^n = V_2T_2^n$$

$$n = \frac{\log V_1 - \log V_2}{\log T_2 - \log T_1} = 0.204$$

Now, for $T_3 = 60$ min, $V_3 = ?$

Using

$$V_1T_1^n = V_3T_3^n$$

$$V_3 = V_1 \times \left(\frac{60}{60}\right)^{0.204} = 30 \text{ m/min}$$

7.35 A tool life of 45 minutes was noted in a particular machining process at a cutting speed of 50 meters per minute (m/min). The tool life dropped to 20 minutes when the cutting speed was raised to 200 meters per minute (m/min). Based on the tool, work, and cutting conditions, estimate the value of constant C.

Solution: Given: $V_1 = 50$ m/min; $T_1 = 45$ min, $V_2 = 200$ m/min, $T_2 = 20$ min, Using Taylor tool life equation, we have

$$V_1T_1^n = V_2T_2^n$$

$$n = \frac{\log V_1 - \log V_2}{\log T_2 - \log T_1} = 1.71$$

Using

$V_1T_1^n = C$

Or C= $50\times (45)^{1.71} = 33570.93$

Unsolved Questions

7.1. Design the down sprue to fill the mould cavity with liquid cast iron (ρ_m=7800 kg/m^3) at a flow rate of 12 kg/s without causing aspiration. Assume there is no pressure head at the bottom of the sprue and neglect all frictional effects. (Ans = Diameter at top of sprue = 4.45 cm, Diameter at bottom of sprue = 2.97 cm)

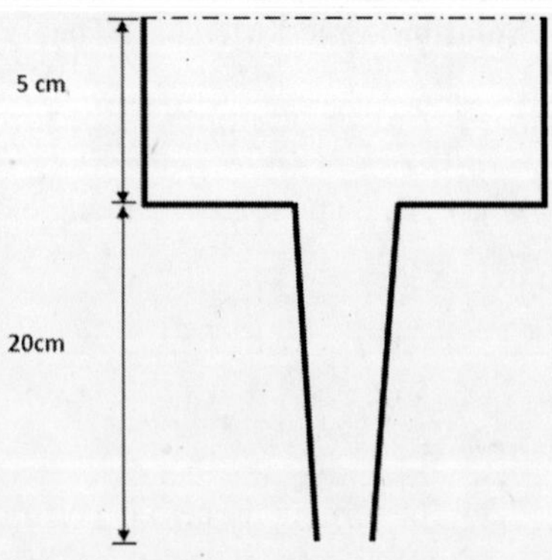

7.2 In a bottom gating design, sprue feeds a horizontal runner to fill a mould with dimensions 1 m × 0.5 m ×

0.25 m. Calculate the mould filling time for a given gate cross-sectional area of 10 cm^2 for gating system as shown in figure. (Ans. 73.17s)

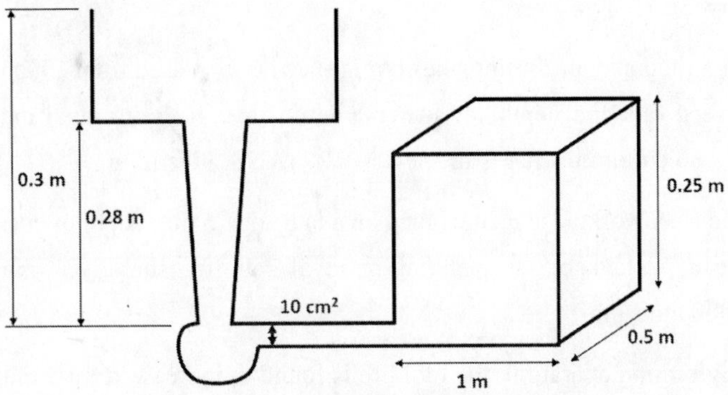

7.3 A heated rolling mill may produce up to 150 horsepower and has 600 mm diameter rolls. A plate that is 30 mm thick must be reduced to 20 mm in a single pass. The width of the starting plate is 200 mm. When warmed, the work material has a strain-hardening exponent of 0.18 and a strength coefficient of 250 MPa. Ascertain the following: (a) the true strain, (b) the rolling mill's limiting force, and (c) the maximum roll speed for the operation.

(True strain: 0.41, Force: 1,976,649.30 N Max. Rolling speed: 18.66 mm/min)

7.4 A connecting rod is to be hot forged in an impression die. The projected area of the part is 8,500 mm^2. Due to the design of the die, flash will form during forging, increasing the total area, including flash, to 10,000 mm^2. The part's geometry is complex, with a shape factor (C_f) of 8.0. The heated work material yields at 95 MPa and does not exhibit strain hardening. Calculate the maximum force needed to perform the operation. (Maximum force:7,600,000 N)

7.5 Using indirect extrusion, a 75mm long cylindrical billet with a 38 mm diameter is made to have a 10mm diameter. There is a 90° die angle. The constants in the Johnson equation are b = 1.5 and a = 0.8. strength coefficient X = 500 MPa and n = 0.22 for the work metal flow curve. If the ram speed is 400 mm/min, calculate the following: (a) extrusion ratio, (b) true strain (homogeneous deformation), (c) extrusion strain, (d) ram pressure, (e) ram force, and (f) power.

(Extrusion ratio: 14.44, True strain (homogeneous deformation): 2.67, extrusion strain: 4.805, Ram pressure: 2,444.20 MPa, Ram force: 2,771,991.66 N, Power: 24.77)

7.6 In a two-pass wire drawing method, the wire's cross-sectional area is reduced by 35% in the first pass and by another 28% in the second. Calculate the percentage reduction in total.

(The overall reduction: 53.2%)

7.7 The chip thickness ratio of mild steel cut orthogonally using a 20° rake angle tool was 0.8. The shear angle calculated using this data, expressed in degrees is? **(ANS:** ϕ = 45.89°)

7.8 In orthogonal machining, the uncut thickness and the chip thickness are 0.45mm and 0.75mm, respectively. Given the rake angle of tool equal to 45°, the shear plane angle is? **(ANS:** $\emptyset = 35.75°$)

7.9 During orthogonal machining, the cutting speed is increased from 100 m/min to 150 m/min, while the feed rate and depth of cut remain constant. If the original material removal rate (MRR) was 60 cm^3/min, what is the new MRR? (**ANS:** 90 cm^3/min)

7.10 A mild steel workpiece is machined on a lathe at 1.5 mm depth of cut, 0.8 mm/rev and 50 m/min speed. Calculate the material removal rate for the given machining condition. (**ANS:** 60000 mm^3/min)

7.11 During turning operation, the tool life is found to increase from 5 minutes to 20 minutes due to decrease in turning speed from 400 rpm to 200 rpm. Determine the tool life if the operation is performed under the same condition but the operating speed is increased to 600 rpm. (**ANS:** Tool life = 0.8 min)

7.12 A single point tool cutting at 50 m/min yields a 20-hour tool life. If the velocity is doubled and Taylor's constant C is 250, calculate the tool life for the given machining condition. (**ANS:** Tool life = 57.64 min)

7.13 The following parameters are used to accomplish an orthogonal cutting operation: chip thickness = 0.12 mm, depth of cut = 0.1 mm, and cutting speed = 4 m/s. Determine the chip's velocity along the tool face under the specified machining conditions. (**ANS:** 3.33 m/s)

KNOW MORE

Explore many new models developed for investigating complex aspects of casting, forming and machining to understand what can be done to enhance the productivity and economy of the manufacturing process. Try to visit a modern manufacturing lab/industry to learn how these principles are applied in practice. Much information about progress and development in the manufacturing modelling area is available in the public domain. Efforts may be made to learn and gain expertise.

Scan me!

SUGGESTED RESOURCES FOR FURTHER READING/LEARNING

1. M P Grover, "Fundamentals of Modern Manufacturing", John Wiley & Sons, (2010)
2. D K Dwivedi, Materials Engineering, AICTE, (2023)
3. D K Dwivedi, NPTEL Course "Fundamentals of Manufacturing Processes" https://archive.nptel.ac.in/courses/112/107/112107219/
4. Kalpakjian and Schmid, "Manufacturing engineering and technology", 7th edition Pearson, (2014).
5. Ghosh and Mallik, "Manufacturing Science", 2nd edition, EWP, (2019)
6. Rao, P. N, "*Manufacturing technology", Volume 1*, McGraw Hill Education, (2013).
7. Rao, P. N, "*Manufacturing technology", Volume 2*, McGraw Hill Education, (2013).

CO AND PO ATTAINMENT TABLE

Course outcomes (COs) for this course can be mapped with the programme outcomes (POs) after the completion of the course and a correlation can be made for the attainment of POs to analyse the gap. After proper analysis of the gap in the attainment of POs necessary measures can be taken to overcome the gaps.

Table for CO and PO attainment

Course Outcomes	Attainment of Programme Outcomes *(1- Weak Correlation; 2- Medium correlation; 3- Strong Correlation)*											
	PO-1	PO-2	PO-3	PO-4	PO-5	PO-6	PO-7	PO-8	PO-9	PO-10	PO-11	PO-12
CO-1												
CO-2												
CO-3												
CO-4												
CO-5												
CO-6												

The data filled in the above table can be used for gap analysis

INDEX